Table of Contents

Introduction . . . . **ix**

Finding Your Best Starting Point ix

About the Companion CD-ROM x

System Requirements. xi

Installing and Using the Sample Files xi

Conventions and Features in This Book xii

Part I Getting Started with Analysis Services

1 Understanding Business Intelligence and Data Warehousing 3

Introducing Business Intelligence 3

Reviewing Data Warehousing Concepts. 5

The Purpose of a Data Warehouse 5

The Structure of a Dimensional Database 6

A Fact Table. 10

Dimension Tables 11

Chapter 1 Quick Reference. 16

2 Understanding OLAP and Analysis Services 17

Understanding OLAP. 17

Consistently Fast Response. 18

Metadata-Based Queries. 20

Spreadsheet-Style Formulas 22

Understanding Analysis Services 23

Analysis Services and Speed. 24

Analysis Services and Metadata. 24

Analysis Services Formulas 26

Analysis Services Tools. 28

Chapter 2 Quick Reference. 29

3 Building Your First Cube 31

Exploring Business Intelligence Development Studio. 31

Examining the Contents of an Analysis Services Project 32
Exploring Menu Commands 35
Preparing to Create a Cube 36
Reviewing the Analysis Requirements 37
Creating a New Analysis Services Project 37
Creating a Cube 38
Using the Cube Wizard Without a Data Source 38
Reviewing the Cube Structure in the Cube Designer. 45
Generating a Schema 47
Using the Schema Generation Wizard 47
Loading Data into the Relational Schema 52
Processing and Browsing a Cube 55
Deploying and Processing a Cube 55
Browsing a Cube 56
Chapter 3 Quick Reference. 58

Part II Design Fundamentals

4 Designing Dimensions 63

Reviewing the Data Warehouse Structure 63
Building a Standard Dimension 64
Adding a Data Source. 65
Creating a Data Source View 67
Using the Dimension Wizard 69
Deploying a Dimension 74
Changing Attribute Properties 76
Working with a Time Dimension 77
Modifying a Data Source View 78
Creating a Time Dimension 79
Working with Role-Playing Dimensions. 84
Creating a Parent-Child Dimension. 85
Adding an Employee Dimension. 86
Totaling Data for Non–Leaf-Level Data Members 88
Managing Levels within a Parent-Child Dimension 92
Chapter 4 Quick Reference. 96

5 Designing Measure Groups and Measures. 99

Adding Measure Groups to a Cube 99

Building a Cube 100
Changing Properties for Measure Groups and Measures 103
Specifying Dimension Usage 104
Browsing Multiple Measure Groups 107
Aggregating Semiadditive Measures. 113
Adding a Measure Group to an Existing Cube 113
Using a Semiadditive Aggregate Function. 115
Calculating Distinct Counts. 117
Creating Simple Calculations 119
Adding a Calculation to a Cube. 120
Applying Conditional Formatting 126
Chapter 5 Quick Reference 127

6 Working with a Finance Measure Group 129

Designing an Account Dimension 129
Working with Account Intelligence. 130
Using Unary Operators 135
Aggregating by Account. 139
Designing Nonadditive Financial Measures 144
Creating a Nonadditive Measure. 145
Chapter 6 Quick Reference 148

7 Designing Aggregations and Hierarchies. 149

Understanding Aggregation Design 149
Using the Aggregation Design Wizard 151
Inspecting Aggregations. 155
Changing Partition Counts 158
Adding Attributes to the Aggregation Design 160
Designing User Hierarchies. 161
Adding a User Hierarchy. 162
Aggregating User Hierarchies 165
Optimizing Aggregations 167
Using the Query Log 168
Viewing Usage Data. 170
Using the Usage-Based Optimization Wizard 171
Maintaining the Query Log 172
Chapter 7 Quick Reference 173

Part III Advanced Design

8 Using MDX 177

Creating Tuple-Based Calculated Members. 177
Creating an MDX Calculation for Percent of Total 182
Creating an MDX Calculation for Percent of Parent. 186
Querying with MDX. 188
Executing MDX Queries 188
Working with Basic MDX Queries 193
Designing Custom Members 197
Creating a Calculated Member Using a Set-Based Function 197
Creating Cumulative Calculations. 200
Working with MDX Scripts 202
Managing the Sequence of Calculations 202
Adding a Script Assignment. 205
Developing Key Performance Indicators 209
Comparing Cube Values to Goals 209
Using MDX Expressions with Key Performance Indicators 212
Chapter 8 Quick Reference. 215

9 Exploring Special Features 217

Defining Dimension Relationships 217
Using a Referenced Relationship Type 217
Using a Many-to-Many Relationship Type 221
Supporting Currency Conversions 229
Localizing Cubes 231
Adding Translations. 231
Browsing Translations 235
Organizing Information with Folders and Perspectives. 236
Organizing Measures 236
Using Perspectives. 238
Chapter 9 Quick Reference. 242

10 Interacting with Cubes 245

Implementing Actions. 245
Using Standard Actions. 246
Linking to Reports 249
Adding Drillthrough 251

Using Writeback 253
Write-Enabling a Dimension 254
Dynamically Adding Members to a Dimension 255
Modifying the Cube Structure for Writeback 257
Writing Values Back to a Cube 261
Chapter 10 Quick Reference 267

Part IV Production Management

11 Implementing Security 271
Using Role-Based Security 271
Creating Security Roles 272
Managing Roles 277
Applying Security to a Dimension 278
Restricting Access to a Dimension 278
Restricting Access to Specific Members of a Dimension 281
Controlling Visual Totals for a Dimension 283
Defining a Default Member for a Dimension 284
Securing Data at the Cell Level 287
Preventing Values in Cells from Being Read 287
Allowing Users to Write to Cells 290
Setting Administration Security 291
Creating Security Roles for Processing 291
Chapter 11 Quick Reference 293

12 Managing Partitions and Database Processing 295
Managing Very Large Databases 295
Understanding Partition Strategies 295
Creating Partitions 296
Merging Partitions 301
Working with Storage 304
Understanding Analysis Services Storage Modes 305
Setting Storage Options 306
Changing Data in a Warehouse 308
Managing OLAP Processing 312
Processing a Dimension 313
Processing a Cube 318
Configuring Proactive Caching 320

Monitoring Cube Activity 326
Profiling Analysis Services Queries 326
Using the Performance Monitor 330
Chapter 12 Quick Reference 333

13 Managing Deployment 335
Reviewing Deployment Options 335
Building a Database 336
Deploying a Database 341
Processing a Database 348
Managing Database Objects Programmatically 351
Working with XMLA Scripts 352
Automating Database Processing 356
Creating a SQL Server Integration Services Package 357
Using the Analysis Services Processing Task 358
Handling Task Failures 359
Scheduling a SQL Server Integration Services Package 361
Planning for Disaster and Recovery 364
Backing Up an Analysis Services Database 365
Restoring an Analysis Services Database 366
Chapter 13 Quick Reference 368

Glossary 369

Index 373

Introduction

Microsoft SQL Server 2005 Analysis Services is the multidimensional online analytical processing (OLAP) component of Microsoft SQL Server 2005 that integrates relational and OLAP data for business intelligence (BI) analytical solutions. The goal of this book is to show you how to use the tools and features of Analysis Services so you can easily create, manage, and share OLAP cubes within your organization. Step-by-step exercises are included to prepare you for producing your own BI solutions.

To help you learn the many features of Analysis Services, this book is organized into four parts. Part I, "Getting Started with Analysis Services," introduces BI and data warehousing, defines OLAP and the benefits an OLAP tool can bring to a data warehouse, and guides you through the development of your first OLAP cube. Part II, "Design Fundamentals," teaches you how to design dimensions, measure groups, and measures, and then how to combine and enhance these objects to create an analytical solution that addresses a variety of analytical requirements. Part III, "Advanced Design," shows you how to use multidimensional expressions (MDX) and key performance indicators (KPIs) to further enhance your analytical solutions and to query an Analysis Services database. In addition, this part covers special Analysis Services features for advanced dimension design, globalization of analytical solutions, and a variety of interactive features that extend the analytical capabilities of cubes. Part IV, "Production Management," explains how to use security to control access to cubes as well as to restrict the data that a particular user can see, how to design partitions to manage database scalability, and how to manage and monitor production databases.

Finding Your Best Starting Point

This book covers the full life cycle of an analytical solution from development to deployment. If you're responsible only for certain activities, you can choose to read the chapters that apply to your situation and skip the remaining chapters. To find the best place to start, use the following table:

If you are	Follow these steps
An information consumer who uses OLAP to make decisions	**1.** Install the sample files as described in "Installing and Using the Sample Files." **2.** Work through Parts I and II to become familiar with the basic capabilities of Analysis Services. **3.** Skim chapters of interest to you in Part III to understand how additional features might meet your analytical requirements.

If you are	Follow these steps
A BI analyst who develops OLAP models and prototypes for business analysis	**1.** Install the sample files as described in "Installing and Using the Sample Files." **2.** Work through Part I to get an overview of Analysis Services. **3.** Complete Part II to develop the necessary skills to create a prototype cube. **4.** Review the chapters that interest you in Parts III and IV to learn about advanced features of Analysis Services and to understand how cubes are accessed by users and how cubes are managed after they are put into production.
An administrator who maintains server resources or production migration processes	**1.** Install the sample files as described in "Installing and Using the Sample Files." **2.** Skim Parts I–III to understand the functionality that is included in Analysis Services. **3.** Complete Part IV to learn how to manage and secure cube access and content on the server as well as how to configure, monitor, and manage server components and performance.
A BI architect who designs and develops analytical solutions	**1.** Install the sample files as described in "Installing and Using the Sample Files." **2.** Complete Part I to become familiar with the benefits of Analysis Services. **3.** Work through Parts II and III to learn how to create dimensions and cubes and how to implement advanced design techniques. **4.** Complete Part IV to understand how to design cubes that implement the security, performance, and processing features of Analysis Services.

About the Companion CD-ROM

The CD that accompanies this book contains the sample files that you need to complete the step-by-step exercises throughout the book. For example, in Chapter 3, "Building Your First Cube," you open a sample solution to learn how files are organized in an analytical solution. In other chapters, you add sample files to the solution you're building so you can focus on a particular concept without spending time to set up the prerequisites for an exercise.

System Requirements

To install Microsoft Analysis Services 2005 and to use the samples provided on the companion CD, your computer will need to be configured as follows:

- Microsoft Windows 2000 Advanced Server, Windows XP Professional, or Windows Server 2003 with the latest service pack applied.
- Microsoft SQL Server 2005 Developer or Enterprise Edition with any available service packs applied. Refer to the Operating System Requirements listed at *http://msdn2.microsoft.com/en-us/library/ms143506(en-US,SQL.90).aspx* to determine which edition is compatible with your operating system.

The step-by-step exercises in this book and the accompanying practice files were tested using Windows XP Professional and Microsoft SQL Server 2005 Analysis Services Developer Edition. If you're using another version of the operating system or a different edition of either application, you might notice some slight differences.

Installing and Using the Sample Files

The sample files require approximately 52 MB of disk space on your computer. To install and prepare the sample files for use with the exercises in this book, follow these steps:

1. Remove the CD-ROM from its package at the back of this book, and insert it into your CD-ROM drive.

Note If the presence of the CD-ROM is automatically detected and a start window is displayed, you can skip to Step 4.

2. Click the Start button, click Run, and then type **D:\startcd** in the Open box, replacing the drive letter with the correct letter for your CD-ROM drive, if necessary.
3. Click Install Sample Files to launch the Setup program, and then follow the directions on the screen.

   The sample files will be copied from the CD-ROM to your local hard drive. The default installation folder is C:\Documents and Settings\<username>\My Documents \Microsoft Press\as2005sbs. If you later change this installation folder to a different location, you'll need to reference the new location when working through the exercises. For each chapter that uses sample files, you'll find a corresponding folder in the installation folder. You will be instructed where to find the appropriate sample files when an exercise requires the use of an existing file.

> **Tip** In the C:\Documents and Settings\<username>\My Documents\Microsoft Press\as2005sbs\Answers folder, you'll find a separate folder for each chapter in which you make changes to the sample files. The files in these folders are copies of these sample files when you complete a chapter. You can refer to these files if you want to preview the results of completing all exercises in a chapter.

4. Remove the CD-ROM from the drive when installation is complete.

   Now that you've completed installation of the sample files, you need to follow some additional steps to prepare your computer to use these files.

5. Click the Start button, click Run, and then type **C:\Documents and Settings\<username>\My Documents\Microsoft Press\as2005sbs\Setup\Restore\Restore_databases.cmd** in the Open box.

   This step attaches the Microsoft SQL Server 2005 database that is the data source for the analytical solution that you will create and use throughout this book.

   Now you're set to begin working through the exercises.

Conventions and Features in This Book

To use your time effectively, be sure that you understand the stylistic conventions that are used throughout this book. The following list explains these conventions:

- Hands-on exercises for you to follow are presented as lists of numbered steps (1, 2, and so on).
- Text that you are to type appears in boldface type.
- Properties that you need to set in SQL Server Business Intelligence Development Studio (BIDS) (a set of templates provided in Microsoft Visual Studio) are sometimes displayed in a table as you work through steps.
- Pressing two keys at the same time is indicated by a plus sign between the two key names, such as Alt+Tab, when you need to hold down the Alt key while pressing the Tab key.
- A note that is labeled as **Note** is used to give you more information about a specific topic.
- A note that is labeled as **Important** is used to point out information that can help you avoid a problem.
- A note that is labeled as **Tip** is used to convey advice that you might find useful when using Analysis Services.

Part I
Getting Started with Analysis Services

In this part:

Chapter 1: Understanding Business Intelligence and Data Warehousing 3
Chapter 2: Understanding OLAP and Analysis Services 17
Chapter 3: Building Your First Cube 31

Chapter 1

Understanding Business Intelligence and Data Warehousing

After completing this chapter, you will be able to:

- Understand the purpose of business intelligence and data warehousing.
- Distinguish between a data warehouse and a transaction database.
- Understand dimensional database design principles.

Microsoft SQL Server 2005 Analysis Services is a tool to help you implement *business intelligence* (BI) in your organization. BI makes use of a data warehouse, often taking advantage of online analytical processing (OLAP) tools. How exactly do BI, data warehousing, OLAP, and Analysis Services relate to each other? In this chapter, you'll learn the purpose of BI in general, and also some basic concepts of data warehousing in a relational database. In the next chapter, you'll learn how OLAP enhances the capabilities of BI, and how Analysis Services makes both OLAP and relational data available for your BI needs.

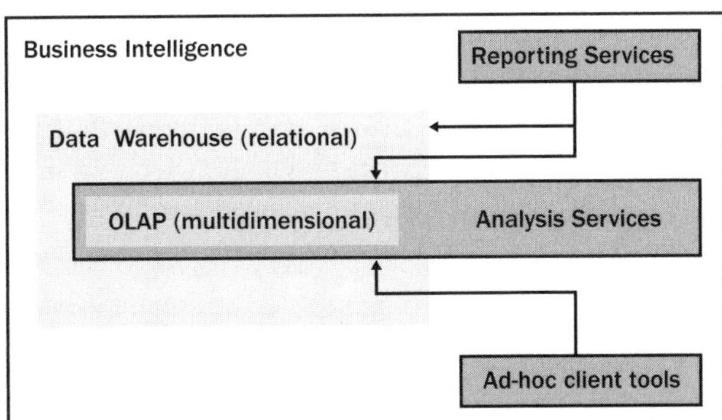

Introducing Business Intelligence

BI is a relatively new term, but it is certainly not a new concept. The concept is simply to make use of information already available in your company to help decision makers make decisions better and faster. Over the past few decades, the same goal has gone by many names. In the early 1980s, executive information system (EIS) applications were very popular.

An EIS, however, often consisted of one person copying key data values from various reports onto a "dashboard" so that an executive could see them at a glance. But the goal was still to help the decision maker make decisions. Later, EIS applications were replaced by decision support system (DSS) applications, which really did essentially the same thing. So what is so different about BI?

The biggest change in the past few decades has been the need to create management reports for all levels of an organization, and all types of decision makers. When you need to provide fast-response reports for many purposes throughout a large organization, having one person type values for another to read is not practical.

One useful way to think about BI is to consider the types of reports—and their respective audiences. Typical reports fall into one of the three following general classes.

- **Dashboard reports** These are highly summarized, often graphical representations of the state of the business. The values on a dashboard report are often key performance indicators (KPIs) for an organization. A dashboard report may display a simple summation of month-to-date sales, or it may include complex calculations such as profitability growth from the same period of the previous year for the current department compared to the company as a whole. A dashboard often includes comparisons to targets. A dashboard report is often customized for the person viewing the report, showing, for example, each manager the results for his or her department. Dashboard reports are often used by executives and strategic decision makers.
- **Production reports** These are typically large, detailed reports that have the same basic structure each time they are produced. They may be printed, or distributed online, either in Web-based reports or as formatted files. One advantage of a production report is that the same information can be found in the same place in each report. A production report may consist of one large report showing information about all parts of the company, or it may be "burst" into individual sections delivered to the relevant audience. Production reports are often used by administrators and tactical decision makers.
- **Analytical reports** These are dynamic, interactive reports that allow the user to "slice and dice" the information in any of thousands of ways. As with dashboard reports, analytical reports can display simple summations or complex calculations. They typically allow drill-down to very detailed information, or drill-up to high-level summaries. This type of report is typically used by analysts or "hands-on" managers who want to understand all aspects of the situation.

Much of the information you need comes from outside the organization. That's why you read the *Wall Street Journal* and keep a bookmark in your browser pointed at *www.bloomberg.com*. But much of the information you need also comes from inside the organization, and much of that information is numerical. This numerical information becomes more useful for decision making when organized into a BI solution.

Reviewing Data Warehousing Concepts

A data warehouse is often a core component of a BI infrastructure within an organization. The procedures that you'll complete throughout this book use a sample data warehouse as the underlying database for the analytical solutions that you'll build. In this section, you'll review the characteristics of a data warehouse, the table structures in a data warehouse, and design considerations, but details for building a data warehouse are beyond the scope of this book. For more information about data warehousing, refer to *http://msdn.microsoft.com/library/default.asp?url=/library/en-us/createdw/createdw_3r51.asp.*

The Purpose of a Data Warehouse

A *data warehouse* is a repository for storing and analyzing numerical information. A data warehouse stores stable, verified data values. You might find it helpful to compare some of the most important differences between a data warehouse and a transaction database.

- A transaction database helps people carry out activities, while a data warehouse helps people make plans. For example, a transaction database might show which seats are available on an airline flight so that a travel agent can book a new reservation. A data warehouse, on the other hand, might show the historical pattern of empty seats by flight so that an airline manager can decide whether to adjust flight schedules in the future.
- A transaction database focuses on the details, while a data warehouse focuses on high-level aggregates. For example, a parent purchasing the latest popular children's book doesn't care about inventory levels for the Juvenile Fiction product line, but a manager planning the rearranging of store shelving may be very interested in a general decline in sales of computer book titles (for subjects other than SQL Server 2005). The implication of this difference is that the core data in a warehouse are typically numeric values that can be summarized.
- A transaction database is typically designed for a specific application, while a data warehouse integrates data from different sources. For example, your order processing application—and its database—probably includes detailed discount information for each order, but nothing about manufacturing cost overruns. Conversely, your manufacturing application—and its database—probably includes detailed cost information, but nothing about sales discounts. By combining the two data sources in a data warehouse, you can calculate the actual profitability of product sales, possibly revealing that the fully discounted price is less than the actual cost to manufacture. But no worries: You can make up for it in volume.
- A transaction database is concerned with now; a data warehouse is concerned with activity over time. For example, in a simple bank account, each transaction—that is, each deposit or withdrawal—creates an instantaneous change in the account balance. The transaction system rarely maintains historical balances, and even transaction logs are usually archived after a month or two. In a data warehouse, you can store many years of

transaction data (perhaps summarized), and you can also store snapshots of historical balances. This allows you to compare what you did today with what you did last month or last year. When making decisions, the ability to see a wide time horizon is critical for distinguishing between trends and random fluctuations.

- A transaction database is volatile; its information constantly changes as new orders are placed or cancelled, as new products are built or shipped, or as new reservations are made. A data warehouse is stable; its information is updated at standard intervals–perhaps monthly, weekly, or even hourly–and, in an ideal world, an update would add values for the new time period only, without changing values previously stored in the warehouse.
- A transaction database must provide rapid retrieval and updating of detailed information; a data warehouse must provide rapid retrieval of highly summarized information. Consequently, the optimal design for a transaction database is opposite to the optimal design for a data warehouse. In addition, querying a live transaction database for management reporting purposes would slow down the transaction application to an unacceptable degree.

There are other reasons to create a data warehouse, but these are several of the key reasons, and should be sufficient to convince you that creating a data warehouse to support management reporting is a good thing.

The Structure of a Dimensional Database

One of the most popular data warehouse designs is called a *multidimensional database*. The term *multidimensional* conjures up images of Albert Einstein's curved space-time, parallel universes, and mathematical formulas that make solving for integrals sound soothingly simple. The bottom line is that calling a database multidimensional is really a bit of a lie. It's a snazzy term, but when applied to databases it has nothing in common with the multidimensional behavior of particles accelerating near the speed of light or even with the multidimensional aspects of Alice's adventures down the rabbit hole. This section will help you understand what multidimensionality really means in a database context.

Suppose that you are the president of a small, new company. Your company needs to grow, but you have limited resources to support the expansion. You have decisions to make, and to make those decisions you must have particular information.

In the world of data warehousing, a summarizable numerical value that you use to monitor your business is called a *measure*. When looking for numerical information, your first question is which measure you want to see. You could look at, say, Sales Dollars, Shipment Units, Total Defects, or Ad Campaign Responses. Suppose that you ask your personal financial analyst to create a report of your company's total Units Sold. Here's what you'll get (imagine that the numbers are in millions, if you prefer):

113

Looking at the one value is useful, but frustrating: You want to break it out into something more informative. For example, how has your company done over time? You ask for a monthly analysis, and here's the new report:

January	February	March	April
14	41	33	25

Your company has been operating for four months, so across the top of the report you'll find four labels for the months. Rather than the one value you had before, you'll now find four values. The months subdivide the original value. The new number of values equals the number of months. This is analogous to calculating linear distances in the physical world: The length of a line is simply the length.

You're still not satisfied with the monthly report. Your company sells more than one product. How did each of those products do over time? You ask for a new report by product and by month:

	January	February	March	April
Road-650			6	17
Mountain-100	6	16	6	8
Cable Lock	8	25	21	

Your young company sells three products, so down the left side of the report are the three product names. Each product subdivides the monthly values. Meanwhile, the four labels for the months are still across the top of the report. You now have 12 values to consider. The number of values equals the number of products times the number of months. This is analogous to calculating the area of a rectangle in the physical world: Area equals the rectangle's length times its width. The report even looks like a rectangle.

The comparison to a rectangle, however, applies only to the arithmetic involved, not to the shape of the report. Your report could be organized differently–it could just as easily look like this:

Road-650	January	
Road-650	February	
Road-650	March	6
Road-650	April	17
Mountain-100	January	6
Mountain-100	February	16
Mountain-100	March	6
Mountain-100	April	8

Cable Lock	January	8
Cable Lock	February	25
Cable Lock	March	21
Cable Lock	April	

Whether you display the values in a list like the one above (where the numerical values form a line) or display them in a grid (where they form a rectangle), you still have the potential for 12 values if you have four monthly values for each of three products. Your report has 12 potential values because the products and the months are independent. Each product gets its own sales value—even if that value is zero—for each month.

Back to the rectangular report. Suppose that your company sells in two different states and you'd like to know how each product is selling each month in each state. Add another set of labels indicating the states your company uses, and you get a new report, one that looks like this:

		January	February	March	April
WA	Road-650			3	10
	Mountain-100	3	16	6	
	Cable Lock	4	16	6	
OR	Road-650			3	7
	Mountain-100	3			8
	Cable Lock	4	9	15	

The report now has two labels for the states, three labels for products (each shown twice), and four labels for months. It has the potential for showing 24 values, even if some of those value cells are blank. The number of potential values equals the number of states times the number of products times the number of months. This is analogous to calculating the volume of a cube in the physical world: Volume equals the length of the cube times its width times its height. Your report doesn't really look like a cube—it looks more like a rectangle. Again, you could rearrange it to look like a list. But whichever way you lay out your report, it has three independent lists of labels, and the total number of potential values in the report equals the number of unique items in the first independent list of labels (for example, two states) times the number of unique items in the second independent list of labels (three products) times the number of unique items in the third independent list of labels (four months).

Because the phrase *independent list of labels* is wordy, and because the arithmetic used to calculate the number of potential values in the report is identical to the arithmetic used to calculate length, area, and volume—measurements of spatial extension—in place of *independent list of labels,* data warehouse designers borrow the term *dimension* from mathematics. Remember that this is a borrowed term. A data analysis dimension is very different from a physical dimension. Thus, your report has three dimensions—State, Product, and Time—and the report's number of values equals the number of items in the first dimension times the number of items in the second dimension, and so forth. Using the term *dimension* doesn't say anything about how the labels and values are displayed in a report or even about how they should be stored in a database.

Each time you've created a new dimension, the items in that dimension have conceptually related to one another–for example, they are all products, or they are all dates. Accordingly, items in a dimension are called *members* of that dimension.

Now complicate the report even more. Perhaps you want to see dollars as well as units. You get a new report that looks like this:

		January		February		March		April	
		U	$	U	$	U	$	U	$
WA	Road-650					3	7.44	10	24.80
	Mountain-100	3	7.95	16	42.40	6	15.90		
	Cable Lock	4	7.32	16	29.28	6	10.98		
OR	Road-650					3	7.44	7	17.36
	Mountain-100	3	7.95					8	21.20
	Cable Lock	4	7.32	9	16.47	15	27.45		

U = Units; $ = Dollars

Because units and dollars are independent of the State, Product, and Time dimensions, they form what you can think of as a new, fourth dimension, which you could call a Measures dimension. The number of values in the report still equals the product of the number of members in each dimension: 2 times 3 times 4 times 2, which equals 48. But there is not–and there does not need to be–any kind of physical world analogue. Remember that the word *dimension* is simply a convenient way of saying *independent list of labels*, and having four (or 20 or 60) independent lists is just as easy as having three. It just makes the report bigger.

In the physical world, the object you're measuring changes depending on how many dimensions there are. For example, a one-dimensional inch is a linear inch, but a two-dimensional inch is a square inch, and a three-dimensional inch is a cubic inch. A cubic inch is a completely different object from a square inch or a linear inch. In your report, however, the object that you measure as you add dimensions is always the same: a numerical value. There is no difference between a numerical value in a "four-dimensional" report and a numerical value in a "one-dimensional" report. In the reporting world, an additional dimension simply creates a new, independent way to subdivide a measure.

Although adding a fourth or fifth dimension to a report does not transport you into hyperspace, that's not to say that adding a new dimension is trivial. Suppose that you start with a report with two dimensions: 30 products and 12 months, or 360 possible values. Adding three new members to the product dimension increases the number of values in the report to 396, a 10 percent increase. Suppose, however, that you add those same three new members as a third dimension—for example, a Scenario dimension with Actual, Forecast, and Plan. Adding three members to a new dimension increases the number of values in the report to 1,080, a 300 percent increase. Consider this extreme example: With 128 members in a single dimension, a report has 128 possible values, but with those same 128 total members split up into 64 dimensions—with two members in each dimension—a report has 18,446,744,073,709,551,616 possible values!

A Fact Table

In a dimensional data warehouse, a table that stores the detailed values for measures, or *facts*, is called a *fact table*. A fact table that stores Units and Dollars by State, by Product, and by Month has five columns, conceptually similar to those in the following sample:

State	Product	Month	Units	Dollars
WA	Mountain-100	January	3	7.95
WA	Cable Lock	January	4	7.32
OR	Mountain-100	January	3	7.95
OR	Cable Lock	January	4	7.32
WA	Mountain-100	February	16	42.40

In these sample rows from a fact table, the first three columns—State, Product, and Month—are key columns. The remaining two columns—Units and Dollars—contain measure values. Each column in a fact table is typically either a key column or a measure column, but it is also possible to have other columns for reference purposes—for example, Purchase Order numbers or Invoice numbers.

A fact table contains a column for each measure. Different fact tables will have different measures. A Sales warehouse might contain two measure columns—one for Dollars and one for Units. A shop-floor warehouse might contain three measure columns—one for Units, one for Minutes, and one for Defects. When you create reports, you can think of measures as simply forming an additional dimension. That is, you can put Units and Dollars side by side as column headings, or you can put Units and Dollars as row headings. In the fact table, however, each measure appears as a separate column.

A fact table contains rows at the lowest level of detail you might want to retrieve for the measures in that fact table. In other words, for each dimension, the fact table contains rows for the most detailed item members of each dimension. If you have measures that have different dimensions, you simply create a separate fact table for those measures and dimensions. Your data warehouse may have several different fact tables with different sets of measures and dimensions.

The sample rows in the preceding table illustrate the conceptual layout of a fact table. Actually, a fact table almost always uses an integer key for each member, rather than a descriptive name. Because a fact table tends to include an incredible number of rows—in a reasonably large warehouse, the fact table might easily have millions of rows–using an integer key can substantially reduce the size of the fact table. The actual layout of a fact table might look more like that of the following sample rows:

STATE_ID	PROD_ID	Month	Sales_Units	Sales_Dollars
1	347	1	3	7.95
1	447	1	4	7.32
2	347	1	3	7.95
2	447	1	4	7.32
1	347	2	16	42.40

When you put integer keys into the fact table, the captions for the dimension members have to be put into a different table–a dimension table. You will typically have a dimension table for each dimension represented in a fact table.

Dimension Tables

A *dimension table* contains the specific name of each member of the dimension. The name of the dimension member is called an *attribute*. For example, if you have three products in a Product dimension, the dimension table might look something like this:

PROD_ID	Product_Name
347	Mountain-100
339	Road-650
447	Cable Lock

Product Name is an attribute of the product member. Because the Product ID in the dimension table matches the Product ID in the fact table, it is called the *key attribute*. Because there is one Product Name for each Product ID, the name is simply what you display instead of the number, so it is still considered to be part of the key attribute.

In the data warehouse, the key attribute in a dimension table must contain a unique value for each member of the dimension. In relational database terms, this key attribute is called a *primary key column*. The primary key column of each dimension table corresponds to one of the key columns in any related fact tables. Each key value that appears once in the dimension table will appear multiple times in the fact table. For example, the Product ID 347, for Mountain-100, should appear in only one dimension table row, but it will appear in many fact table rows. This is called a *one-to-many* relationship. In the fact table, a key column (which is on the many side of the one-to-many relationship) is called a *foreign key column*. The relational database uses the matching values from the primary key column (in the dimension table) and the foreign key column (in the fact table) to *join* a dimension table to a fact table.

In addition to making the fact table smaller, moving the dimension information into a separate table has an additional advantage—you can add additional information about each dimension member. For example, your dimension table might include the Category for each product, like this:

PROD_ID	Product_Name	Category
347	Mountain-100	Bikes
339	Road-650	Bikes
447	Cable Lock	Accessories

Category is now an additional attribute of the Product. If you know the Product ID, you can determine not only the Product Name, but also the Category. The key attribute name will probably be unique—because there is one name for each key, but other attributes don't have to be unique. The Category attribute, for example, may appear multiple times. This allows you to create reports that group the fact table information by Category as well as by product.

A dimension table may have many attributes besides the name. Essentially, an attribute corresponds to a column in a dimension table. Here's an example of our small three-member Product dimension table with additional attributes:

PROD_ID	Product_Name	Category	Color	Size	Price
347	Mountain-100	Bikes	Black	44	782.99
339	Road-650	Bikes	Silver	48	3,399.99
447	Cable Lock	Accessories	NA	NA	25.00

Dimension attributes can be either groupable or nongroupable. In other words, would you ever have a report in which you want to show the measure grouped by that attribute? In our example, Category, Size, and Color are all groupable attributes. It is easy to imagine a report in which you group sales by color, by size, or by category. But Price is not likely to be a groupable attribute—at least not by itself. You might have a different attribute—say, Price Group—that would be meaningful on a report, but Price by itself is too variable to be meaningful on a report. Likewise, a Product Description attribute would not be a meaningful grouping for a report. In a Customer dimension, City, Country, Gender, and Marital Status are all examples of attributes that would be meaningful to put on a report, but Street Address or Nickname are attributes that would most likely not be groupable. Nongroupable attributes are sometimes called *member properties*.

Some groupable attributes can be combined to create a *natural hierarchy*. For example, if a Product key attribute has Category and Subcategory as attributes, in most cases, a single product would go into a single Subcategory, and a single Subcategory would go into a single Category. That would form a natural hierarchy. In a report, you might want to display Categories, and then allow a user to drill-down from the Category to the Subcategories, and finally to the Products.

Hierarchies—or drill-down paths—don't have to be natural (i.e., where each lower-level member determines the next higher member). For example, you could create a report that shows products grouped by Color, but then allow the user to drill-down to see the different Sizes available for each Color. Because of the drill-down capability in the report, Color and Size form a hierarchy, but there is nothing about Size that determines which Color the product will be. This is a hierarchy, but is it not a natural hierarchy—which is not to say that it is an unnatural hierarchy. There is nothing wrong with Color and Size as a hierarchy; it is simply a fact that the same Size can appear in multiple Colors.

Attributes That Change over Time

One reason for using an integer key for dimension members is to reduce the size of the fact table. Also, an integer key allows seemingly duplicate members to exist in a dimension table. In a Customer dimension, for example, you might have two different customers named John Smith, but each one will be assigned a unique Customer ID, guaranteeing that each member key will appear only once in the dimension table.

Of course, because the data warehouse is generated by extracting data from a production system, the two John Smiths will undoubtedly have unique keys already. One may be C125423A and the other F234654B. These are called *application keys* because they came from the source application. If you already have unique keys for each customer (or product or region), does the data warehouse really need to generate new keys for its own purposes, or can it just use the application keys to guarantee uniqueness?

Most successful data warehouses do generate their own unique keys. These extra, redundant unique keys are called *surrogate keys*. Sometimes people who are accustomed to working with production databases have a hard time understanding why a data warehouse should create new surrogate keys when there are already unique application keys available. There are basically three reasons for creating unique surrogate keys in a data warehouse:

1. Surrogate keys can be integers even if the application key is not. This can make the data warehouse fact table consume less space. It takes less space in the fact table to store an integer such as 54352 rather than a string such as C125423A. This is the least important reason for creating surrogate keys.
2. A data warehouse integrates data from multiple source systems. It is common for source systems to have different application keys for the same person, or, conversely, the same application key for different people. For example, in the Sales system, the product application key A543 might refer to a Mountain-100 bike, while in the manufacturing system (which was created by a completely different group of people), the product application key A543 might refer to a Road-650 bike. A more realistic example is one that happens when two companies merge (a euphemism for one company swallowing up the other). In the parent company's sales system, customer C125423A may refer to John Smith, while in the subsidiary's sales system, C125423A might coincidentally refer to Tsing-Mun To. Even such supposedly unique values as an American Social Security Number

can be granted to a new person, once the government believes that the original person is deceased. Using surrogate keys in the data warehouse prepares the warehouse for such eventualities.

3. One of the most compelling reasons for using surrogate keys in a data warehouse has to do with what happens when the value of an attribute changes over time. For example, at the moment, our Road-650 bike has a list price of 3,399.99. What happens when next year, due to inescapable market forces, we reduce the list price to 3,199.99? In a production order processing system, you simply change the price in the master product list and any new orders use the new price. In a data warehouse, you have history to consider. Do we want to pretend that the Road-650 bicycle has always sold for 3,199.99? Or do we want the data warehouse to reflect the fact that this year the price is in the 3,300-3,500 price range, while next year the price is in the 3,000-3,299 price range? If you simply use the application key to represent the bicycle, you don't have a lot of choice. If, on the other hand, you had the foresight to create surrogate keys for the product, you could simply create a new surrogate key for the less expensive version of the same bicycle, and keep the application key as just another attribute. The ability to create multiple instances of the same product–or the same customer–is an extremely important benefit of surrogate keys, and it is particularly important in a data warehouse where you are maintaining historical information for comparison.

Surrogate keys are a critical part of most data warehouse design. The foreign key in the fact table and the primary key in the dimension table are then completely under the control of the data warehouse.

Stars and Snowflakes

In a production database, it is critical for changing values to be consistent across the entire application: If you change a customer's address in one part of the system, you want the changed address to be immediately visible in all parts of the system. Because of this need for consistency, production databases tend to be broken up into many tables so that any value is stored only once, with links (or joins) to any other places it may be used. Ensuring that a value is stored in only one place is called *normalization*, and it is very important in production database systems.

In a data warehouse dimension, you may have multiple attributes that form a natural hierarchy. For example, several products might belong to a subcategory, and several subcategories are grouped into a category. A database designer who is familiar with creating production databases will want to normalize the dimension so that there is a separate Subcategory table where each subcategory appears only once, and then a separate Category table where each category appears only once. This, of course, requires foreign keys in the Product and Subcategory tables that join to unique primary keys in the Subcategory and Category tables, respectively.

If you are creating reports against the data warehouse, however, many joins can make the query slow. For example, if you want to see the total sales for the Bikes Category for the year 2006, you would have to join each row in the fact table to the Product table, and then to the Subcategory table, and then the Category table, and also to the Date table, the Month table, then the Quarter table, and finally to the Year table. And you would have to do all those joins to all the rows in the fact table, just to find out which ones to discard. This makes the query for a relational report much slower than it needs to be. The fact is that values in a data warehouse are not changing as dynamically as they would in a production database, so storing the values redundantly is less important than is retrieving the values as quickly as possible for a report.

Consequently, in many data warehouses, all the attributes for a dimension are stored in a single dimension table–even if that means that categories and years are stored redundantly many times. Storing redundant values in a single table is called *denormalizing* the data. The concept is that dimension tables are relatively small (compared to the fact tables), and that performing a single join to find out the Year and the Category is much faster with only a couple of joins, so denormalizing is worth doing.

Storing all the attributes for each dimension in a single denormalized dimension table produces what is called a *star schema*, because you end up with a single fact table surrounded by a single table for each dimension, and the result looks a bit like a star. Normalizing each of the dimension tables so that there are many joins for each dimension results in a *snowflake schema*, because the "points" of the star get broken up into little branches that look like a snowflake. In reality, it isn't the database that is star or snowflake, because one dimension might be fully normalized (i.e., a snowflake), while another dimension in the same data warehouse might be fully denormalized (i.e., a star). In fact, even within a single dimension, some attributes might be normalized into a snowflake while others are denormalized into a star.

If you are creating a data warehouse for the purpose of creating reports directly from a relational database, the more snowflaking you do with attributes, the slower the query that populates the report will run. If, however, you will use the warehouse primarily as a data source for Analysis Services, then the difference between star or snowflake dimension attributes is much less significant, and you can use other reasons (such as which database structure is easier to create and update) as the basis for a design decision.

Alternative Dimension Table Structures

In an idealized form, each dimension in a warehouse has a separate dimension table, and each lowest-level member appears only once in a dimension table. Some dimensions, however, are a little more complicated. For example, in an Employee dimension, everybody is an employee, so there is a primary key for each employee. But some of the employees are also managers of other employees. Unlike in a standard dimension, where the parent attribute is in a new column (and possibly in a new table), in an Employee dimension, the parent attribute simply points back to a new row of the original Employee primary key. This is called a *parent-child* dimension because both the parent member and the child member are in the same attribute.

In relational database terms, this pointing back from one attribute to the key of the same table is called a *self-referential join*. It allows for a lot of flexibility in an organizational structure, but can complicate the way that you generate reports.

This chapter has dealt with BI in general, and with relational data warehouses in particular. A relational data warehouse is very valuable, but it does not provide all the benefits you might want. For example, just because Category and Subcategory are attributes of the Product dimension, there is nothing in the relational database that indicates that there is a natural hierarchy from Category to Subcategory to Product, and there is certainly nothing to indicate that you might want to show Size and Color in a hierarchical relationship. Adding this information is the role of OLAP in general, and Analysis Services specifically, and the benefits provided by OLAP and Analysis Services will be covered in the next chapter.

Chapter 1 Quick Reference

This term	Means this
Attribute	Information about a specific dimension member
Data warehouse	A relational database designed to store management information
Dimension	A list of labels that can be used to cross-tabulate values from other dimensions
Fact table	The relational database table that contains values for one or more measures at the lowest level of detail for one or more dimensions
Foreign key column	A column in a database table that contains many values for each value in the primary key column of another database table
Join	The processes of linking the primary key of one table to the foreign key of another table
Measure	A summarizable numerical value used to monitor business activity
Member	A single item within a dimension
Member property	An attribute of a member that is not meaningful when grouping values for a report, but contains valuable information about a different attribute
Primary key column	A column in a database dimension table that contains values that uniquely identify each row
Snowflake design	A database arrangement in which attributes of a dimension are stored in a separate (normalized) table
Star design	A database arrangement in which multiple attributes of a dimension are redundantly stored in a single (denormalized) dimension table

Chapter 2

Understanding OLAP and Analysis Services

After completing this chapter, you will be able to:

- Understand the definition of OLAP and the benefits an OLAP tool can add to a data warehouse.
- Understand how Microsoft SQL Server Analysis Services 2005 implements OLAP.
- Understand tools for developing and managing an Analysis Services database.

Business intelligence (BI) is a way of thinking. A data warehouse is a general structure for storing the data needed for good BI. But data in a warehouse is of little use until it is converted into the information that decision makers need. The large relational databases typical of data warehouses need additional help to convert the data into information. In this chapter, you will first learn the general benefits of online analytical processing (OLAP)—one of the best technologies for converting data into information—and then you will learn about how Microsoft Analysis Services implements the benefits of OLAP.

Understanding OLAP

The first version of Analysis Services was named OLAP Services. Even though the name now reflects the purpose of the product, rather than the technology, the technology is still important. Understanding the history of the term OLAP can help you understand its meaning.

In 1985, E. F. Codd coined the term *online transaction processing* (OLTP) and proposed 12 criteria that define an OLTP database. His terminology and criteria became widely accepted as the standard for databases used to manage the day-to-day operations (transactions) of a company. In 1993, Codd came up with the term *online analytical processing* (OLAP) and again proposed 12 criteria to define an OLAP database. This time, his criteria did not gain wide acceptance, but the term OLAP did, seeming perfect to many for describing databases designed to facilitate decision making (analysis) in an organization.

Some people use OLAP simply as a synonym for dimensional data warehousing. Usually, however, the term OLAP describes specialized tools that make warehouse data easily accessible. One term that is almost always associated with OLAP—but never associated with relational databases—is the word *cube*. As you learned in the previous chapter, the term *dimension* was appropriated from geometry for use in a relational warehouse. In a similar way, OLAP borrowed the word *cube* to describe what in the relational world would be the integration of the fact table with dimension tables. In geometry, a cube has three dimensions. In OLAP, a cube can have anywhere from one to however many dimensions you need. The word does make some sense because, in geometry, you calculate the size of the cube by multiplying the size of each of the three dimensions. Likewise, in OLAP, you calculate the theoretical maximum size of a cube by multiplying the size of each of the dimensions. Different OLAP tools define, store, and manage cubes differently, but when you hear the word "cube," you're in the OLAP world.

So what is the benefit of an OLAP cube over a relational database? Typically, OLAP tools add the following three benefits to a relational database:

- Consistently fast response
- Metadata-based queries
- Spreadsheet-style formulas

Before looking specifically at Analysis Services, consider how OLAP in general provides these benefits.

Consistently Fast Response

One of the ways that OLAP obtains a consistently fast response is by prestoring calculated values. Basically, the idea is that you either pay for the time of the calculation at query time or you pay for it in advance. OLAP allows you to pay for the calculation time in advance. In terms of how data is physically stored, OLAP tools fall into two basic types: a spreadsheet model and a database model. Analysis Services storage is basically the database model, but it will be useful for you to understand some of the issues and benefits of a spreadsheet model OLAP.

- **Spreadsheet model OLAP** In a spreadsheet, you can insert a value or a formula into any cell. Spreadsheets are very useful for complex formulas because they give you a great deal of control. One problem with spreadsheets is that they are limited in size, and a spreadsheet is essentially a two-dimensional structure. An OLAP cube built using a spreadsheet storage model expands the model into multiple dimensions, and can be much larger than a regular spreadsheet. With OLAP based on a spreadsheet model, any cell in the entire cube space has the potential to be physically stored. That is both a good thing and a bad thing. It's a good thing because you can enter constant values at any point in the cube space, and you can also store the results of a calculation at any point in the cube space. It's a bad thing because it limits the size of the OLAP cube due to a little problem called data explosion.

You have perhaps heard the story of the man who invented chess. He lived in India, and according to legend, his name was Sessa. The king of India was very impressed with the game of chess and asked Sessa to name his reward. Sessa's request was so modest that it offended the king: He asked simply for one grain of rice for the first square of his chess board, two grains for the second square, four grains for the third, and so forth, doubling for each of the 64 squares of the board. Of course, by the time the king's magicians calculated the total amount of rice needed to pay the reward, they realized that—had they known the metric system and the distance to the sun—it would require a warehouse 3 meters by 5 meters by twice the distance to the sun to pay the reward. In one version of the legend, the king simply solved the problem by cutting off Sessa's head. In another version, the king was more noble and also more clever. He gave Sessa a sack, pointed him to the warehouse and told him to go count out his reward—no rush.

The problem Sessa gave the king was the result of a geometric progression: When numbers increase geometrically, they get very large very quickly, and the size of a cube increases geometrically with the number of dimensions. That is the problem with OLAP stored using a spreadsheet model. Because any cell in cube space has the potential for being stored physically, data explosion becomes a very real problem that must be managed. The more dimensions you include in the cube, and the more members in each dimension, the greater the data explosion potential. Spreadsheet-based OLAP tools typically have elaborate—and complicated—techniques for managing data explosion, but even so, they are still very limited in size.

Spreadsheet-based OLAP tools are typically associated with financial applications. Most financial applications involve relatively small databases coupled with complex, nonadditive calculations.

- **Database model OLAP** OLAP tools that store cube data by using a database model behave very differently. They take advantage of the fact that most reporting requires addition, and that addition is an associative operation. For example, when adding the numbers 3, 5, and 7, it doesn't matter whether you add 3 and 5 to get 8 before adding the 7, or whether you add 5 and 7 to get 12 before adding 3. In either case, the final answer is 15. In a purely relational database, you can get fast query results by creating aggregate tables. In an aggregate table, you presummarize values that will be needed in a report. For example, in a fact table that includes thousands of products, five years of daily data, and perhaps several other dimensions, you may have millions of rows in the fact table, requiring many minutes to generate a report by product subcategory and by quarter, even if there are only 50 subcategories and 20 quarters. But if you presummarize the data into an aggregate table that includes only subcategories and quarters, the aggregate table will have at most one thousand rows, and a report requesting totals by subcategory and by quarter will be extremely fast. In fact, because of the associative nature of addition, a report requesting totals by category and by year can use the same aggregate table, again producing the results very quickly.

Perhaps the biggest benefit of OLAP stored using the database model is the ability to avoid data explosion. Because you need relatively few aggregate tables to provide fast results, you can have much larger cubes with many more dimensions and attributes than by using a spreadsheet model. Perhaps the biggest disadvantage of OLAP stored by using a database model is that there is no inherent way to physically store values that are calculated using nonassociative operators. An extreme example of a difficult financial calculation is Retained Earnings Since Inception. To calculate this value, you must first calculate Net Income—itself a hodgepodge of various additions, subtractions, and multiplications. And you must calculate Net Income for every period back to the beginning of time so that you can sum them together. This is not an associative calculation, so calculating for all of the business units does not make it any easier to calculate the value for the total company.

Even OLAP cubes that are stored by using the database model can calculate some nonassociative values very quickly. For example, an Average Selling Price is not an additive value—you can't simply add prices together. But to calculate the Average Selling Price for an entire product line, you simply sum the Sales Amount and Sales Quantity across the product line, and then, at the product line level, you divide the total Sales Amount by the total Sales Quantity. Because you are calculating a simple ratio of two additive values, the result is essentially just as fast as retrieving a simple additive value.

Database-style OLAP tools are usually associated with sales or similar databases. Sales cubes are often huge—both with hundreds of millions of fact-table rows, and with multiple dimensions with many attributes. Sales cubes also often involve additive measures (dollars and units are generally additive) or formulas that can be calculated quickly based on additive values.

One of the major benefits of OLAP is the ability to precalculate values so that reports can be rendered very quickly. Different OLAP technologies may have different strengths and weaknesses, but a good OLAP implementation will be much faster than the equivalent relational query whenever highly summarized values are involved.

Metadata-Based Queries

When you write queries against a relational data source, you use Structured Query Language (SQL). SQL is an excellent language, but it was developed primarily for transaction systems, not for reporting applications. One of the problems with SQL is not the language itself, but the fact that the database provides relatively little information about itself. Information about how the data is stored and structured, and perhaps more importantly, what the data means, is called *metadata*. Relational databases contain a small amount of metadata, but most of the information about the database has to come from you—the person writing the SQL query.

An OLAP cube, on the other hand, contains a great deal of metadata. For example, when you create an OLAP cube, you define not only what the measures are, but also how they should be aggregated, what the caption should be, and even how the number should best be formatted. Likewise, in an OLAP cube, when you create a dimension with many attributes, you define which attributes are groupable, and whether any of the groupable attributes should be linked together into a hierarchy. Unfortunately, SQL is not able to take advantage of this metadata as you create queries.

Consequently, when you use an OLAP data source, you use a different query language, most likely multidimensional expressions, or MDX. MDX was originally developed by Microsoft, and many OLAP vendors have their own proprietary query languages. But in 2001, Microsoft, Hyperion, and SAS formed the XML for Analysis (XMLA) council to formulate a common specification for working with OLAP data sources. The query language chosen for the XMLA specification is MDX. Most major OLAP vendors have joined the XMLA council and now have XMLA providers. (For more information about XMLA, check out the council's Web site at *www.xmla.org*.)

In this section, you will be introduced to some of the benefits of MDX as a metadata-based query language. You don't need to try to learn the details of how to write MDX; you'll learn more about MDX specifics in a later chapter. Everything you learn about MDX queries in this book definitely applies to Microsoft Analysis Services. Most of it will also apply to most other OLAP providers, but some of the details may be different.

One of the key benefits of a query language that can work with the metadata of an OLAP source is that you can use a general-purpose browser to query a specific data source. For example, with a Microsoft Analysis Services cube, you can choose to use Microsoft client tools such as those included in Microsoft Office, or you can choose tools from any of dozens of other vendors. Any client tool that uses MDX or XMLA can understand your cube and generate meaningful reports without the need for you to create custom queries. In other words, because MDX query statements are based on metadata stored in the OLAP cube, you can probably use a tool that will generate the query for you, and you won't have to write any MDX query statements at all.

If you do have a reason for writing custom MDX queries, the metadata makes it much easier than writing SQL queries. As a simple example, in SQL, if you create a query that calculates the total Sales Units for each customer's City, you still need to add a clause to make sure that the cities are sorted properly; but in an MDX query, you simply state that you want the members of the City attribute and you automatically get the default sort order as defined in the metadata. As another example, in a SQL table that contains both Country and City columns, there is nothing to suggest that Cities belong to specific countries, so if you want to show all the cities from Germany, you have to explicitly include the fact the you want to filter by Germany but show cities; in an OLAP cube, where Country is defined as the parent of City, you can specify the query using the expression *[Germany].Children*. In fact, if you later inserted a Region attribute between Country and City, the MDX query would automatically return the regions in Germany, based on the hierarchical relationships defined in the metadata.

These are just a taste of the kind of benefits MDX brings to the area of reporting queries. Many other kinds of reporting queries that are difficult in SQL—such as a cross-tabulation that shows the best-selling products as column headings and the best-selling regions as row headings—are very simple by using MDX queries. Some reports that are simply impossible in SQL—such as nesting multiple layers of attributes as column headings—are also very simple by using MDX queries.

Spreadsheet-Style Formulas

Arguably half the world's businesses are managed by using spreadsheets. Spreadsheets are notoriously decentralized, error-prone, difficult to consolidate, and impossible to manage. So why are they such a key component of business management? Because spreadsheet formulas are intuitive to create. To calculate the percentage of the total for a given product, you point at the product cell, add a division sign (/), point at the total cell, and you're done. With a little fiddling with the formula, you can copy it to calculate the percentage for any product. When you're creating the percentage formula, you don't need to worry about how the total got calculated; you solved that with a different formula, so now you can simply use the result. The same is true for other formulas such as month-to-month growth, or growth from the same month of the previous year and many other useful analytical formulas. Many very useful formulas that would be very difficult to create using pure relational SQL queries are easy to create in a spreadsheet.

But even from a spreadsheet user's perspective, formulas have inherent problems. A spreadsheet formula is inherently two-dimensional: You have numbers for rows and letters for columns. If you need to replicate the same spreadsheet for a different time period—particularly one in which there are different products or different dates—it is cumbersome to modify the formulas. And it is easy to make mistakes: There is nothing about the reference C12 that reassures you that you are indeed getting the value for March and not for April. As formulas become long and complex, it can be difficult even for the original creator to figure out what the formula really means. In addition, you can easily replace a formula in the middle of a range with an "adjusted" formula, or a constant value, and then forget that you made the change.

From a management perspective, spreadsheet formulas have even bigger problems: The formulas in a spreadsheet are key "business logic," and yet they are spread out all over the organization. The growth calculation created by Rajif may have some subtle differences from the one created by Sayoko, even though they ostensibly (and apparently) use the same logic.

Formulas in OLAP cubes have many of the same benefits as a spreadsheet formula: While creating a formula, you can reference any cell in the entire cube without concern for how that value was calculated.

Most OLAP providers have their own proprietary formula languages. Even providers who support MDX queries as part of the XMLA specification may not support the full potential of MDX formulas. Microsoft Analysis Services has a very rich implementation of MDX formulas. Here are a few examples of ways that MDX formulas are even easier than spreadsheet formulas:

- References in a spreadsheet formula are cryptic. In MDX, formulas can have meaningful names in references. Thus, instead of =C14/D14, the formula might be [Actual]/[Budget].
- In a spreadsheet, a formula must be explicitly copied to each cell that needs it. In MDX, a formula is defined generically, so that switching a report to show 500 products instead of just 50 requires you to make sure that the formulas apply properly to the new rows.

Likewise, if you create a new worksheet—say, for a new region—you must make sure that the formulas on the new worksheet point to the proper cells. In MDX, switching to a new region automatically uses the same generic formula.

- The nature of a spreadsheet reference is two-dimensional, with a letter for the column and a number for the row. This inherently limits the number of dimensions you can easily incorporate into a formula. MDX references use a structure (similar to that used for geometric coordinates) that is not tied to a two-dimensional physical location, and can explicitly include dozens of dimensions, if necessary. In addition, an MDX reference simplifies the use of multiple dimensions by taking advantage of the concept of a "current" member. For example, in the same way that copying the formula =C14/D14 to multiple sheets in a single workbook automatically uses the values from cells on the current sheet, using the MDX formula [Actual]/[Budget] automatically uses the current time period, or the current department, or the current product.
- A spreadsheet formula has no knowledge of the logical relationships between other cells; it has no knowledge of metadata. MDX formulas, on the other hand, can take advantage of a cube metadata to calculate relationships that would be difficult in a spreadsheet. For example, in a spreadsheet, it is easy to calculate the percentage each product contributes to the grand total, but it is very difficult to calculate the percentage each product contributes to its product group. In MDX, because the metadata can include information about hierarchical relationships, calculating the Percent of Parent within a product hierarchy is very easy.
- A spreadsheet formula can only refer to values that are on the same worksheet (or perhaps another worksheet in the same workbook). An MDX formula has access to any value anywhere in the cube space. This allows you to create *bubble-up* or *exception* formulas. An example of a bubble-up exception formula would be a report that shows the total sales at the region level, but displays the value in red if any of the districts within the region is significantly lower than its target. It does this even though the districts don't appear on the report.

This is just a taste of the ways that an MDX formula can be more powerful than a simple spreadsheet formula. In addition, MDX formulas are stored on the server, putting business logic into a centralized, manageable location, rather than spreading the business logic across hundreds of independent spreadsheets.

Understanding Analysis Services

You don't need Analysis Services to create a data warehouse; you create a data warehouse in a relational database. Even if you want to add the benefits of OLAP, you can choose any of several OLAP vendors. So why use Analysis Services for OLAP? Some people say that Microsoft products are popular because they have an inexpensive licensing model. But buying a cheap tool can be an expensive mistake. For something as important as BI, you want to be sure that the tools you use are the best you can use. So what makes Microsoft SQL Server 2005 Analysis

Services a good choice? In order to answer that, you need to understand some of the fundamental architecture of Analysis Services. In the first half of this chapter, you learned three major benefits of OLAP technology. Now you will learn how Analysis Services implements those three main benefits.

Analysis Services and Speed

Speed comes from precalculating values. Querying a 100-million-row table for a grand total is going to take much more time than querying a 100-row summary table. Because most very large data warehouse databases use addition for *aggregations*, Analysis Services stores data in a database style, using the equivalent of summary tables for aggregations. Of course, it can store the data in a special format that is particularly efficient for storage and retrieval, but conceptually, creating aggregations in Analysis Services is the same as creating summary tables in a relational database. Because the values are additive (or similar), you don't need to create a space for every possible value. Rather, you create "strategic" aggregations, so that relatively few aggregations can support hundreds or thousands of possible types of queries.

The biggest problem with creating summary tables in a relational data warehouse is that there is an incredible amount of administrative work involved.

- First, you must decide which of the potential millions of possible aggregate tables you will actually create.
- Second, you must create, populate, and update the aggregate tables.
- Finally, you must change reports to use the appropriate aggregate tables.

Each one of these steps is a major undertaking. Analysis Services basically takes care of all of them for you. (You can do some tuning, but the process is essentially automatic.) Analysis Services has sophisticated tools to simplify the process of designing, creating, maintaining, and querying aggregate tables, which it then stores in its extremely efficient proprietary structures. Managing aggregations has always been an extremely strong feature of Analysis Services. Because of its ability to avoid data explosion issues, Analysis Services can handle extremely large–multiterabyte–databases.

Analysis Services and Metadata

Analysis Services in SQL Server 2005 has significantly re-architected the way that metadata is defined–both for dimensions and for cubes.

Dimension Metadata

Consider a Customer dimension. In a relational data warehouse, you would typically have a table with a primary key–one that uniquely identifies each customer. Then you have a number of attributes that relate to that customer. For example, you might have Street Address, City, Country, Region, Age, Age Group, Gender, and potentially many other attributes. In Analysis

Services 2005, you simply define the dimension as a key with attributes. The metadata matches the logic of the data.

Some attributes—such as Street Address—will never be used for grouping or selecting customers, so you flag them in the metadata.

Some attributes—such as Gender—can be used for grouping on a report, and can also be added into a total, which essentially ignores the attribute. This is the automatic, default behavior of an attribute in Analysis Services. A single-level groupable attribute is called an *attribute hierarchy*.

A single dimension can have many attribute hierarchies. Again, the metadata matches the logic of the data.

Some attributes form a natural hierarchy. For example, each customer has an age, and each age belongs to an age group. Analysis Services allows you to create a multilevel hierarchy of attributes that reflects this relationship. A customer might belong to multiple hierarchies. For example, in your organization, you might have each customer belong to a city, which belongs to a country, which then belongs to a region. In Analysis Services, you can define multiple multilevel hierarchies from attributes in a single dimension—again, making the metadata match the logic of the data.

In previous versions of Analysis Services, each hierarchy essentially became a separate dimension, even though they all came from the same underlying relational dimension. In Analysis Services 2005, all the attributes and hierarchies of a logical dimension belong to that dimension in the Analysis Services dimension. In fact, even without creating multilevel hierarchies, if you nest attributes on a report—putting, for example, Gender and then Age Group on the rows of a report—Analysis Services automatically recognizes the combinations that actually exist in the dimension and ignores any that do not. This allows incredible flexibility in reporting without hurting query performance.

Cube Metadata

Suppose you decide to design a cube before you create the data warehouse to support it—which, incidentally, you can do in Analysis Services 2005. First, you select a measure—say, Sales Amount. Next, decide what dimensions you would like for that measure, and at what level of detail—say, Product by Customer, by Date. This defines the *grain* for the measure. Finally, decide if there are any other measures that have the same grain—perhaps Sales Units. You would then create a *measure group* that contains all the measures that have the same dimensions at the same grain.

Suppose you select a new measure requiring a different grain. For example, suppose you want Sales Target to have product categories by calendar quarter by scenario. This measure does not have the same grain as Sales Amount and Sales Quantity, so you create a new measure group. If there are any other measures that require the same grain as Sales Target, you can add them to the same measure group.

A measure group is simply the *group* of *measures* that share the same grain. When you go to build your data warehouse, you would create a separate fact table for each measure group. Conversely, if you already have a data warehouse with several fact tables, you simply create a measure group for each fact table.

A *cube* is then the combination of all the measure groups. This means that a single cube can contain measures with different grains. This pushes the meaning of *cube* even further from its geometrical origins. Perhaps you can visualize a cube as a cluster of crystals of varying sizes and shapes, many of which share common sides. In this new way of thinking, a single cube can contain all the metadata for all the data in your data warehouse. Because of this, a cube is now sometimes called a *Unified Dimensional Model,* or UDM. Sometimes a cube has more information than is manageable by a single person. For example, a procurement manager may not care about how sales discounts are applied. Analysis Services allows you to create a *perspective* that is like a cube that contains only a subset of the measures and dimensions of the whole cube. You can create as many perspectives as you want within a cube.

A cube is a logical structure, not a physical one. The same is true for a measure group. It defines the metadata so that client tools can access the data. You define measures and dimensions, and specify how measures should be aggregated across the dimensions.

Conceptually, each measure group contains all the detail values stored in the fact table, but that doesn't mean that the measure group must physically copy all the detail values from the fact table. If you choose, you can make the measure group dynamically retrieve values as needed from the fact table. In this case, you're using the measure group only to define metadata. This is called relational OLAP, or ROLAP. For faster query performance, you can tell the measure group to copy the detail values into a proprietary structure that allows for extremely fast retrieval. This is called multidimensional OLAP, or MOLAP. Analysis Services allows you, as the cube designer, to decide whether to store the values as MOLAP or ROLAP. Aside from performance differences, where the detail values are physically stored is completely invisible to a user of a cube. Whether you use MOLAP or ROLAP, values are stored in a memory *cache*—on a space-available basis—to make subsequent queries faster. You can think of MOLAP storage as a disk-based cache that allows the Analysis Server to load the memory cache much faster than if it had to go to the relational database.

Analysis Services Formulas

Even without any explicit formulas, an Analysis Services cube contains many calculations—the totals that aggregate up the hierarchies in each dimension are calculations, and they happen automatically. If you create a cube that consists primarily of additive measures—for example, a cube that summarizes sales or other transactions—the basic cube engine does most of the calculation work. When you create MOLAP aggregations, Analysis Services physically stores the values needed to query sum, count, min, and max calculations extremely quickly. In addition, you can create *calculated members* that perform calculations on aggregated values. Calculated members make it easy to create values such as average prices, weighted averages, ratios, growth calculations, and other key performance indicators (KPIs) to analyze your data. In addition to including sophisticated built-in tools for creating calculated members, Analysis Services allows you to access external functions from Microsoft Visual Basic for Applications (VBA) or Microsoft Excel, or even write your own external functions.

Because a cube contains multiple measure groups, it is easy to create calculations that include measures from different fact tables. For example, you could calculate a percentage by dividing Sales Amount by Sales Target even though the two measures are in different measure groups.

Finance Formulas

Financial applications typically require much more sophisticated formulas than simple addition. This is one of the reasons spreadsheets are very popular for financial analysis. Analysis Services has special features to support financial analysis:

- **Unary operators** Most financial analysts expect expenses (which are really negative) to show up as positive numbers. Some accounts–such as the number of employees–are called memo accounts and should not be added or subtracted. Analysis Services provides a mechanism for properly managing these types of accounts.
- **Semiadditive calculations** Some measures are actually snapshots at a point in time. Typical examples include inventory quantities and bank account balances. These measures should be added up over all dimensions *except* time. Analysis Services supports semiadditive calculations.
- **By account aggregations** Sometimes a single measure should behave differently depending on what type of account it is. For example, a Revenues account should add up over time, but a Balance account should not. The By Account aggregation type allows you to have different aggregation definitions for different account types within a single measure.
- **Script assignments** For certain complex financial calculations, you need to change a value that would otherwise be calculated in the cube–and then allow that value to be reaggregated within the normal dimension aggregation rules. You can think of it as changing a specific formula in a spreadsheet, even when other formulas depend on it. This was possible in Analysis Services 2000, but was very obscure and difficult. In Analysis Services 2005, the method for assigning formulas to portions of the cube has become much more simple and straightforward.

MDX formulas have always been very powerful for complex spreadsheet-like calculations. Even with the advent of XMLA for making MDX a standardized query language, Analysis Services has a much stronger implementation of MDX as a formula language than any other OLAP tool.

Analysis Services Tools

When you are responsible for an Analysis Services cube—or UDM—you perform two basic roles. On the one hand, you act as a developer—designing and creating the dimensions and cubes. On the other hand, you act as an administrator—keeping deployed cubes up-to-date and performing properly. In a large-scale implementation, it is common for these roles to be performed by different people, or even for multiple people to be involved in each part. Analysis Services in SQL Server 2005 recognizes that these are completely different roles and gives you two completely different tools for performing them.

For the developer, there is Business Intelligence Development Studio (BIDS). This is actually a copy of Visual Studio 2005, but with business intelligence designers installed instead of designers for C#.NET or VB.NET. If you use Visual Studio to write .NET applications, BIDS integrates smoothly with your existing installation. If you do not use Visual Studio for any other purpose, the Visual Studio shell, along with the business intelligence designers, is included with SQL Server 2005. Within BIDS, you can have multiple developers working on different parts of a single project, using XMLA to deploy the Analysis Services application to the development, test, or production server as appropriate. You can even integrate the project with Microsoft Visual Source Safe (VSS) so that you can safely manage the "source code" for an Analysis Services cube. If you want to automate either development or production tasks, you can use the .NET libraries in Analysis Management Objects (AMO), or you can use XMLA scripts.

Analysis Services 2005 is very effective at implementing the three benefits of OLAP. It uses a database model—with automatic management of aggregations—to handle extremely fast response from huge databases with little or no data explosion. It allows you to create a metadata model that accurately represents the true nature of both dimensions and cubes. And it supports a powerful implementation of the MDX formula language with capabilities that range from simple calculated ratios to complex financial calculations with sophisticated ripple effects. In essence, Analysis Services is simple enough for small, uncomplicated organizations, and powerful enough for large or complex organizations, allowing all types of organizations to add analytical power to their BI solutions.

Chapter 2 Quick Reference

This term	Means this
Aggregation	Summarized values of a measure
Cache	Server-based storage locations both in memory (automatic) or on disk (designed) that enhance query performance
Calculated member	A mechanism for aggregating measures using formulas more complex than those stored in a cube
Cube	A collection of one or more related measure groups and their associated dimensions
Cube metadata	Instructions for creating and querying OLAP structures such as cubes and dimensions
Hierarchy	Levels of aggregation within a single dimension
Measure group	The conceptual container of detail values from a single fact table, along with all possible aggregations for one or more dimension hierarchies
Online analytical processing (OLAP)	A database system optimized to support decision-making processes
Online transaction processing (OLTP)	A database system used to manage transactions such as order processing
Unified Dimensional Model (UDM)	The measure groups and dimensions that define your organization's BI data; essentially synonymous with a cube

Chapter 3

Building Your First Cube

After completing this chapter, you will be able to:

- Navigate an Analysis Services project in Microsoft Visual Studio.
- Use the Cube Wizard to build a simple cube from a template.
- Use the Generate Schema Wizard to build a relational schema as a data source for the cube.
- Deploy and process an Analysis Services project to the Analysis Server.
- Browse a cube.

In Chapter 2, "Understanding OLAP and Analysis Services," you were introduced to the key components of an Analysis Services cube and the role of a cube in a business intelligence (BI) solution. Now you're ready to learn how to build a cube by using the business intelligence templates available in Microsoft Visual Studio. In this chapter, you'll begin by familiarizing yourself with the organization of objects within this integrated development environment. The best way to do this is to examine an existing project. Next, you'll learn how to use a top-down approach to developing a cube, which means you'll design the cube first and then you'll build and load the data source afterwards. (You'll learn how to develop a cube using the bottom-up approach in Chapter 4, "Designing Dimensions," and Chapter 5, "Designing Measure Groups and Measures.")

After you design the cube, you will use the cube's structure to build a relational database (known as a star schema) to house the data for the cube. Once you load data into the relational database, and then into the cube, you'll be able to see how attributes, dimensions, measures, and measure groups fit together within a cube to create a powerful analytical tool.

Exploring Business Intelligence Development Studio

To develop BI solutions in SQL Server 2005, you use special designers integrated into Microsoft Visual Studio 2005. If you have used any recent version of Visual Studio to develop applications, the development environment will be familiar. By using Visual Studio, you can organize your development work into a project. This is particularly useful in a large-scale environment, because you can have multiple developers working on a single cube project, and you can use Microsoft Visual Source Safe or Microsoft Team Foundation to store backup copies of all the project files. If you have never used Visual Studio, you may see some windows and toolbars that are not familiar to you. Many of the environment tools simplify the process of building a BI application. Some of the tools, however, do not relate to BI projects, and you can simply ignore them.

If you originally acquire Visual Studio as part of SQL Server 2005, it will include only the business intelligence designers. If you acquire other Visual Studio tools—for example, VB.NET or C#.NET—those design tools are integrated into the same environment. Within the Visual Studio environment, the business intelligence designers are grouped together. For convenience, we will refer to the business intelligence designers of Visual Studio as Business Intelligence Development Studio (BIDS).

Within the BIDS environment, you can create Analysis Services projects that structure data for high-performance analysis, develop Integration Services packages that prepare and load data for use with your Analysis Services projects, and build Reporting Services reports that present the results of analysis to the business user community. If you also have other development tools, you can include C#.NET or ASP.NET applications in the same solution as your BI projects. This book focuses only on Analysis Services, but many resources exist to help you take full advantage of any Visual Studio tools that you own.

When you use BIDS to develop an Analysis Services project, that project becomes a database when you deploy it to an Analysis Server. You can also create an Analysis Services project in BIDS to make design changes to an existing Analysis Services database. To perform general maintenance tasks on a production database—for example, to process a database object—you use SQL Server Management Studio (SSMS) instead. You will learn about SSMS in Chapter 13, "Managing Deployment."

Examining the Contents of an Analysis Services Project

When you first open BIDS after installation, you will see the Start page displayed in the main window. This page contains a list of your Recent Projects, quick links for Getting Started and for Visual Studio Headlines, as well as links to recent articles from Microsoft Developers Network (MSDN): Visual Studio 2005. If this is the first time you have used this application, the Recent Projects pane will be empty. Once you start building projects, this pane will contain links to those projects, which makes it a helpful tool for locating and opening recent work.

If this is your first time working with BIDS and if you have never worked with Visual Studio, you might not be familiar with the way items are organized in this environment. A solution is a container for one or more projects. You view the contents of a solution in the Solution Explorer window which is displayed by default in the upper right window of the development environment. If the Solution Explorer is not visible, you can click the Solution Explorer button in the toolbar, or click Solution Explorer in the View menu. A solution could contain multiple Analysis Services projects, for example, or a solution could contain one or more Analysis Services, Integration Services, Report Model, or Reporting Services projects. In turn, each project is a container for one or more collections of objects. These objects are grouped by folders, such as Data Source Views, Cubes, or Dimensions. You can work with only one solution at a time, but you can access any object in any project within the solution while that solution is open in Visual Studio.

When you create a new Analysis Services project or open an existing project of this type, the Solution Explorer window displays a set of folders: Data Sources, Data Source Views, Cubes, Dimensions, Mining Structures, Roles, Assemblies, and Miscellaneous. As you design your analytical solution, you add objects to these folders as needed, typically starting with data sources, continuing with data source views, and then building dimensions and cubes. If you are building a solution without a data source, you can launch a wizard that guides you through the required steps. This approach would be appropriate when you want to prototype an analytical solution before a data warehouse is available.

In this procedure, you'll begin your tour of the Visual Studio interface by opening the finished version of the Analysis Services project that you will build as you progress through the chapters of this book.

Open the SSAS Step by Step solution

1. Start SQL Server Business Intelligence Development Studio.

   Your screen looks similar to this:

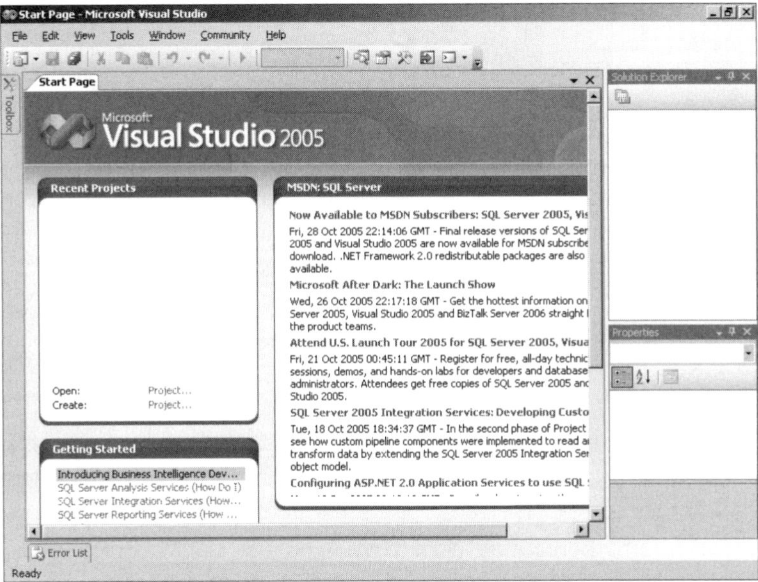

> **Note** In order to complete this procedure, you must first complete the setup procedures outlined in the Introduction.

2. On the File menu, point to Open, and then click Project/Solution.
3. Browse to open the SSAS Step by Step solution in the C:\Documents and Settings\<username>\My Documents\Microsoft Press\as2005sbs\chap03\Step by Step folder, where <username> is your login name on your computer.

4. Select SSAS Step by Step.sln, and then click Open.

   The sample solution looks like this:

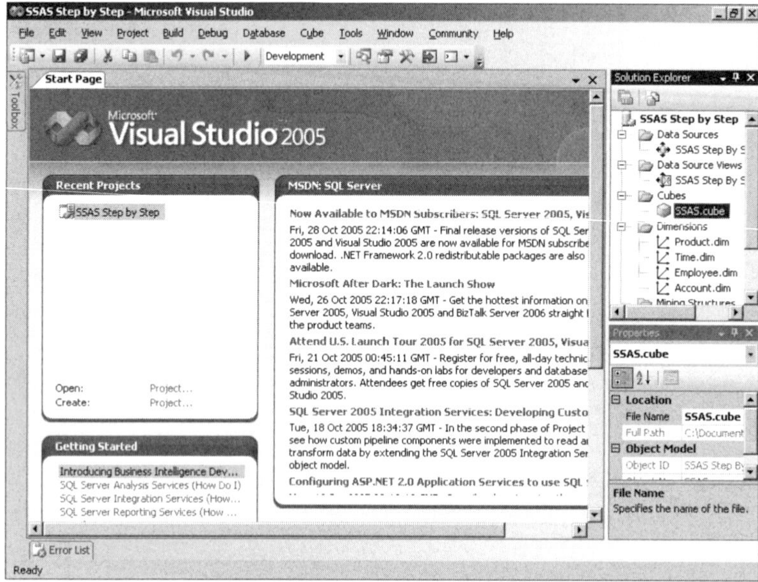

   This sample solution contains many examples which highlight the new features available in this new version of Analysis Services. Notice the folders in the database project in the Solution Explorer window. Each folder contains a particular type of object used in an Analysis Services database.

5. In the Solution Explorer window, double-click SSAS Step by Step DW.ds in the Data Sources folder.

   The Data Source Designer contains the connection string and credentials used to retrieve data from a relational database. A single solution can contain more than one *data source*, and the Data Sources folder stores the list of connected relational databases. An Analysis Services database must contain at least one data source.

6. Click Cancel, and then double-click SSAS Step by Step DW.dsv in the Data Source Views folder.

   An Analysis Services database must also contain at least one *data source view* (DSV) in the Data Source Views folder. A DSV contains the logical representations of tables from one or more data sources. In the DSV, you can add a logical primary key to any table or view that does not have a physical primary key. You define relationships between tables, even for tables that come from different data sources. You can also create calculated columns or logical views (named queries) without making the changes in the source databases.

7. Double-click Product.dim in the Dimensions folder.

   An Analysis Services project also contains at least one dimension and at least one cube. Each of these objects has its own folder. The Mining Structures folder is used for the data mining functionality that is included in SQL Server 2005 Analysis Services. The Roles folder is used to support both client and administration security. You can use the Assemblies folder for class libraries that you develop to extend the capabilities of your project. The Miscellaneous folder is for project-related files, such as documentation or notes about remaining tasks. Most of the time, you'll work with a DSV, a cube, or a dimension.

Exploring Menu Commands

The development environment includes the standard Visual Studio menus–such as File, Edit, View, Project, Build, Debug, and so on. The Project menu is context-sensitive–that is, the commands that appear on the menu change depending on the type of project that contains the object you select in Solution Explorer. Some of the other Visual Studio commands might not be relevant to an Analysis Services project. As with many Microsoft applications, you can configure which toolbars are visible on your screen at any time.

In addition to the standard menus, when you select a dimension or cube object in Solution Explorer, a Dimension or Cube menu, respectively, appears in the menu bar. This menu is also context-sensitive. Because different commands are available for different objects, you can't simply scan through all the menus on the menu bar, hoping to recognize the command you want, as you can in most Windows applications. Rather, you must think of the object the command applies to, select that object, and then find the command on the menu or toolbar.

The best way to understand the menus and options in Visual Studio is to explore them, which is what you will do in this procedure.

Explore menu commands

1. Click the SSAS.cube object in Solution Explorer.

   The Cube menu appears in the Visual Studio menu bar.

2. Review the commands available in the Cube menu, and then right-click the SSAS.cube object in Solution Explorer.

   There are more commands in the shortcut menu because the shortcut menu also allows you to cut, copy, delete, or rename the cube within Solution Explorer as part of managing the Analysis Services project, as well as to access properties related to the cube.

3. Double-click the SSAS.cube object in Solution Explorer to open the Cube Designer.

The Cube Designer looks like this:

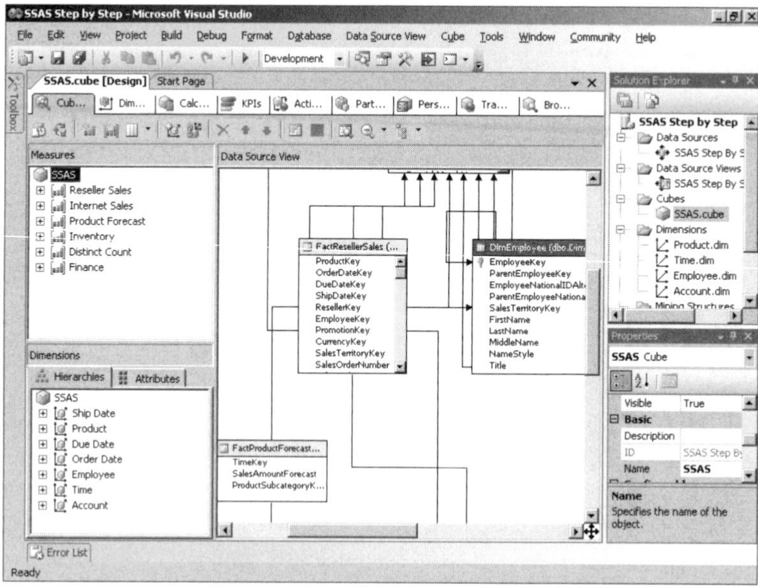

4. Review the commands now available in the Cube menu.

   The Cube menu now contains commands related to the Cube Designer. Some of these commands are displayed with icons that also appear on the designer toolbar.

5. Click the Calculations tab in the Cube Designer, and then compare the commands in the Cube menu with the toolbar.

   The commands in the menu and the toolbar change to correspond to the current designer window.

6. Right-click any item in the Script Organizer to review the shortcut menu for this area of the designer.

   The list of commands available in the Script Organizer is a subset of the commands that you can access from the menu or the toolbar.

7. On the File menu, click Close Project.

   Now that you've learned how to navigate within Visual Studio, you're ready to create a project of your own to continue your exploration of the capabilities of Analysis Services.

Preparing to Create a Cube

In this section, you will create a cube that is not based on an existing data source, so you have complete freedom to create the type of cube you want as a basis for reporting. To simplify the process, you'll use a standard template provided by the Cube Wizard in Analysis Services.

Creating a cube by using a wizard template is remarkably quick, but before you begin you need to make a few preparations.

Reviewing the Analysis Requirements

Sometimes you might prefer to work out the cube design before building and populating the relational database used to load the cube with data. You'll use this approach to create a cube later in this chapter. You will not create a relational database structure for your cube until *after* you design the cube. Once you understand your project's requirements so that you can build the cube properly, you can create the cube, allow Analysis Services to create an empty source database, import the appropriate data from the SSAS Step by Step DW relational database, and finally process the cube so that you can see the results from the cube.

The analysis objective of your first project is to enable users to analyze sales dollars and the number of products sold by product and by time. Your cube will need two measures–Sales Dollars and Sales Units. As you learned in Chapter 1, "Understanding Business Intelligence and Data Warehousing," a measure is a numeric value that will be summarized in the cube. You will also need two dimensions–Product and Time. In Chapter 1, you learned that a dimension consists of attributes that group measure values. The Product dimension you create will use standard attributes as defined by the wizard template. The Time dimension you create should support both calendar and fiscal calendars which include date, month, quarter, and year attributes organized into appropriate hierarchies.

Creating a New Analysis Services Project

In Visual Studio, before creating a cube, you must first create an Analysis Services project in which to store it. An Analysis Services project can contain more than one cube, but a cube cannot exist outside a project. When you deploy the project, a database that corresponds to the project is created on the Analysis Server.

In this procedure, you'll create an Analysis Services project named My First Cube to store your first cube.

Start a new Analysis Services project

1. On the File menu, point to New, and then click Project.

   The New Project dialog box displays the available designers for the Business Intelligence project types. If you have Visual Studio installed on your computer, you can also use other Visual Studio designers to add other projects to the same solution if you need to integrate your BI project with a custom application.

2. Ensure that the Project Type is set to Business Intelligence Projects, and then click the Analysis Services Project template.

3. Type a name for the project: **My First Cube**.

Notice that the text in the Solution Name box changes automatically to match the project name. When you are planning to create a solution with multiple projects, you can change the solution name. For now, leave it as My First Cube.

4. Change the location for the project to **C:\Documents and Settings\<username>\My Documents\Microsoft Press\as2005sbs\Workspace** and confirm that the Create Directory For Solution check box is selected.

   The New Project dialog box looks like this:

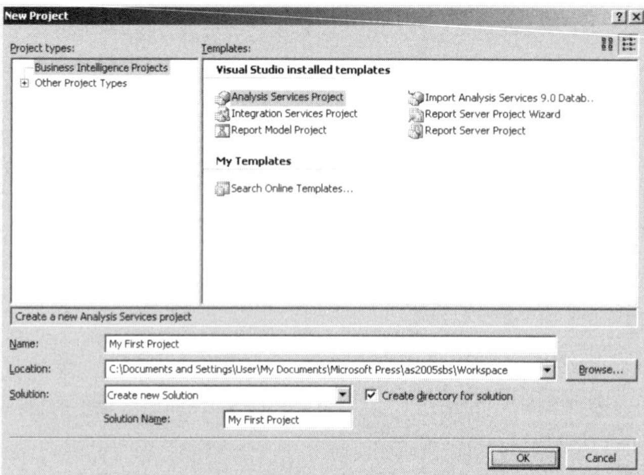

5. Click OK to continue.

   The Solution Explorer window now contains a set of empty folders that will later contain objects as you build your Analysis Services project. There are also several other windows available in Visual Studio that you use to create and manage objects within your project, which you will learn how to do in later chapters of this book.

Creating a Cube

Once you've created an Analysis Services project, you can build a cube with or without fact and dimension tables ready for use as a data source. A cube consists of one or more measures (such as Sales or Quantity) from a fact table, and one or more dimensions (such as Product or Time) from dimension tables. When you build a cube with a data source already in place, the Cube Wizard helps you select the appropriate fact and dimension tables.

Using the Cube Wizard Without a Data Source

If you decide to build a cube without a data source, you have the option to use a built-in template that helps define the cube structure. After selecting the desired template, you select measures and dimensions from the template to include in the cube and specify which dimensions will be associated with each measure group. You have the option to generate the relational schema immediately after completing the wizard. However, before taking this step, you might want to modify or delete the analysis objects created from the template first.

In this procedure, you'll start the Cube Wizard to create a new cube.

Build a new cube

1. In Solution Explorer, right-click the Cubes folder, and then click New Cube.

   The Welcome page of the Cube Wizard is displayed. If you want to bypass this page in the future, just select the Don't Show This Page Again check box to disable the page permanently.

2. Click Next.

In this procedure, you'll select the option to create a cube using a template, but without an underlying database.

Specify a data source

1. Click Build The Cube Without Using A Data Source.
2. Select the Use A Cube Template check box, and then select Adventure Works Standard Edition from the template drop-down list.

   The Select Build Method page of the Cube Wizard now looks like this:

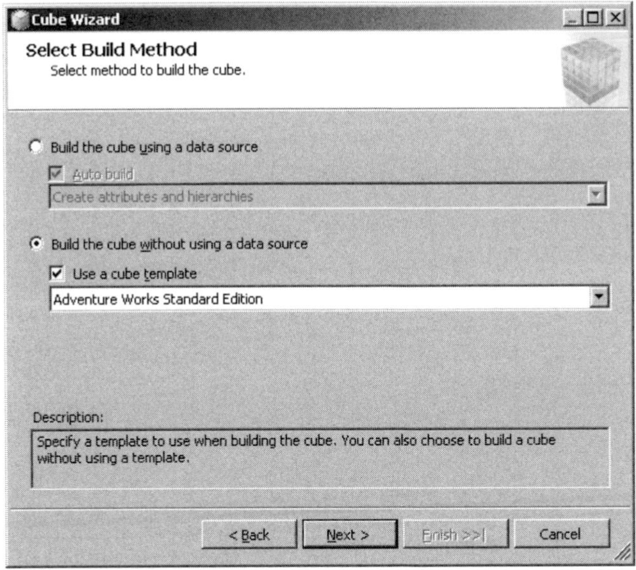

3. Click Next.

If you were using a data source, the Cube Wizard would lead you through the necessary steps. Without a data source, the next step is to create measures and dimensions. The templates make this process easy.

In this procedure, you'll define two measures for the cube, Sales Amount and Order Quantity.

Add measures

1. To clear the selection of all measures, click the box in the header row to the left of Measure Name, and then select the check boxes to the left of Internet Sales Amount and Internet Order Quantity.

   Notice that these measures are part of a measure group called Internet Sales. If you scroll through the list of measures, you'll see there are other measure groups: Internet Orders, Internet Customers, Sales Reasons, Reseller Sales, Reseller Orders, Sales Summary, Sales Orders, and Sales Targets. Each measure group is a collection of measures that comes from the same fact table.

2. Scroll back to the top of the list of measures, click the box that contains the measure name Internet Sales Amount, and change the measure name to **Sales Dollars**.

3. Repeat the previous step to change Internet Order Quantity to **Sales Units**.

   The measure names provided by each template can be changed to something more suitable for your needs. If you forget to change the name in this step of the Cube Wizard, you can change it later in the Cube Designer.

4. In the Measure Group column for the Sales Dollars and Sales Units rows, change the name of the Internet Sales measure group to **Sales**.

   The Define New Measures page of the Cube Wizard will now look like this:

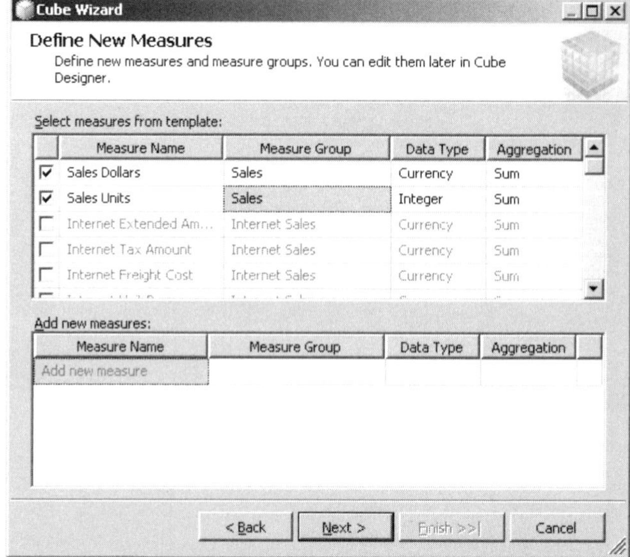

5. Click Next.

In this procedure, you'll add the Product and Time dimensions to the cube.

Add dimensions

1. To clear the selection of the template dimensions, click the box in the header row to the left of Type.

   The template contains several dimensions that you can include in your cube. Each dimension contains several stock attributes which you cannot change within the Cube Wizard, but you can change them freely after you complete the wizard. Select the SCD box if you want to include attributes for Slowly Changing Dimensions for tracking the start and end dates as well as the current status of a dimension record.

2. Click the respective check boxes to select the Products and Time dimensions.

3. Maximize the Cube Wizard window to view all of the dimension's attributes from the template.

   Your screen looks like this:

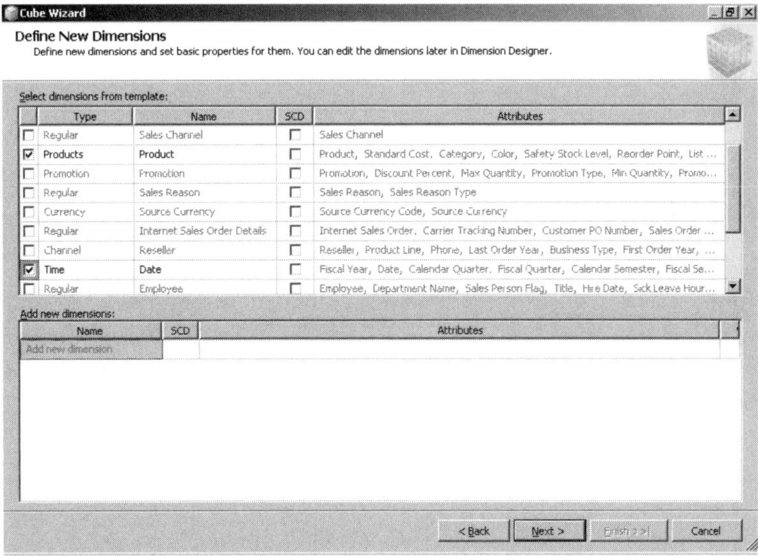

   Notice the default attributes for each dimension. You always have the option to remove unneeded attributes or add desired attributes after you complete the Cube Wizard.

   You now have all the dimensions that you need added to the cube. You're ready to move to the next step.

4. Click Next.

In this procedure, you'll specify the beginning and ending dates of the data that you wish to analyze as July 1, 2001, and December 31, 2006, respectively.

Define time periods

1. Click the First Calendar Day drop-down list, click the left arrow in the calendar control to scroll back to July 2001, and then click the appropriate day in the calendar to set the starting date as July 1, 2001.

   When you use the template's Time dimension, you must define the date range for this dimension. You must also specify the time attributes to include in the dimension, such as year, quarter, and month.

2. In the Last Calendar Day drop-down list, click 2005, and then type **2006**.

   You can either type date values in the boxes, or use the calendar control.

3. In the Time Periods pane, select the following: Year, Quarter, and Month.
4. Clear the Date check box in the Time Periods pane.

   When you clear the date, you'll see a warning message at the bottom of the wizard dialog box: "The date frequency level is required. If you do not want it to be visible, you can hide this attribute in the dimension editor." Since the Date attribute is the key attribute for the Time dimension, it must be included. A key attribute is used internally by Analysis Services to uniquely identify each record. Notice that you cannot move forward to the next page of the wizard until you include Date.

5. Click Date, and then click Next.

In this procedure, you'll add a fiscal calendar hierarchy that starts July 1 and ends June 30.

Add a special calendar

1. Select the Fiscal Calendar check box.

   Additional calendars are optional. You have up to four calendar types that will be used to create alternate hierarchies for Time: Fiscal, Reporting, Manufacturing, and ISO 8601. For each calendar type, except ISO 8601, you can specify the starting time period to properly allocate days into the correct time period. For example, if you change the start day of the Fiscal Calendar to 1 July, then any day in the month of July will display in the first month of the year when using the Fiscal Calendar during a cube browsing session.

2. Set Start Day And Month to **1 July**.
3. Click Next.

In this procedure, you'll specify how the dimensions and the measure groups are related and how the dimensions are used.

Relate dimensions to measures

1. Review the default settings in the Define Dimension Usage page of the Cube Wizard, which looks like this:

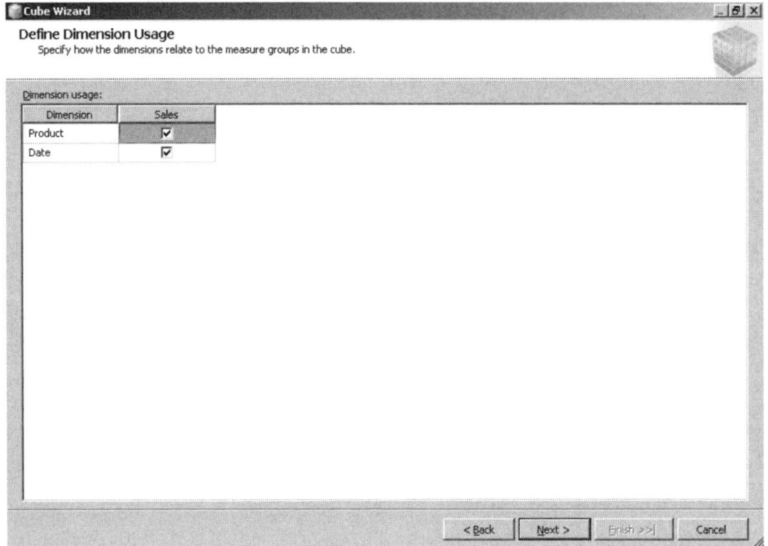

The selected check boxes indicate that both the Product and Date dimensions will be related to measures in the Sales measure group. Since you are building a very simple cube, both dimensions should be related to the single measure group.

Note The wizard always associates a measure group with the key attribute of each dimension. In many cases, that is appropriate. For example, if the key attribute of the Time dimension is Date and the key attribute of the Product dimension is Product, and you have sales data available by day and by product, the wizard will produce the correct association. But what if you also had a budget measure group included in the cube? Budget data is typically less granular than sales data, perhaps by month and by product category instead of by day and by product. You will not be able to define this relationship between budget and nonkey attributes of the Product dimension by using the wizard, but you will be able to define it later in the Cube Designer. You will learn about dimension usage in greater detail in Chapter 9, "Exploring Special Features."

2. Click Next.

In this procedure, you'll provide a name for your cube, the final step to completing the wizard.

Finish the Cube Wizard

1. In the Cube Name box, type **My Sales Cube**.

The cube name is automatically supplied when you select a template. In this case, the default name is Adventure Works. If you don't use a template when building the cube, the default name is the DSV name. You can always edit this name later if you're not sure what name to provide on this page.

2. Expand the Product node, and then expand the Attributes folder to view the attributes that will be created for this dimension.

   The preview of the cube structure on this page of the Cube Wizard is your first comprehensive view of the cube. If you see something that requires a change, you can move back to the appropriate page of the Cube Wizard, but remember that you can always make changes to this structure later if you want to add or delete objects.

   If you select the Generate Schema Now option, you will begin the Schema Generation Wizard. A *schema* is a denormalized relational database containing tables for the measure groups and dimensions that you use in the cube. You will learn more about generating a schema when you run the Schema Generation Wizard later in this chapter.

3. Click Finish to complete the Cube Wizard.

   The main window now displays the Cube Structure tab of the Cube Designer, as shown below:

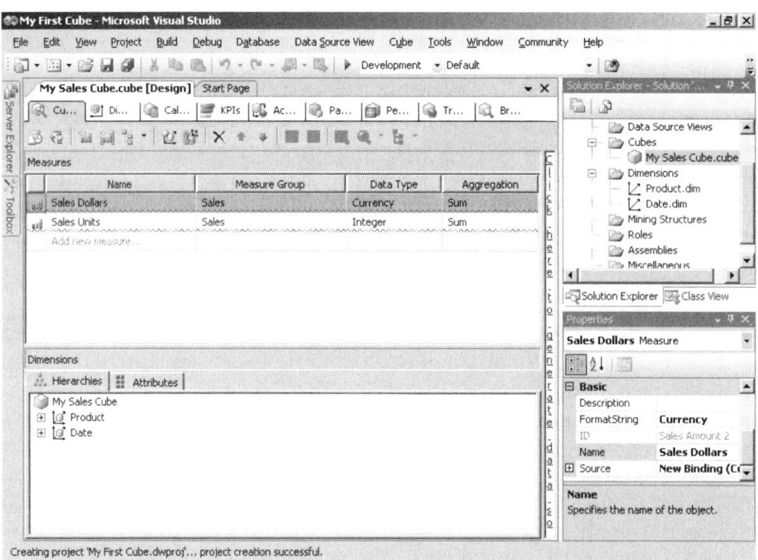

Note The red lines in the Measures pane indicate there is a problem with the measures. Because there is no DSV associated with the measures, an error condition results. You'll fix the error condition later in this chapter when you generate a schema.

Congratulations! You've just built your first cube. You can see in the lower left corner there is a Dimensions pane that displays the two dimensions in the cube. In the upper left corner, in the Measures pane, you can see one measure group that contains two measures. Since the cube is not connected to a data source yet, there isn't a DSV visible in the center window. However, you can still review the cube structure, and you can add to the cube structure or modify it until you get it just right. The Cube Wizard does not create the actual cube files or load values from the data warehouse. To use the cube, you must first process it, which you will do later in this chapter.

Reviewing the Cube Structure in the Cube Designer

The Cube Structure tab of the Cube Designer organizes the dimension and measure objects that are defined for the cube. In this workspace, you can review and change the properties of each object. As you select an object on the Cube Structure tab, the object's properties are available for editing in the Properties window. The Cube Structure tab also provides a diagram pane in which you can view the underlying table structures for the cube to see columns in the dimension and fact tables that are related. If the tables are not yet created, you will see a link, Click Here To Generate Data Source View. This link launches the Generate Schema Wizard, which you'll learn more about later in this chapter.

In this procedure, you'll change the default measure to Sales Dollars and explore the Cube Structure tab of the Cube Designer.

Review and modify the cube structure

1. On the Cube Structure tab, click Sales Dollars.

   Notice the Properties window below the Solution Explorer window. It currently displays all available properties for the selected object, which in this case is Sales Dollars.

2. In the Cube Structure toolbar, click the Show Measures Tree button.

   The Measures pane now displays the Sales measure group and its related measures in a tree view.

3. Click Sales in the Measures Tree.

   In the Properties window, you can view all of the properties associated with the Sales measure group. When you view measures in the Grid View, which was the default view in the Cube Structure after building a cube from a template, you cannot access the properties for measure groups. You can, however, use the toolbar buttons to toggle between Grid View and Tree View.

4. Click My Sales cube in the Measures pane.

   As with measure groups, there are certain properties for the cube that you can change only when you use Tree View for measures. The *DefaultMeasure* property is associated with the cube and might need to be changed if you build a cube from a template, but exclude the template's default measure from the cube. In this case, Reseller Sales

Amount is not a valid measure for your cube, so you need to change the *DefaultMeasure* property for your cube.

5. In the Properties window, locate the *DefaultMeasure* property (near the top of the list of properties), and then click Sales Dollars in the property's drop-down list.

Caution If you forget to reset this property, the cube will not process successfully.

6. Expand the Date dimension in the Dimensions pane.

   Your screen looks like this:

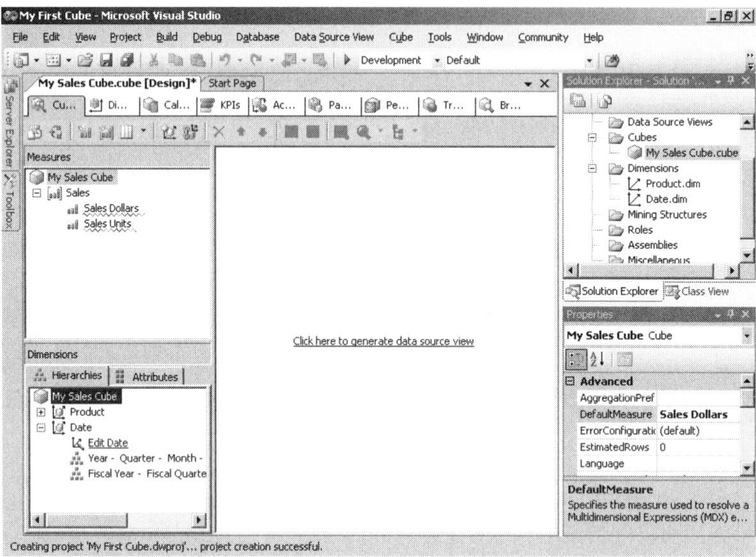

   Notice the two hierarchies built by the Cube Wizard:

   - Year – Quarter – Month – Date
   - Fiscal Year – Fiscal Quarter – Fiscal Month – Fiscal Day

   The Edit Date link above these hierarchies is one way that you can open the Dimension Structure for this dimension. The Dimension Structure is a workspace in the Dimension Designer where you can edit the properties of attributes and hierarchies in a dimension. You'll learn about dimensions, attributes, and hierarchies in greater detail in Chapter 4.

7. Click the Attributes tab in the Dimensions pane, and then expand Product.

The Dimensions pane looks like this:

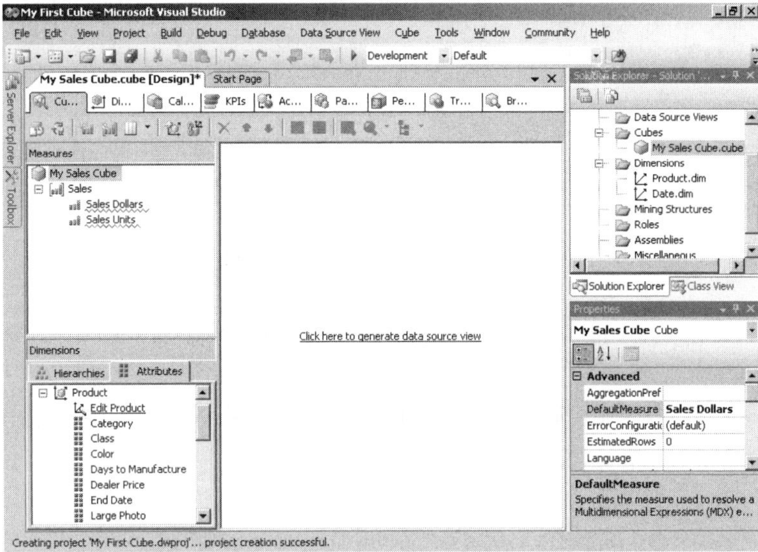

All the attributes from the Adventure Works Standard Edition template that you used to create this cube are listed here. If you don't want to include some of these attributes in the dimension, you won't be able to delete them here. You can only change or delete attributes of a dimension in the Dimension Designer.

Generating a Schema

When you use the Cube Wizard to build a cube without a data source, you will need to create a relational database to hold the data used to load values into the cube. You can create the necessary dimension and fact tables manually, but an easier method is to use the Schema Generation Wizard. Once the schema is built, you can insert data into the dimension and fact tables in preparation for viewing that data in the cube.

Using the Schema Generation Wizard

The Schema Generation Wizard guides you through the process of building a relational schema. Before you begin, you will need to create the database to which the Schema Generation Wizard will add the dimension and fact tables needed to load data into your cube. Once the relational structures are built, the Schema Generation Wizard adds a DSV to the Analysis Services project based on a data source that you specify. The data source defines the connection information for the source database, while the DSV is a representation of the table structures and relationships that are used when making modifications to the cube and when loading data into the cube.

In this procedure, you'll run the Schema Generation Wizard.

Create a relational schema

1. Start Microsoft SQL Server Management Studio, click Database Engine in the Server Type box, ensure the server name is correct, and then click Connect.

> **Note** Throughout this book, it is assumed that you are working on a local server using Windows authentication. You will need to change the server name and provide credentials if your environment is configured differently.

2. In the Object Explorer window, right-click the Databases folder, and then click New Database.
3. Type a name for the database, **My Simple Database**, and then click OK.
4. Switch to Visual Studio, and then, in the Diagram pane on the Cube Structure tab, click the link labeled Click Here To Generate Data Source View.

   The Schema Generation Wizard launches.
5. Click Next, and then, on the Specify Target page of the wizard, click New.

   The Data Source Wizard opens.

> **Note** If you had previously added a data source to your project, you could select it in the Data Source list box instead of creating a new data source.

6. Click Next, and then, on the Select How To Define The Connection page of the Data Source Wizard, click New.
7. In the Connection Manager dialog box, type the server name: **localhost**.
8. Click Use Windows Authentication to log on to the server.
9. In the Select Or Enter A Database Name list box, click My Simple Database.
10. Click the Test Connection button, and then click the OK button to close the Test Connection Succeeded message box.
11. Click OK to close the Connection Manager dialog box, and then click Next.
12. On the Impersonation Information page of the Data Source Wizard, click Use the Service Account, and then click Next.

> **Important** If you choose another option on this page, you will not be able to deploy your cube to the Analysis Server later in this chapter.

The Data Source Name defaults to the name of the selected database, My Simple Database.

Click Finish to complete the Data Source Wizard.

13. Your screen now looks like this:

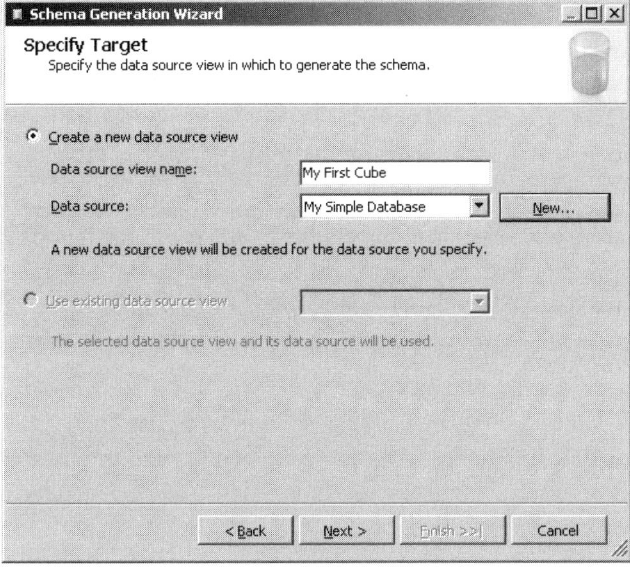

Now that a data source is available, you are ready to continue with the Schema Generation Wizard.

14. Click Next.

The Subject Area Database Schema Options page looks like this:

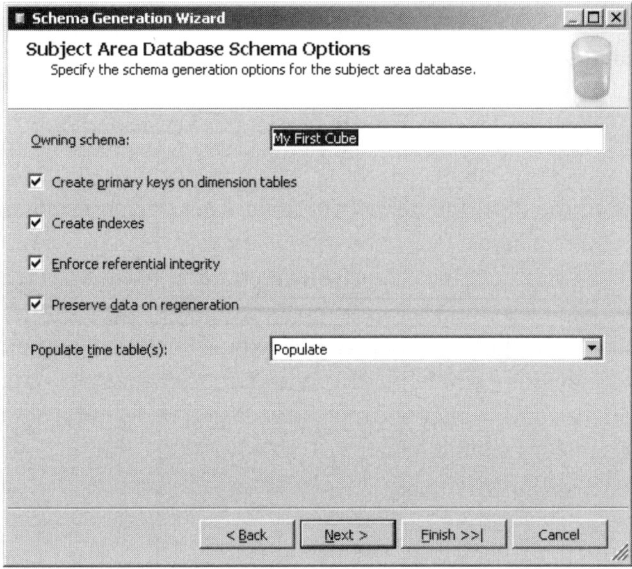

On this page of the wizard, you must specify an owner for the schema in the target database. By default, the Analysis Services project will be designated as the schema owner. Multiple schemas can coexist within the same target database, each distinguished by a project name to keep tables generated for one project from conflicting with tables generated for other projects.

Notice that, by default, all the options are selected because they are all recommended strategies for designing a relational schema. However, if your goal is to produce a prototype quickly and you aren't concerned about processing performance or data integrity, you can clear the selection of these options. For the purposes of this procedure, you will leave them selected.

a. You can gain some performance benefits by having the Schema Generation Wizard create primary keys in the physical dimension tables. If you choose not to have them created, the DSV will automatically create logical primary keys for each dimension anyway since they are required for Analysis Services.

b. Another performance enhancement is the creation of indexes on the foreign key columns in the fact table. Usually, these indexes boost Analysis Services processing because data can be retrieved more efficiently from the database due to the many joins between dimension and fact tables. However, you have the option to bypass creation of these indexes.

c. Referential integrity between the fact table and the dimension tables is important for maintaining data quality in an analytical application. You can choose whether or not to enforce referential integrity in the relational schema. Regardless of your choice, the physical tables and the data source view will include the foreign key relationships between the fact and dimension tables so that they can be properly joined for processing queries.

d. You will also need to indicate whether data in the tables should be preserved if you decided later to regenerate the schema. If you choose the setting to preserve data, but a problem resulting from the schema change requires rows to be deleted, you will receive a warning before the deletion of rows is carried out.

e. Next, you need to decide whether the Schema Generation Wizard should automatically load the time dimension with data. This operation can be performed each time you regenerate the schema or when there is no data in the tables when the schema is generated. You can also choose never to load the time tables with data. If the time dimension uses attributes defined in a Cube Wizard template, then all attributes will be populated. However, if you add a new attribute to the time dimension after completing the wizard, the Schema Generation Wizard will create a column for that attribute in the dimension table, but it has no way of determining what values should be used to populate that column. You will need to come up with your own method for updating that column with data.

15. Click Next.

    The Schema Generation Wizard now looks like this:

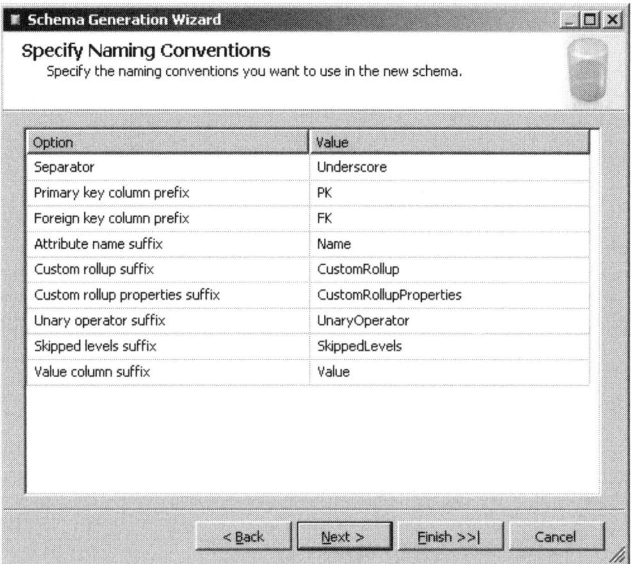

    On this page, you can adjust the naming conventions used by the Schema Generation Wizard if you already have standards that you want to use. The default separator is an underscore, but you can instead choose to use a space or no separator. For primary key and foreign key prefixes, you can change the defaults of PK and FK, respectively, to other values of your own choosing. When an attribute has both a key column and a name column, the default naming convention for the suffix of the name column is Name, which you can change as long as no other suffix has the same value. All of the other naming conventions apply to suffixes used for columns that support special Analysis Services features: custom rollup, custom rollup properties, unary operators, and skipped levels. You can change the default suffix values for each of these column types as long as each is unique across all suffixes.

16. Click Next, and then click Finish.

    The Schema Generation Progress window shows the processing status and provides details on the steps being performed. When processing is completed, the Close button becomes active.

17. Click Close.

Your screen now looks like this:

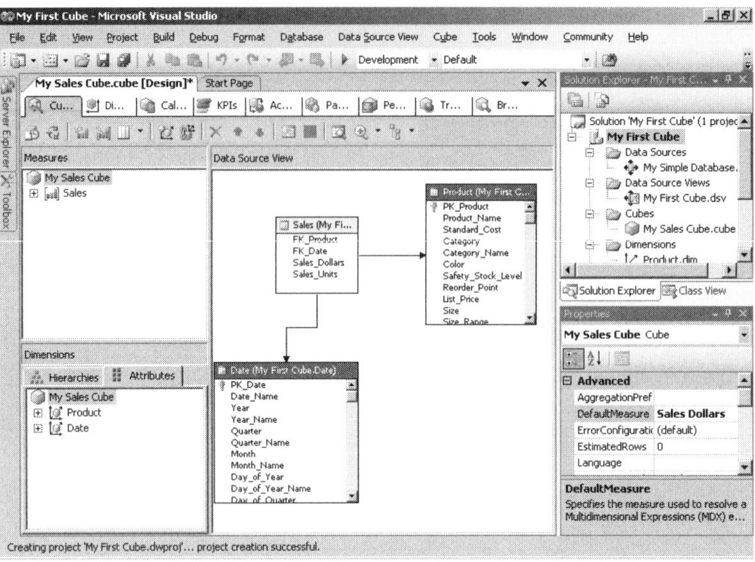

Loading Data into the Relational Schema

Now that the fact table and dimension tables exist in the database that you created, My Simple Database, you are able to populate the tables with data in preparation for processing the cube. Processing the cube is the operation that actually loads data into the cube and dimension files from the relational tables. A discussion of all of the best practices to follow to prepare data for loading in a data warehouse is well beyond the scope of this book. For now, to complete the procedures in this chapter, you'll just need to copy a subset of data from the SSAS Step by Step DW database to the newly built fact and dimension tables in My Simple Database.

In this procedure, you'll copy data from the DimProduct and FactResellerSales tables in the SSAS Step by Step DW database to My Simple Database by using the SQL Server Import and Export Wizard.

Loading the schema with data

1. If necessary, open SQL Server Management Studio and connect to the Database Engine.
2. In the Databases folder, right-click SSAS Step by Step DW, scroll to Tasks, and then click Export Data.
3. The SQL Server Import and Export Wizard appears. Click Next.
4. The Choose a Data Source Page automatically fills in the data source, server, and database to create a connection to SSAS Step by Step DW. Click Next.
5. On the Choose a Destination page, select My Simple Database in the Database dropdown list.

6. On the Specify Table Copy Or Query page, select Write A Query To Specify The Data To Transfer. Click Next.

7. Type the following query into the SQL Statement box on the Provide a Source Query page:

```
Select ProductKey, EnglishProductName, Weight from DimProduct
```

8. Click Next, and then click [My Simple Database].[My First Cube].[Product] in the Destination drop-down list.

9. Click Edit in the Mapping column, and then in the Column Mappings dialog box, click in the Destination box for each source column to select the corresponding destination column, as specified in this table:

Source	Destination
ProductKey	PK_Product
EnglishProductName	Product_Name
Weight	Weight

Your screen should look like this:

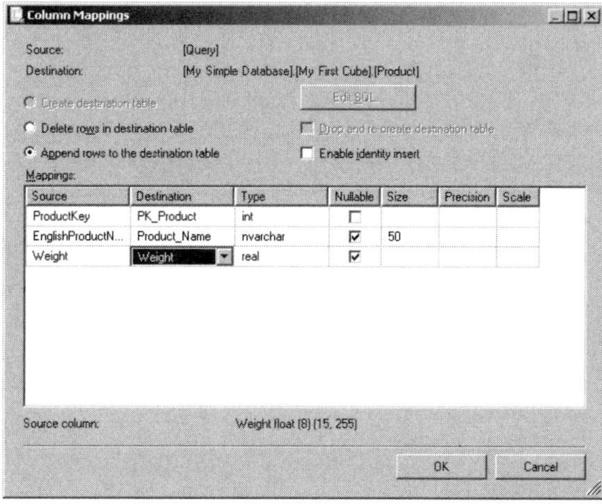

10. Click OK to close the Column Mappings dialog box, click Next, and then click Finish twice.

    The Performing Operation page of the wizard will display the progress of the copy operation.

11. When complete, click Close.

12. In the Databases folder, right-click SSAS Step by Step DW, scroll to Tasks, and then click Export Data.

13. Click Next twice, and then click My Simple Database in the Database drop-down list.

14. On the Specify Table Copy Or Query page, click Write A Query To Specify The Data To Transfer. Click Next.
15. Type the following query into the SQL Statement box on the Provide a Source Query page:

```
Select ProductKey, FullDateAlternateKey, SalesAmount, OrderQuantity
from FactResellerSales, DimTime
where DimTime.TimeKey = FactResellerSales.OrderDateKey
```

16. Click Next, and then click [My Simple Database].[My First Cube].[Sales] in the Destination drop-down list.

Tip You may need to maximize the dialog box and resize the Destination column to see the full table name.

17. Click Edit in the Mapping column, and then in the Column Mappings dialog box, click in the Destination box for each source column to select the corresponding destination column, as specified in this table:

Source	Destination
ProductKey	FK_Product
FullDateAlternateKey	FK_Date
SalesAmount	Sales_Dollars
OrderQuantity	Sales_Units

Your screen should look like this:

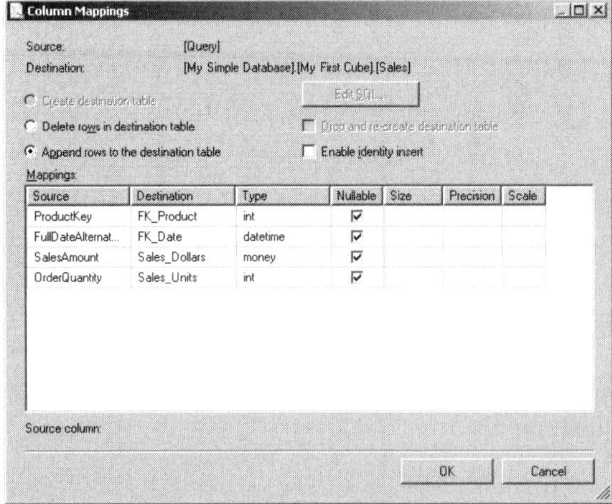

18. Click OK to close the Column Mappings dialog box, click Next, and then click Finish twice. When processing has finished, click Close.

    Now data is in My Simple Database. The time dimension table, My First Cube.Date, was populated with data by the Schema Generation Wizard automatically. Then, you created two export jobs which loaded My First Cube.Product and My First Cube.Sales with data from similar tables in the SSAS Step by Step DW database. However, this data has not yet been loaded into the cube. You'll complete that goal in the next procedure.

Processing and Browsing a Cube

Processing a dimension and processing a cube are two separate tasks. When you process a dimension, Analysis Services reads in the information from the dimension tables and constructs a map of the dimension based on each attribute. Within the map, each value in a dimension column is an attribute member which is stored in a two-level attribute hierarchy for the dimension. For example, suppose that Washington and Oregon are members of the State attribute in the Geography dimension. The map stores these members in the State attribute hierarchy like this: All⇱ Washington and All⇱ Oregon. By storing each member of an attribute hierarchy in two levels in the dimension map, Analysis Services can use the map to quickly find relationships between members when you query the cube. Of course, the dimension map is compressed and very efficient.

When you process a cube, Analysis Services first combines the dimension maps from all the dimensions used in the cube into a multidimensional cube map. It then reads the detail records from the fact table, storing detail values in a data storage area. The data storage area is efficiently organized and does not take up any room for key combinations that do not contain a value.

Deploying and Processing a Cube

As you work with a project on your computer workstation, solution files, project files, and XML-based definition files for cubes and dimensions are stored on your local drive by default. You cannot browse a cube using only the files on your workstation. Instead, you must deploy these files to the Analysis Server where they can be processed and read into storage. There are several ways that you can move the required files to the Analysis Server, which you will learn about in Chapter 13. In this chapter, you will use Visual Studio to deploy your project.

When you process a cube, the Analysis server automatically processes any dimensions that are used in the cube that have not yet been processed. So, to process the cube and all its dimensions, you need to execute only one command.

In this procedure, you'll deploy the My First Cube project to the Analysis Server where it is processed and made available for viewing.

Deploy and process an Analysis Services project

1. In Visual Studio, right-click the My First Cube project in Solution Explorer, and then click Deploy.

   When the deployment is complete, the Deployment Progress window looks like this:

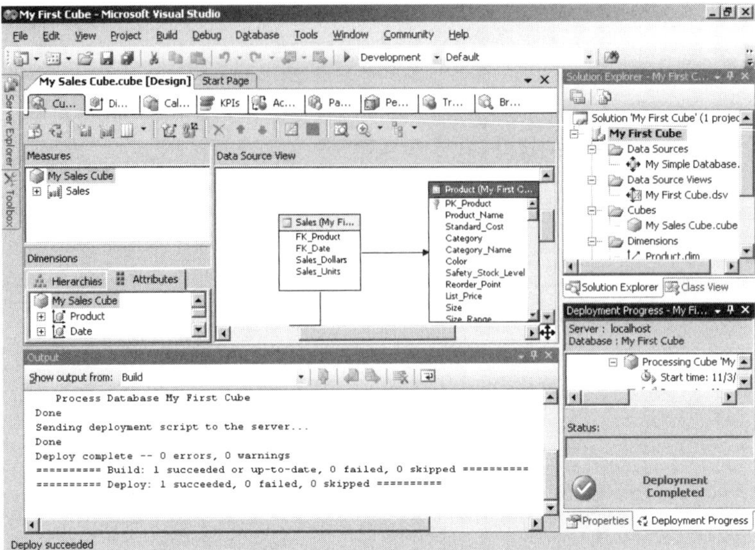

   The Deployment Progress window monitors the current activity being executed as part of the deployment process. A log appears in this window to show the progress. As each dimension is processed, a group of entries appears in the log. As the cube is processed, a corresponding group of entries appears in the log.

2. By default, deployment from Visual Studio also processes the dimensions and cubes when they are first moved to the Analysis Server. When you process a cube, Analysis Services copies the detail values from the fact table into proprietary data structures. It does not store any aggregated values unless you design aggregations (which you'll learn how to do in Chapter 7, "Designing Aggregations and Hierarchies"). For a small cube such as this one, the lack of aggregations will not hinder your ability to browse the cube.

3. Close the deployment log window.

Browsing a Cube

The Cube Designer in Visual Studio provides a browser for viewing cubes. This browser is not intended for business users, but for developers of cubes so they can easily test and validate cube values after the cube has been processed. When you first open the Cube Browser, you see an empty data grid. In order to browse the cube, you drag measures and dimension objects to the grid.

In this procedure, you'll learn how to browse cube data.

Browse a cube

1. Click the Browser tab.

   The Cube Browser looks like this:

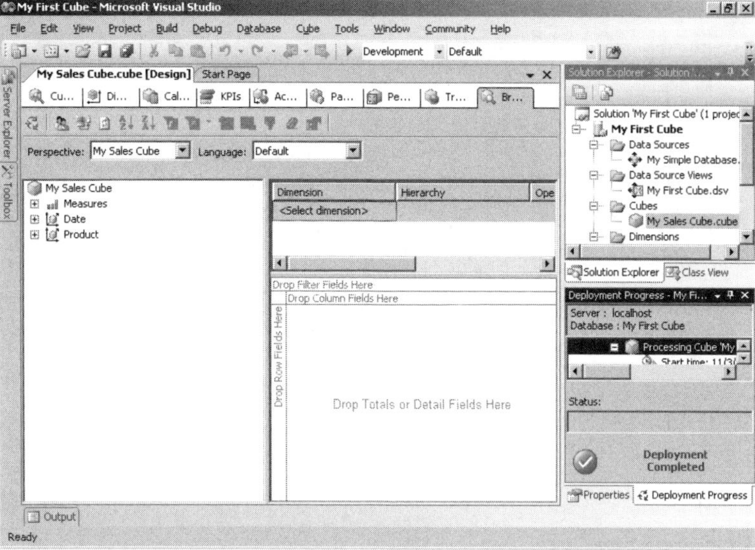

2. Drag the Measures object from the cube metadata tree on the left side of your screen to the area of the grid labeled Drop Totals Or Detail Fields Here.

   The Sales Dollars and Sales Units values in the grid represent the grand total of these two measures in the cube. These values are the equivalent of using the Sum function with each measure column in the fact table to derive a grand total value.

   You can drag measures one by one to the grid if you expand the Measures object in the cube metadata tree. Or you can drag the Measures object to the grid to add all measures at once to the grid.

3. Expand Product in the cube metadata tree, and then drag the Product attribute to the area of the grid labeled Drop Row Fields Here.

   This placement of the Product attribute in the grid is also known as placing Product on the rows axis.

4. In the cube metadata tree, expand Date, and then drag the Year – Quarter – Month – Date hierarchy to the area of the grid labeled Drop Column Fields Here.

   This step is also known as placing the selected hierarchy on the columns axis.

5. Click the plus sign next to Calendar 2002 to view the measure by quarter in 2002.

Your screen looks like this:

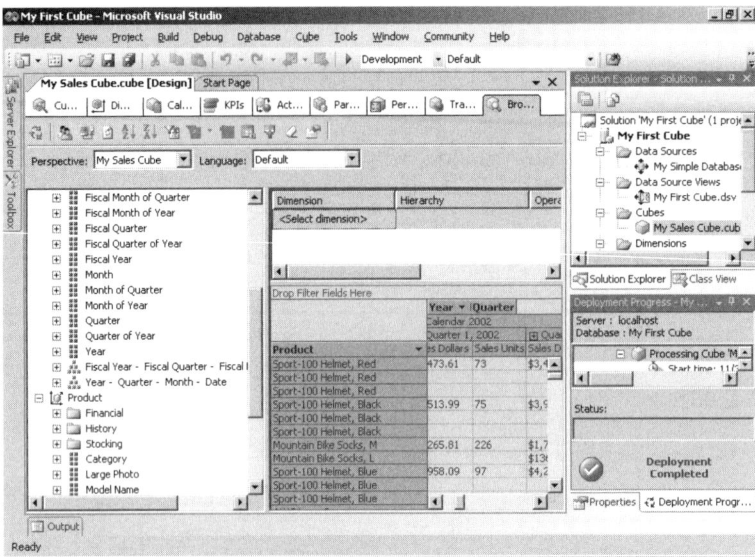

6. On the File menu, click Close Project.

   Congratulations! You have successfully created and browsed your first cube. You will learn more about browsing a cube in later chapters of this book. Using the Cube Wizard and the template provided with Analysis Services, you are able to design a cube independently of an existing data source. The cubes and dimensions you create by using this wizard, however, might not be precisely what you need. You can make any desired changes to the cube structure or dimension structures by deleting objects or changing properties. Once you've made these changes, you can then use the Schema Generation Wizard and SQL Server Import and Export Wizard to generate tables and load data into these tables in preparation for processing your cube.

Chapter 3 Quick Reference

To	Do this
Start a new Analysis Services Project	Start a new project in Business Intelligence Development Studio (Visual Studio) and select Analysis Services Project from the Business Intelligence Projects folder. Provide a name for the project and solution, and designate a folder location for the solution.
Build a cube without a data source by using a template	In Solution Explorer, right-click the Cubes folder, click New Cube, select a template, and then choose measures and dimensions from the template to include in the cube.

To	Do this
Generate a relational schema based on a cube that was created without a data source	Create an empty database in Microsoft SQL Server Management Studio; launch the Schema Generation Wizard in Visual Studio by choosing this option on the final page of the Cube Wizard, by clicking the link in the Diagram pane of the Cube Structure tab within the Cube Designer, or by clicking Generate Relational Schema from the Database menu; and then, in the wizard, specify a target database and select database schema options.
Deploy and process a cube	In Solution Explorer, right-click the Analysis Services project that contains the cube, and then click Deploy.
Browse a cube	In Solution Explorer, double-click the .cube file in the Cubes folder to open the Cube Designer, and then click the Browser tab.

Part II
Design Fundamentals

In this part:

Chapter 4: Designing Dimensions 63
Chapter 5: Designing Measure Groups and Measures 99
Chapter 6: Working with a Finance Measure Group 129
Chapter 7: Designing Aggregations and Hierarchies 149

In Part I, "Getting Started with Analysis Services," you learned about the purpose of business intelligence (BI), the structures used in data warehousing, and the value of an online analytical processing (OLAP) solution. You were also introduced to the role of the Unified Dimensional Model (UDM) in Analysis Services and built your first cube by using a template in a top-down approach. Throughout the chapters of Part II, you'll build a more complex cube based on tables in a data warehouse. You'll learn design fundamentals and then apply what you learn by creating Analysis Services objects—attributes, dimensions, measure groups, aggregations, and hierarchies—to construct a cube using a bottom-up approach. Later, in Part III, "Advanced Design," you'll work with advanced design techniques to enhance your cube with greater functionality.

Chapter 4

Designing Dimensions

After completing this chapter, you will be able to:

- Define a data source for an Analysis Services project.
- Create a data source view (DSV).
- Use the Dimension Wizard to build standard, time, and parent-child dimensions.
- Deploy Analysis Services database objects.
- Change dimension properties.
- Work with special properties of parent-child dimensions.

In Chapter 3, "Building Your First Cube," you created dimensions from a template and then used the Schema Generation Wizard to build tables in a Structured Query Language (SQL) Server database to correspond to the dimension design. In this chapter, you'll use the Dimension Wizard to create dimensions from existing tables and work with the Dimension Designer to review a dimension's structure, modify its properties, and browse its data. You'll work with three different kinds of dimensions–standard, time, and parent-child–to become familiar with the range of options available to you when designing and building dimensions.

Reviewing the Data Warehouse Structure

The dimensions and the cube you'll create in this chapter and in Chapter 5, "Designing Measure Groups and Measures," are based on a simple Microsoft SQL Server database supplied on this book's companion CD. The database file (SSAS Step by Step DW.mdf) is an extremely simplified version of the Adventure Works DW database that ships with Microsoft SQL Server 2005, with a few modifications to aid your exploration of Analysis Services. The SSAS Step by Step DW database is small enough that you should be able to clearly understand its structure, but it illustrates the common dimension types that are the focus of this chapter.

The SSAS Step by Step DW database contains data for a fictitious manufacturing company called Adventure Works. It is designed as a small data warehouse to support analysis of products, customers, employees, financial accounting, sales, and much more. The following table provides a brief description of the tables that you'll be using to create dimensions in this chapter and to create measures in Chapter 5:

Table Name	Description
DimEmployee	Personal information for all employees: Employee Names, Addresses, Titles, Managers, Hire Date, etc.
DimProduct	Product information: Name, Cost, Color, Size, etc.
DimProductSubcategory	Classifications of products within categories: Bikes can be Mountain Bikes, Road Bikes, or Touring Bikes. Accessories can be Pedals, Chains, Wheels, etc. Clothing can be Gloves, Jerseys, Shorts, etc.
DimProductCategory	Major classifications of products: Bikes, Accessories, Clothing, and Components.
DimTime	Contains date-related data for the business: Year, Quarter, Month, Date, etc.
FactInternetSales	Transaction details for sales made through an Internet e-commerce site.
FactResellerSales	Transaction details for sales made through the reseller's channel.

The two fact tables, FactResellerSales and FactInternetSales, both have some dimension keys in common–ProductKey, OrderDateKey, DueDateKey, and ShipDateKey. They also have two measures in common–SalesAmount and OrderQuantity. ProductKey is joined to a chain of dimension tables (snowflake schema): DimProduct, DimProductSubcategory, and DimProductCategory. OrderDateKey, DueDateKey, and ShipDateKey all join to a single DimTime table. FactResellerSales also has a dimension key, EmployeeKey, that is joined to the DimEmployee dimension table (parent-child). You'll work with other tables in the database in later chapters as you focus on special design features of Analysis Services.

Building a Standard Dimension

A cube must contain at least one dimension. Unless you are building a cube from a template, as you did in Chapter 3, you will probably create most of your dimensions before creating the cube. Standard dimensions are the most common kind of dimension in a cube. Time and parent-child dimensions have additional properties to address specific analytical requirements, which you'll learn about later in this chapter.

Before you get started with your first dimension, you'll need to create a data source so that Analysis Services can connect to the data warehouse. You'll also need to create a data source view (DSV) so that Analysis Services knows which tables from the data warehouse contain the data to load into the dimension. Once you have a data source and a DSV in place, you're ready to build dimensions. When you build a standard dimension, you can use a single table (star schema) or you can use multiple related tables (snowflake schema) from the data warehouse.

Adding a Data Source

One of the first tasks in building a cube from the bottom up is to add a data source. The data source is the connection information that Analysis Services uses to connect to the database that hosts the data. The data source contains the connection string which specifies the server and the database hosting the data as well as any necessary authentication credentials.

The data source can be a .NET provider or a native OLE DB provider. OLE DB is an industry-standard technology that is a generalized replacement for the Open Database Connectivity (ODBC) standard used for many years. When accessing data from Microsoft SQL Server 2005 relational databases, you should use the SQL Native Client, which is the SQL OLE DB and SQL ODBC providers rolled into one with some added functionality to support new SQL Server 2005 features. This provider type is selected by default when you create a new data source for your Analysis Services projects.

In this procedure, you'll create a data source that defines a connection to the SSAS Step by Step DW database in your local SQL Server using Microsoft Windows authentication.

Add a data source to an Analysis Services project

1. If necessary, start SQL Server Business Intelligence Development Studio (BIDS).
2. On the File menu, point to New, and then click Project.
3. In the New Project dialog box, click the Analysis Services Project template in the Templates pane.
4. Type a name for the project: **SSAS Step by Step**.
5. If necessary, change the location for the project to **C:\Documents and Settings\<username>\My Documents\Microsoft Press\as2005sbs\Workspace**, and click OK.
6. In Solution Explorer, right-click the Data Sources folder, click New Data Source, and then click Next.
7. Click the New button to create a new connection.
8. In the Connection Manager dialog box, type a server name: **localhost.**
9. In the Select Or Enter A Database Name list box, select SSAS Step by Step DW.

The Connection Manager dialog box looks like this:

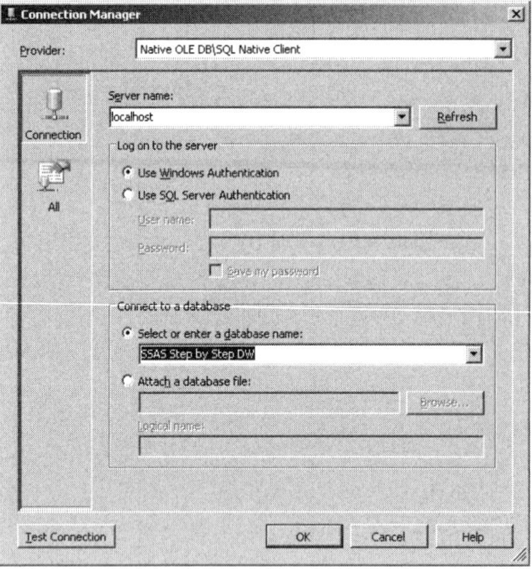

10. Click Test Connection and then click OK to close the message box.
11. Click OK to close the Connection Manager dialog box.
12. Click Next.
13. On the Impersonation Information page of the Data Source Wizard, click Use The Service Account and click Next.

    Here you can see that the default data source name matches the name of the database that you selected in the Connection Manager dialog box. It's generally recommended to keep the data source name in your project consistent with the name of the database so that anyone reviewing the project files can tell at a glance where to find the source data for cube.
14. To complete the wizard, click Finish.

The Solution Explorer window looks like this:

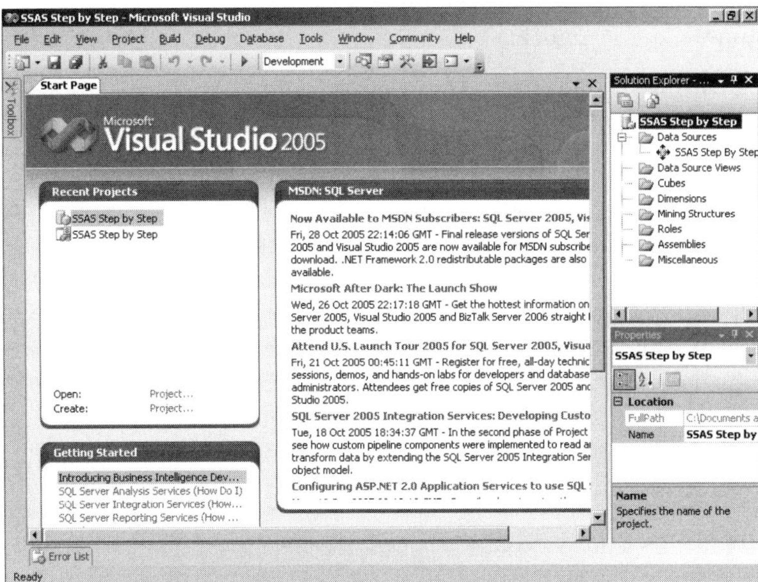

Notice that the Data Sources folder now contains a data source item, SSAS Step by Step DW.ds. You can change the name of the data source at any time, but you must retain the .ds file extension in the name of this item or the data source will not be recognizable by the Dimension Designer and Cube Designer in Visual Studio.

15. Save the solution.

Creating a Data Source View

In Chapter 2, "Understanding OLAP and Analysis Services," you were introduced to the concept of the Unified Dimensional Model (UDM) that is the centerpiece of an online analytical processing (OLAP) solution. The UDM provides an intermediate logical layer between the physical relational database that is used as a data source and the proprietary cube and dimension structures that are used to resolve user queries. There are at least four good reasons for creating a UDM for analysis instead of allowing users to directly access data in the data sources:

1. Manipulating data sources is easier for system administrators and developers, and more difficult for business users. With a UDM, the initial setup of data sources is left to system administrators and developers so that business users can focus on analyzing data.
2. Companies often use multiple databases, systems, files, and services to store data. You spare each business user the effort of locating all the pertinent data and systems, and figuring out how to work with it, by combining this disparate data into a single UDM.

3. Data must be consolidated into a unified format and summarized across systems. If you don't already have a data warehouse, a UDM can help you present the data in a unified and summarized manner.
4. The business user must research the business rules associated with each system and apply them consistently. Using a UDM, you can define those business rules in one place for consistent application.

An important component of the UDM in Analysis Services is the DSV. Because the scope of analysis within a single cube can be more limited than the scope of a data warehouse, you can pick and choose the data that you need for the dimensions and for the cube by creating a subset view of the data warehouse. This subset view is called a DSV. Selecting objects to study from the data warehouse is like aiming a telescope at the sky and selecting only the celestial objects within its scope to analyze. Further, just as you can aim your telescope at a different section of the sky, you can aim the scope of your DSV at a different section of the data. You can also add and remove tables as you change the features built into your cube, which you will learn how to do throughout the chapters of this book.

In this procedure, you'll create a DSV that includes the DimProduct, DimProductSubcategory, and DimProductCategory tables.

Use the Data Source View Wizard

1. In Solution Explorer, right-click the Data Source Views folder, click New Data Source View, and then click Next.
2. Click SSAS Step by Step DW to select the relational data source, and then click Next.
3. Double-click dbo.DimProduct to add it to the Included Objects list.

   Alternatively, you can click on a table and then click the arrow pointing to the right (which looks like a greater-than sign) to move it to the Included Objects list. You can select multiple tables by pressing the Ctrl key while clicking on each table.
4. Repeat the previous step to add dbo.DimProductCategory and dbo.DimProductSubcategory to the Included Objects list.

   There is an existing relationship defined in the data warehouse among these three tables. Products are organized into Product Subcategories and Product Subcategories are organized into Product Categories. For example, note the relationships in the following table:

Product Category	Product Subcategory	Product
Bikes	Mountain Bikes	Mountain-100 Silver, 38
Bikes	Mountain Bikes	Mountain-100 Black, 44
Bikes	Road Bikes	Road-150 Red, 62
Bikes	Road Bikes	Road-650 Black, 52
Bikes	Touring Bikes	Touring-2000 Blue, 60
Bikes	Touring Bikes	Touring-1000 Yellow, 46

You will build a dimension in the next procedure that uses data from these three tables, so all three tables must be included in the DSV.

In addition, you could add a Named Query to the table to reference data from these three tables without adding them explicitly to the DSV. A Named Query is analogous to a view in a relational database. You create a Transact-SQL statement to define the tables and columns that you want to combine into a single object. You need to create the data source view with at least one object before you can add a Named Query to it.

5. Click Next, and then click Finish.

   You have the option to change the default DSV name before completing the wizard.

6. Save the solution.

Using the Dimension Wizard

With the data source and the DSV added to the project, Analysis Services now has access to the underlying data that will be loaded into your dimension. The next step in building a standard dimension is to use the Dimension Wizard to create the initial structure of the dimension. When using the Visual Studio development environment, the only way to build a new dimension is to use this wizard.

The Dimension Wizard is a flexible tool that will guide you through the steps required to create the dimension. First, you choose whether or not to use an underlying data source. The next step is to define the dimension type. If the dimension will be based on a database table, then the next steps are to specify the main table of the dimension, identify the key column and name column for the leaf-level attribute, select attributes for inclusion in the dimension, and associate related tables with the dimension.

In this procedure, you'll create a Product dimension that is based upon the DimProduct, DimProductSubcategory, and DimProductCategory tables in the DSV.

Create a standard dimension

1. In Solution Explorer, right-click the Dimensions folder, click New Dimension, and then click Next.

   If you choose to build the dimension with an underlying database and to use Auto Build, the Dimension Wizard will analyze the data in the source tables and create attributes and hierarchies for you. If you prefer more control over the structure of your dimension, you should disable Auto Build. On the other hand, if your goal is to build a prototype cube, building the dimension without an underlying data source will allow you to work out a structure and get a model quickly built. Later, you can load data into it. As you saw in Chapter 3, you can even use templates to help you build the model. For now, you will build a dimension manually to learn how the process works and to give you greater control over the structure of the new dimension as you work through this chapter.

2. Clear the Auto Build check box, and then click Next.
3. Click the SSAS Step by Step DW data source view.

   You can review the diagram for the DSV if you click Browse on this page of the wizard. This feature is helpful when you have multiple DSV in a project and want to be sure that you select the correct one.
4. Click Next.

   The Select The Dimension Type page of the Dimension Wizard looks like this:

   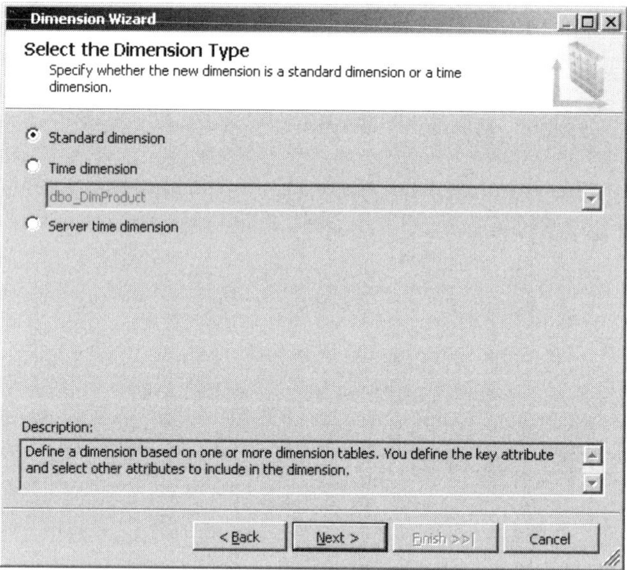

   You'll use the default option, Standard Dimension, in this procedure. You'll learn more about the options to create a Time Dimension and a Server Time Dimension later in this chapter.
5. Click Next.

   The Main Table defaults to dbo.DimProduct since it is first alphabetically in the list of tables contained in the DSV. When necessary, you can choose a different table from the list to represent the leaf level of the dimension. In this case, the DimProduct table contains the most granular level of detail required for this dimension, so you will keep this default selection for Main Table.

   On this page of the wizard, you'll also need to select the key column(s) that uniquely identify each dimension member. For this dimension, ProductKey is unique for each row in the DimProduct table. As a default, a dimension uses the same column for the member keys and for the member names, but you can also specify a name for each member that's separate from the member key. A member name is the text that appears in a heading row or column on a report, so you should make these names meaningful and descriptive. Because ProductKey is not useful for reporting, you should designate EnglishProductName as the member name column.

6. In the Key Columns list, select ProductKey, and then select EnglishProductName in the Column Containing The Member Name drop-down list.

   The current page of the wizard looks like this:

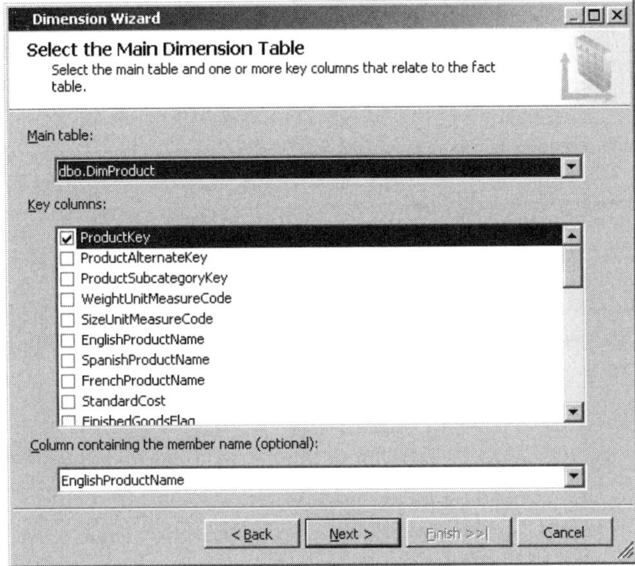

7. Click Next.

   The Select Related Tables page of the wizard looks like this:

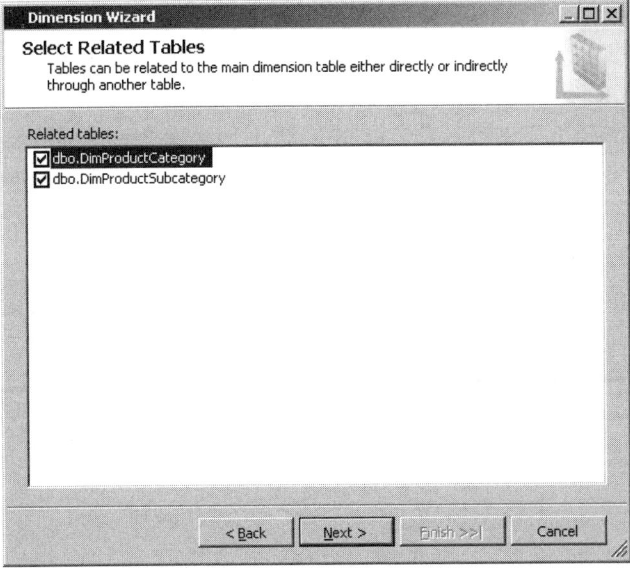

The dbo.DimProductCategory and dbo.DimProductSubcategory tables are already selected as related tables because these two tables are joined to the main table, dbo.DimProduct, in the selected DSV. Because you want to include attributes from these two tables in the dimension, you should accept the default selection of these tables on this page.

8. Click Next, and then, on the Select Dimension Attributes page of the wizard, select the check box next to the following attributes: Color, List Price, and Size.

   All columns from the main table and related tables are available for selection as dimension attributes. You can choose all columns from all tables, or you can select a few of the available columns.

9. Select the check box to the left of Dim Product Subcategory, and then, in the same row, click dbo.DimProductCategory.EnglishProductSubcategoryName in the Attribute Name Column drop-down list.

> **Note** You may need to resize the wizard dialog box or the width of the columns (or both) to be able to view the names in the list box.

   Color, List Price, and Size do not have separate key and name columns like Product, Product Category, and Product Subcategory. When there are separate columns in the dimension table to represent the unique key of an attribute and its user-friendly name, you should adjust the Attribute Key Column or Attribute Name Column as necessary on this page of the wizard. Be careful to select the correct column!

   You can also change the name of the attribute on this page of the wizard. For example, you probably don't want users to see attributes named Dim Product Category or Dim Product Subcategory. You can click in the Attribute Name column and type in a more appropriate name here. However, since you will learn an alternative method for fixing the attribute name later in this chapter, you can keep the default attribute names here.

10. Select the check box to the left of Dim Product Category, and then, in the same row, click dbo.DimProductCategory.EnglishProductCategoryName in the Attribute Name Column drop-down list.

11. Click Next.

    On the Specify Dimension Type page of the wizard, the default dimension type is Regular. You'll learn more about specifying dimension types in Chapter 6, "Working with a Finance Measure Group." Some dimension types are used by client applications that query Analysis Services, while other dimension types direct the behavior of a dimension, such as applying special aggregation rules for an accounts dimension. Keep the default setting for this dimension.

12. On the Specify Dimension Type page, click Next.

13. On the Define Parent-Child Relationship page, click Next.

    Since you're not currently building a parent-child dimension, you don't need to change the Define Parent-Child Relationship page of the wizard. Later in this chapter, you will learn more about working with this page of the wizard.

14. Change the name of the dimension from Dim Product to **Product**, and then click Finish.

    Your screen looks like this:

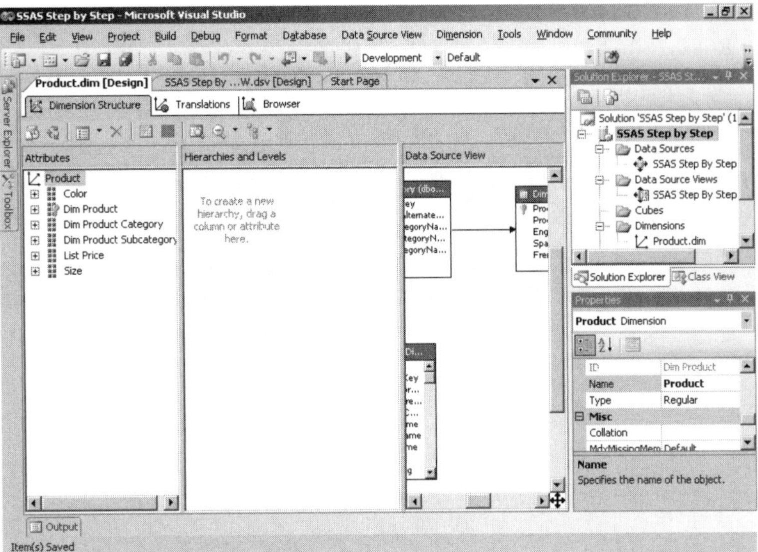

    After completing the dimension wizard, you'll see Product.dim as an object in the Dimensions folder of the Solution Explorer window. In the main window of Visual Studio, you see the Dimension Designer. The Dimension Designer has three tabs–Dimension Structure, Translations, and Browser.

    On the Dimension Structure tab, you can review the list of attributes for the dimension as well as view a diagram of the tables from the DSV that were used to create the dimension. Notice also the Properties window in the lower right corner. The Properties window displays all properties for the object currently selected in the main window, which is the dimension object in the Attributes pane when you first finish the wizard.

15. In the Attributes pane of the Dimension Structure tab, right-click Dim Product, click Rename, and then type **Product**.

16. Repeat the previous step to rename Dim Product Category as **Category**, and Dim Product Subcategory as **Subcategory**.

    Alternatively, you can change the *Name* property of an attribute which you will do later in this chapter.

17. Save the solution.

Deploying a Dimension

Although the Dimension Structure tab of the Cube Designer is useful for reviewing the attributes of a dimension and their properties, you can't browse the members of a dimension here. Instead, you use the Browser of the Dimension Designer to review the members of a dimension within their respective attribute hierarchies. You should browse a dimension early in the development cycle to make sure you get the right columns selected for the member name column and that the sort order of members is correct.

However, right now your dimension is defined only in an XML file, Product.dim, that is contained in an Analysis Services project on your workstation. If you try to browse the dimension now, you will get an error message because the dimension must first be deployed to the Analysis Server. Deploying the dimension to the server copies your local XML file to the server's data folder, creates a dimension object on the server, and then processes the dimension to load data into the new object.

In this procedure, you'll deploy the SSAS Step by Step solution to the local Analysis Server and browse the processed Product dimension.

Deploy a dimension to the Analysis Server

1. Click the Browser tab.

   Your screen looks like this:

   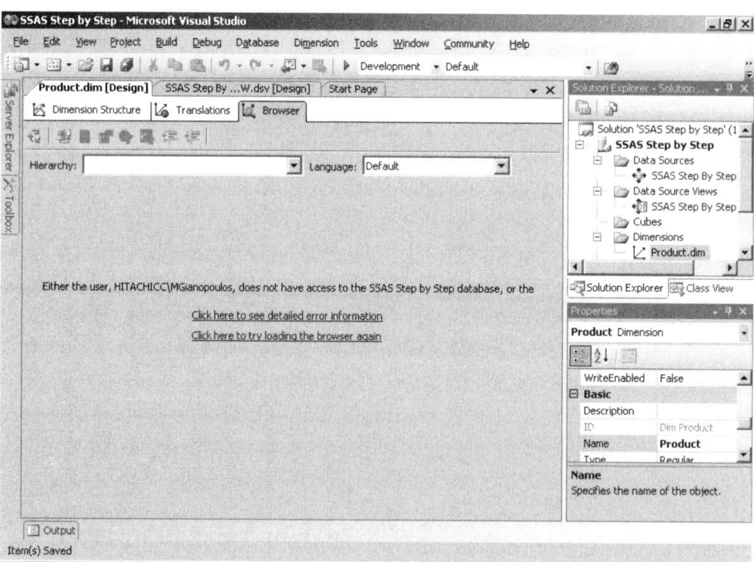

   Because the dimension has not yet been deployed to the Analysis Server, it is unavailable for browsing.

2. Right-click the SSAS Step by Step project in the Solution Explorer window, and then click Deploy.

The default target server for deployment is the local server.

> **Tip** If you want to deploy to a different server, you should first right-click on the SSAS Step by Step project in the Solution Explorer window, click Properties, click Deployment in the Configuration Properties tree, and then change the *Server* property to the correct target server.

The Deployment Progress window displays the current status of the operation.

3. When deployment is complete, click the Reconnect button in the Browser toolbar.

   Your screen now looks like this:

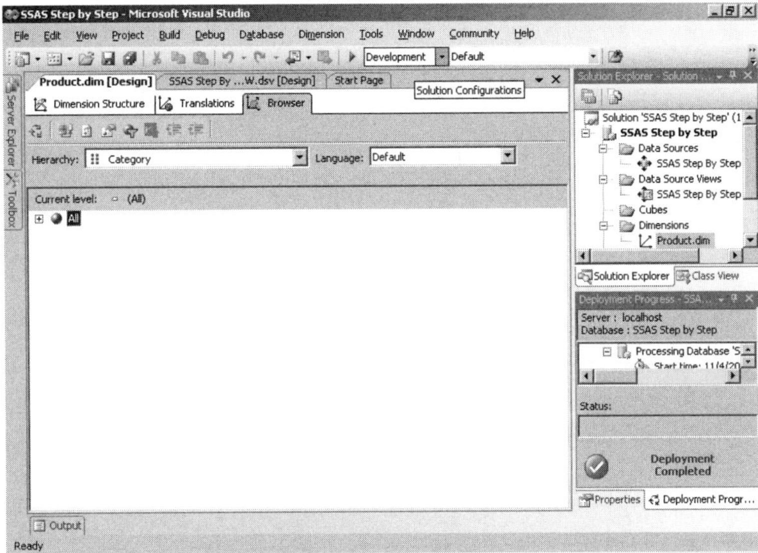

   Each time that you make changes to objects in an Analysis Services project and deploy those changes to the server, you must use the Reconnect button in the Browser tab of a designer if you have previously attempted to browse a database object.

4. In the Hierarchy drop-down list, select Category.

   Each attribute is available for selection in the Hierarchy drop-down list. By default, an attribute defined for a dimension results in the creation of an attribute hierarchy. Attribute hierarchies are useful for grouping information for analysis. For example, in this dimension, you can group information about products by category, by subcategory, or by individual product. You can also group product information by color or by size. When you select an attribute hierarchy in the browser, you can view the members of that attribute in a two-level hierarchy. The top level of each hierarchy is the All member, which is used to display the aggregated value of the attribute members for each measure when viewed in a cube.

5. Click the plus sign to the left of the All member in the Category hierarchy tree.
6. Click Subcategory in the Hierarchy drop-down list, and then expand All to view the members of this attribute hierarchy.
7. Repeat the previous step to view the members of each remaining hierarchy.

Changing Attribute Properties

You can modify attribute properties when you want to change the appearance of members within an attribute hierarchy. For example, you can use the *Order* property to control the sort sequence of members, or you can specify a different member name column for an attribute by changing its *NameColumn* property. Some properties control how an attribute functions, such as the *Type* and *Usage* properties, which you'll learn more about in Chapter 6. Other properties that you'll learn about later in this chapter and in Chapter 7, "Designing Aggregations and Hierarchies," such as the *IsAggregatable* and *AggregationUsage* properties, affect how an attribute hierarchy is aggregated (or not).

After you create a dimension, one of the first properties that you should consider changing is *AttributeHierarchyEnabled*. Every attribute that you add to a dimension becomes an attribute hierarchy, as you saw in the previous procedure. When users browse a cube, they select attribute hierarchies for grouping measure values, so you should be careful about which attribute hierarchies are available for grouping data. In the current dimension, for example, grouping by Category, Subcategory, Product, Color, or Size seems logical and desirable. However, grouping by List Price is probably not useful. Typically, an attribute like this, which can have a high number of distinct members relative to the leaf-level attribute, is used for filtering purposes or for detailed reporting.

In this procedure, you'll disable the *AttributeHierarchyEnabled* property of the List Price attribute.

Disable the *AttributeHierarchyEnabled* property

1. Click the Dimension Structure tab, right-click the List Price attribute, and then click Properties.
2. In the Properties window, scroll to the *AttributeHierarchyEnabled* property, and then select False in the property's drop-down list.

   Notice that the icon in the Attributes pane next to List Price is now gray, while all the other icons remain blue. The gray icon in the Attributes pane indicates that the attribute hierarchy is disabled for this attribute.
3. Right-click the SSAS Step by Step project in the Solution Explorer window, and then click Deploy.

   Each time you want to view the results of a change that you have made to a dimension, you must deploy the project to the server before you can browse the dimension.

4. When deployment is complete, click the Reconnect button in the Browser toolbar.

   Notice that List Price is no longer available as a hierarchy in the Hierarchy list box.

The Unknown Member

Oftentimes when you are dealing with relational databases, data integrity issues will be a problem, especially when you are in a prototyping stage of development or when you are building a cube from a source that is not a standard data warehouse. In these situations, it's possible that a record referencing a new dimension record is loaded into a fact table prior to the addition of the new dimension record to the dimension table. Or perhaps the cube is processed before the dimension is processed. You'll learn more about the challenges of managing new data in fact and dimension tables in Chapter 12, "Managing Partitions and Database Processing."

Normally, if you try to process a cube from a fact table that contains a dimension key that is not yet found in the dimension, the processing operation will fail. However, when you are building a prototype or when your solution requires near real-time information, you may want to ignore this type of error and allow processing to continue. By enabling the *UnknownMember* property of a dimension and by setting the value of the *KeyErrorAction* property of a cube to ConvertToUnknown, you can avoid processing errors when a fact table contains a missing or invalid key for that dimension. The aggregated values of each measure in the cube will consequently always equal the corresponding aggregated values in the fact table as a result.

The *UnknownMember* property has three possible values: Visible, Hidden, and None. The default setting for the *UnknownMember* property is Visible, so you'll notice a member named Unknown in each attribute hierarchy of a new dimension, even though you don't have a record with that name in your dimension table. If you prefer a different name for this member, set the value of the *UnknownMemberName* property.

Working with a Time Dimension

There's practically no such thing as an OLAP database without a Time dimension. Often, a Time dimension contains months as the lowest level of detail–aggregated into quarters and years. Sometimes, a Time dimension will contain days as the lowest level of detail. On occasion, particularly if you're monitoring a manufacturing operation or Internet activity, you might create a dimension with minutes or even seconds as the lowest level of detail. Whatever the level of detail, a Time dimension has certain unique qualities.

For example, time typically occurs in regular intervals. Each hour contains 60 minutes, each day contains 24 hours, each quarter contains 3 months, and each year contains 4 quarters. This repetitive nature of time encourages certain questions, such as, "How does this month compare to the same month of last year?" The multidimensional expressions (MDX) language, which you'll learn about in Chapter 8, "Using MDX," has functions that make it easy to answer this type of question. By flagging certain dimensions as Time dimensions, and certain levels within a dimension as specific units of time, you can make those functions easy to use.

Of course, time isn't completely uniform because the 365 days in a year aren't evenly divisible by the 7 days in a week or the 12 months in a year. Some months have 30 days; some have 31, or 28, or occasionally 29. Months begin on different days of the week. Irregularities are a fact of life in Time dimensions, and when working with time, you need to be prepared for both the regularities and the irregularities.

One irregularity that frequently arises when dealing with time is that many organizations use a fiscal year—where the starting day of the year isn't January 1. As you saw in Chapter 3, Analysis Services can build a Time dimension based on a specified date range and add a special calendar to this dimension for Fiscal Year. For greater flexibility, you should use a dimension table from your data warehouse because you include special properties for a date, such as the season for a month if this information is important to analysis over time in your organization.

Modifying a Data Source View

As you learned previously in this chapter, the DSV is a very flexible structure that can be modified as you add dimensions and cubes to your project. You can add tables to the DSV at any time. In addition, you can add a *Named Query* to limit the columns available from a single table or to construct a logical view by combining columns from multiple tables. As another alternative, you can add a derived column, known as a *Named Calculation*, to a table. Using a Named Query or a Named Calculation gives you the ability to manipulate the data structures for use by Analysis Services even if you don't have permissions to make similar changes at the database level.

If you use Analysis Services to generate a Server Time dimension for you based on a range of dates, you need to use a Date/Time column in the fact table to use this dimension. (Creating a Server Time dimension is discussed later in this chapter.) However, it's generally recommended that you use a separate dimension table for dates rather than use a Date/Time column in the fact table. As with other dimension tables, you would then use an integer key to join the date dimension table with the fact table. This difference in data types in the fact table—date/time which requires 8 bytes versus integer which requires 4 bytes—can have a big impact on the amount of space required to store the fact table in your data warehouse when the fact table contains millions of records. Further, as already noted, you can create a Time dimension table that includes special time-based attributes that your business uses when analyzing data that won't be available if you rely solely on the Server Time dimension.

In this procedure, you'll add tables to the DSV.

Add tables to a data source view

1. In Solution Explorer, double-click SSAS Step by Step DW.dsv to open the Data Source View Designer.

   Alternatively, if the designer is still open in the main window of Visual Studio, you can click the SSAS Step by Step DW.dsv [Design] tab to continue working with the DSV.

2. Right-click the background of the Data Source View Diagram pane, and then click Add/Remove Tables.

3. In the Add/Remove Tables dialog box, double-click both dbo.DimTime and dbo.FactResellerSales in the Available Objects list to move these two tables to the Included Objects list, and then click OK.

   You'll use the DimTime table as the main table for the Time dimension that you create in the next procedure. In a later procedure, you'll use the FactResellerSales table to learn how the same time dimension can be used in different contexts, known as role-playing. Notice in the data source view diagram that there are three relationships between FactResellerSales and DimTime.

Creating a Time Dimension

When you create a Standard dimension using the Dimension Wizard, you first specify the table(s) used to create the dimension and then you select the desired attributes. You'll notice that the process is slightly different when you create a Time Dimension because you can specify only one dimension table and you then map its columns to special time-related attributes, such as year, quarter, or month, to name a few. After the dimension is created, you might need to rename objects and adjust attribute properties to display dimension members correctly in each attribute hierarchy.

In this procedure, you'll add a Time dimension to your Analysis Services project.

Build a time dimension

1. In Solution Explorer, right-click the Dimensions folder, click New Dimension, and then click Next.

2. Clear the Auto Build check box, and then click Next.

3. Click the SSAS Step by Step DW DSV, and then click Next.

4. On the Select the Dimension Type page of the wizard, click Time Dimension, and then click dbo_DimTime in the corresponding drop-down list.

   All tables in the DSV are available in the drop-down list. Since the wizard is unable to identify which table is the time dimension, you must select the appropriate table here.

5. Click Next.

6. On the Define Time Periods page, click the drop-down list for Year in the Time Table Columns, scroll through the list of columns, and then click CalendarYear to assign this column to the Year time property.
7. Repeat the previous step to assign table columns to specific time properties, as shown in the following table:

Time Property	Time Table Columns
Quarter	CalendarQuarter
Month	EnglishMonthName
Fiscal Quarter	FiscalQuarter
Fiscal Year	FiscalYear

8. Click Next.

   The Review New Hierarchies page of the wizard shows you the user hierarchies that will be created based on your selection of time properties on the previous page of the wizard. You'll learn more about user hierarchies in Chapter 7. You have the option here to remove the autogenerated hierarchies or to remove levels from a hierarchy. For now, you'll leave the hierarchies as they are.

9. Click Next, change the dimension name from Dim Time to **Time**, and then click Finish to complete the wizard.

   Your screen looks like this:

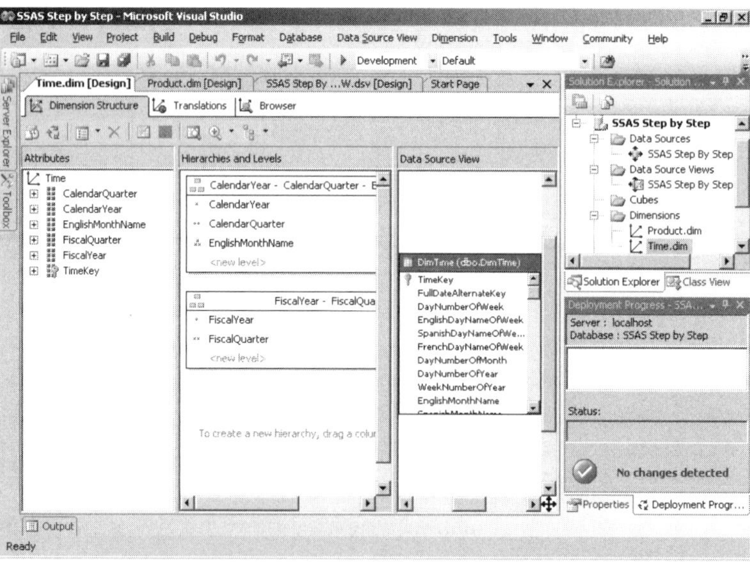

   Now Time.dim is available in the Dimensions folder of the Solution Explorer window and the Dimension Designer for the new dimension is open in Visual Studio.

10. Rename attributes as shown in the following table:

Rename this	As this
CalendarQuarter	Calendar Quarter
CalendarYear	Calendar Year
EnglishMonthName	Month
FiscalQuarter	Fiscal Quarter
FiscalYear	Fiscal Year
TimeKey	Date

Attribute names are often used as row or column headings in reports, so you might need to alter the default attribute names to a more suitable name for reporting purposes.

11. Rename user hierarchies as shown in the following table:

Rename this	As this
CalendarYear - CalendarQuarter - EnglishMonthName	Calendar
FiscalYear - FiscalQuarter	Fiscal

Notice that the level names displayed in the user hierarchy were not changed when you renamed attributes. For example, EnglishMonthName is still visible and was not renamed as Month. For consistency in a production database, you should rename levels in the user hierarchy to match the current attribute name, but since this dimension is for learning purposes only, you can leave the level names as they are.

12. In the Attributes list, right-click Date, click Properties, and then, in the Properties window, scroll to the *NameColumn* property, click (new) in the property's drop-down list, click FullDateAlternateKey, and then click OK.

The key column for this attribute is still TimeKey, which is used to join the dimension to related fact tables, but the key has no meaning to users. Instead, you can use the *NameColumn* property to display the name of an attribute member. In this case, users will see the value from the FullDateAlternateKey column of the DimTime table, which is a date value in a mm/dd/yy format.

13. Right-click the SSAS Step by Step project in the Solution Explorer window, and then click Deploy.

14. When deployment is complete, click the Browser tab, and then, in the Hierarchy drop-down list, click Calendar.

15. Expand the All member in the Calendar hierarchy tree, expand 2001, and then expand 3.

Your screen looks like this:

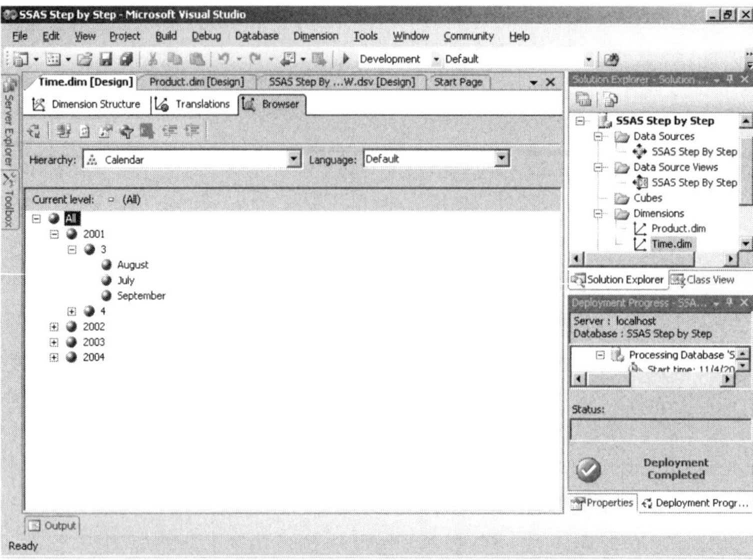

Notice that the months are sorted alphabetically: August, July, September. Sort order of attributes within the attribute hierarchy is determined by the *OrderBy* property which defaults to Key. Because the key value for Month is DimTime.EnglishMonthName, the result is an alphabetical sort based on the name of the month. However, you can produce the correct sort order by using another column in the DimTime table–Month-NumberOfYear.

16. Click the Dimension Structure tab, right-click Month, click Properties, and then, in the Properties window, scroll to the *KeyColumns* property.
17. Click the ellipsis button (...) in the property's list box, and then click the ellipsis button in the *Source* property in the DataItem Collection Editor dialog box.

18. Click MonthNumberOfYear in the Source Columns list, and then click OK. Your screen looks like this:

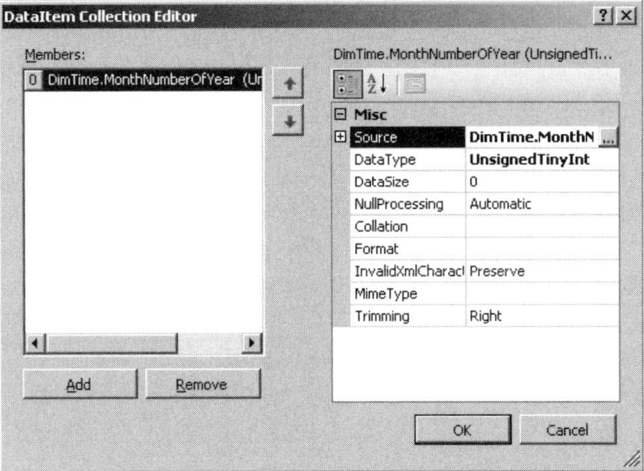

19. Click OK to close the DataItem Collection Editor dialog box.
20. Right-click the SSAS Step by Step project in the Solution Explorer window, and then click Deploy.
21. When deployment is complete, click the Browser tab, and then click the Reconnect button in the Browser toolbar. If necessary, expand the All member in the Calendar hierarchy tree, expand 2001, and then expand 3.

    Your screen now looks like this:

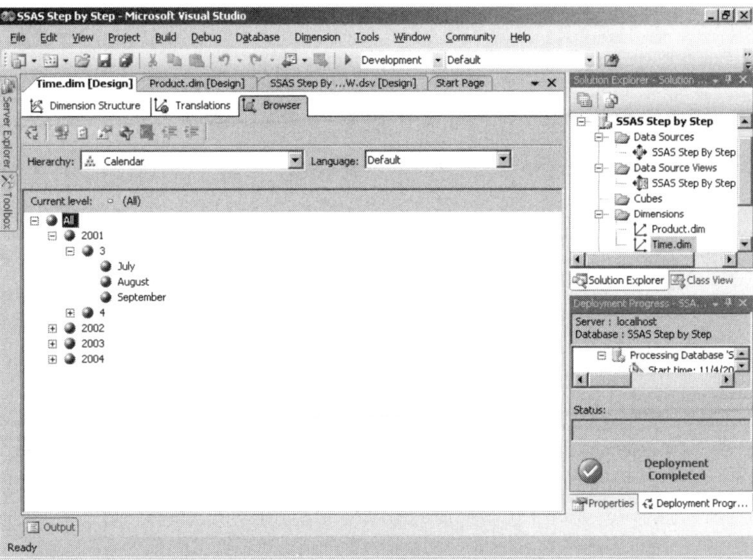

22. The months are now correctly sorted.

The Server Time Dimension

Using the Dimension Wizard, you can create a Standard dimension, a Time dimension, or a Server Time dimension. The Server Time dimension is unique because the data for this dimension does not come from a dimension table in your data warehouse, but is generated by Analysis Services and stored in a proprietary file structure on the server. You simply specify the beginning date and end date of the dimension, select the time periods to include such as year, quarter, month, or date, and choose the special calendars, if any, to add to the dimension. In fact, the process to define a Server Time dimension is identical to the process you used to define the Time dimension in Chapter 3. In Chapter 3, however, you generated a schema to hold data for the dimension which Analysis Services populated for you. When you create a Server Time dimension, no such table is created. The data available to this dimension type is maintained solely by Analysis Services. To use this dimension with a fact table, you will need to have a date/time column instead of a dimension key in the fact table. Analysis Services will use the date in this column to join the fact table with the Server Time dimension.

Working with Role-Playing Dimensions

As you learned previously in this chapter, a dimension can play different roles in a fact table. You can recognize a *role-playing dimension* when there are multiple columns in a fact table that each have foreign keys to the same dimension table. For example, in the SSAS Step by Step DW database, there are three dimension keys in the FactInternetSales and FactResellerSales tables which all refer to the DimTime table. The same time dimension is used to track sales by order date, by shipment date, and by delivery date. If you add the Time dimension to a cube that contains either of these fact tables, the corresponding role-playing dimensions are automatically added to the cube.

In this procedure, you'll add a predefined cube object to your Analysis Services project.

Add an object to a project

1. In Solution Explorer, right-click the SSAS Step by Step project, point to Add, and then click Existing Item.
2. Browse to C:\Documents and Settings\<username>\My Documents\Microsoft Press \as2005sbs\chap04, and then double-click Simple Cube.cube to add it to your project.

   When you use the same DSV across multiple projects, you can also reuse object files in different projects. By adding an existing item, you created a copy of the item's file that is now associated with your current project. Changes to this file in the SSAS Step by Step project do not affect the original version of Simple Cube.cube in the C:\Documents and Settings\<username>\My Documents\Microsoft Press\as2005sbs\chap04 folder.

In this procedure, you add role-playing time dimensions to a cube.

Add role-playing time dimensions to a cube

1. In Solution Explorer, double-click Simple Cube.cube to open the Cube Designer.
2. In the Dimensions pane of the Cube Designer, right-click the background, and then click Add Cube Dimension.
3. Click Time in the Select Dimension list, and then click OK.

   Your screen looks like this:

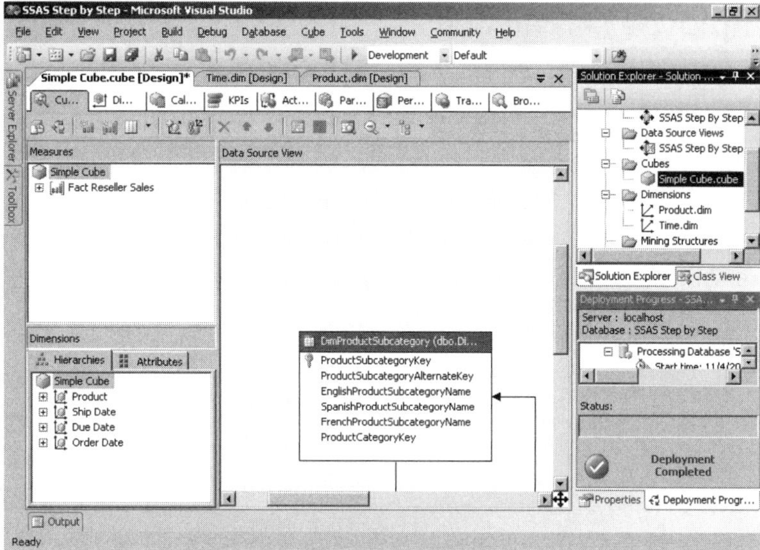

   Notice that Time is not added to the Dimensions pane, but there are three new dimensions: Ship Date, Due Date, and Order Date. Notice also there are no corresponding .dim files for these dimensions in the Dimensions folder of Solution Explorer. All that you see is the Time Dimension that you added previously. That is because the three new dimensions are role-playing dimensions for time.

Creating a Parent-Child Dimension

A Parent-Child dimension has a different table structure than most dimension tables. So far in this chapter, you have created a Product dimension which is a snowflake schema because it is based on multiple tables. You have also created a Time dimension which is a star schema because it is based on a single table. A Parent-Child dimension is also built from a single table, but it contains a built-in recursive hierarchical structure that you use to aggregate values across levels within each branch of the hierarchy.

For example, organizational data is often structured as a recursive hierarchy. An employee table includes records for each employee which, at their simplest, include a column to hold the unique employee key, a column for the employee name, and a column to hold the key to the record for the employee's manager. Because managers are also employees, there is another record in the same table that forms a branch of the employee hierarchy. You can recognize these parent-child relationships in your DSV by the self-referencing relationship that links the foreign key column of a table to the primary key column of the same table.

Adding an Employee Dimension

Just as with any other standard dimension, you use the Dimension Wizard to create a Parent-Child dimension. After specifying the dimension table and selecting attributes, you confirm the parent-child relationship in the table that the wizard detected by the self-referencing join on the table.

In this procedure, you'll add the DimEmployee table to the DSV and then use the table to create a parent-child dimension.

Create a parent-child dimension

1. Open SSAS Step by Step DW.dsv.
2. Right-click the background of the Data Source View Diagram pane, and then click Add/Remove Tables.
3. In the Add/Remove Tables dialog box, double-click dbo.DimEmployee in the Available Objects list to move this table to the Included Objects list, and then click OK.

   Notice the self-referencing relationship for the DimEmployee table in the DSV. This relationship is indicated by the arrow leading from the DimEmployee table back to itself.
4. In Solution Explorer, right-click the Dimensions folder, click New Dimension, click Next, clear the Auto Build check box, click Next, click the SSAS Step by Step DW DSV, and then click Next twice.
5. Click dbo.DimEmployee in the Main Table drop-down list, click EmployeeKey in the Key Columns list, click LastName in the Column Containing The Member Name drop-down list, and then click Next.
6. On the Select Dimension Attributes page of the wizard, select the check box next to ParentEmployeeKey.

   You must include the attribute that defines the foreign key column of a record in a parent-child dimension.
7. Click Next twice.

The Define Parent-Child Relationship page of the wizard looks like this:

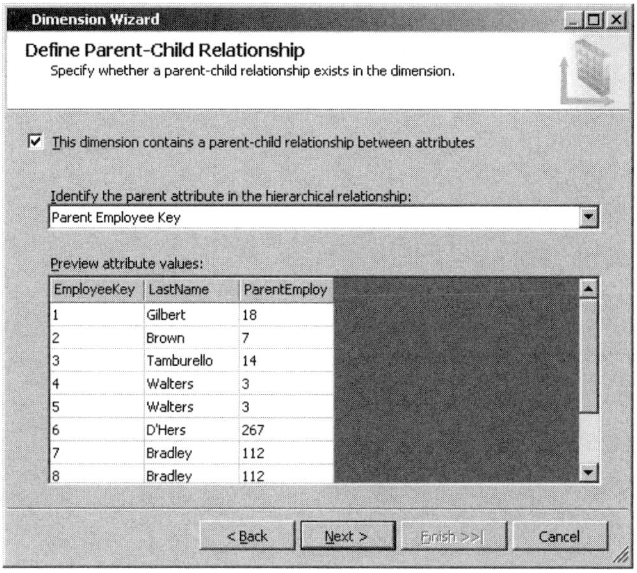

Notice that the This Dimension Contains A Parent-Child Relationship Between Attributes check box is selected. This relationship was automatically detected by the wizard based on the self-referencing join on this table in the DSV. ParentEmployeeKey is also correctly detected as the parent attribute as a result of the self-referencing join. This page of the wizard also allows you to preview attribute keys, attribute values, and the corresponding parent attribute keys for the top records in the table so that you can verify that the parent-child structure has been set up correctly.

8. Click Next, change the name of the dimension from Dim Employee to **Employee**, and then click Finish.

   The Employee parent-child dimension is now added to your project.

9. In the Attributes pane of the Dimension Structure tab, right-click Dim Employee, click Rename, and then type **Employee**.

10. Repeat the previous step to rename Parent Employee Key as **Employees**.

11. Keeping Employees selected in the Attributes pane, open the Properties window and locate the *Usage* property.

    Valid values for the *Usage* property are Key, Parent, and Regular. When you create a Parent-Child dimension, the Dimension Wizard automatically sets the value of this property to Parent for the parent attribute. There can be only one attribute with *Usage* set to Parent within a dimension. Similarly, there can be only one attribute with *Usage* set to Key. All other attributes must have a *Usage* value equal to Regular or dimension processing will fail.

12. Right-click the SSAS Step by Step project in the Solution Explorer window, and then click Deploy.

13. When deployment is complete, click the Browser tab, and then, in the Hierarchy drop-down list, click Employees.

14. Expand the All member in the Employees hierarchy tree, and then expand Sánchez, Trenary, Ajenstat, Welcker, and Abbas.

    Your screen looks like this:

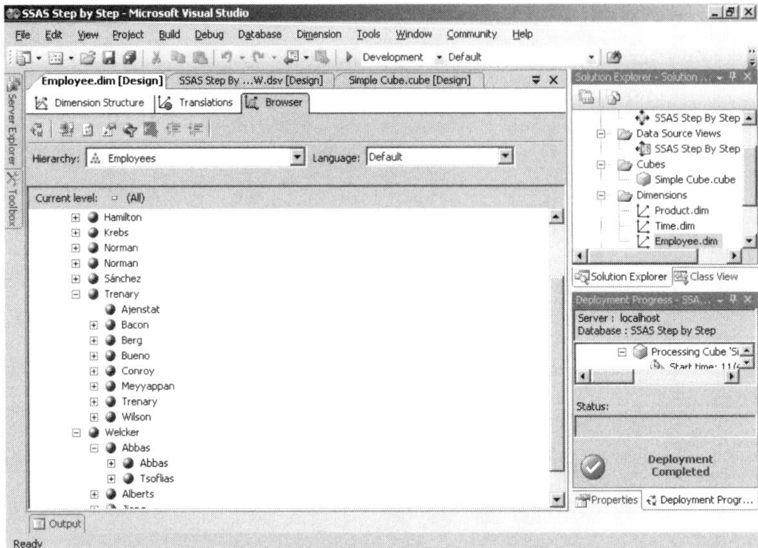

You can see that there are a different number of levels within the hierarchy. Notice that Trenary is a parent member with several child members. Only one of the child members–Conroy–is also a parent member. Trenary contains a data member also named Trenary. This type of structure is called a ragged hierarchy because the leaf-level members (those without child members) do not all share the same number of ancestors. For example, Ajenstat has three ancestor members–Trenary, Sánchez, and the All member, whereas Tsoflias has four ancestor members–Abbas, Welcker, Sánchez, and the All member.

Totaling Data for Non–Leaf-Level Data Members

In a standard dimension, only the leaf-level members can correspond to values in the fact table. For example, in a Time dimension, you can't have some rows in the fact table with monthly values and other rows with quarterly values. In a parent-child dimension, on the other hand, it's common to have values in the fact table at both the leaf level and at a parent level. For example, in the SSAS Step by Step DW database, Abbas is a manager, but is also directly responsible for some of the sales in the SalesFact table, as well as being indirectly responsible for the sales of direct reports. You need to decide whether or not cube browsers can see sales that Abbas made or only the sales for the direct reports.

In this procedure, you'll change the *MembersWithData* property value to compare the difference between the available options.

Set the *MembersWithData* property

1. Open the Simple Cube cube designer, and then, in the Dimensions pane, right-click the background, and then click Add Cube Dimension.
2. Click Employee in the Select Dimension list, and then click OK.
3. Deploy the project, and then click the Browser tab of the Cube Designer when deployment is complete.
4. In the cube metadata tree, expand Employee, drag the Employees hierarchy (not the Employee hierarchy!) to the area of the grid labeled Drop Row Fields Here, and then drag the Measures object to the area of the grid labeled Drop Totals or Detail Fields Here.
5. Click the plus sign next to Sánchez to drill down one level, click the plus sign next to Welcker to drill down another level, and then click the plus sign next to Abbas to drill down one more level.

   Your screen looks like this:

   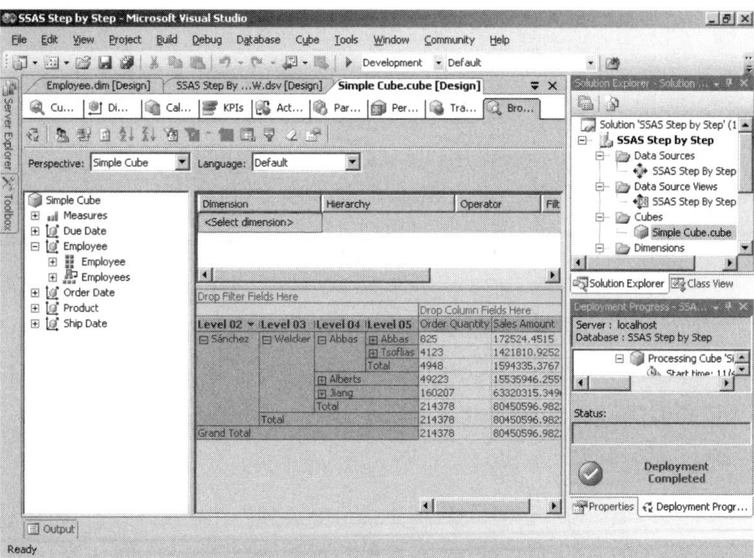

   Notice that when you expand Abbas, you can see on Level 05 the total sales of 172,524.4515 for Abbas and total sales of 1,421,810.9252 for Tsoflias. The combined sales for these two individuals is 1,594,335.3767, which appears on the total row beneath these two members.

6. Click the minus sign next to Abbas in Level 04 to collapse this branch of the hierarchy.

   The total sales amount for Abbas is 1,594,335.3767, which, as you saw in the previous step, is actually total sales for both Abbas and Tsoflias.

   Other than the fact that you saw one Abbas member in Level 04 and another Abbas member in Level 05, it was not obvious from the member names which member represented the aggregated totals from child members and which were the aggregated values for the parent member from the fact table. You can change the template that creates the new member name to make a distinction.

7. Open the Employee Dimension Designer, click the Dimension Structure tab if necessary, right-click the Employees attribute in the Attributes pane, and then click Properties.

8. In the Properties window, change the *MembersWithDataCaption* to * **(data)**.

   The asterisk is a placeholder for the member name.

9. Deploy the project, and then click the Browser tab of the Cube Designer when deployment is complete. Click the Reconnect button, and then drill down to Level 05 of the Employee hierarchy.

   Your screen looks like this:

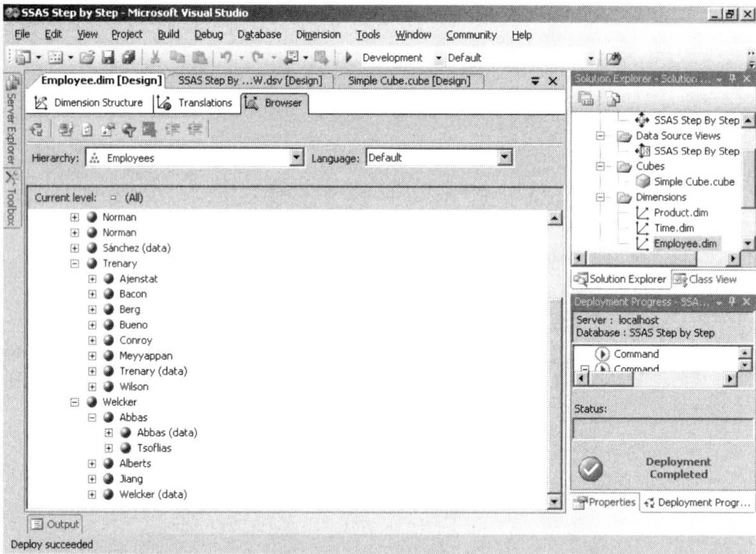

   The managers' data members now are more easily distinguished from the other child members as well as their parent member.

10. Switch back to the Dimension Structure tab in the Employee Dimension Designer, right-click the Employees attribute in the Attributes pane, and then click Properties.

11. In the Properties window, click NonLeafDataHidden in the *MembersWithData* property drop-down list to review the available values.

The Properties window looks like this:

The *MembersWithData* property is available only for a parent-child dimension, and more specifically is available only for an attribute with its *Usage* property set to Parent. The *MembersWithData* property has two possible values: NonLeafDataVisible and NonLeafDataHidden.

NonLeafDataVisible (the default) creates a new member for each parent. That new member can display the values linked to that member in the fact table. This option is appropriate when you want to directly compare a manager's sales with those of the direct reports. NonLeafDataHidden does not create a new member for each parent. However, the total for a parent member may be greater than the sum of its visible children.

12. Click NonLeafDataHidden in the *MembersWithData* property drop-down list.
13. Deploy the project, and then click the Browser tab of the Cube Designer when deployment is complete. Click the Reconnect button, and then drill down to Level 05 of the Employee hierarchy.

Your screen looks like this:

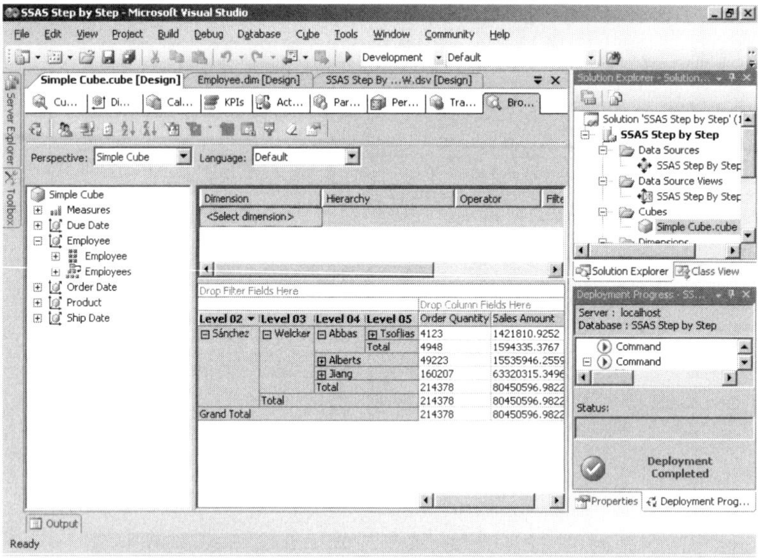

Notice that you can no longer see the individual sales contribution of Abbas, only that of Tsoflias. However, the total sales for Abbas are still 1,594,335.3767. Non–leaf-level data is always included in the aggregated values at each level of the hierarchy. The *MembersWithData* property simply controls whether or not you see this data allocated to a parent member.

Managing Levels within a Parent-Child Dimension

In a parent-child dimension, sometimes there is only one member that does not truly have a parent. For example, the values for the manager at the top level of the Employee dimension are the same values for the All member. In your Employee dimension, there's no need to have an All level above Sánchez. The All level can be removed for other dimension types as well, such as a time dimension when you have a business rule that time should not be aggregated for all years in the cube.

Besides removing the All level, you can also manage the names of levels for a parent-child hierarchy. Recall that when you browsed the cube in the previous procedure, each level was numbered sequentially, beginning with Level 02 and continuing through Level 05. A parent-child dimension has an exclusive property that you can use to provide a more meaningful name to each level.

In this procedure, you'll remove the All level from the Employees hierarchy.

Remove the All level from a hierarchy

1. Open the Employee Dim Designer, right-click Employees in the Attributes pane of the Dimension Structure tab, and then click Properties.
2. Scroll to the *IsAggregatable* property, and then click False in the property's drop-down list.
3. Deploy the project, and then click the Browser tab of the Dimension Designer when deployment is complete. Click the Reconnect button.

   Your screen looks like this:

   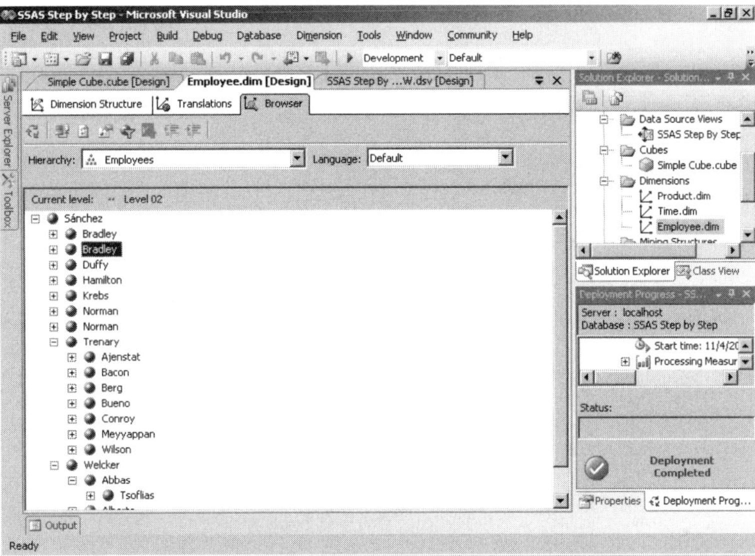

   The All level is now removed. Since the All level for this parent-child hierarchy is not visible in the cube browser, you will not notice any change there. This property only affects queries that return the list of members contained in the hierarchy for which this property has been set to False.

In this procedure, you'll define a level naming template for the Employees hierarchy.

Create a level naming template for a parent-child hierarchy

1. Click the Dimension Structure tab, right-click Employees in the Attributes pane, and then click Properties.
2. Scroll to the *NamingTemplate* property, and then click the ellipsis button in the property's list box.
3. Click in the Name box to the right of the asterisk (*), and type **CEO**.

Your screen looks like this:

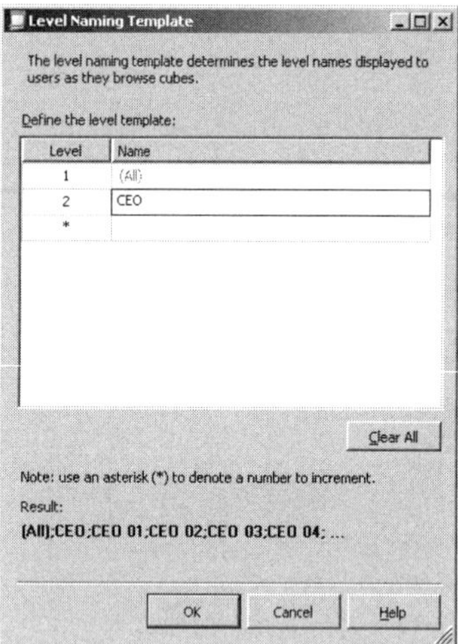

As soon as you begin typing, the asterisk changes to a 2, and a new row, with an asterisk, appears.

4. Click in the Name box in the new row, and type **Manager**. In the box of the next row, type **Supervisor**, and in the box of the final row, type **Individual Contributor**.

   Your screen looks like this:

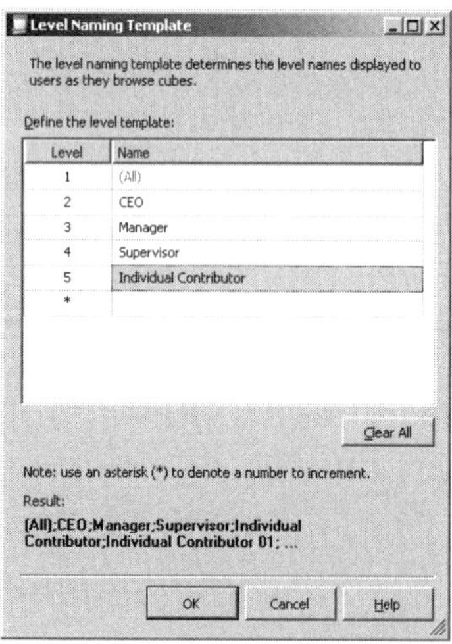

   As you enter values into the level naming template grid, the result is displayed at the bottom of the grid. Any levels that are automatically created below the lowest level specified in the template are given sequentially incremented numbers.

5. Click OK to close the Level Naming Template dialog box.

6. Deploy the project, click the Browser tab of the Cube Designer when deployment is complete, and then click the Reconnect button.
7. Drag the Employees hierarchy to the grid area labeled Drop Row Fields Here, and then drill down until you can see five levels displayed.

   Your screen looks like this:

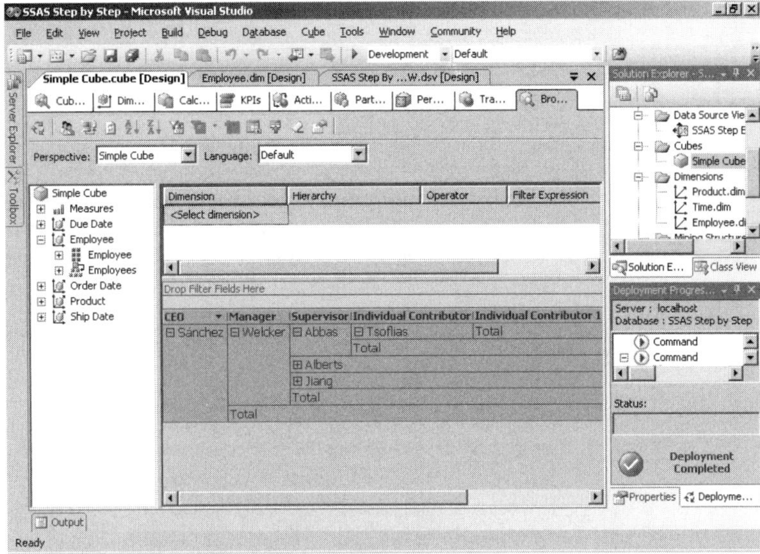

   Notice that instead of Level 01, Level 02, etc. as the column labels for the Employees hierarchy, you now see the names of each level that you specified: CEO, Manager, Supervisor, and Individual Contributor. Any levels below the lowest level specified in the template are given sequentially incremented numbers.
8. Save the solution.

Linked Dimensions

A *linked dimension* is based on a dimension that is stored in a separate Analysis Services database which may or may not be on the same server. You can create and maintain a dimension in just one database and then reuse that dimension by creating linked dimensions for use in multiple databases. Users will not notice any difference between a regular dimension and a linked dimension. As a developer, you will be able to browse the members of a linked dimension in the Dimension Designer, but you can only modify the dimension within its original Analysis Services database.

Chapter 4 Quick Reference

To	Do this
Add a data source to an Analysis Services project	In Solution Explorer, right-click the Data Sources folder, click New Data Source, click New, select a provider, enter a server name, specify the authentication method and credentials for authentication, and, if needed, select a database name, and then specify the credentials for Analysis Services to impersonate when accessing the data source during processing.
Create a data source view (DSV)	In Solution Explorer, right-click the Data Source Views folder, click New Data Source View, select an existing data source (or create a new one), and then add tables or views to the Included Objects list.
Create a standard dimension from an existing data source without using Auto Build	In Solution Explorer, right-click the Dimensions folder, click New Dimension, clear the Auto Build check box, select a data source view, select Standard Dimension, specify the main table, select the key column, optionally select the member name column, include any related tables, select attributes, and name the dimension.
Deploy an Analysis Services project	In Solution Explorer, right-click the Analysis Services project, and then click Deploy.
Browse a dimension	In the Dimension Designer, click the Browser tab, and then, if the project has been recently deployed, click the Reconnect button on the Browser toolbar. Select the appropriate hierarchy in the drop-down list and expand the attribute hierarchy tree to view the hierarchy members.
Disable an attribute hierarchy	In the Attributes pane of the Dimension Structure tab in the Dimension Designer, click an attribute, and then, in the Properties window, change the *AttributeHierarchyEnabled* property to False.
Add a table to a DSV	In the Data Source View Designer, right-click the Data Source View Diagram pane, click Add/Remove Tables, and add tables or views to the Included Objects list.
Create a time dimension from an existing data source	In Solution Explorer, right-click the Dimensions folder, click New Dimension, clear the Auto Build check box, select a DSV, select Time Dimension, specify the time dimension table, assign columns from the dimension table to built-in time periods, and then name the dimension.
Add an object file to a project	Right-click the project in the Solution Explorer, point to Add, click Existing Item, and then navigate to the folder containing the object to open the file.
Add role-playing dimensions to a cube	Ensure multiple relations are defined between a fact table and a dimension, create the dimension by using the Dimension Wizard, open the Cube Designer, right-click the background of the Dimension pane of the Cube Structure tab, click Add Cube Dimension, click the dimension in the list, and then click OK.
Create a parent-child dimension manually	Follow the procedure for creating a standard dimension and, on the Define Parent-Child Relationship page of the Dimension Wizard, select the check box This Dimension Contains a Parent-Child Relationship Between Attributes and identify the parent attribute key.

To	Do this
Hide data for non–leaf-level data members	In the Attributes pane of the Dimension Structure of the Dimension Designer, click the parent attribute of a parent-child dimension, and then, in the Properties window, change the *MembersWithData* property to NonLeafDataHidden.
Remove the All level of a hierarchy	In the Attributes pane of the Dimension Structure of the Dimension Designer, click an attribute, and then, in the Properties window, change the *IsAggregatable* property to False.
Apply a level naming template to a parent-child hierarchy	In the Attributes pane of the Dimension Structure of the Dimension Designer, click the parent attribute of a parent-child dimension, and then, in the Properties window, click the ellipsis button for the *NamingTemplate* property, and then type in a name for each level.

Chapter 5

Designing Measure Groups and Measures

After completing this chapter, you will be able to:

- Build a cube based upon an underlying data source using the New Cube Wizard.
- Create, modify, and browse measures and measure groups.
- Define the relationship between dimensions and measure groups.
- Work with aggregations of semiadditive measures.
- Add distinct count measures.
- Create calculations to provide additional functionality.

In Chapter 4, "Designing Dimensions," you focused on the use of the Dimension Wizard to create different types of dimensions, and the Dimension Designer to enhance those dimensions by changing certain properties, and to review the results of those enhancements. In this chapter, you'll shift your focus to the Cube Wizard to build a cube from measure groups, measures, and dimensions. You also use the Cube Designer to make any necessary changes to the cube structure and to check the impact of these changes by browsing the cube. There are many ways to create measures from quantitative data; in this chapter, you learn some of the more common methods by creating additive measures, semiadditive measures, distinct counts, and simple calculations.

Adding Measure Groups to a Cube

A cube not only requires at least one dimension, as you learned in Chapter 4, but it also requires at least one measure group which in turn must contain at least one measure. Multiple measure groups in the same cube are most meaningful when they have at least one dimension in common. When you build a cube, you identify the fact table that serves as the data source for a measure group and you select one or more measures from that fact table to include in each measure group. This measure can be as simple as a count of the rows in the fact table used as a source for the measure group, or it can be associated with a column in the fact table. You also specify the dimensions used to summarize these measures and define the dimension's attributes that represent the lowest level of detail within each measure group.

After a cube is built, you will likely want to change certain properties, such as the formatting string used to display the measure value or the aggregation function used to produce summary values. You can even hide a measure if it should be used as part of calculation and isn't useful by itself for analysis. Of course, you can always add new measure groups or new measures to an existing cube.

Building a Cube

As with building a dimension using a bottom-up approach, you must add the required tables to your project's data source view (DSV) before you can begin building a cube in the same manner. In the case of a cube, you need to add at least one fact table to the DSV. If you're not using a data warehouse, you can add a table that contains a numeric column that also has foreign keys for your dimensions. The Cube Wizard makes it easy for you to build a cube quickly. It guides you through the process of creating measure groups from fact tables and relating dimensions to the measure groups.

In this procedure, you'll add fact tables to the existing DSV and then use the Cube Wizard to create a cube from this underlying data source.

Use the Cube Wizard

1. Start SQL Server Business Intelligence Development Studio (BIDS), and open the SSAS Step by Step solution that you saved in the C:\Documents and Settings\<username>\My Documents\Microsoft Press\as2005sbs\Workspace folder.

> **Note** If you skipped Chapter 4, open the SSAS Step by Step solution in the C:\Documents and Settings\<username>\My Documents\Microsoft Press\as2005sbs\Answers\chap04\SSAS Step by Step folder.

2. In Solution Explorer, double-click SSAS Step by Step DW.dsv to open the Data Source View Designer.
3. Right-click the background of the Data Source View Diagram pane, and then click Add/Remove Tables.
4. In the Add/Remove Tables dialog box, double-click both dbo.FactInternetSales and dbo.FactProductForecast in the Available Objects list to move these two tables to the Included Objects list, and then click OK.
5. In Solution Explorer, right-click the Cubes folder, and then click New Cube to launch the Cube Wizard.
6. Click Next, clear the Auto Build check box, and then click Next twice.

   The beginning steps of the Cube Wizard are similar to the beginning steps of the Dimension Wizard. You can build the object with or without a data source. If you choose to use a data source, you also choose whether or not to use Auto Build to suggest the structure.

So that you can become more familiar with the cube structure, you will not use Auto Build to build this cube.

7. On the Identify Fact and Dimension Tables page of the Cube Wizard, select the check boxes in the Dimension column that correspond to dbo.DimProduct, dbo.DimTime, and dbo.DimEmployee.

   Notice the warning that says at least one fact table must be selected. It identifies dimension tables that are not related to a fact table. Right now, all the dimensions are listed because you haven't yet identified the fact tables.

8. Select the check boxes in the Fact column that correspond to FactResellerSales, FactInternetSales, and FactProductForecast.

   Your screen looks like this:

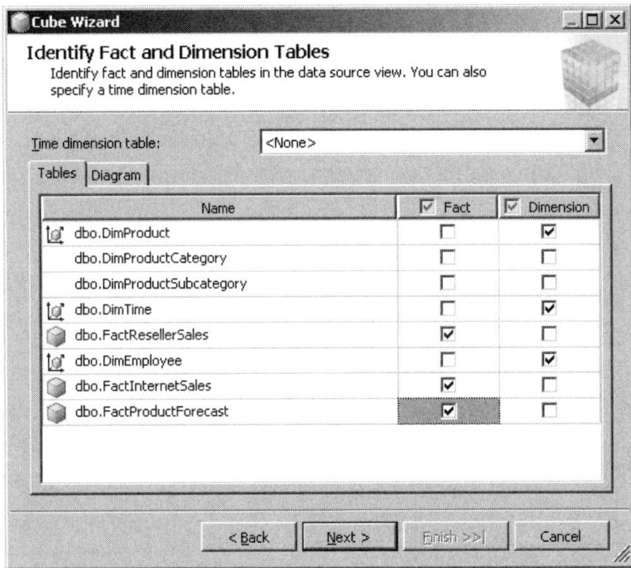

   Notice that the warning disappears when you select the first fact table.

   At this point in the wizard, you're specifying which tables in the DSV will be used to build the cube. You will define the relationship between each dimension and each measure group later. At this point, the wizard verifies that for each fact table selected, there is at least one related dimension table selected based on the foreign key relationships defined in the DSV.

9. Click Next, and then click the >> button to move all available dimensions–Product, Employee, and Time–to the Cube Dimensions list, and then click Next.

10. Clear the check box in the header row to the left of Measure Groups/Measures to clear the default selection of all measures, and then select the check box to the left of Order Quantity (in the Fact Reseller Sales measure group).

    Notice that for each measure group there is one measure per numeric column in the fact table. Because foreign key columns are often integer columns, these columns are also included as potential measures. (You'll learn how to use a foreign key column for a distinct count measure later in this chapter.)

    The list of candidate measures also includes a count measure. This measure is not dependent on a column in the fact table, but instead is made available as a convenience to you. When added to a cube, this type of measure will return a count of the fact table rows summarized by dimension. Count measures are useful when each row of the fact table represents a discrete transaction or event.

11. Change the measure name from Order Quantity to **Reseller Order Quantity**.

    Notice that the first item in the available measures list, Fact Reseller Sales, is also selected when you select Order Quantity. Fact Reseller Sales will become the Measure Group that holds the Order Quantity and the other measures from the FactResellerSales table. By default, the name of the measure group is the same as the underlying fact table name. You can edit this name here, but instead you'll use the Cube Designer to rename the measure groups in the next procedure.

12. Select the check box to the left of Sales Amount, and then change the measure name to **Reseller Sales Amount**.

13. Scroll to find the Fact Internet Sales measure group, select the check boxes to select Order Quantity – Fact Internet Sales and Sales Amount – Fact Internet Sales, and change the names of these measures to **Internet Order Quantity** and **Internet Sales Amount**, respectively.

    Two measures with the same name, even if they come from different measure groups, are not allowed in the same cube.

14. Scroll to find the Fact Product Forecast measure group, select the check box to select Sales Amount Forecast, and then click Next.

15. Change the cube name to **SSAS**, and then click Finish.

Your screen looks like this:

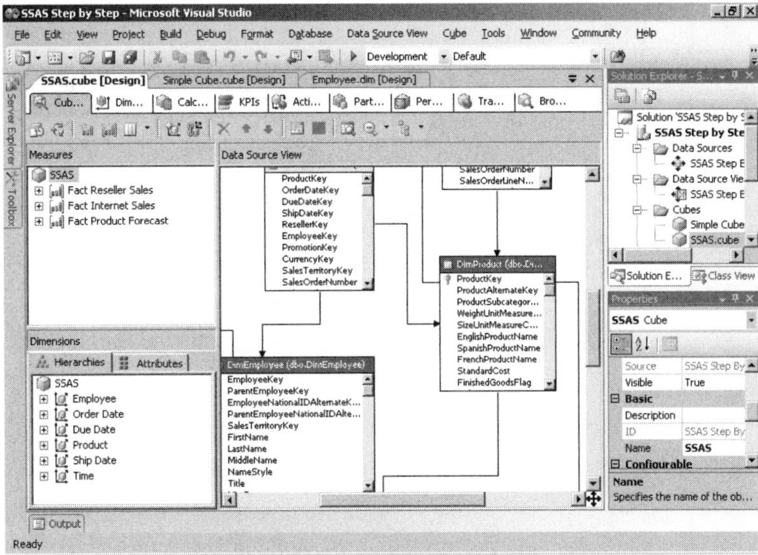

Notice that the measures pane in the Cube Designer displays a measure group for each fact table that you selected in the wizard: Fact Internet Sales, Fact Reseller Sales, and Fact Product Forecast. When users browse this cube, they will see measures organized by measure group. The word Fact in the name of these measure groups will likely be confusing to users and, just as you changed dimension names to be more user-friendly, you'll change these later in this chapter.

Changing Properties for Measure Groups and Measures

Measure groups and measures have properties that you can modify, just like dimensions and attributes, as you learned in Chapter 3, "Building Your First Cube." You might want to change the *Name* property of these objects if the name from the underlying fact table is less user-friendly than you'd like. While most front-end tools include a feature that allows users to apply formatting to measures, it's a good practice to set the *FormatString* property for each measure in the cube. (It makes it easier for you to compare values during the development stage as well.) Even more important than setting properties related to appearance, though, is ensuring that the *AggregateFunction* property of each measure is set correctly. Other properties determine how measure groups are processed or stored on the server, how errors during processing are handled, how measures are stored, and how they can be used. The best way to become familiar with the available properties is to examine the description of each property in the Properties window of Visual Studio after selecting a measure group or measure in the Cube Structure workspace of the Cube Design.

In this procedure, you'll rename the measure groups.

Rename measure groups

1. In the Measures pane, right-click the Fact Reseller Sales measure group, click Properties, and then change the *Name* property value to **Reseller Sales**.
2. Repeat the previous step to rename Fact Internet Sales and Fact Product Forecast to **Internet Sales** and **Product Forecast**, respectively.

> **Tip** You can also right-click an item in the Measures pane, and then click Rename. Renaming the item also updates the *Name* property.

In this procedure, you'll format each measure.

Format measures

1. In the Measures pane, expand Resellers Sales, click the Reseller Order Quantity measure, and then select #,# in the *FormatString* property drop-down list.

   Now this measure will display without decimal places and with a thousands separator. You can select a format string from the list of available values for this property, or you can type in a valid custom format string, as you'll see in the next step.
2. Repeat the previous step to select or type a new value in the *FormatString* property box for the remaining measures, as shown in the following table:

For this measure	Change *FormatString* to
Reseller Sales Amount	$#,#
Internet Order Quantity	#,#
Internet Sales Amount	$#,#
Sales Amount Forecast	$#,#

   This custom string $#,# is similar to the Currency format, but Currency has two decimal places and the custom string displays values without decimal places.

Specifying Dimension Usage

The relationships between dimension tables and fact tables should be defined in the DSV. When you use the Cube Wizard to select specific dimensions and fact tables, these defined relationships are also included in the cube, where they are referred to as *dimension usage*. The Cube Designer contains a tab where you can review the dimension usage settings determined by the wizard and where you can make adjustments as you refine the design of the cube.

In this procedure, you'll review how each dimension relates to each measure group.

Review the relationship between cube dimensions and measure groups

1. In the Cube Designer, click the Dimension Usage tab.

   Your screen looks like this:

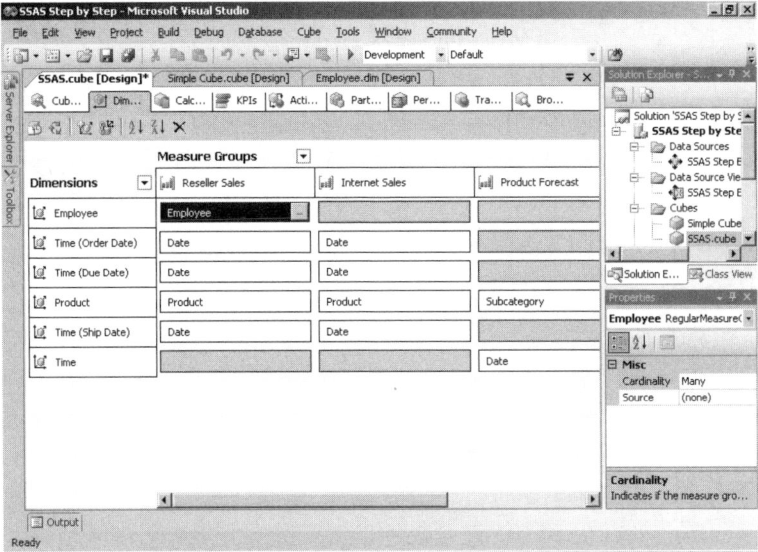

   The grid on this tab places each measure group in the cube in a column and each dimension in a row. At each intersection of a measure group and a dimension, you specify dimension usage—that is, you specify how the dimension is related to the measure group. For example, you can see in this layout that the Employee dimension is related to the Reseller Sales measure group by way of the Employee attribute. This relationship is the cube's representation of the relationship between the DimEmployee and FactResellerSales tables based on EmployeeKey, as defined in the DSV. Because no other fact table contains an EmployeeKey column, there are no other relationships with a measure group defined for the Employee dimension.

   Now take a look at the Time dimension. As you learned in Chapter 4, the Time dimension can be a role-playing dimension when a fact table contains multiple foreign key columns for this one dimension. The fact tables underlying the Reseller Sales and Internet Sales measure groups fit this description, and, accordingly, you see each of the role-playing dimensions—Order Date, Due Date, and Ship Date—associated with these two measure groups. On the other hand, the fact table underlying Product Forecast has only one foreign key column to the DimTime table and therefore is related only to the base dimension, Time. Whether using the role-playing dimension or the base dimension, all of the measure groups are related to the dimensions by way of the Date attribute, which is the key attribute for the Time dimension.

   Finally, notice how the Product Dimension intersects with all three measure groups. For the Reseller Sales and Internet Sales measure groups, the relationship is defined by the

Product attribute, which happens to be the key attribute of the Product dimension. The Product Forecast measure group relates to the Product dimension at a different level of granularity–Subcategory. That is, the foreign key in the FactProductForecast table relates to the Subcategory attribute in the set of tables that comprises the Product dimension. It's common to have data in forecast and budget fact tables that is more summarized than fact tables that contain transaction details. By using measure groups with different levels of granularity such as this, you can easily compare actual results (in this case, Reseller Sales and Internet Sales) against the plan (ProductForecast).

2. Click the intersection of Product and Product Forecast, and then click on the ellipsis button that appears in the box.

   Your screen looks like this:

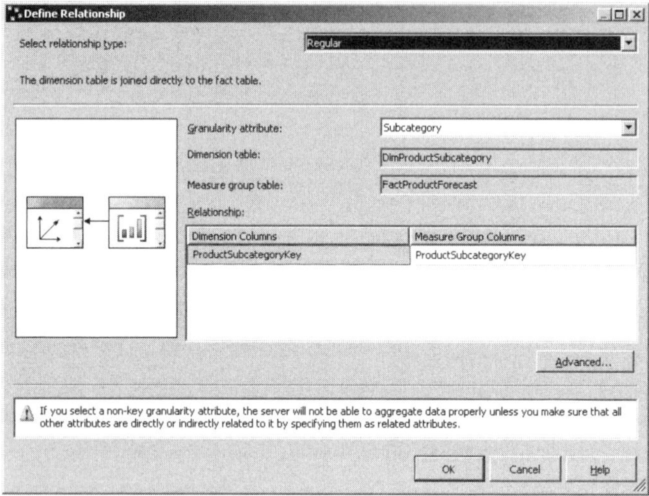

You'll notice that this relationship is set up as a Regular relationship. When a regular relationship exists between a measure group and a dimension, at least one column in the fact table is joined to one column in the dimension table according to the DSV. (Remember that you can create relationships in the DSV that don't actually exist in the physical relational tables.)

When the relationship type is Regular, you must specify a *granularity attribute*, which is the dimension attribute that represents the lowest level of detail in the fact table. Put another way, it's simply the attribute for which there is a column in the measure group's fact table. In this case, Subcategory is an attribute that has a key column and a name column defined, but Subcategory is the name of the attribute and therefore is the value assigned to the Granularity Attribute box.

If you look at the Relationship table below the Granularity Attribute box, you'll see the Dimension Column is defined as ProductSubcategoryKey, which is the key column for the Subcategory attribute. This value is populated in the Dimension Columns list automatically when you make a selection in the Granularity Attribute list box. The Measure Group Columns list is used to identify the foreign key column in the fact table that corresponds to the dimension key column.

All of the settings in this dialog box are set automatically by the Cube Wizard if relationships in the data source view are correctly defined. When defining regular relationships, you shouldn't need to make changes here unless the structure of your dimensions or fact tables changes later. There are several other relationship types that will require manual configuration here, and you'll learn more about them in Chapter 9, "Exploring Special Features."

Before moving on to the next section, notice the warning message at the bottom of the Define Relationship dialog box: "If you select a non-key granularity attribute, the server will not be able to aggregate data properly unless you make sure that all other attributes are directly or indirectly related to it by specifying them as related attributes." This message appears because ProductSubcategoryKey is not the key attribute for the Product dimension, even though it is a key column for an attribute. Remember that each dimension can have only one key attribute to uniquely identify the leaf-level of the dimension. If ProductSubcategoryKey is not correctly related to other attributes in the same dimension, then you will get incorrect results when browsing the cube. You'll see how this works in the next section.

3. Click OK to close the Define Relationship dialog box.

Browsing Multiple Measure Groups

A benefit of using multiple measure groups in the same cube is the ability to make comparisons even when the granularity of a dimension in each measure group is different. For example, sales measure groups might contain actual sales information at the product level, while a forecast measure group might contain forecasted values at the subcategory level. By placing these measure groups in the same cube, you can easily compare forecast units with sales units at the subcategory level. If you have relationships between attributes correctly defined, you can further summarize measures in these measure groups to compare forecast units with sales units at the category level. After building a cube, you should review the aggregated values for each dimension across all measure groups to make sure you get the expected results.

In this procedure, you'll deploy and browse a cube that contains multiple measure groups and modify attribute relationships to examine their interaction with measure groups.

Examine the interaction between attributes and measure groups in a cube

1. Click the Browser tab in the Cube Designer.

Your screen looks like this:

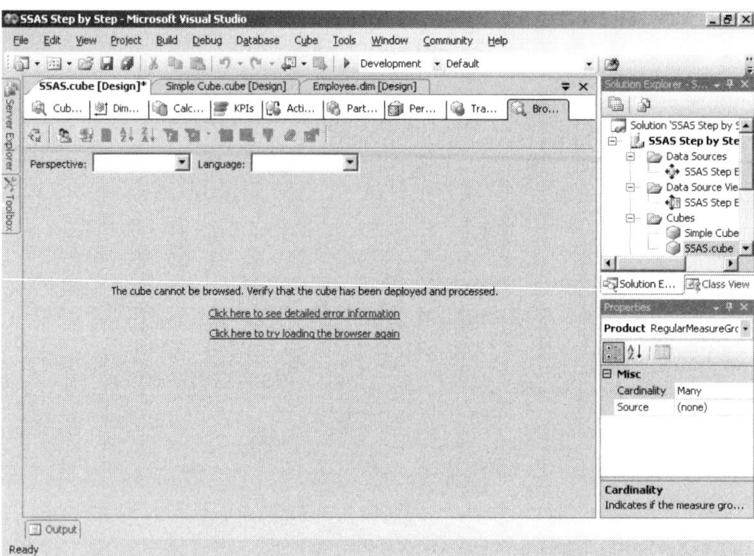

Notice the error message: "The cube cannot be browsed. Verify that the cube has been deployed and processed." As with dimensions, you cannot browse a cube immediately after building it with the wizard because the cube must be deployed to the server where it is processed. Remember that processing is the operation that loads data into the cube structure. Also, it's important to note if you later make changes to the cube by using the Cube Designer, including something as simple as changing a *FormatString* property, you must still deploy the cube to the Analysis Server before browsing.

2. In Solution Explorer, right-click the SSAS Step by Step project, and then click Deploy.
3. When deployment has completed successfully, click the Reconnect button on the Browser toolbar.
4. Drag Measures from the metadata pane, and drop it in the area of the grid labeled Drop Totals or Detail Fields Here.

   When you drag the Measures object, all measures–regardless of measure group–are added to the grid as a group. Notice the formatting strings have been applied to each measure, which makes it a lot easier to read the values than if you had skipped that step. However, this browser interface aligns the numbers to the left, which makes comparing values more challenging.
5. Click the Reseller Order Quantity column caption to select the entire column, right-click the caption, and then select Commands and Options.
6. On the Format tab, click the Align Right button.
7. Click the Reseller Sales Amount caption, and then click the Align Right button.

The dialog box remains open even when you click on a different measure. All formatting changes are applied to the currently selected item in the grid.

8. Repeat the previous step for all of the remaining measures, and then close the dialog box when you are finished.

   Your screen looks like this:

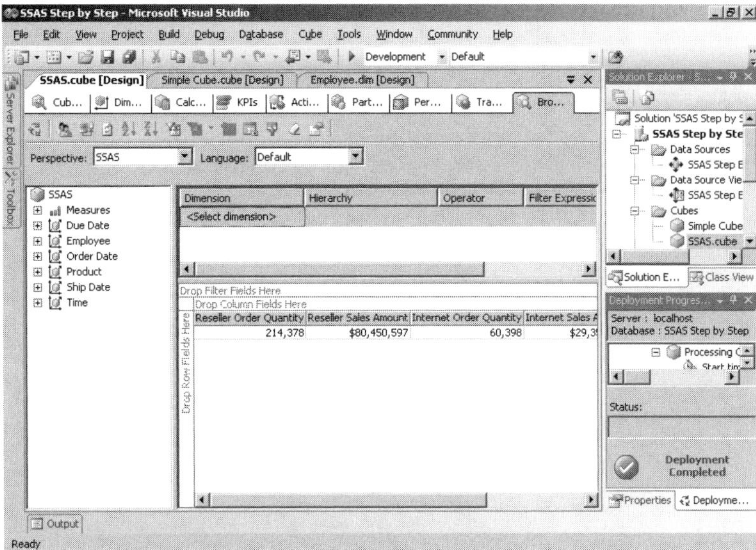

You can also be selective about which measures are visible in the browser. If, after placing measures on the grid, you decide you want to focus on just a few measures, you can remove the other measures one by one.

9. In the grid, click the Reseller Order Quantity caption, drag it to any spot in the metadata pane, and drop it when you see the Delete symbol (the letter X).

   This action doesn't change the measure's position in the metadata tree; it simply removes it from the browser grid.

10. Repeat the previous step to remove Internet Order Quantity from the browser grid.

11. Expand Product, drag Subcategory to the grid, and then drop it in the area labeled Drop Row Fields Here.

    Remember that Reseller Sales Amount and Internet Sales Amount come from measure groups that have Product as a granularity attribute, while Product Forecast comes from a measure group that has Subcategory as a granularity attribute. The values you see in the grid for all measures are summarized by Subcategory. Even though Subcategory is not represented in the fact tables underlying Reseller Sales and Internet Sales measure groups, there is a defined relationship between their granularity attribute, Product, and the Subcategory attribute. This relationship allows the measures to be added up to show product sales by Subcategory. You can see this relationship in the Dimension Designer for the Product dimension.

12. In Solution Explorer, double-click Product.dim. If necessary, click the Dimension Structure tab. Expand Product in the Attributes pane.

    Your screen looks like this:

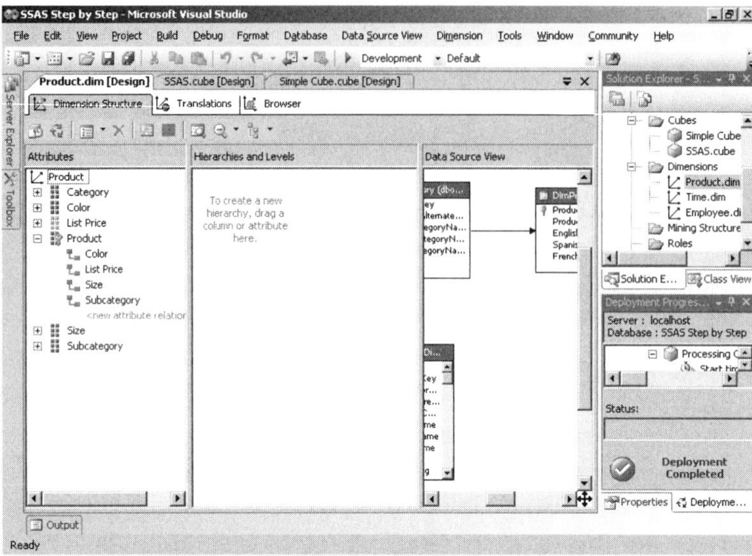

In this example, Product is the *target attribute* and the others listed under it–Color, List Price, Size, and Subcategory–are *source attributes*. The relationship between a target attribute and its source attributes is known as a *direct attribute relationship*; it is used by the cube to compute aggregated values for each of the source attributes when the fact table contains only the Product key.

13. Expand the Subcategory target attribute.

    Subcategory only has one direct attribute relationship–with Category. Because Category is related to Subcategory and Subcategory is related to Product, the cube can derive the Category values when it has the Product key from FactResellerSales or FactInternetSales. This relationship between Product and Category is known as an *indirect attribute relationship*.

    Remember the message in the Define Relationship dialog box at the end of the previous procedure? It was a reminder that the cube can only aggregate data when there is a direct or indirect relationship between attributes in the same dimension. You have now seen that all attributes of the Product dimension are directly or indirectly related to Product, which is the granularity attribute for the Reseller Sales and Internet Sales measure groups. Therefore, any of these attributes can be used to view the aggregated measures for these two measure groups.

In the previous procedure, you confirmed that Subcategory is the granularity attribute for the Product Forecast measure group. You can see here that there is a direct attribute relationship with Category, so you know that you can use the Category attribute to view aggregated measures for that measure group as well. Are there any indirect relationships?

14. Expand the Category target attribute.

    Category has no direct attribute relationships defined. Therefore, you will only be able to use two attributes–Subcategory and Category–when working with Product Forecast measures.

15. Switch to the browser in the Cube Designer, remove Subcategory from the grid, and then drag Category to the rows axis.

    The measures from each measure group aggregate properly because they are directly or indirectly related to the granularity attribute of each measure group.

16. Now remove Category from the grid, and then drag Color to the rows axis.

    Your screen looks like this:

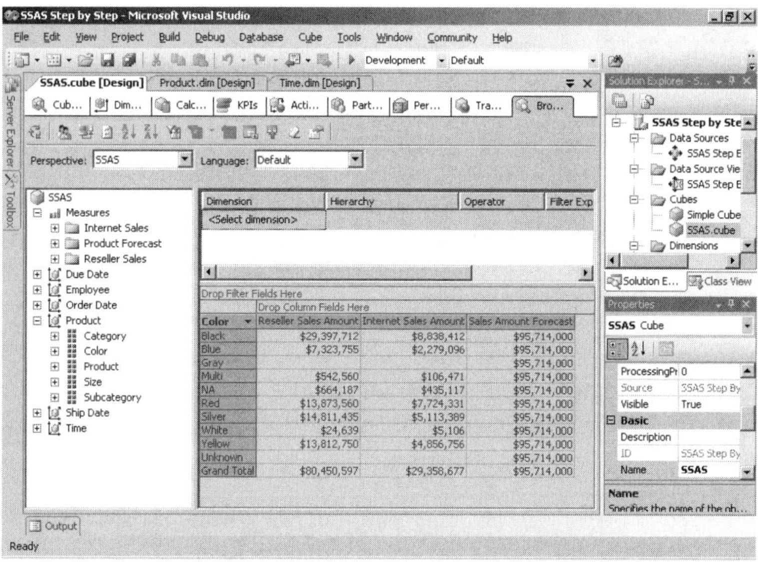

It looks like something is wrong. The Sales Amount Forecast for each color is the same amount. What has really happened is that, because Color is not directly or indirectly related to Subcategory, the cube is unable to aggregate this measure by color and instead displays the total Sales Amount Forecast for each color.

The relationships defined in the DSV are used to build the attribute relationships in the dimension. You can remove these attribute relationships if you prefer, and you can create new attribute relationships if necessary. Be sure to test your changes to ensure the resulting aggregated values are what you expected. Try this out by removing the relationship between Subcategory and Category.

17. Switch to the Dimension Designer for Product, and then in the Dimension Structure tab, right-click the Category source attribute beneath the Subcategory attribute, click Delete, and then click OK to confirm the deletion.

18. Deploy the project.

    Notice the error message that the Category attribute is not related (directly or indirectly) to the "Product" key attribute. Removing the attribute relationship between Category and Subcategory left Category as an orphaned attribute. Because it's not related to the key attribute of the dimension directly or indirectly, the dimension cannot be processed.

19. Close the Error List dialog box.

20. Drag the Category attribute to the space labeled <New Attribute Relationship> beneath Product.

    Now Category is directly related to Product, but has no relationship with Subcategory. The dimension can now be processed, but what will happen when you view measures with the Category attribute?

21. Deploy the project, switch to the Cube Designer, click the Reconnect button on the toolbar of the Browser tab, drag Color off of the grid, and then drag Category to the grid on rows.

    With Category, you see the same behavior with Sales Amount Forecast that you saw previously when Color was on rows. Even though the DSV has a join between Subcategory and Category, it is the attribute relationship in the dimension structure that determines whether or not aggregated values can be derived for an attribute that is not the granularity attribute for a measure group.

22. Now that you've seen how attribute relationships affect the aggregated values of measures, restore the attribute relationships in the Product dimension to the original state by removing the Category source attribute from the Product target attribute and placing it under the Subcategory target attribute.

23. Switch to the Dimension Designer for Product, drag Category from beneath Product, and drop it in the space labeled <New Attribute Relationship> beneath Subcategory.

    The next time that you browse the cube, after the project is deployed, you'll see the correct aggregated values for Category across all measure groups.

Aggregating Semiadditive Measures

A *semiadditive measure* is different from the additive measures you've seen thus far because it can be summed along some, but not all, dimensions in a cube. A common use of a semiadditive measure is a value for a fixed point in time (also known as a snapshot), such as inventory quantity. Inventory quantity can be summed up along the Product dimension to find out how many bikes are in stock on a given day, but you can't sum this measure across the Time dimension. For example, the number of bikes you had in stock at the end of the first quarter can't be added to the number of bikes you had in stock at the end of the second quarter (at least, not if you want the correct result!). The measure of inventory on hand over time requires you to look at the value at the end of the time period only, not the sum of all values over the period. When you add a semiadditive measure to a cube, whether using the Cube Wizard or manually adding it by using the Cube Designer, you must change its default aggregation behavior.

Adding a Measure Group to an Existing Cube

Now that your cube is created, can you enhance it with additional measure groups and measures? Of course! Sometimes, you'll need to add another fact table to your DSV to create a new measure group. Other times, you'll simply add more measures to an existing measure group from the underlying fact table. You can easily make these additions to your cube by using the Cube Designer. But first, be sure the supporting data for the measure is available in the DSV—either by adding new tables to the DSV or by confirming that an existing fact table contains the desired measure.

In this procedure, you'll add the Inventory measure group to the cube.

Add a measure group to a cube

1. In Solution Explorer, double-click SSAS Step by Step DW.dsv, right-click the background of the Diagram pane, and then click Add/Remove Tables.
2. Double-click dbo.FactInventory in the list of Available Objects to add it to the Included Objects list, and then click OK.

   The TimeKey column in this table joins to the DimTime table and ProductKey joins to the DimProduct table. The InStkUnit column is the only measure in this table and contains a count of each product's inventory on the first day of the month.
3. Switch to the SSAS Cube Designer, right-click anywhere in the Measures pane on the Cube Structure tab, click New Measure Group, click FactInventory, and then click OK.
4. Rename the new measure group as **Inventory**.
5. Expand the Inventory measure group.

Your screen looks like this:

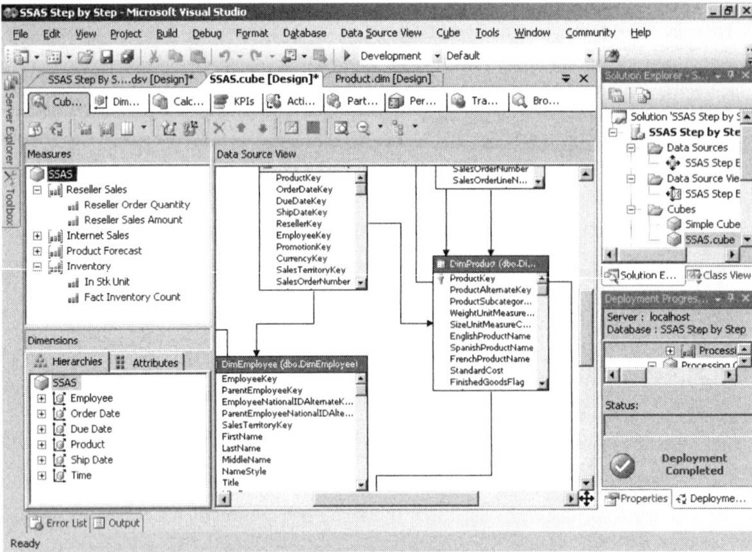

Even though the fact table contained only one measure, another measure—FactInventoryCount—is automatically included. Because count measures are commonly found in cubes, the Cube Wizard and the Cube Designer both suggest this measure when you add a measure group. You have the option of including this measure or not.

6. Right-click Fact InventoryCount, click Delete, and then click OK to confirm deletion of the object.
7. Rename In Stk Unit as **Units In Stock**, and then change its *FormatString* property value to **#,#**.
8. In Solution Explorer, right-click the SSAS Step by Step project, click Deploy, click the Browser tab, and then click the Reconnect button on the Browser toolbar.
9. Click anywhere in the grid to activate the Browser toolbar, and then click the Clear Results button in the Browser toolbar to remove all dimensions and measures from the grid.
10. In the metadata tree, expand Measures, expand Inventory, and then drag Units in Stock to the area of the grid labeled Drop Total or Detail Fields Here.
11. Expand Time, and then drag Time.Calendar, the calendar hierarchy, to the area of the grid labeled Drop Column Fields Here.
12. Expand Product, and then drag Category to the area of the grid labeled Drop Row Fields Here.

13. Right-click the Units in Stock caption in the grid, click Commands and Options, click the Format tab, click the Align Right button on the Format tab, and then close the Commands and Options dialog box.

14. In the grid, expand 2004, and then expand 1 to see the year, quarter, and month levels of the Calendar hierarchy.

    Your screen looks like this:

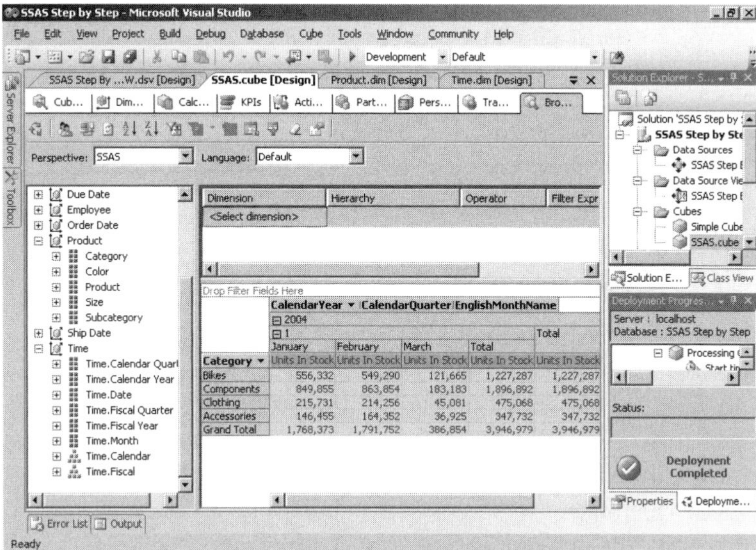

Notice the two Total columns as well as the Grand Total column each display the sum of Units In Stock from January through March for each Category, while the Grand Total row displays the sum of all Categories for each month. Adding up the category values within a month is fine, but you need to prevent the addition of values across months. You'll correct this behavior in the next procedure.

Using a Semiadditive Aggregate Function

Each measure in a cube has an *AggregateFunction* property, which by default is set to Sum. As you've already seen in this chapter, the Sum function is not appropriate for a semiadditive measure. Analysis Services provides several alternative functions for semiadditive measures, which are shown in the following table.

Use this aggregate function	To do this
ByAccount	Apply the aggregation function assigned to the member's account type (in an account dimension only).
AverageOfChildren	Average the value of all nonempty children of the current member.
FirstChild	Get the value of the first child of the current member.

Use this aggregate function	To do this
LastChild	Get the value of the last child of the current member.
FirstNonEmpty	Get the value of the first child of the current member that is not empty.
LastNonEmpty	Get the value of the last child of the current member that is not empty.

The ByAccount aggregate function is a special type of behavior that you'll learn more about in Chapter 6, "Working with a Finance Measure Group." Notice the other aggregate functions involve one or more child members. Child members are all members that are one level below a specified member. As an example, consider that each attribute hierarchy is a two-level hierarchy, with an All member at the top level and the attribute members on the bottom level. These attribute members are children of the All member. This family relationship also applies to user hierarchies, like the Calendar hierarchy in the Time dimension, which has three levels–Year, Quarter, and EnglishMonthName. Each month is a child of a quarter and each quarter is a child of a year.

Before selecting an aggregate function, you need to understand the business rules within your organizations for each semiadditive measure. Sometimes, you might need to average the value of each month to derive the quarter value. Similarly, you would average each quarter to derive the year value. To accomplish this objective, you use the AverageOfChildren aggregate function. Other times, the correct calculation should use the value of the first or last child only. For a variation of this approach, you can use FirstNonEmpty or LastNonEmpty. With these two aggregate functions, the first or last child, respectively, with a value for the selected measure (referred to as nonempty), will be used.

In this procedure, you'll change the *AggregateFunction* property of the Units In Stock measure to LastNonEmpty.

Use the LastNonEmpty aggregate function

1. Click the Cube Structure tab, right-click Units In Stock in the Measures pane, click Properties, and then select LastNonEmpty in the *AggregateFunction* property's drop-down list.

2. Deploy the project, click the Browser tab, and then click the Reconnect button.

Your screen looks like this:

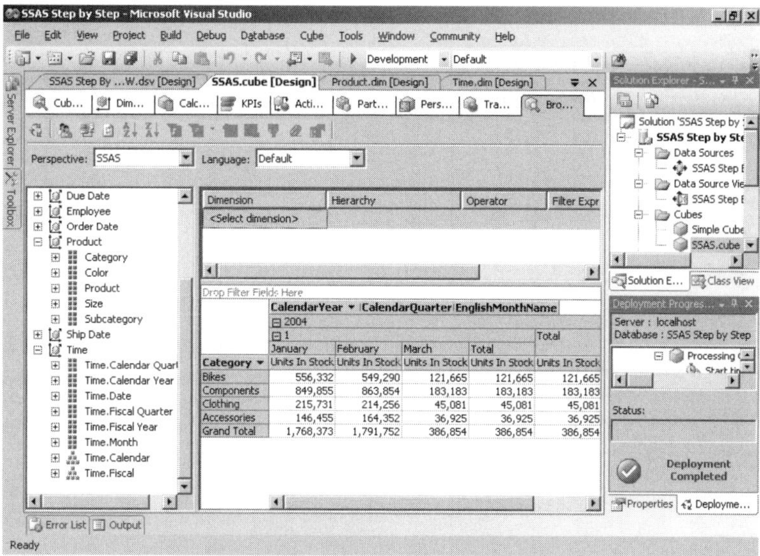

Notice the inventory measure Units In Stock is now aggregating correctly, both over time and by product. The Grand Total column reflects only the March value for each product category instead of summing all months. The quarter value and the year value also both show the March value, since March is the last month of the quarter with a nonempty value as well as the last month of the year with a nonempty value. If, for example, a category had a value for February, but no value for March, then the quarter and year value would show the February value instead of the empty March value.

> **Note** If you use this aggregate function and a given product has no inventory on a given date, the fact table should include a row for this product with a measure value of zero so that it will not be treated as empty.

Calculating Distinct Counts

Another useful aggregate function is DistinctCount, which returns the number of unique members represented in a fact table. For example, if a fact table that contains sales data also includes a column for CustomerKey, then the DistinctCount aggregate function would count the number of unique CustomerKeys in the fact table, not the number of CustomerKeys. (The total number of CustomerKeys would equal the total number of fact rows.) Measuring the number of distinct customers that are buying products can help a company monitor whether the customer base is growing or shrinking over time.

In this procedure, you'll add the Unique Customers measure to the cube and set its *Aggregate-Function* property to DistinctCount.

Adding a Distinct Count Measure

1. Click the Cube Structure tab, right-click anywhere in the Measures pane, and then click New Measure.
2. In the Usage drop-down list, select Distinct Count, select FactInternetSales in the Source Table drop-down list, and then click CustomerKey in the Source Columns list.

   Your screen looks like this:

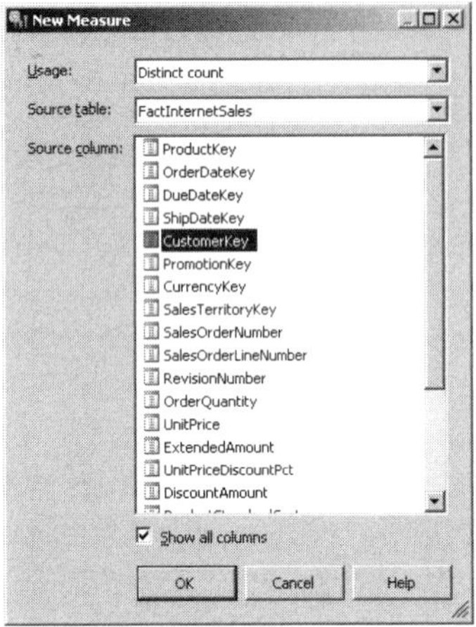

3. Click OK.

   The Measures pane looks like this:

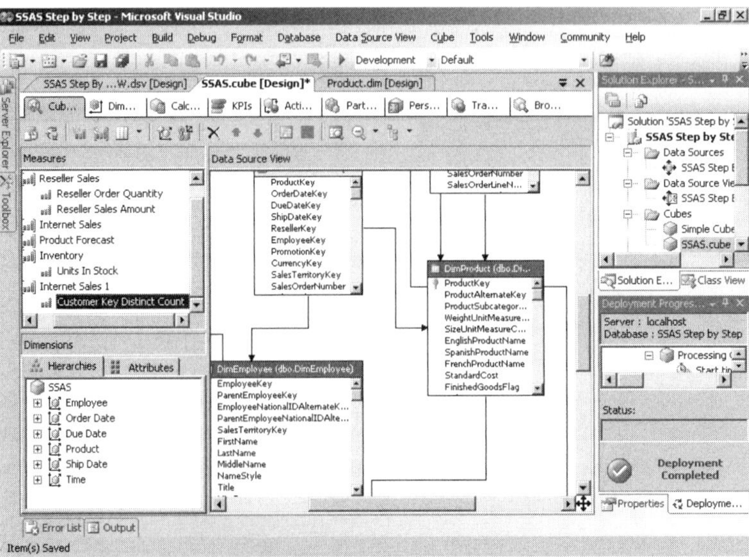

Notice that a new measure group, Internet Sales 1, is created for the new measure. Because you specified Distinct Count for this measure, and because distinct count measures must be contained in a separate measure group, Analysis Services automatically created a new measure group.

Distinct Measures require their own measure group to optimize processing performance. The New Measure wizard automatically places the Distinct Count Measure into its own measure group in the Cube Structure.

4. Rename Internet Sales 1 as **Distinct Count** and rename Customer Key Distinct Count as **Unique Customers**.
5. Deploy the project, click the Browser tab, click the Reconnect button, click anywhere in the grid, and then click the Clear Results button to reset the cube browser.
6. Expand Measures, and then expand the Distinct Count folder.

Your screen looks like this:

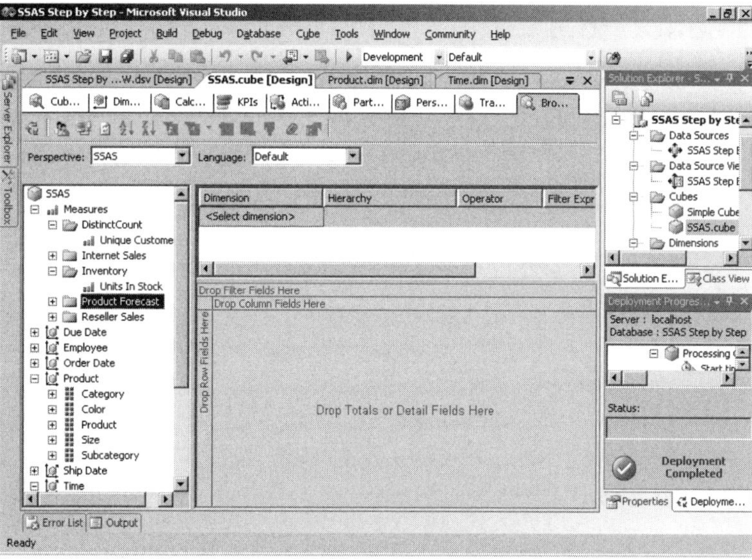

Distinct counts will always be kept in a separate folder. You'll use this new measure in the next procedure.

Creating Simple Calculations

MDX is a pseudoacronym for *multidimensional expressions*. MDX was created expressly for use with multidimensional online analytical processing (MOLAP) data sources. MDX is used in two different ways within Analysis Services. First, it is a query language–the tool for retrieving reports from an OLAP cube. In other words, MDX is the tool used by client applications to retrieve values. Second, MDX is an expression language–the tool used to calculate single values. For example, MDX is what you use to add calculations to a cube. This chapter will give you a brief introduction to MDX expressions by showing you how to use them to create simple calculations in your cube. In Chapter 8, "Using MDX," you'll learn how to create more complex calculations and how to execute and debug MDX queries. If you understand MDX, you can create sophisticated expressions that put the A (for *analytical*) into OLAP.

MDX is not exclusive to Analysis Services. It's part of a specification called OLE DB for OLAP, which Microsoft has sponsored to industry standards boards as a tool for querying a multidimensional data source. MDX is a standardized language that is supported by several OLAP providers, just as Structured Query Language (SQL) is a standardized language that is supported by many relational database providers. Of course, just as relational database providers make modifications to the SQL standard, so OLAP providers will make minor customizations to the MDX standard. In fact, the MDX implemented in Analysis Services does vary somewhat from the OLE DB for OLAP specification. This book will refer only to the Analysis Services version of MDX.

Adding a Calculation to a Cube

Calculations extend the analytical capability of your cube. You can use expressions to add additional measures to a cube. You can create a *derived measure* if you add a Named Calculation to a fact table in the DSV. To create a Named Calculation, you use a SQL expression to perform arithmetic operations using other columns in the fact table. For example, you could multiply an amount by a quantity to derive an extended amount. Derived measures calculate as part of the SQL statement that retrieves values from the fact table. The expression always calculates before any aggregations are performed.

Earlier in this chapter, you learned that you can manage the aggregation behavior of a measure by specifying the correct *AggregateFunction* property. The default aggregation function is *Sum*, which adds lower level values to get higher level values. With some derived measure expressions, however, you get incorrect values if you use the *Sum* function to aggregate the values. For example, if you want to calculate average sales correctly using dollars and units sold, you must perform the calculation after the dollars and units are summed. To do that, you must create a *calculated measure*. A calculated measure is a calculation that is added to the Measures dimension.

The difference between a derived measure and a calculated measure is when the calculation is performed. A derived measure is calculated before aggregations are created, and the values of the derived measure are stored in the cube. A calculated measure is calculated after aggregations are created, and the values of a calculated measure aren't stored in the cube. The primary criterion for choosing between a derived measure and a calculated measure is not efficiency, but accuracy.

If a calculation contains only addition or subtraction, you can choose whether to create a derived measure or a calculated measure based purely upon convenience or efficiency, since addition and subtraction can be done in any order. For example, you could create a Gross Profit measure by subtracting a Cost Of Goods Sold measure from a Net Sales Dollars measure. Since this calculation involves only subtraction, the values will be the same whether you choose to make it a derived measure–using columns from the fact table–or a calculated measure–using measures in a cube. If the measure will be used frequently, make it a derived measure; if infrequently, make it a calculated measure.

If a calculation involves multiplication by a constant, you'll get the same value regardless of whether you use a calculated or a derived measure. Again, base the decision on how frequently the measure will be accessed. If a calculation involves multiplying or dividing one column by another–as in calculating a price or a ratio–the choice between a calculated measure and a derived measure is important. If you want to aggregate by summing and the expression for the measure involves multiplication or division, you'll almost always want to create a calculated measure. If, however, you use a *Min* or *Max* aggregation function, you might want to create a derived measure that calculates before the aggregation takes place.

In this procedure, you'll create a simple calculation to determine the average Internet sales per unique customer.

Add a weighted average calculation

1. Click the Calculations tab in the Cube Designer.

   Your screen looks like this:

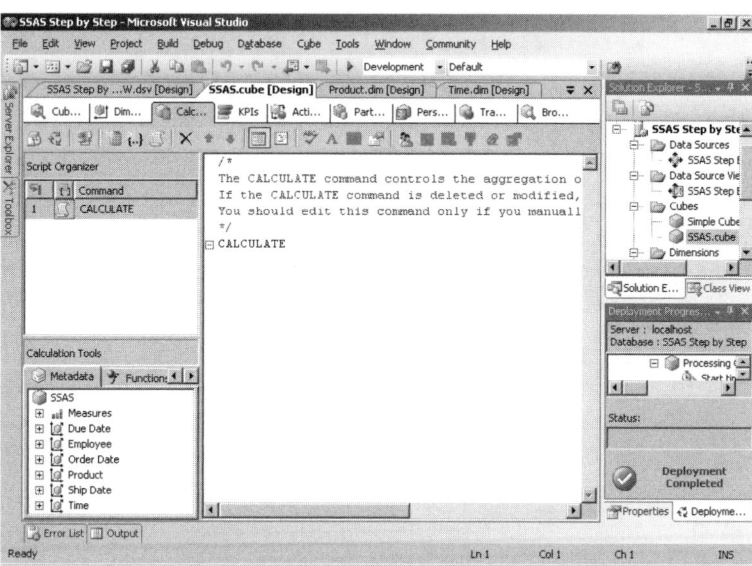

   If you're already familiar with MDX scripting, you might prefer to click the Script View button on the toolbar to switch views. Otherwise, you'll find it easier to create a new calculated member using the Form View which is the default view when you first open the Calculations tab.

2. Click the New Calculated Member button on the Calculations toolbar.

   The Script Organizer pane looks like this:

   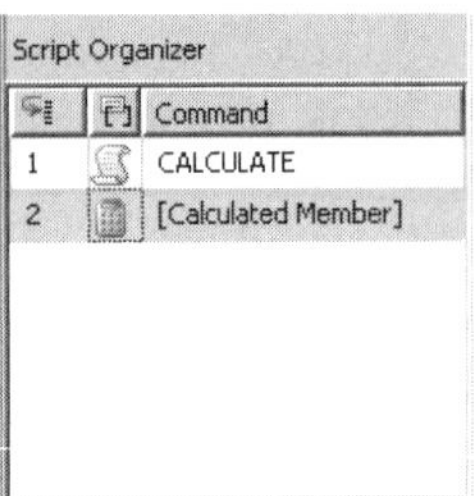

   Notice that a new row was added to the Script Organizer pane. The Script Organizer lists all calculations in the cube. The first row must always be CALCULATE in order for the cube calculations to return a value at query time. You'll learn about the importance of sequencing calculations correctly in the Organize Scripts procedure in Chapter 8. If you right-click a calculation in the Script Organizer, you can rearrange the selected calculation or delete it. Selecting a calculation in the Script Organizer displays the calculation in the current view.

3. In the Name box, type **Avg Internet Sales Per Customer**.

   Notice the red symbol that appears to the right of the Name box. This symbol indicates that there is a problem with the name that you entered. If you want to include spaces in the name of the calculation, then you need to enclose the name in square brackets.

4. Correct the name of the calculation by typing **[** (left square bracket) in front of the name and **]** (right square bracket) at the end of the name.

   Now that the name is valid, the red symbol disappears. Valid names for calculated members contain only letters or digits. The name may only contain a space or other characters if the name is enclosed by square brackets, [and].

5. Expand Measures in the cube metadata tree located in the Calculation Tools pane, expand the Internet Sales measure group, and then Drag Internet Sales Amount into the Expression box.

   You have the option with Form View to type in the MDX expression directly or to drag and drop objects from the Calculation Tools pane. By dragging an object from the cube metadata tree, the object is added to the Expressions box as a fully qualified expression, such as [Measures].[Internet Sales Amount]. Alternatively, you can type this expression directly into the box, but it's recommended to use the graphical interface to avoid typing errors and ensure proper syntax.

   In addition to the metadata tree, which contains all of the objects in your cube, the Calculation Tools pane has a Functions tab and a Templates tab. MDX includes a large number of functions which are all listed on the Functions tab, organized by function type. When you drag a function from the Functions tab, it shows you the syntax for the function, using placeholder tokens enclosed in double pointed brackets. You need to replace these tokens with an appropriate item by typing or dragging an item into the Expression box. Similarly, you can use templates to build a more complex MDX script to perform a specific calculation.

6. In the Expressions box, type / to continue building the expression.
7. To complete the calculation expression, expand the Distinct Count folder in the metadata tree, drag Unique Customers into the Expressions box, and drop it at the end of the current expression string.

   Your screen looks like this:

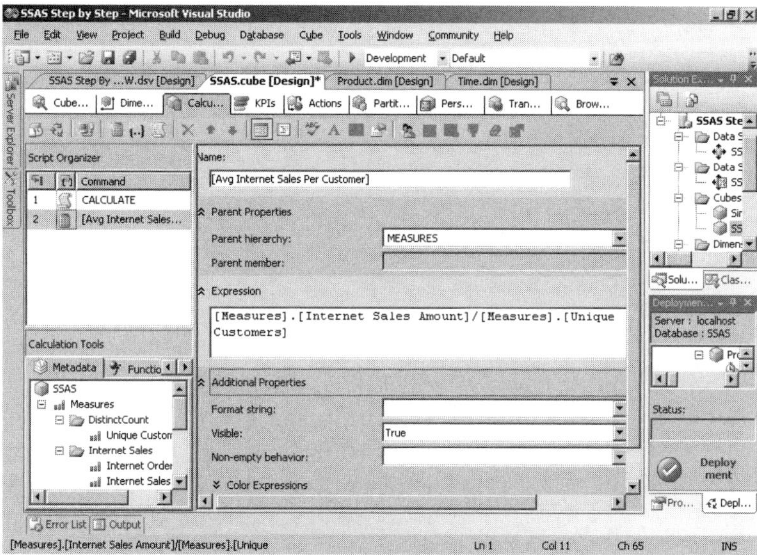

8. Click Currency in the Format String list box.

   All of the standard formatting strings are available for selection here. You can also type in a custom format string in the Format String drop-down list.

   Notice the *Visible* property value is True. The *Visible* property determines whether the object will be visible to the end user. When this property value is set to False, the calculation can still be used in other MDX expressions and scripts, but will not be available in the Measures folder when users browse the cube.

9. Select Unique Customers in the Non-Empty Behavior drop-down list, and then click OK.

   Nonempty behavior is an important property for ratio calculations. If the denominator is empty, an MDX expression will return an error just as it would if the denominator were equal to zero. By selecting one or more measures for the *Non-Empty Behavior* property, you are establishing a requirement that each selected measure first be evaluated before the calculation expression is evaluated. If each selected measure is empty, then the expression is also treated as empty and no error is returned.

10. Click the Check Syntax button on the toolbar, and then click OK.

    Making this step a standard procedure after creating a calculation is a good idea.

11. To test the calculated member, deploy the project, click the Browser tab, and then click Reconnect.

12. Expand Measures, and then drag Avg Internet Sales Per Customer into the grid, drag Category from the Product dimension to rows, and then drag Time.Calendar from the Time dimension to columns.

    Your screen looks like this:

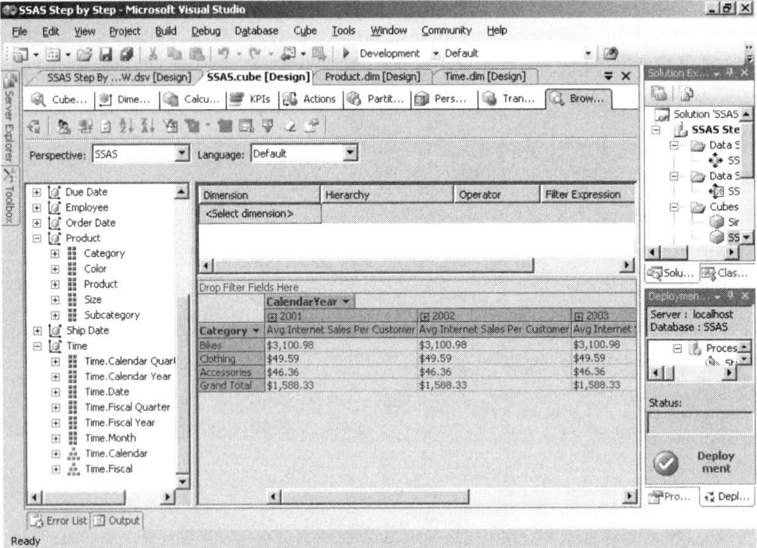

Notice that the values are different across Category, but are the same across Time. Whenever you see the same values repeat like this, and you know that the measure is not semiadditive, then the first thing you should check is the relationship between the cube dimension and the fact table which is defined on the Dimension Usage tab.

13. Click the Dimension Usage tab.

Your screen looks like this:

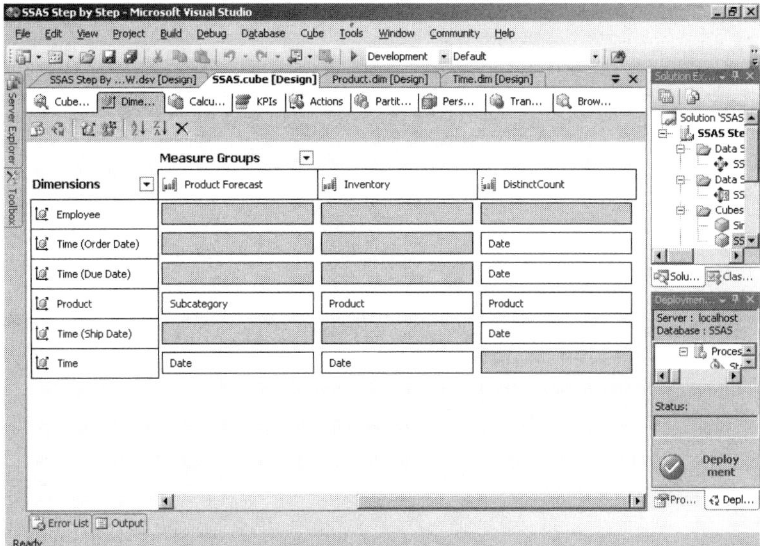

Recall that the denominator of the calculated measure is Unique Customers, which is in the Distinct Count measure group. In the cube browser, you noticed the problem with the measure's interaction with the Time dimension. You can see here that the Time dimension doesn't intersect with Distinct Count. When there's no dimension usage specified for an intersection between a dimension and a measure group, the cube browser displays the total for the All level of the dimension.

Ordinarily, to correct the problem that you're seeing in the cube, you fix the dimension usage between Time and Distinct Count. However, in this fact table, there are actually three columns that contain a TimeKey–ShipDateKey, Due DateKey, and OrderDateKey. You learned in Chapter 3 that these are role-playing dimensions. Because each of these roles does in fact have a relationship defined with Distinct Count, the problem that you see in the browser is really an issue with placing the correct dimension on columns.

14. Click the Browser tab, drag the Time dimension out of the grid, expand Order Date in the metadata tree, and then drag the Order Date.Calendar hierarchy to the columns of the grid.

Your screen looks like this:

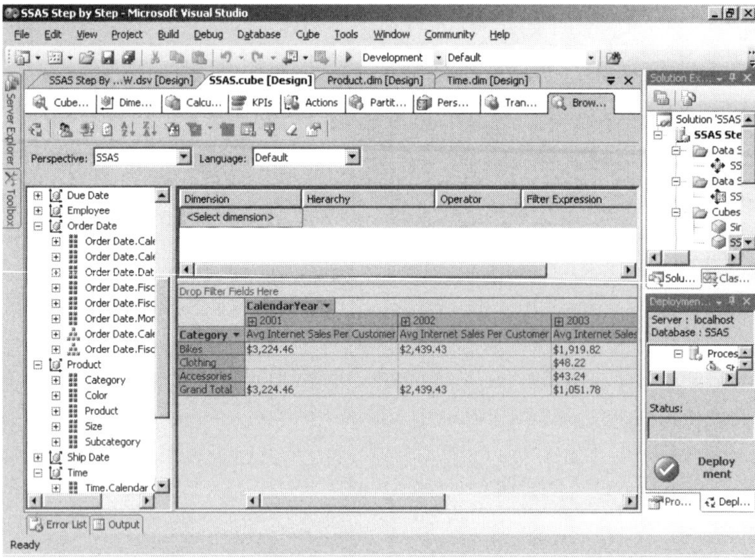

Now the values vary correctly over time. In the Grand Total column, you can see the calculated values that had previously displayed for each year when the Time dimension was on columns. To prevent confusion for users, you might consider deleting a cube dimension that has no relationship to fact tables in your cube. when there are other role-playing dimensions that do have a relationship.

Applying Conditional Formatting

Conditional formatting allows you to set appearance characteristics, such as foreground and background color, based upon the values returned by the expression. For example, you can set green text or a green background to indicate that a measure is on track with expectations, while using red to indicate that a measure is below expectations. To apply conditional formatting, you use the IIF function with MDX expressions. This function is similar to an If–Then–Else statement in which a condition is evaluated as true or false. If it's true, then take some action, or else take a different action.

In this procedure, you'll add a color expression to display the calculation with a green font when the value exceeds a specific threshold and with a red font when the value is below another threshold.

Add a color expression to a calculation

1. Click the Calculations tab and ensure that Avg Internet Sales Per Customer is selected in the Script Organizer list.
2. Click the arrows icon next to Color Expressions to expand this section of the form.

3. In the Fore Color box, type this expression:

```
IIf( [Measures].[Avg Internet Sales Per Customer] > 2000 , 65280 /*Lime*/, 255 /*Red*/)
```

This expression follows the standard syntax for an MDX If statement of `IIf(Logical_Expression, {Expression1, Expression2}`. Embedded within the expression are comments, which are enclosed within the /* and */ symbols. Comments are ignored when evaluating an expression, and can be helpful for clarifying complex expressions or, as in this case, labeling a color code.

If you don't already know the color code that you want to use, you can click the button to the right of the Fore Color box and choose a color. The code associated with that color will be inserted in the Fore Color expression box.

Notice that you can also add an expression to the Back Color box to define a color for the background of a cell in the cube browser.

4. Click the Check Syntax button.
5. Deploy the project, click the Browser tab, and then click the Reconnect button.

You should see the intersection of Bikes and 2001 as well as Bikes and 2002 display using a green font, since these values exceed the threshold of $2,000, and all other values display using a red font because they are below $2,000.

6. Save and close the solution.

Chapter 5 Quick Reference

To	Do this
Create a cube from an existing data source	In Solution Explorer, right-click the Cubes folder, click New Cube, clear the Auto Build check box, select a data source view (DSV), select dimension and fact tables, select cube dimensions, select measures, and name the cube.
Rename a measure group	On the Cube Structure tab of the Cube Designer, right-click the measure group, and then select Rename or change the *Name* property in the Properties window.
Format a measure	On the Cube Structure tab of the Cube Designer, click the measure, and then change its *FormatString* property in the Properties window.
Define a regular relationship between a dimension and a measure group	On the Dimension Usage tab of the Cube Designer, click the cell intersection of the dimension and the measure group, click the ellipsis button in the cell, click Regular in the Relationship Type box, click an attribute in the Granularity Attribute list box, and then select the corresponding fact table column in the Measure Group Columns list box.
Right-align measure values in the browser	Right-click the measure caption on the Browser tab of the Cube Designer, click Commands and Options, click the Format tab, and then click the Align Right button.

To	Do this
Define a direct attribute relationship between two attributes	On the Dimension Structure tab of the Dimension Designer, expand the target attribute, and then drag the source attribute to the space labeled <New Attribute Relationship> beneath the target attribute.
Add a measure group to an existing cube	On the Cube Structure tab of the Cube Designer, right-click anywhere in the Measures pane, select New Measure, and then select the applicable fact table.
Specify an aggregation function	On the Cube Structure tab of the Cube Designer, click the measure, and then change its *AggregateFunction* property in the Properties window.
Add a distinct count measure	On the Cube Structure tab of the Cube Designer, right-click anywhere in the Measures pane, click New Measure, select Distinct Count in the Usage drop-down list, select the source fact table in the Source Table drop-down list, and then click the source column.
Create a simple calculation	On the Calculations tab of the Cube Designer, click the New Calculated Member button on the toolbar, type a name for the measure in the Name box, and enter an MDX expression in the Expression box.
Apply conditional formatting to a calculation	On the Calculations tab of the Cube Designer, expand the Color Expressions section, and enter an MDX expression that uses the IIF function in the Fore Color box, the Back Color box, or both.

Chapter 6

Working with a Finance Measure Group

After completing this chapter, you will be able to:

- Build an account dimension to support financial analysis.
- Use custom rollup operators.
- Aggregate an account dimension.
- Create nonadditive measures.

In the previous two chapters, you learned how to build dimensions and measure groups from standard warehouse tables. You can use the techniques you learned to meet most analytical requirements, but financial analysis has special requirements. In this chapter, you'll learn about the special tools that Analysis Services provides to handle these special requirements by building an account dimension and a financial measure group. You'll also get more experience working with calculations by building a financial ratio.

Designing an Account Dimension

A finance department deals with many types of financial reporting–profit and loss statements, balance sheets, and so forth. Creating a dimension for use in financial analysis is tricky because of the way account values aggregate: Sometimes accounts sum to a parent, sometimes an account is subtracted from its parent, and sometimes an account does not aggregate into the parent value at all. Consider, for example, a profit and loss report:

Level 02	Level 03	Level 04	Amount
⊟ Net Income	⊟ Operating Profit	⊞ Gross Margin	$83,519,884
		⊞ Operating Expenses	$48,394,979
		Total	$35,124,906
	⊞ Other Income and Expense		$50,780
	⊞ Taxes		$7,030,480
	Total		$28,145,206
⊟ Statistical Accounts	⊞ Average Unit Price		
	⊞ Headcount		$280
	⊞ Square Footage		$390,000
	⊞ Statistical Accounts		
	⊞ Units		$9,596
	Total		
Grand Total			$28,145,206

The components of Net Income are Operating Profit, Other Income and Expenses, and Taxes. All values are positive numbers. But, to calculate Net Income Total, you must subtract the Taxes Total value from the sum of Operating Profit Total and Taxes Total. Likewise, to calculate Operating Profit Total, you must subtract the Operating Expenses value from the Gross

Margin value. Often, a Statistical section of the report contains a line for Head Count, but the values from the Head Count line are for information only; they should not be added into the Balance Sheet Total or Net Income Total values.

In this section, you'll learn how to create a simple finance cube. A finance cube requires three components to create the correct behavior for a dimension representing a chart of accounts: specifying the dimension type, identifying a unary operator field, and using the ByAccount aggregation function. With these components in place, balance sheet items such as assets and liabilities, which cannot be summed across time, will be set up to display correctly. Likewise, income statement items, such as revenues and cost of goods sold, which can be summed across time, will also display correctly.

Working with Account Intelligence

The Dimension Wizard lets you add Account Intelligence to an account dimension. Account Intelligence identifies and maps standard account types to the dimension, like Asset, Liability, Income, and Expense. This mapping of account types is used in combination with attribute properties to produce the correct aggregation behavior for each account.

Note Account Intelligence only applies to dimensions with underlying data sources because of its dependency on the table structure.

When you create an Account dimension, you specify the dimension type–Accounts. This dimension type tells Analysis Services that the dimension contains a chart of accounts and will be used for financial analysis. You also map specific columns in the underlying dimension table to attribute types, as shown in this table:

This attribute type	Does this
Chart of Accounts	Identifies the parent attribute that arranges accounts into the correct hierarchy using parent-child relationships
Account Name	Specifies an attribute as an Account Name for client applications
Account Number	Specifies an attribute as an Account Number for client applications
Account Type	Flags the attribute in a dimension that contains the classification for each account, such as Asset, Income, Expense, etc.

In this procedure, you'll add a dimension table to your data source view (DSV) and create a new dimension that uses the added table.

Create an Account dimension

1. Start SQL Server Business Intelligence Development Studio (BIDS), and then open the SSAS Step by Step solution that you saved in the C:\Documents and Settings\<username>\My Documents\Microsoft Press\as2005sbs\Workspace folder.

> **Note** If you skipped Chapter 5, "Designing Measure Groups and Measures," open the SSAS Step by Step solution in the C:\Documents and Settings\<username>\My Documents\Microsoft Press\as2005sbs\Answers\chap05\SSAS Step by Step folder.

2. In Solution Explorer, double-click SSAS Step by Step DW.dsv, right-click the background of the DSV diagram pane, click Add/Remove Tables, and then double-click dbo.DimAccount to add this table to the Included Objects list, and then click OK.

   Your screen looks like this:

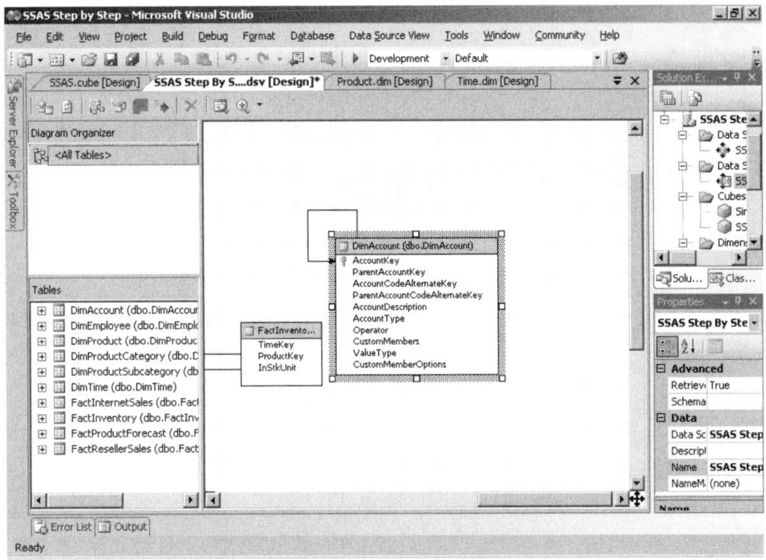

   Notice the DimAccount table has a self-referencing relationship, which is also referred to as a parent-child relationship, as you learned in Chapter 4, "Designing Dimensions."

3. In the Solution Explorer, right-click the Dimensions folder, select New Dimension, and then click Next.
4. Clear the Auto Build check box, and then click Next.
5. Click SSAS Step by Step DW in the Available Data Source Views list, and then click Next.
6. On the Select the Dimension Type page, keep the default selection, Standard Dimension, and click Next.
7. Select dbo.DimAccount in the Main Table drop-down list, select the check box to the left of AccountKey in the Key Columns list, and then click AccountDescription in the Column Containing The Member Name (Optional) drop-down list.

Your screen looks like this:

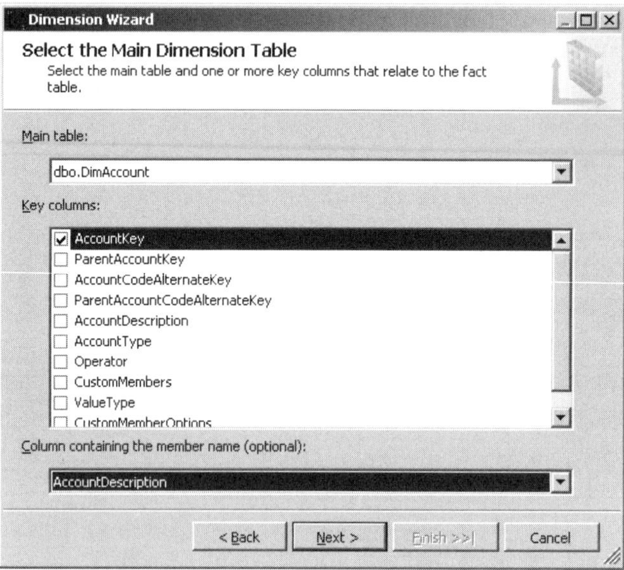

8. Click Next and then, on the Select Dimension Attributes page, select the check boxes to the left of Parent Account Key and Account Type.

   The Parent Account Key is a required attribute that is used to define the parent-child relationship. In order to create a parent-child hierarchy, you must not only have this column in the underlying dimension table, but you must also explicitly select it as an attribute in the Dimension Wizard. Similarly, the Account Type is another required attribute that is used to determine the correct aggregation behavior for each account. Other columns in the table are used to set attribute properties, such as Operator, but these other columns do not need to be explicitly selected as attributes.

9. Click Next, and click Accounts in the Dimension Type drop-down list.
10. Select the check box in the Include column to the left of Chart of Accounts, and then, in the same row, select Parent Account Key in the Dimension Attribute drop-down list.

    Attribute types assign special properties to specific attributes in a dimension. When you select an attribute type, the wizard suggests an attribute from the group that you specified on previous pages of the wizard, but you can override the suggested mapping.

11. Select the Account Name check box, and then select Dim Account in the corresponding Dimension Attribute drop-down list, if necessary.
12. Select the Account Type check box.

Your screen looks like this:

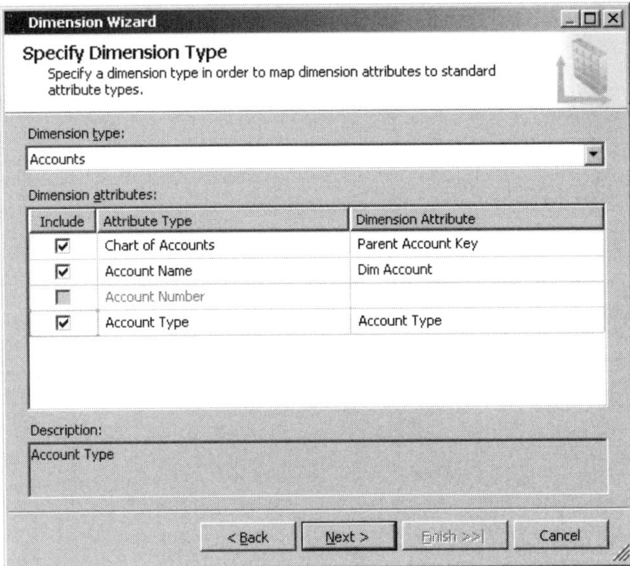

13. Click Account Type in the Dimension Attribute drop-down list, and then click Next.
14. Change the selected value in the Built-In Account Types drop-down lists for each account type to match this screen, and then click Next.

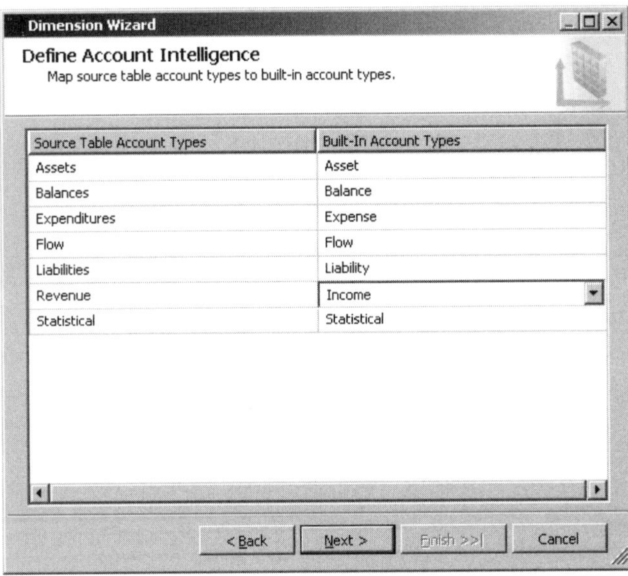

The names of account types that you use in your organization might be different from the standard account types available in Analysis Services. This page of the dimension wizard provides you with an easy way to associate your own account types to the standard types.

The Define Parent-Child Relationship page looks like this:

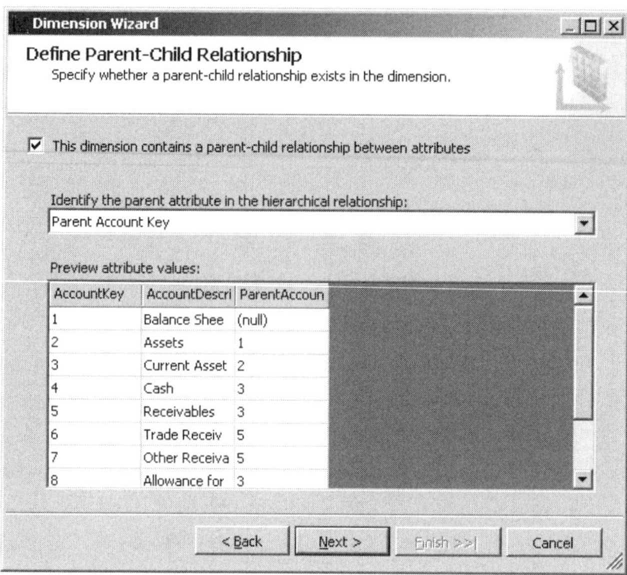

If your dimension table has the correct relationships defined between the attribute key and the parent key, then the check box labeled This Dimension Contains A Parent-Child Relationship Between Attributes is selected. The default parent attribute in this case is the Parent Account Key because it is defined as the foreign key in the dimension table. On this page of the wizard, you can preview the attributes of the dimension so that you can confirm that the relationship between parent and child members is correct.

15. Click Next, change the dimension name to **Account**, and then click Finish.

16. In the Attributes pane of the dimension designer, click the Dim Account attribute, and then, in the Properties window, change the *Name* property to **Account**.

17. Click the Account Type attribute, and then, in the Properties window, scroll through the properties to find the *Type* property.

    Notice the value of the *Type* property is AccountType, which was set by the Dimension Wizard when you included Account Type as an attribute type for this dimension.

18. In the Attributes pane of the Dimension Designer, click the Parent Account Key attribute, and change its *Name* property to **Accounts** in the Properties window.

    Notice here the value of the *Type* property is Account and its usage is set to Parent. Setting this property correctly, as well as that of the Account Type and the dimension, is required for financial aggregations to work correctly.

19. Open the Cube Designer for the SSAS cube and, on the Cube Structure tab, right-click the Dimensions pane, click Add Cube Dimension, click Account in the Select Dimension list, and then click OK.

The dimension is now in the cube, but it is not related to any measure group already in the cube. You add a related measure group to the cube in the next procedure.

Using the Dimension *Type* Property

The *Type* property of a dimension has many possible values. You can use the Dimension Wizard to automatically set the type, or you can change the property manually in the Dimension Designer. Analysis Server uses this type to manage the behavior of account and time dimensions, but otherwise, the value of the *Type* property has no direct effect on the server. This property is available for a client application to inspect. For example, some Graphical Information Systems (GIS) applications can use a dimension with its *Type* property set to Geography to display analytical data on maps. You should refer to the documentation of your client application to determine whether this feature is supported and to learn how to configure a dimension correctly for the client application.

Using Unary Operators

To properly aggregate the values along the Account dimension, each member of the dimension needs its own aggregation rule. The rule for Current Assets should be: "Add me to my parent." The rule for Taxes should be: "Subtract me from my parent." The rule for Headcount should be: "Don't aggregate me at all." With a parent-child dimension, you can include a column in the dimension table that specifies a unique rule for each member.

The aggregation rule consists of a single-character code. The codes are simply the arithmetic operators: plus (+) for addition, minus (-) for subtraction, asterisk (*) for multiplication, and slash (/) for division. In addition, a tilde (~) is used to prevent the member from aggregating at all. These codes are called *unary operators* because each value gets its own operator.

Note The word *unary* is related to the word *unit* and means "one."

Analysis Services has a special property called the *UnaryOperatorColumn* which applies only to the parent attribute in a parent-child dimension. You use this property to specify the column in a dimension table that is used to store the unary operator (+, -, *, /, and ~).

In this procedure, you'll add a new measure group to the cube and then browse the cube to see how values incorrectly aggregate before you specify the *UnaryOperatorColumn* for the Account dimension.

Browse the default aggregations of an Account dimension

1. In Solution Explorer, double-click SSAS Step by Step DW.dsv, right-click the background of the diagram pane, click Add/Remove Tables, double-click dbo.FactFinance to add the table to the Included Objects list, and then click OK.

Your screen looks like this:

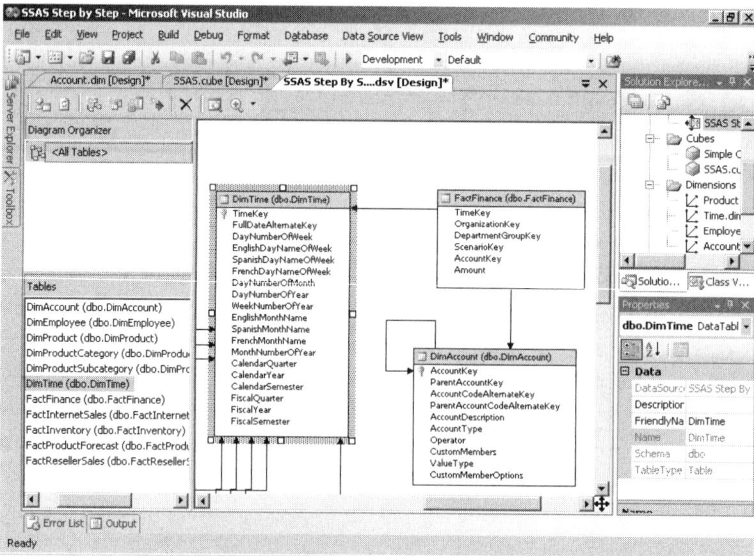

Notice the relationship between DimAccount and FactFinance using the AccountKey in each table.

2. Open the Cube Designer for the SSAS cube, and, on the Cube Structure tab, right-click the Measures pane background, and then click New Measure.

   Alternatively, you could choose the option to add a new measure group, but this would add every numeric column in the selected table which, in the case of FactFinance, includes key columns that you would not want to use as measures.

3. Select FactFinance in the Source Table drop-down list, click Amount in the Source Column list, and then click OK.

   You have the option to change the aggregate function in the New Measure dialog box by changing the Usage value, but for now you will use the Sum aggregate function in order to observe how aggregation behavior changes when you later change the aggregate function.

4. With the Amount measure selected in the Measures pane, find the *FormatString* property in the Properties pane and type **$#,#**.

5. Right-click FactFinance in the measures pane, click Rename, and then type **Finance**.

6. Deploy the project. When deployment is complete, click the Browser tab of the Cube Designer, and then click the Reconnect button.

7. Expand Measures, expand Finance, and then drag Amount to the area of the grid labeled Drop Totals Or Detail Fields Here.

8. Right-click the Amount value displayed in the grid, click Commands And Options, click the Align Right button, and then close the Commands And Options dialog box.

9. Expand the Account dimension, and then drag the Accounts hierarchy to the rows area of the grid.

10. Click the plus sign (+) to the left of Net Income in the grid to drill down to the next level.

    Your screen looks like this:

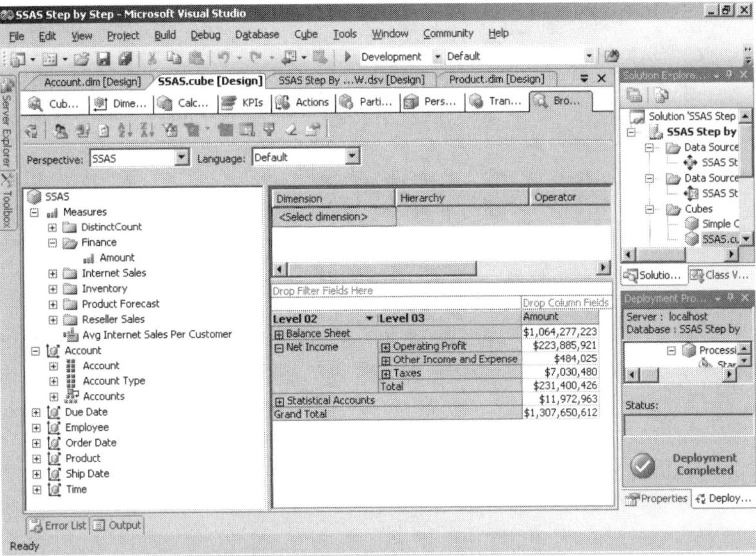

Notice that the Total for Net Income is equal to the sum of Operating Profit, Other Income and Expense, and Taxes. The table below compares the correct calculation to the current calculation in the cube.

Cube Calculation	Correct Calculation
Operating Profit	Operating Profit
+ Other Income and Expense	+ Other Income and Expense
+ Expenses	- Expenses
+ Taxes	- Taxes
= Net Income	= Net Income

All account values are added together in the cube because the current aggregate function assigned to the Amount measure is Sum. However, as you can see from the table, sometimes financial accounts should be added together and at other times should be subtracted. To see the correct aggregation behavior in the cube, you need to use unary operators in the Account dimension.

In this procedure, you'll set the *UnaryOperatorColumn* property for the Accounts attribute hierarchy to apply unary operators to the aggregation of measure values.

Set the *UnaryOperatorColumn* property

1. Switch to the Dimension Designer for the Account dimension.

2. Right-click the DimAccount table heading in the Data Source View pane, and then click Explore Data.

   Your screen looks like this:

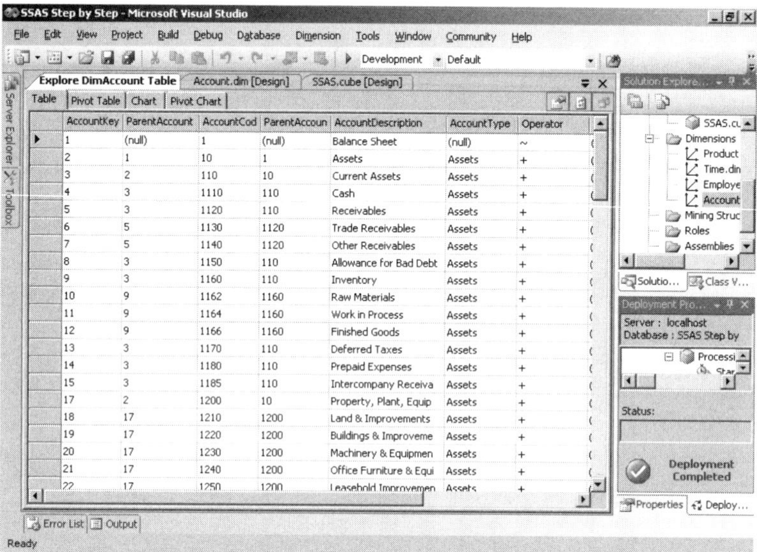

   The DimAccount table contains a column named Operator that includes the appropriate unary code (+, -, ~) for each account.

3. Close the Explore DimAccount Table window.

4. In the Attributes pane on the Dimension Structure page, click the Accounts attribute, and then, in the Properties window, change the *UnaryOperatorColumn* property in the drop-down list from (none) to (new).

   The Object Binding dialog looks like this:

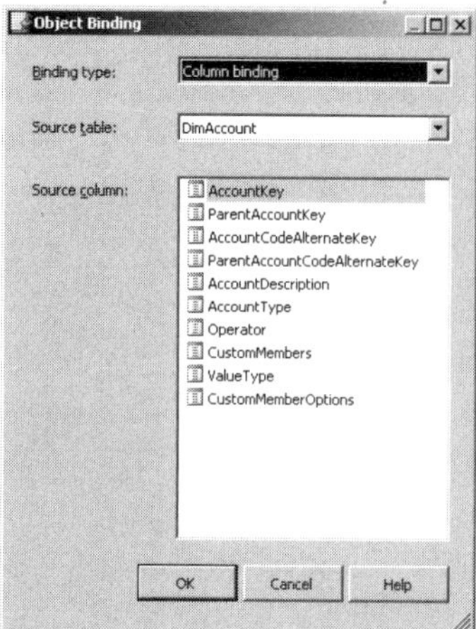

5. Click Operator in the Source Column list, and then click OK.

   Before you can see the effect of the unary operators, you must deploy the cube.

6. Deploy the project. When deployment finishes, switch to the Cube Designer, and then click the Reconnect button on the Browser toolbar.

   Your screen looks like this:

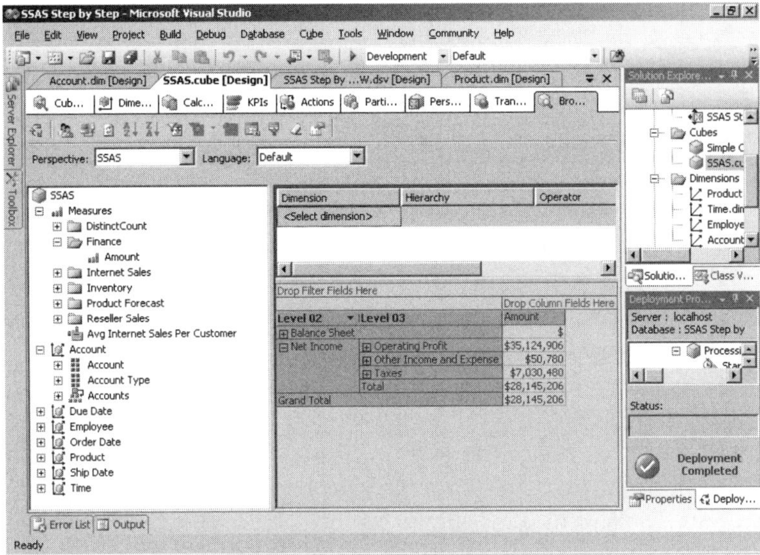

   Notice that the Total for Net Income is now correctly calculated.

Aggregating by Account

Specifying a unary operator for the Account dimension affects only the aggregation behavior of members within that dimension. If you were to slice the Account dimension by the Time dimension, the cube would aggregate the values for each account using the Sum function. For example, Net Income for one year would be added to Net Income for the next year, as simplified in the table below.

Net Income	2003	2004	Total
Operating Profit	11,362,042	2,636,170	**13,998,212**
Other Income and Expense	17,085	8,397	**25,482**
Taxes	2,815,544	909,590	**3,725,134**
Total	**8,563,583**	**1,734,977**	**10,298,560**

This behavior is fine for profit and loss accounts like Net Income which should accumulate the Amount value over time, which means Amount is an *additive* measure in this scenario. However, balance sheet accounts like Assets and Liabilities should not accumulate Amount over time. You cannot add the Amount for Assets from one year to the Amount for Assets of another year to come up with a total for both years. Instead, the correct Amount for Assets is the value for the last day of the time period that you are analyzing, as simplified in the table below.

Balance Sheet	2003	2004	Total
Current Assets	20,330,894	19,102,999	**19,102,999**
Other Assets	227,251	234,259	**234,259**
Property, Plant, Equipment	1,641,662	1,631,215	**1,631,215**
Total Assets	**22,199,807**	**20,968,473**	**20,968,473**
Liabilities and Owners Equity	**22,199,807**	**20,968,473**	**20,968,473**

For balance sheet accounts, then, Amount is semiadditive–that is, it can be aggregated across any dimension except time, in which case it must use the last available value. You learned about semiadditive aggregations in Chapter 5. For handling balance sheet accounts, the best option is the LastNonEmpty aggregate function, but that would not work well with the profit and loss accounts. Instead, you can use the ByAccount aggregate function. This function applies different aggregate functions to different attributes at query time, based on the specified account type for each attribute. For example, LastNonEmpty is applied to asset accounts and the Sum function is applied to revenue accounts. To use the ByAccount aggregate function, you must have one (and only one) dimension in the cube for which the *Type* property equals Accounts. You also must be sure to set the parent key attribute's *Type* property to Account and its *Usage* property to Parent. If you specify the Account dimension type when using the New Dimension Wizard to build the dimension, these property settings will be applied automatically.

In this procedure, you'll change the *AggregateFunction* property of the Account measure to LastNonEmpty to observe the aggregation behavior.

Use the *LastNonEmpty* function with an Account dimension

1. On the Browser tab of the Cube Designer, drag the Time.Calendar hierarchy to columns.
2. Expand Balance Sheet to drill down to the next level, and expand 2004 to drill down to Quarters.

Your screen looks like this:

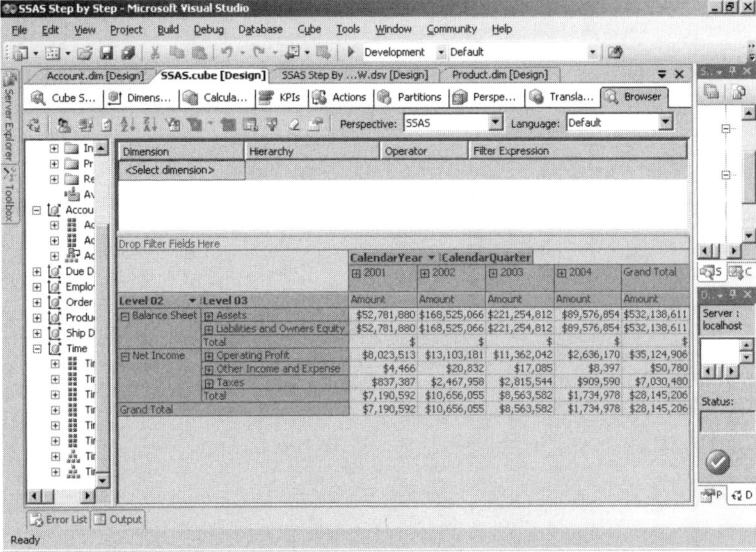

Notice the Grand Total for Assets is the sum of each year's value for Assets, when it should be the value for the last available day in 2004.

3. On the Cube Structure tab, expand the Finance measure group, right-click Amount, click Properties, and then change the *AggregateFunction* property from Sum to LastNonEmpty.

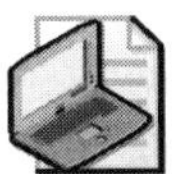

> **Note** This is not the correct value to use for the *AggregateFunction* property of this measure, but you use it here to compare its behavior with ByAccount, which you'll use in the next procedure.

4. Deploy the project. When it is deployed, click the Browser tab of the Cube Designer, and then click the Reconnect button. If necessary, drill down from Balance Sheet to Level 03, which displays Assets, Liabilities and Owners Equity, and Total.

Your screen looks like this:

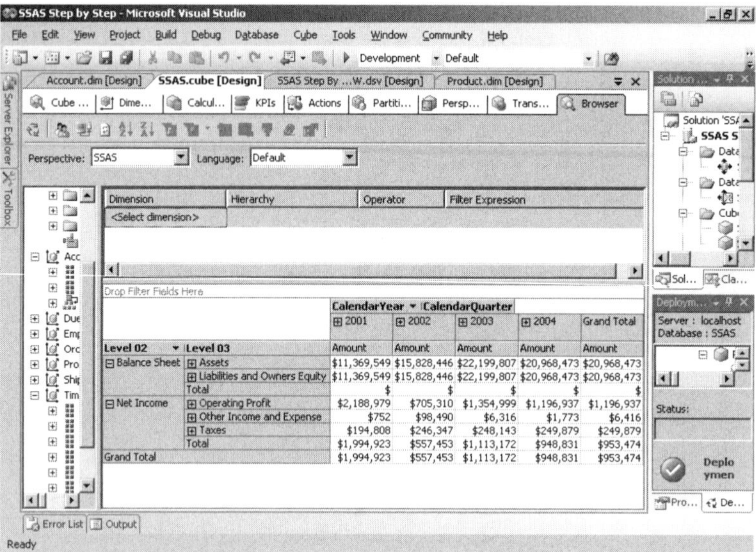

Compare the Asset account from the last year value, 2004, to the Grand Total. The Grand Total value now equals the value for 2004. Each year value will be equal to the value on the last day of the respective year for which Balance Sheet values were added to the fact table.

5. Expand 2004, and then expand 2 to drill down to the Month level.

   Notice that the value for Assets is the same for the last month of the quarter, the quarter, the year, and the Grand Total for all Assets in the grid. This value is carried to the year-end total even though the last time period in the cube isn't the last month or quarter in the year. It is carried over because it is the last nonempty value for the year. The other empty quarters are ignored.

   This behavior is fine for assets, but what about for revenues?

6. Expand Net Income, Operating Profit, and Gross Margin to drill down to Total Cost of Sales, and close the 2004 node.

Your screen looks like this:

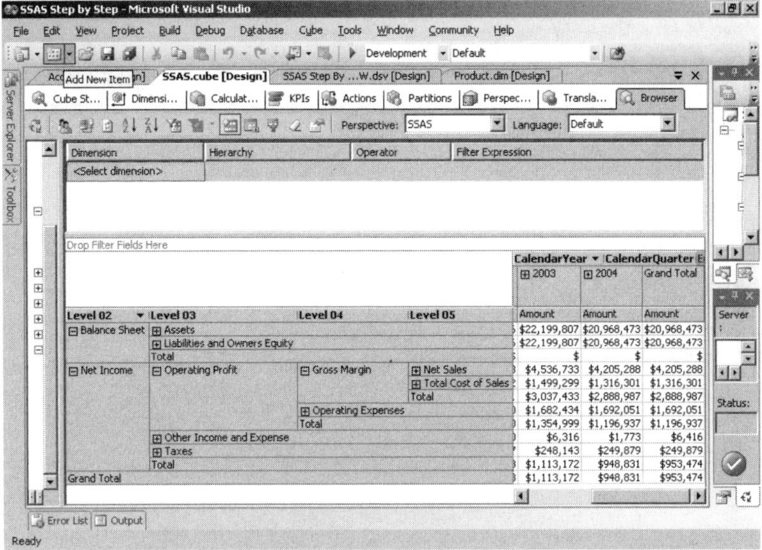

The Grand Total for Net Sales equals the value for the last year, 2004, and the year value equals the last quarter value. The correct aggregation for Net Sales should be calculated by adding each year's Net Sales across time. The LastNonEmpty aggregate function applies to all types of accounts, both Balance Sheet and Net Income accounts.

Recall that, in the previous procedure, the Sum function was fine for the measure for Net Income accounts, but not for the Balance Sheet accounts. Now you can see that the LastNonEmpty function works well with the Balance Sheet accounts, but not with the Net Income accounts. To solve this very type of problem, you'll use the ByAccount aggregate function.

In this procedure, you'll change the *AggregateFunction* property of the Account measure to ByAccount.

Use the ByAccount aggregate function

1. On the Cube Structure tab, expand the Finance measure group, click the Amount measure, and then, in the Properties window, change the *AggregateFunction* property from LastNonEmpty to ByAccount.

2. Deploy the project. When the project deploys successfully, switch to the Cube Designer, click the Browser tab, and then click the Reconnect button.

Your screen looks like this:

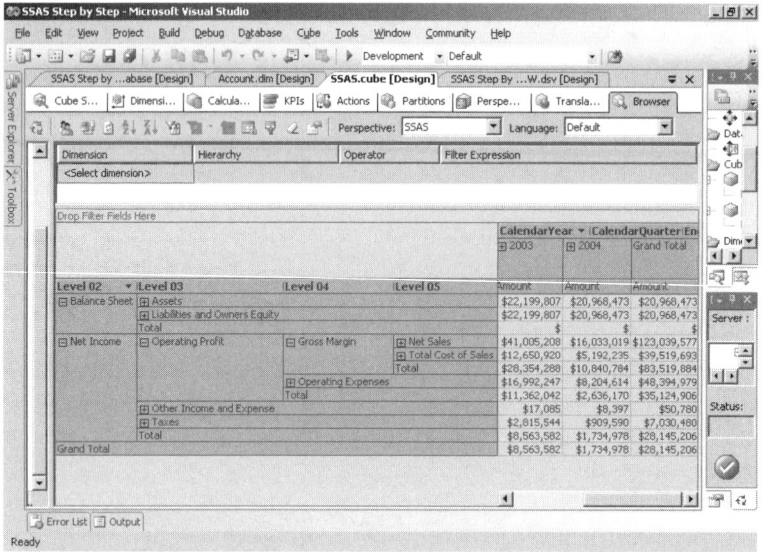

Compare the Grand Total for Assets to the 2004 value to confirm that both values are now equal. You can see also that the Grand Total for Operating Profit is the sum of all years. The ByAccount aggregation function uses the account types defined for each account to determine which accounts are additive across time and which are semiadditive.

Designing Nonadditive Financial Measures

Quantitative analysis isn't always limited to additive or semiadditive measures. Often, averages, ratios, and percentages can reveal important trends and are consequently relevant to many types of analysis. As you learned in Chapter 5, these types of calculations must be added to a cube as calculated measures because they won't aggregate correctly across any dimension. The components of the calculations must be summed separately and then the necessary multiplication or division can be performed. These types of calculations are known as *nonadditive measures*.

You created two types of nonadditive measures by completing the procedures in Chapter 5 when you created a distinct count measure and an average measure. The distinct count measure counts unique occurrences of a customer within a sales fact table. The average measure aggregates two measures separately, and then divides one measure by the other. In this section, you create another type of nonadditive measure, commonly used in financial analysis, which divides the value of a single measure for one financial account by the value of the same measure for a different financial account.

Creating a Nonadditive Measure

Financial analysis often includes ratios that are derived from monetary and statistical values. One such ratio is Operating Profit Per Employee, calculated by dividing Operating Profit by Headcount, which are two members of the Account dimension in the SSAS Step by Step project. More accurately, the numerator in this operation is the Amount measure for Operating Profit, which is the aggregation of its children accounts. Likewise, the denominator for this ratio is the Amount measure for Headcount, which is a statistical account often available in financial systems to track the number of employees over time. The Amount for Headcount is also aggregated before it is used in the calculation.

In this procedure, you'll create the nonadditive Operating Profit Per Employee measure.

Add an Operating Profit Per Employee measure

1. Click the Calculations tab of the Cube Designer.
2. Click the New Calculated Member button on the toolbar.
3. Type **[Operating Profit Per Employee]** in the Name box.

> **Important** Be sure to include the brackets surrounding the name when the name includes spaces.

4. Type ((open parenthesis) in the Expression box.
5. Expand Measures in the Calculation Tools pane, and then expand the Account dimension. Expand the Accounts hierarchy, then the Members folder, the All member, and the Net Income member.

   The Metadata tab looks like this:

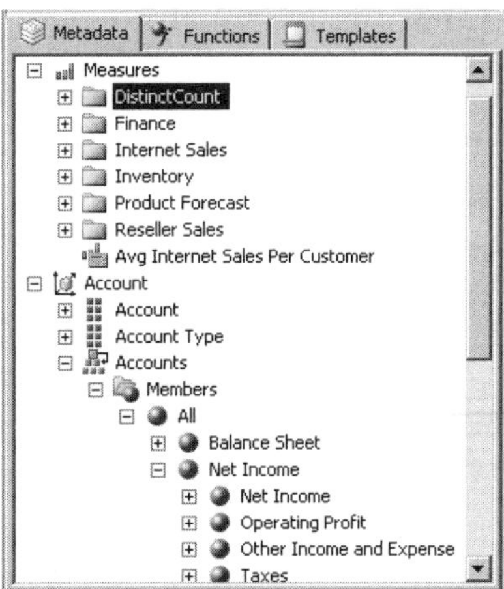

6. Drag Operating Profit to the Expression box.

   The expression looks like this:

   ```
   ([Account].[Accounts].&[48]
   ```

   This representation of Operating Profit is a valid member name for this dimension. This name includes the dimension (Account), the hierarchy (Accounts), and the member key value (48). Often, it's preferable to use the member key value since keys should not change within a dimension but names sometimes do. Fortunately, you don't have to know the member key value. When you drag a member from the metadata tree, the key is inserted automatically, when possible.

7. Position your cursor at the end of the expression, and type , (comma).

8. In Measures, expand Finance, and then drag Amount to the Expression box to the right of the comma, and then type) (closing parenthesis).

   The expression looks like this:

   ```
   ([Account].[Accounts].&[48], [Measures].[Amount])
   ```

   This expression is a *tuple*, which you'll learn more about in Chapter 8, "Using MDX." A tuple refers to a specific value in the cube. In this case, the tuple refers to the Amount value for Operating Profit.

9. Position your cursor at the end of the expression, and then type /((division operator followed by an open parenthesis).

10. Expand the Statistical Accounts member in the Accounts hierarchy, drag Headcount to the Expression box, dropping it at the end of the expression, type , (comma) to continue the expression, and then, from under the Finance folder, drag Amount to the right of the comma.

11. Position your cursor at the end of the expression, and then type) (closing parenthesis) so that your expression looks like this:

    ```
    ([Account].[Accounts].&[48],[Measures].[Amount])/
    ([Account].[Accounts].&[96],[Measures].[Amount])
    ```

12. Click the Check Syntax button in the toolbar to ensure that you created the expression correctly, and then click OK to close the message box.

13. Select "Currency" in the Format String drop-down list.

14. Set the Non-Empty Behavior to Amount.

Your screen looks like this:

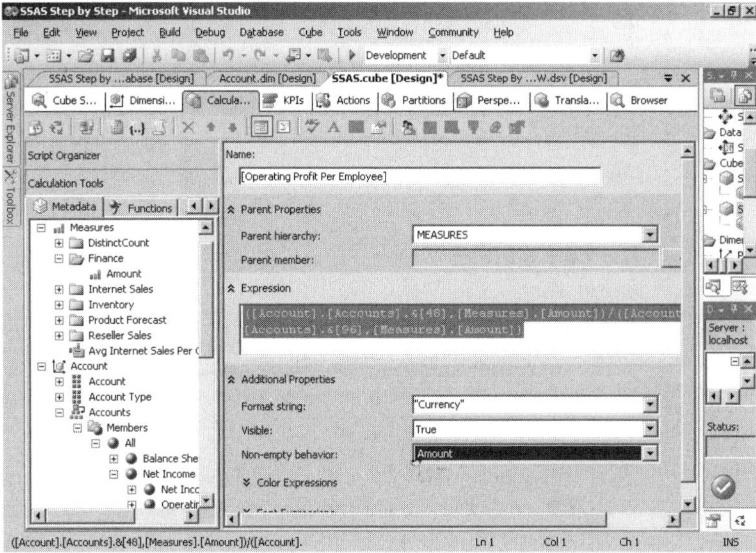

15. Deploy the project, click the Browser tab, and then click the Reconnect button.
16. Click anywhere in the grid to enable the Browser toolbar buttons, click the Clear Results button, expand Measures, and then drag Operating Profit Per Employee to the grid.
17. Drag the Time.Calendar hierarchy to rows on the grid.

Your screen looks like this:

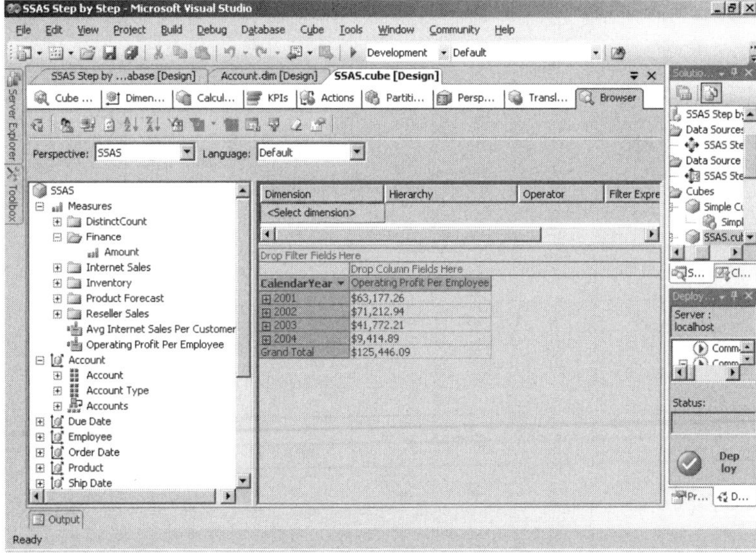

Notice that the Operating Profit Per Employee has declined in 2003 and 2004. This could be a result of rapid growth in the number of employees in the company, or this could be an indication of a problem in the customer channel, sales strategy, or purchasing process, for example. You would need to do additional analysis to find the answers. By including this type of calculation in the cube, you enable users to spot potential problem areas more easily and to ask the questions that will help find out the answers to why this trend is occurring.

Chapter 6 Quick Reference

To	Do this
Specify a dimension type	On the Specify Dimension Type page of the Dimension Wizard, click the dimension type in the Dimension Type drop-down list. *or* On the Dimension Structure tab of the dimension designer, click the background of the Attributes pane and, in the Properties window, click the dimension type in the *Type* property's drop-down list.
Define aggregation rules for financial accounts	Add a column to the dimension table containing the codes + for addition, - for subtraction, and ~ for no aggregation; on the Dimension Structure tab of the dimension designer, assign that column to the *UnaryOperatorColumn* property for the parent key attribute of the dimension; and then set the *AggregateFunction* property for the financial measure to ByAccount.
Retrieve a value from a cell in a calculation	On the Calculations tab of the Cube Designer, build an expression from a tuple, with attribute members separated by commas and enclosed in parentheses.

Chapter 7

Designing Aggregations and Hierarchies

After completing this chapter, you will be able to:

- Use the Aggregation Design Wizard to design aggregations.
- Create user hierarchies and attribute relationships for dimensions.
- Control aggregation levels for individual dimensions.
- Create aggregations that optimize actual usage patterns.

In the previous three chapters, you designed the measures and dimensions for a cube. Now it's time to consider how to optimize that design by creating aggregations and user hierarchies. In this chapter, you'll learn how to build aggregations that improve query performance without excessively increasing the disk space required to store cube data. In addition, you'll learn how to create user hierarchies that not only enable users to browse a cube more efficiently, but also contribute to enhanced query performance. Finally, you'll fine-tune the aggregation design to factor in common queries generated by user interactions with the cube.

Understanding Aggregation Design

As you learned in Chapter 2, "Understanding OLAP and Analysis Services," an online analytical processing (OLAP) cube appears to contain every possible summarized value by every attribute for every dimension. For example, the SSAS cube created in Chapter 5, "Designing Measure Groups and Measures," contains Reseller Order Quantity and Reseller Sales Amount, to name a few, and Product, Employee, and Time as dimensions. If you query the cube at the lowest level of detail, for example, Reseller Sales Amount for Half-Finger Gloves, L sold by Rachel B. Valdez in May 2004, the cube returns the number $852 as if it were stored directly in the cube. At the same time, if you query the cube at a much higher level of detail, for example, Reseller Sales Amount for Gloves sold by all employees during 2004, the cube returns the number $207,775, again, as if that number were stored directly in the cube.

The sample SSAS Step by Step DW data warehouse on this book's companion CD contains information to support many dimensions. So far, you've worked with the Product, Employee, and the Time dimensions. (Ignore the role-playing dimensions and the Account dimension just for the purposes of this example.) At the level of detail stored in the warehouse, there are 606 products for sales, 17 employees with sales of these products, and 1,158 dates. That means there are 606 x 17 x 1,158, or 11,929,716 possible combinations, which means there could theoretically be 11,929,716 rows in the fact table. In reality, products and employees were introduced gradually over time, and each product isn't sold every day by every employee, so only 60,858 combinations actually appear as rows in the FactResellerSales table. Even though the fact table contains only 60,858 detail values, the cube can display up to 11,929,716 detail level cells–most of which would be empty.

In addition, because a cube appears to contain every possible summarized value at every possible level of detail for every dimension, the cube must appear to contain not only the 11,929,716 possible detail combinations, but also all possible summary values. Counting all the members in each attribute hierarchy of these three dimensions, the SSAS Step by Step DW warehouse database has a lot of possible combinations. In the Product dimension, there are 647 members comprising the 606 members in the Product attribute hierarchy, 37 members in the Subcategory attribute hierarchy, and four members in the Category attribute hierarchy. There are 296 members in the Employee dimension. In the Time dimension, there are 1,186 members, which include the 1,158 members in the Date attribute hierarchy, 12 members in the Month attribute hierarchy, four members in the Calendar Quarter attribute hierarchy, four members in the Fiscal Quarter attribute hierarchy, four members in the Calendar Year attribute hierarchy, and four members in the Fiscal Year attribute hierarchy. Finally, there are the two measures for the Reseller Sales measure group. The cube must therefore appear to contain 647 x 296 x 1,186 x 2, or 454,266,464 values, just for this one measure group. In this small sample database, the cube appears to contain over 7,464 times as many values as the fact table contains rows! This is called data explosion, which was explained in Chapter 2. Data explosion is a major issue with OLAP cubes, and all OLAP products must deal with it in some way.

The simplest way to avoid data explosion is to avoid storing aggregations altogether and, instead, calculate them on demand. But when you have a large data warehouse, this option quickly takes its toll on performance because requesting a single high-level summarized value from the cube would require retrieving and summing hundreds or thousands of values from the source data. The challenge of OLAP is to make queries as fast as possible while avoiding data explosion. Microsoft SQL Server 2005 Analysis Services provides several features that allow the database administrator to control and fine-tune the relationship between the physical size of the cube and the speed of the queries. In fact, Analysis Services provides options in many cases that allow *both* compact data files *and* responsive queries.

Aggregations are precalculated summaries of detailed data that enable the Analysis server to answer queries quickly. While you can easily create a cube without aggregations–none of the cubes used previously in this book have any aggregations–aggregations can make a tremendous difference in query time for a large cube. Regardless of how many aggregations you design, the cube always appears to contain every possible aggregated value. When you request a value from a cube, Analysis Services uses whatever aggregations are available to retrieve the value as quickly as possible.

You also don't need to store all the possible aggregations for a cube. The Analysis server can use aggregations that do exist to quickly calculate additional values as needed. For example, say you request the total Sales Amount for 2004 from a Sales cube and that aggregated value is not physically stored in the cube, but the quarter totals are. The Analysis server will retrieve the four quarter totals and quickly calculate the year total.

Don't confuse an *aggregated value* with an aggregation. An aggregated value is a single, summary value retrieved from a cube. An aggregation consists of all the possible combinations of one attribute hierarchy with all other attribute hierarchies in the cube. If you use relational OLAP (ROLAP) storage–which stores the aggregations in a relational table–you can actually see what aggregations look like. (You'll learn more about ROLAP in Chapter 12, "Managing Partitions and Database Processing.") This storage mode is not generally recommended when query performance is critical, but it is useful for learning about aggregations. You can design aggregations for a single partition, and then look at the aggregation tables in the relational database as well as the aggregation definition in the partition file.

A partition in Analysis Services is the physical location of stored cube data. Every cube has at least one partition by default. Each time you create a measure group, another partition is created. Queries run faster against a partitioned cube because Analysis Services only needs to read data from the partitions that contain the answers to the queries. Queries can run even faster when the partition also stores aggregations, the precalculated totals for additive measures. Analysis Services can often retrieve the aggregated value faster than it can calculate the same value from the detail data at query time. You can control how much or how little the data is aggregated for each partition.

Using the Aggregation Design Wizard

The Aggregation Design Wizard is the tool you use to decide which of the possible aggregations for a cube will be created. If the cube already has aggregations designed, the Aggregation Design Wizard offers to add to or replace existing aggregations. The aggregation options screen of the Aggregation Design Wizard performs a single task–selecting aggregations from the available pool. The Reseller Sales partition in the SSAS Chapter 7 cube has three dimensions. The Product is a standard dimension with five attribute hierarchies, each with two levels (counting the All level). Just within this one dimension, there are 32 possible aggregations to cover every combination of five hierarchies over two levels. The Time dimension is also a standard dimension; it has six attribute hierarchies, each with two levels (counting the All level), for a total of 64 possible aggregations. The Employee dimension is a parent-child dimension, which behaves as if it has two levels (counting the All level) so this dimension has only two possible aggregations. Theoretically, there are 4,096 possible aggregations that could be created for this partition (32 x 64 x 2). The goal of the Aggregation Design Wizard is to select the best aggregations for a given amount of storage space.

In this procedure, you'll learn how to use the Aggregation Design Wizard to add aggregations to the Reseller Sales partition.

Design aggregations for a cube partition

1. Start SQL Server Business Intelligence Development Studio (BIDS), and open the SSAS Step by Step solution that you saved in C:\Documents and Settings\<username>\My Documents\Microsoft Press\as2005sbs\Workspace.

> **Note** If you skipped Chapter 6, "Working with a Finance Measure Group," open the SSAS Step by Step solution in the C:\Documents and Settings\<username>\My Documents\Microsoft Press\as2005sbs\Answers\chap06\SSAS Step by Step folder.

2. In Solution Explorer, right-click the SSAS Step by Step project, point to Add, click Existing Item, navigate to C:\Documents and Settings\<username>\My Documents \Microsoft Press\as2005sbs\chap07\SSAS Step by Step\SSAS Step by Step, and add the SSAS Chapter 7.cube.
3. Double-click the SSAS Chapter 7 cube in Solution Explorer, and then click the Partitions tab.

   Your screen looks like this:

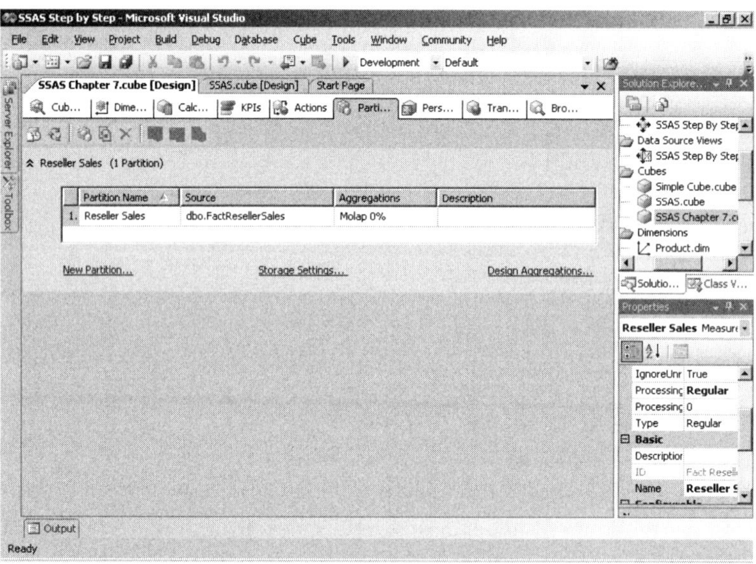

Notice the Reseller Sales partition is open. Information about the partition displays in a table: Partition Name, Source, Aggregations, and Description. The Aggregations value, Molap 0%, is the default value assigned to each partition. Molap indicates the storage mode of the cube data which you'll learn more about in Chapter 12. The percentage value, 0%, indicates that no aggregations have been designed for this partition. Queries can run against a partition without aggregations, but they may not run at an optimal speed.

4. Right-click the first row in the table for the Resellers Sales partition, click Design Aggregations to launch the Aggregation Design Wizard, and then click Next.

   You can also click the Design Aggregations link on the partition page to start the Aggregation Design Wizard.

5. On the Specify Storage and Caching Options page, click Next.

   You learn more about these options in Chapter 12.

6. Click Count.

   Your screen looks like this:

   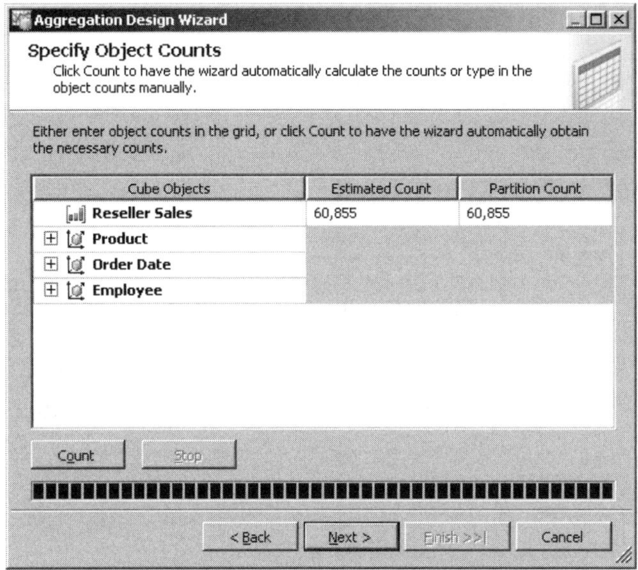

   The wizard counts rows in the fact table as well as rows in the partition. In this case, the partition includes the entire fact table, so the counts are the same. Alternatively, you can enter an Estimated Count or a Partition Count directly, which you'll do in a later procedure. Estimated Count is the default count for the partition. If you specify a Partition Count, that number is used instead of Estimated Count when designing aggregations. If both Estimated Count and Partition Count are zero, you cannot design aggregations. For now, you'll use the count generated by the wizard. In a later step, you'll change these values to observe how counts influence aggregation design.

7. Click Next, and on the Set Aggregation Options page of the wizard, select Performance Gain Reaches, and then click Start.

When initialization is complete, your screen looks like this:

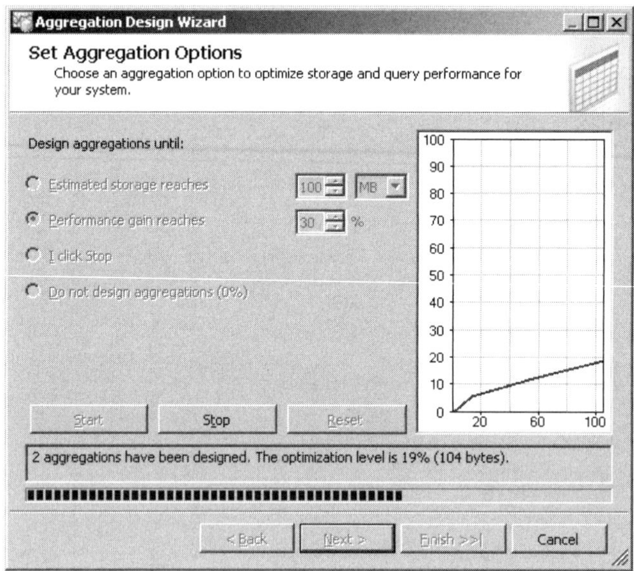

By choosing this option to design aggregations, the wizard will calculate possible aggregations until it exhausts all possibilities for the specified performance gain (unless you click Stop first). You have no control over which aggregations it selects. For most databases, the default performance gain setting provides enough aggregation for very good performance. If you later find that queries are executing too slowly, you can add aggregations then. As you increase the performance percentage, remember that the disk space required to reach 10 percent optimization is less, sometimes by an order of magnitude, than the amount required to go from 10 percent to 20 percent.

As the wizard designs aggregations, you can watch its progress in the graph. You can stop the wizard at any time if you decide to change the options for designing aggregations and want to restart the design process. When the wizard finishes its calculations, the number of aggregations that have been designed displays at the bottom of the page.

In the graph, you can see the relationship between the increase in performance (on the Y-axis) and the amount of disk space consumed (on the X-axis) as a result of the current aggregation design. At some point, the amount of disk space required is more costly than the benefits gained by relatively little improved query performance. The goal of aggregation optimization is to get the best performance increase without unnecessarily consuming disk space.

8. Click Next, select Deploy And Process Now, and then click Finish.

Your screen looks like this:

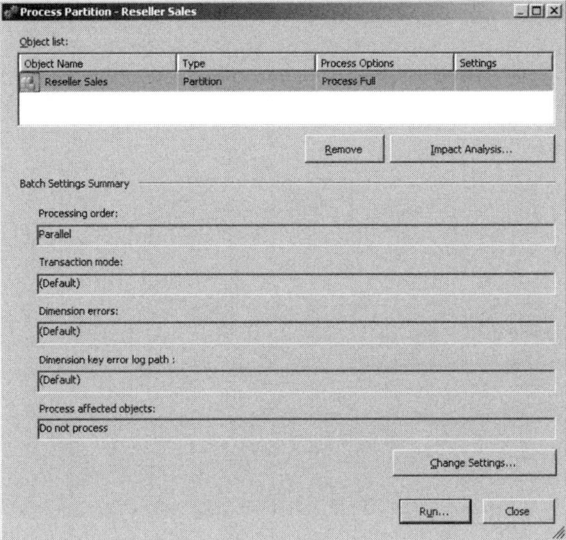

9. Click Run. When processing is complete, expand each processing step to view the details.

   Processing the partition runs one or more SQL queries against the underlying tables to load data into the cube and to calculate aggregations. In the Process Progress dialog box, you can view the status of processing, the duration of processing by partition, and the query string used for processing. If multiple partitions were ready for processing when you started this operation, the progress of each partition would be listed separately in this dialog box.

10. Click Close twice to close all dialog boxes.

Inspecting Aggregations

When you process the aggregations, the cube updates an XML for Analysis (XMLA) file that corresponds to the partition. This file contains information that Analysis Services uses to load the cube data, as well as to create storage for aggregations and load aggregated data into storage. The aggregation definitions are numbered beginning with number 0 and include information on each dimension and any attributes used in the aggregation.

In this procedure, you'll review the aggregation definitions in the partition's XMLA file.

Examine aggregations for a dimension in a cube partition

1. In the Solution Explorer toolbar, click the Show All Files button.

The Solution Explorer window looks like this:

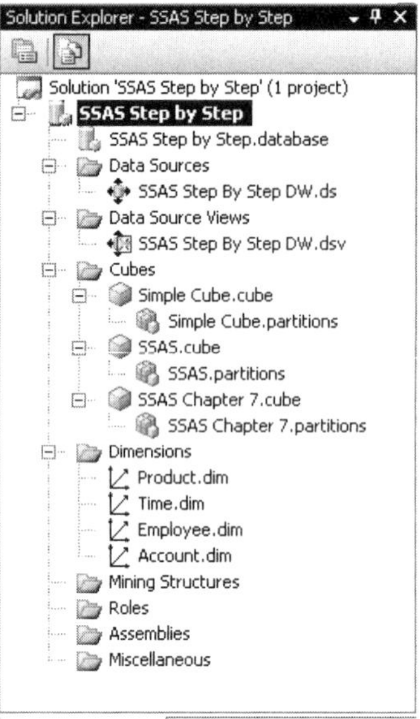

2. Right-click SSAS Chapter 7.partitions in Solution Explorer, and then click View Code.
3. Press Ctrl+F, type **<Aggregations>** in the Find What: box, click Find Next, and then close the Find and Replace dialog box.

   Your screen looks like this:

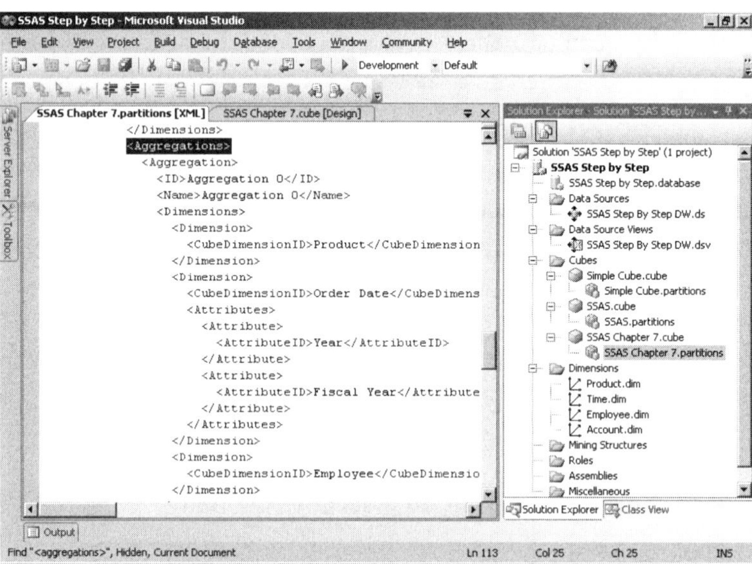

By viewing the code for the partition file, you can review the aggregation information for each partition. The section of the file that contains the aggregation definitions begins with the <Aggregations> tag. If aggregations have not been designed for a partition, then there will not be an <Aggregations> tag in the file. If aggregations have been designed, then each aggregation definition will follow the <Aggregations> tag, with each new definition identified by the <Aggregation> tag. As you scroll through this section of the partitions file, you can see the aggregation definitions for the Reseller Sales partition similar to those shown in this table:

Aggregation	Employee	Order Date	Product
0		Year Fiscal Year	
1	Dim Employee		
2			Dim Product

Notice that, while all dimensions related to the measure group in the partition are included in the aggregation definition, sometimes the dimension elements do not include an <Attribute ID>. When this element is missing for a dimension, that aggregation uses the All level of that particular dimension. Therefore, by looking at the aggregation definition, you can tell which dimensions are being aggregated at the attribute level and which are being summarized at the All level.

For each aggregation definition, the Analysis server stores aggregated values for the specified attributes in combination with the All level of the specified dimensions that did not have an attribute. You can think of each aggregation as a separate table. Using the example from the previous table for Aggregation 0, the table might look like this:

Year	Fiscal Year	Sales Amount	Order Quantity
2001	2002	$ 8,065,435	10,835
2002	2002	$ 8,223,006	11,055
2002	2003	$ 15,921,423	47,186
2003	2003	$ 12,000,247	31,773
2003	2004	$ 20,202,422	68,399
2004	2004	$ 16,038,063	45,130
2004	2005	$ 1,140	3

This aggregation would be used by the server to answer queries that requested either Sales Amount or Order Quantity (or both) by Year or by Fiscal Year (or, again, both) for All Employees and All Products. For example, if a user asked for sales in 2003, then Analysis Services can add together $12,000,247 and $20,202,422 to respond to the query with $32,202,669 much more quickly than it could add up the Sales Amount for all the fact table rows with a TimeKey that represents a date in 2003.

4. Close the SSAS Chapter 7.partitions [XML] code page.

Changing Partition Counts

One of the key pieces of information that the Aggregation Design Wizard requires is the count of fact table rows as well as the count of granularity attributes within each dimension. When you are developing a database, you are often using a subset of data, so the count of rows currently in the fact table likely differs from the actual row count expected in a production database. To get a more accurate aggregation design for your production database, even while working with a smaller development version, you can enter a long-term estimated value. You don't need to be precise, but don't underestimate either. The counts are used only for aggregation design, but may result in an aggregation design that is less than optimal if you underestimate the row count.

In this procedure, you'll change the estimated count of the fact table and the granularity attributes to observe the impact on the aggregation design.

Edit fact table and granularity attribute counts

1. Return to the Partitions tab of the Cube Designer.
2. Right-click the first row in the table for the Resellers Sales partition, click Design Aggregations, and then click Next twice.
3. Before changing the estimated count for the fact table, establish a baseline by designing aggregations for the fact table based on the current count. Click Next, click Performance Gain Reaches and type **100** in the spin box to the right of this option, and then click Start.

   A total of 13 aggregations were designed by the wizard based on the current size of the fact table and dimensions.
4. Click Back, and on the Specify Object Counts page of the wizard, type **100,000,000** in the Partition Count box for Reseller Sales.
5. Expand Product and type **100** in the Partition Count box for Product.

   Notice that the only row that accepts input in the Partition Count is the granularity attribute, the attribute that represents the leaf level, which is Product in this dimension. Later in this chapter, you'll learn how to include other attributes in the pool of potential aggregations.
6. Repeat the previous step to override the Partition Count with a value of **100** for the granularity attribute for each dimension, as shown in this table:

Dimension	Granularity Attribute
Order Date	Date
Employee	Employee

Your screen looks like this:

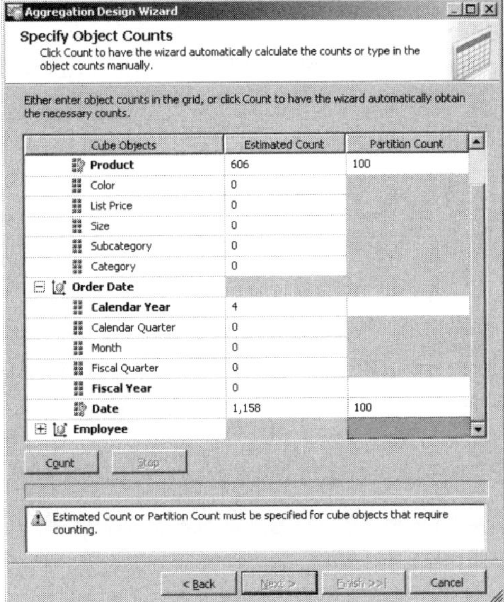

In the Order Date and Employee dimensions, you have nongranularity attributes available for specification of a partition count. With Order Date, the Year and Fiscal Year attributes are available because they are each top-level attributes of user hierarchies. In the case of Employee, the Employees attribute is the parent attribute for this parent-child dimension.

7. Click Next.
8. With the current setting to design for a performance gain of 100%, click Start.

   The number of aggregations is increased to 19 because the number of rows for each granularity attribute is relatively low compared to the large fact table. In this type of situation, query performance can be improved considerably by a large number of aggregations to save the time of computing the aggregated values on demand.
9. Click Back, and then change the Partition Count for both Date and Product to **100,000**.
10. Click Next, and then click Start.

    Notice when one or more of your attributes has a large partition count relative to the fact table, the number of aggregations designed is different from what the number would be if the attribute had a low partition count. Generally speaking, this aggregation count, while lower than the previous example, has a greater number of aggregations than that produced by using just the estimated count.

    In practice, you should rely on the 30% performance gain method of designing aggregations after you specify reasonably close estimates of the counts you expect in the fact and dimension tables after six months or so. The wizard will design a basic set of aggregations that will help queries perform better until the cube has been in production long enough for you to tune the aggregations by using the Usage-Based Optimization Wizard. You'll learn how to use that wizard later in this chapter.

11. Click Finish twice to complete the wizard without processing the partition.

Adding Attributes to the Aggregation Design

What if you want to make other attributes available for consideration in the aggregation design? Currently, only the granularity attribute and the top-level attributes in any user hierarchies are available for consideration by the Aggregation Design Wizard. The *Aggregation-Usage* property can be set for each attribute of a dimension. Most of the time you can leave the default value of Default for this property and get adequate aggregation designs. However, when you have certain attributes that are used frequently, and have a relatively small number of members, you might consider adding them to the pool of potential candidates for aggregation. In the Product dimension, for example, there are a lot of Products, but only a few colors. If Color is queried frequently, then it might be a good candidate for aggregations.

In this procedure, you'll add the Color attribute to the aggregation design pool.

Set the *AggregationUsage* property for an attribute

1. Click the Cube Structure tab of the Cube Designer for the SSAS Chapter 7 cube, and then click the Attributes tab in the Dimensions pane.
2. Expand Product.
3. Click Color, and then in the Properties window, select Full in the *AggregationUsage* property's drop-down list.

   After changing this property, you'll need to run the Aggregation Design Wizard to have the attribute considered for aggregations.
4. Click the Partitions tab, click in the Aggregations column for Fact Reseller Sales partition, and then click the ellipsis button to launch the wizard.

Tip You can click the ellipsis button in the Aggregations column, right-click the partition row and click Design Aggregations, or click the Design Aggregations link to start the wizard.

5. Click Next twice, and then, on the Specify Objects Count page, expand Product.

   Notice that you can now specify a Partition Count for Color, and you cannot complete the wizard without providing a count. Color is now available to the aggregation pool.

Why not have all of the attributes in the pool? The number of possible combinations of aggregations is so large that it would take a very long time to calculate the best choice. You always want to weigh performance against its cost in terms of processing speed and disk space. Therefore, choose only the attributes for which aggregations would be most useful.

6. Click Count.

   Your screen looks like this:

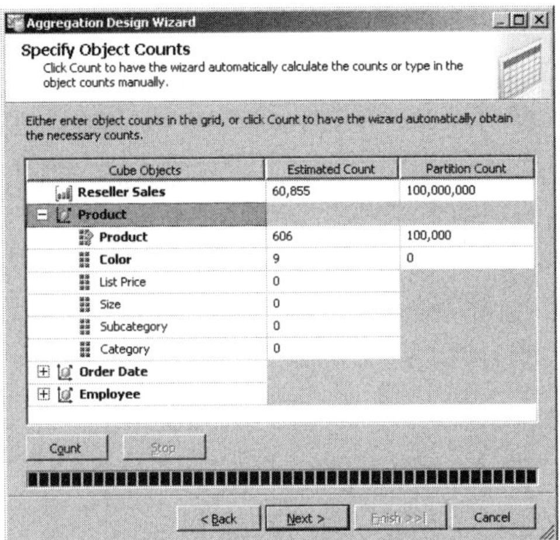

   The number of colors, 9, is added to the Estimated Count for this attribute. Remember that if you don't enter a Partition Count for this attribute, the Estimated Count value is used by default. Because you previously specified a Partition Count of 100,000 for Product, that count remains and is used by default.

7. Click Next, select Performance Gain Reaches, type **100** in the % spin box, and then click Start.

   Compare the number of aggregations designed in this step to the number of aggregations designed in the previous procedure. Adding an attribute doesn't necessarily result in an increase in aggregations.

8. Click Finish twice to complete the wizard without processing the partition.

Designing User Hierarchies

When browsing a cube, attribute hierarchies can be nested on rows or columns to create a drill path from one attribute in one attribute hierarchy to another attribute in a second attribute hierarchy where a relationship between the attributes exists. Rather than force users to drag each attribute hierarchy onto an axis (either rows or columns) one by one each time they want to work with a particular dimension, you can design *user hierarchies* to "prepackage" this collection of attributes as a hierarchy. You've already seen examples of user hierarchies in the Time dimension for Calendar and Fiscal hierarchies that progress from Year to Quarter to Month. The top-level attribute of these hierarchies can be considered for aggregations, but, otherwise, user hierarchies are created for navigational purposes when querying a cube. By default, all other levels of these hierarchies have no effect on aggregations.

Adding a User Hierarchy

Creating a user hierarchy is quite simple. You drag and drop attributes onto the Hierarchy and Levels pane in the preferred drill sequence. If you change your mind, it is easy to drag and drop the attributes into a different sequence, or to remove an attribute from the hierarchy altogether. Each user hierarchy is given a default name starting with Hierarchy, then Hierarchy 1, Hierarchy 2, and so forth. After it is created, you should rename the hierarchy to something more meaningful to users.

> **Note** A user hierarchy may or may not have supporting relationships defined in the data source view (DSV). This hierarchy is primarily for navigational purposes.

In this procedure, you'll create a Category user hierarchy from the Category, Subcategory, and Product attributes, and a Color-Size user hierarchy from the Color and Size attributes.

Add user hierarchies to a dimension

1. In Solution Explorer, double-click Product.dim to open the Dimension Designer.
2. Drag Category from the Attributes pane to the Hierarchies and Levels pane.

   A single-level hierarchy is created based on the Category attribute, but this is not a very useful hierarchy right now. A user hierarchy should have two levels at a minimum; otherwise it is really just an attribute, not a hierarchy.
3. Drag Subcategory from the Attributes pane and drop it below Category in the area labeled <New Level>.
4. Repeat the previous step to add Product beneath Subcategory.

Your screen looks like this:

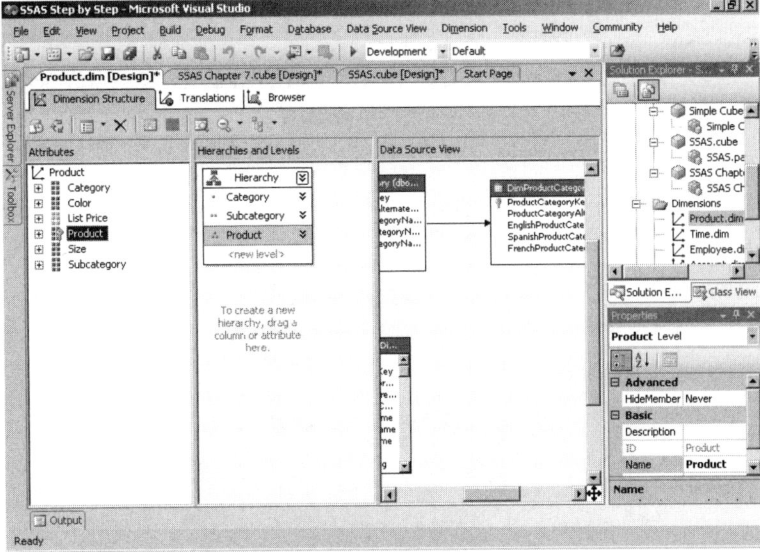

Even though a natural relationship among Category, Subcategory, and Product exists in the DSV based on the foreign key relationships defined between the tables, the navigation path from one level to the next isn't automatically included as a user hierarchy in the dimension (unless you use Auto Build in the Dimension Wizard).

You're not limited to creating user hierarchies based on existing relationships. Any combination of attributes can be included in a user hierarchy, as you'll see in the next few steps.

5. Drag Color to the Hierarchies and Levels pane from the Attributes pane.

   Take care to place Color anywhere on the Hierarchies and Levels pane except within the existing hierarchy, so that a new hierarchy is created.

6. Drag Size and drop it below Color in the area labeled <New Level>.

   Notice that the default name for the first hierarchy is Hierarchy and the second hierarchy is Hierarchy 1. Each new user hierarchy added will be numbered sequentially, such as Hierarchy 2, Hierarchy 3, and so on. These are the names that users will see when browsing the cube. Because these hierarchy names are not very meaningful, you should change them.

7. Right-click the caption of the first hierarchy, Hierarchy, click Rename, and then type **Product Category**.

   All names within a dimension must be unique, regardless of whether they are attribute or user hierarchy names. Since there is an attribute named Category, you can't reuse that name for the hierarchy.

8. Repeat the previous step to rename Hierarchy1 as **Color-Size**.

9. Deploy the project, and then, when deployment is complete, click the Browser tab of the Dimension Designer.

10. Click Product Category in the Hierarchy list box, and then expand the All member, the Bikes member, and the Mountain Bikes member.

    Your screen looks like this:

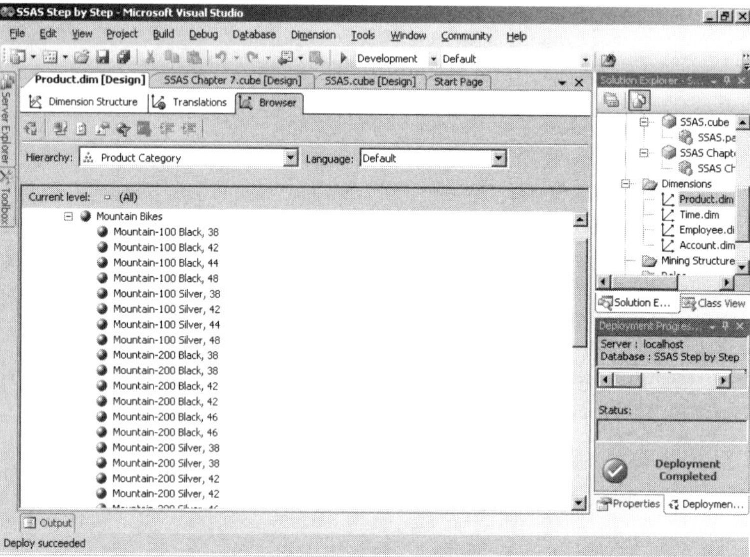

    This user hierarchy will enable users to drill from Category to Subcategory to Product without having to physically nest these attributes in the cube browser.

11. Click Color-Size in the Hierarchy list box, and then expand the All member, the Black member, and the Blue member.

Your screen looks like this:

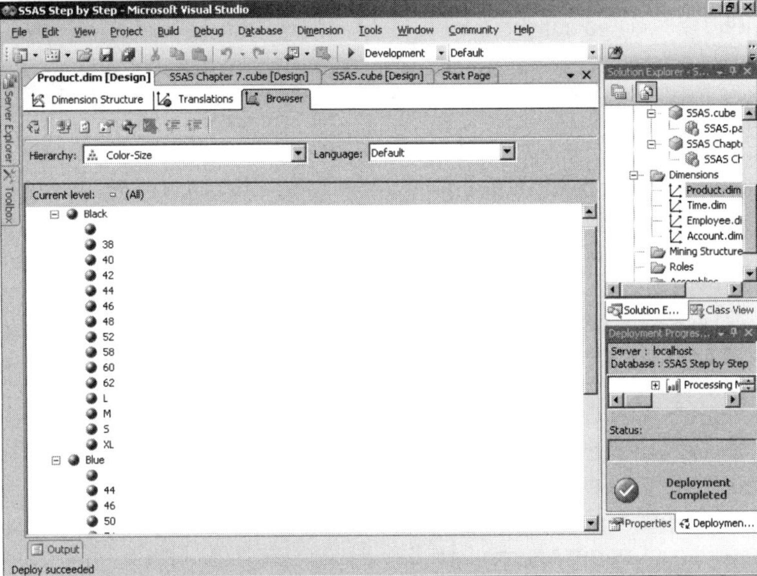

Notice that different Color members list the same Size members in their user hierarchy. The list of Size members will display within each of their related Color attributes when browsing this user hierarchy in the cube.

> **Auto Build**
>
> Auto Build is a feature that reviews the database metadata and structure to makes recommendations about how to structure a cube or a dimension. When using the Dimension Wizard with Auto Build enabled, you have the option for the wizard to suggest attributes only or to suggest both attributes and user hierarchies. Similarly, the Cube Wizard can examine the DSV, and identify the fact and dimension tables and suggest new dimensions. You'll still need to select measures and cube dimensions yourself. You can accept or override the Auto Build recommendations while using either wizard, and, of course, you can edit the cube or dimension after completing the wizard.

Aggregating User Hierarchies

Attribute relationships are initially created based on the table structure in the data DSV. You first encountered attribute relationships in Chapter 5 when you explored the interaction between attributes and measure groups. As you learned, these attribute relationships are required for the calculation of aggregated values when a query includes an attribute other than the granularity attribute. For example, to calculate the value of a measure for a Category, say Bikes, Analysis Services determines which Subcategories are related to the Category. In this example, the related subcategories are Mountain Bikes, Road Bikes, and Touring Bikes. The cube then aggregates the products related to these Subcategories to come up with the subcategory total, and then combines subcategory totals to determine the aggregated value for the Bikes category.

Even though attribute relationships define how values are aggregated across attributes within a dimension, they do not, by default, affect the aggregation design for the dimension. Because aggregations can improve query performance, there might be circumstances where it would be very useful to have the Aggregation Design Wizard consider creating aggregations for the levels of a user hierarchy. For example, storing precalculated values for the Category or Subcategory levels of the Product Category user hierarchy could be beneficial.

You already know that you can change the *AggregationUsage* property to have an attribute added to the pool of aggregation candidates. You can also take advantage of attribute relationships when you have a chain of relationships, such as exists among the attributes Category, Subcategory, and Product. When you create a user hierarchy that mimics this chain of relationships, you can use the Aggregation Design Wizard to include additional attributes in the aggregation pool and thereby speed up queries.

In this procedure, you'll increase the aggregation pool by including a user hierarchy based on attribute relationships.

Update the aggregation design with attributes from a user hierarchy

1. Click the Partitions tab of the SSAS Chapter 7 Cube Designer, right-click the Reseller Sales partition, and then click Design Aggregations.
2. Click Next twice, and then, on the Specify Objects Count page, expand Product.

   Notice you can now specify a Partition Count for Subcategory and Category. However, Size is not available because, even though it is also in a user hierarchy, it has no attribute relationship with Color.
3. Click Count, click Next, select Performance Gain Reaches, type **100** in the % box, and then click Start.
4. Click Finish twice to complete the wizard without processing the partition.
5. Right-click SSAS Chapter 7.partitions in Solution Explorer, and then click View Code.
6. Press Ctrl+F, type **Subcategory** in the Find What: box, click Find Next, and then close the Find and Replace dialog box.

Your screen looks similar to this:

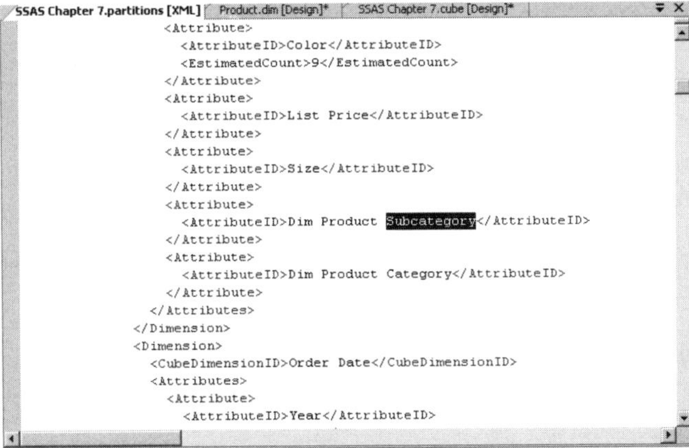

You have now created aggregations for your cube in several ways. Some aggregations were designed based upon the structure of the cube, using the counts of cube objects like the measure groups and the granularity attribute for the dimension. Other aggregations were built because you changed the *AttributeUsage* property to add an attribute to the pool of aggregations. Lastly, you created a user hierarchy for which there is a chain of attribute relationships from one attribute to the next.

Optimizing Aggregations

The Aggregation Design Wizard selects aggregations from a pool of potential aggregations. As you learned previously in this chapter, the default pool of potential aggregations includes all the granularity attributes from each dimension. You can increase this pool by changing attribute properties and adding user hierarchies from related attributes. This design strategy is good for a new cube that you are putting into production, but it might not be optimized for your users. The best way to design optimized aggregations is to consider the actual data that users request from the cube and the frequency with which they request it after they've had a chance to use the cube for a while.

One of the most powerful features of Analysis Services is usage-based optimization. It allows you to select aggregations based on actual queries submitted to the server—that is, on the usage of real-world users. The Usage-Based Optimization Wizard behaves exactly like the Aggregation Design Wizard except that it factors into the equation the actual usage patterns.

Using the Query Log

Usage patterns come from the query log. The query log can be stored in a relational database or in a file located in a folder of your choosing. By default, the server logs 1 out of 10 queries.

If you want to experiment with usage-based optimization, increase the sampling frequency temporarily to make it easier to add entries to the log. You can change the sampling frequency in Microsoft SQL Server Management Studio by changing a property of the Analysis server.

In this procedure, you'll create a query log and execute queries to populate the query log with entries.

Populate the query log

1. Open Microsoft SQL Server Management Studio, click Database Engine in the Server Type box, ensure the server name is correct, and then click Connect.
2. In the Object Explorer window, right-click the Databases folder, and then click New Database.
3. Type a name for the database, **ASQueryLog**, and then click OK.

   Next, you will connect to Analysis Services to start the logging process.
4. In the Object Explorer, click Connect, click Analysis Services, ensure the server name is correct, and then click Connect.
5. Right-click the Analysis Server in the Object Explorer window, and then click Properties.
6. Locate the *Log \ QueryLog \ CreateQueryLogTable* property, and then select True in the Value drop-down list for this property.
7. Click the button in the Value box for the *Log \ QueryLog \ QueryLogConnectionString* property, type **localhost** in the Server Name box, select Use Windows Authentication, select ASQueryLog in the Select Or Enter A Database Name drop-down list, and then click OK.
8. Type **1** in the Value box for the *Log \ QueryLog \ QueryLogSampling* property.

Your screen looks like this:

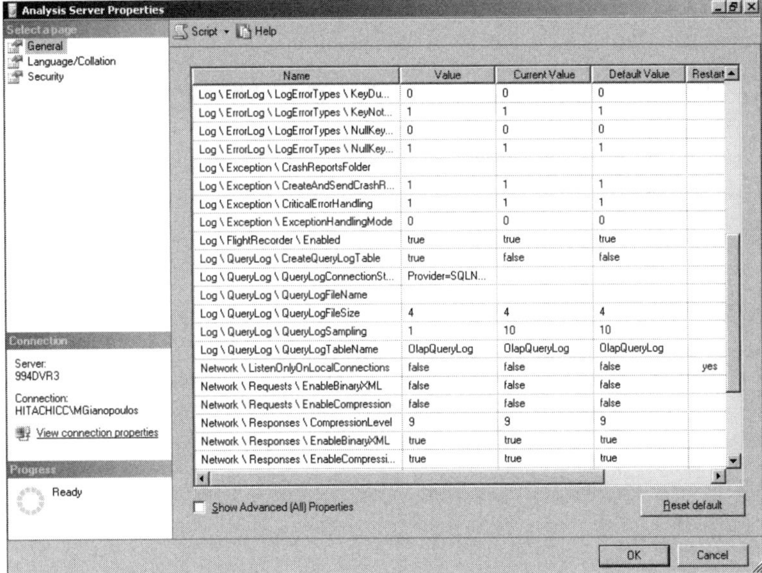

This value will create an entry in the log for each query to an Analysis Services database. Generally, this frequency of sampling would be excessive, but for now, you need to quickly build up data for the Usage-Based Optimization Wizard.

Notice that the *Log \ QueryLog \ QueryLogTableName* property defaults to OlapQuery-Log. When you close the Properties, the table called OlapQueryLog is added to the ASQueryLog database that you created. Of course, the table name can be edited if you prefer.

9. Click OK.

10. Right-click the Databases folder for the SQL Server, click Refresh, expand the Databases folder, expand ASQueryLog, expand Tables, right-click dbo.OlapQueryLog, and then click Open Table.

    The table is currently empty. Now you will perform queries against the cube to log some usage. Each query that you perform will create a new record in the ASQueryLog data-base. Later, the Usage-Based Optimization Wizard will analyze this usage to make opti-mization recommendations for aggregations.

11. Keep the table open in SQL Server Management Studio, expand the Databases folder for the Analysis Server, expand the SSAS Step by Step folder, expand the Cubes folder, right-click SSAS Chapter 7, click Process to apply the designed aggregations, click OK, and then click Close.

12. Right-click SSAS Chapter 7, and then click Browse.

You can browse a cube using the same interface you use in Visual Studio when developing and testing a cube.

13. Spend a few minutes browsing the Sales cube.

    For example, you might drag over some dimensions into the grid, drill to browse members on different levels, and perform various queries to add entries to the query log. Be sure to drill down within your dimensions. Each manipulation of the browser layout generates a new query to the server.

14. Close the browser window.

Viewing Usage Data

You don't need to review the usage data in the query log before you apply usage-based optimization. The data in this table won't be particularly useful to you, but it's good to confirm that you have usage data available before running the Usage-Based Optimization Wizard.

In the next procedure, you'll review data in the query log.

Browse the query log

1. With the dbo.OlapQueryLog window open in SQL Server Management Studio, click the Execute SQL button in the toolbar to refresh the contents of the window.

   Your screen looks similar to this:

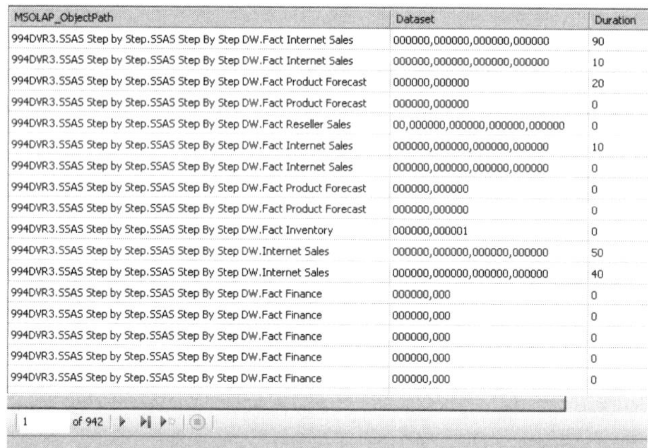

MSOLAP_ObjectPath	Dataset	Duration
994DVR3.SSAS Step by Step.SSAS Step By Step DW.Fact Internet Sales	000000,000000,000000,000000	90
994DVR3.SSAS Step by Step.SSAS Step By Step DW.Fact Internet Sales	000000,000000,000000,000000	10
994DVR3.SSAS Step by Step.SSAS Step By Step DW.Fact Product Forecast	000000,000000	20
994DVR3.SSAS Step by Step.SSAS Step By Step DW.Fact Product Forecast	000000,000000	0
994DVR3.SSAS Step by Step.SSAS Step By Step DW.Fact Reseller Sales	00,000000,000000,000000,000000	0
994DVR3.SSAS Step by Step.SSAS Step By Step DW.Fact Internet Sales	000000,000000,000000,000000	10
994DVR3.SSAS Step by Step.SSAS Step By Step DW.Fact Internet Sales	000000,000000,000000,000000	0
994DVR3.SSAS Step by Step.SSAS Step By Step DW.Fact Product Forecast	000000,000000	0
994DVR3.SSAS Step by Step.SSAS Step By Step DW.Fact Product Forecast	000000,000000	0
994DVR3.SSAS Step by Step.SSAS Step By Step DW.Fact Inventory	000000,000001	0
994DVR3.SSAS Step by Step.SSAS Step By Step DW.Internet Sales	000000,000000,000000,000000	50
994DVR3.SSAS Step by Step.SSAS Step By Step DW.Internet Sales	000000,000000,000000,000000	40
994DVR3.SSAS Step by Step.SSAS Step By Step DW.Fact Finance	000000,000	0
994DVR3.SSAS Step by Step.SSAS Step By Step DW.Fact Finance	000000,000	0
994DVR3.SSAS Step by Step.SSAS Step By Step DW.Fact Finance	000000,000	0
994DVR3.SSAS Step by Step.SSAS Step By Step DW.Fact Finance	000000,000	0
994DVR3.SSAS Step by Step.SSAS Step By Step DW.Fact Finance	000000,000	0

1 of 942

   Each time you added a dimension or a measure to the grid, moved items off the grid, or drilled up or down within a hierarchy, a new record was inserted into the OlapQueryLog. Review the record count at the bottom of the screen to see how quickly your queries added data into the log.

2. Close the table window, but keep SQL Server Management Studio open.

Using the Usage-Based Optimization Wizard

Once you've accumulated a set of queries in the usage log, you can use the Usage-Based Optimization Wizard to design aggregations. The Usage-Based Optimization Wizard is essentially the Usage Analysis Wizard attached to the front of the Aggregation Design Wizard. First, you select the logged queries that should apply, and then you design aggregations.

In this procedure, you'll use the Usage-Based Optimization Wizard to analyze the logged queries and design aggregations optimized for these queries.

Design usage-based aggregations

1. In Visual Studio, open the Cube Designer for the SSAS Chapter 7 cube, click the Partition tab, right-click the first row in the table for the Resellers Sales partition, click Usage-Based Optimization, and then click Next.

   Your screen looks like this:

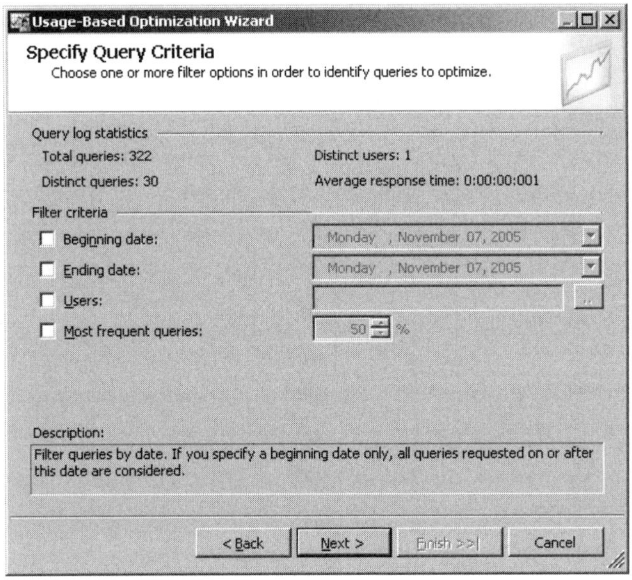

   On the Specify Query Criteria page, there are several different filters that you can use to customize the optimization process: Beginning Date, Ending Date, Users, and Most Frequent Queries. Since this query log has only been tracking data on one day, for one user, and only for a very short period, changing the filter criteria won't make much difference right now. When you work with a database that has been placed in production, however, these filters can be quite useful. For example, you can base the optimization on the queries created by power users, so that the query performance is best for the people who use the data the most frequently.

2. Click Next.

Your screen looks similar to this:

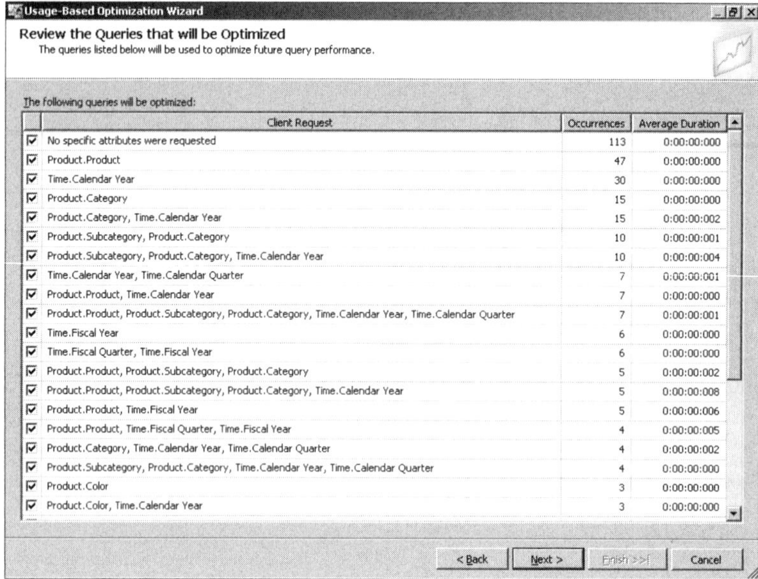

On the Review The Queries That Will Be Optimized page, you can see the frequency with which specific attribute combinations occur and the average duration of queries that include these combinations.

3. Click Next three times, select Performance Gain Reaches, type **100** in the % box, and then click Start on the Set Aggregation Options page.

   How did your usage-based aggregations compare to the previously designed aggregations? If the number of aggregations isn't lower, it's possible you didn't create enough queries to change the default aggregation behavior.

4. When aggregation design is complete, click Finish twice to complete the wizard without processing the partition.

> **Important** Be sure to reset the sampling rate of the query log to a more suitable value, such as the default value of 10, if you plan to use this optimization technique on your own databases.

Maintaining the Query Log

Suppose that you have accumulated a significant number of entries in the log for a cube. You then change the definition of the cube, which makes the entries in the query log no longer meaningful. Leaving those entries in the log as you perform usage-based optimization could lead to invalid optimization. If you no longer need the old log data, you can execute a DELETE query to remove records from the log for that one cube.

If you do want to retain the old query logs, you can extract them from the log database or you can filter for only new log entries when optimizing aggregations. On the Usage Based Optimization Wizard's criteria screen, set the Beginning Date to the date the cube structure was last modified.

In this procedure, you'll delete records from the query log for the Reseller Sales partition.

Delete records from the query log

1. Switch to SQL Server Management Studio, and then click New Query on the toolbar.
2. Click Database Engine in the Server Type list box, and then click Connect.
3. Click ASQueryLog in the database drop-down list that appears on the toolbar.
4. In the Query window, type the following query:

```
DELETE FROM OlapQueryLog
WHERE
MSOLAP_Database = 'SSAS Step by Step'
```

5. Press the Execute button on the toolbar.

   Deleting records from the log has no effect on any aggregations designed by the Usage-Based Optimization Wizard.

Chapter 7 Quick Reference

To	Do this
Design aggregations	On the Partitions tab of the Cube Designer, right-click a partition, click Design Aggregations, specify object counts, select one of the three options for limiting aggregations, and then click Start.
Control the number of aggregations used in a partition	In the Aggregation Design Wizard, change the partition counts, and/or select one of three options: Design aggregations until the storage meets a certain size, until the performance gain meets a certain percentage, or until you click Stop.
Inspect aggregation definitions	In Solution Explorer, click the Show All button, right-click the cube's partition file, and then click View Code.
Add an attribute to the pool of potential aggregations	On the Cube Structure tab of the Cube Designer, click the attribute, change the *AggregationUsage* property to Full, run the Aggregation Design Wizard, and add a count for the attribute.
Create a user hierarchy	On the Dimension Structure tab of the Dimension Designer, drag attributes to the Hierarchy and Levels pane in hierarchical order.

To	Do this
Add attributes of a user hierarchy to the pool of potential aggregations	On the Dimension Structure tab of the Dimension Designer, create a direct attribute relationship between each pair of attributes from level to level (but only if the relationship also exists in the Data Source View), create a user hierarchy using these attributes, run the Aggregation Design Wizard, and add a count for each attribute.
Create a query log	In SQL Server Management Studio, create a new database, connect to Analysis Services, right-click the server, click Properties, set the *CreateQueryLogTable* property to True, set the *QueryLog-ConnectionString* to localhost, using the query log database name, and set the *QueryLogSampling* to the desired sampling rate value.
Apply usage-based optimization to a cube	After creating a query log and allowing users to browse the cube for a period of time, on the Partition tab of the Cube Designer, right-click a partition row, click Usage Based Optimization, filter the query log if necessary, specify object counts, select one of the three options for limiting aggregations, and then click Start.

Part III
Advanced Design

In this part:

Chapter 8: Using MDX 177

Chapter 9: Exploring Special Features 217

Chapter 10: Interacting with Cubes 245

In Part II, "Design Fundamentals," you learned the basics for designing dimensions and measure groups to create a useful analytical solution with Analysis Services. You also learned how to design objects to handle certain unique financial analysis requirements. Throughout the chapters of Part III, you'll work with advanced design techniques to support sophisticated analysis on the one hand and to simplify access to analysis on the other hand. Later in Part IV, "Production Management," you'll shift your focus from building a solution to implementing, managing, and maintaining that solution.

Chapter 8
Using MDX

After completing this chapter, you will be able to:

- Use multidimensional expressions (MDX) to calculate contribution percentages.
- Execute MDX queries using SQL Server Management Studio.
- Use set functions.
- Create calculated members that aggregate sets of values.
- Use script assignments to change cube values.
- Create key performance indicators (KPIs).

In the chapters of Part II "Design Fundamentals," you were introduced to MDX by creating calculations that added new measures to your cube. In this chapter, you'll expand your understanding of MDX by creating more complex calculated measures as well as calculations that create new dimension members. You'll also learn how to construct MDX queries so that you can build analytical reports in custom applications or troubleshoot a cube by retrieving values from a cube with more specificity than is possible through the cube browser. Then you'll take a closer look at the MDX script containing the cube's complete set of calculations by observing how calculation sequence and script assignments influence query results. To complete the chapter, you'll build KPIs using MDX expressions to illustrate how cube values compare to established goals and prior performance or other benchmarks.

Creating Tuple-Based Calculated Members

If you have worked with spreadsheet applications, you already know how to think about data in two dimensions–rows and columns. Working with multidimensional data is not much different, although it is a bit harder to visualize and requires a different language, like MDX, to retrieve values from cells. To see how MDX refers to values in cells in a multidimensional cube, consider first how a Microsoft Excel formula refers to values in other cells in a two-dimensional spreadsheet.

Imagine that you are creating a spreadsheet that calculates the margin (sales minus cost) for three product categories. Traditionally, spreadsheet formulas have used addresses to refer to cells.

	A	B	C	D
1	**Category**	**Sales**	**Cost**	**Margin**
2	Bikes	$66,302,382	$67,293,081	-$990,699
3	Components	$11,799,077	$10,766,110	=B3-C3
4	Clothing	$1,777,841	$1,545,417	$232,424
5	Accessories	$571,298	$375,505	$195,793
6	Grand Total	$80,450,598	$79,980,113	$470,485

The formula in cell D3 uses the address B3 to refer to Components Sales. The address B3 refers to the *position* of the cell, not to its *meaning*. When you copy the formula from cell D3 to cell D4, the address B3 must change to B4. This type of formula is called a *relative reference*; the formula's operands are relative to the cell's position and each copy of the formula appears slightly different.

You can also create formulas that use cell labels. The same worksheet could have formulas that look like these:

	A	B	C	D
1	**Category**	**Sales**	**Cost**	**Margin**
2	Bikes	$66,302,382	$67,293,081	-$990,699
3	Components	$11,799,077	$10,766,110	=Sales-Cost
4	Clothing	$1,777,841	$1,545,417	$232,424
5	Accessories	$571,298	$375,505	$195,793
6	Grand Total	$80,450,598	$79,980,113	$470,485

The new formula in cell D3 uses the label Sales to refer to bike sales. This time, the word *Sales* refers to the *meaning* of the cell (as defined by its column label), not to its *position*. The formula assumes that you want the Sales value for the product category that is on the *same row* as the formula. When you copy the formula from cell D3 to cell D4, the formula doesn't change. In MDX terminology, the formula implicitly uses the current member of the row axis.

Excel formulas that use labels are easy to understand. MDX expressions work in a very similar way. You can create a new calculated measure that automatically refers to the current state, or you can create a new calculated member of the Product dimension that automatically refers to the current measure. By creating a calculated member using MDX, you are in effect entering formulas into a set of cube cells the same way that you copy and paste formulas across a set of cells in an Excel spreadsheet. The power of an MDX calculated member comes from the fact that you don't have to enter the formula into each cell; a single formula automatically propagates to all the necessary cells. This works even when you change the dimensions on the axes.

A spreadsheet formula must often refer to a cell that is not on the same row or column as the cell containing the formula. For example, suppose you want to calculate the percent a specific product category contributed to total sales. Using traditional spreadsheet references, you would need to create a formula similar to the following:

	A	B	C
1	**Category**	**Sales**	**% of Total Sales**
2	Bikes	$66,302,382	82%
3	Components	$11,799,077	=B3/B$6
4	Clothing	$1,777,841	2%
5	Accessories	$571,298	1%
6	Grand Total	$80,450,598	100%

The formula in cell C3 refers to cell B6. To be able to copy the formula to the other cells in column C, it's necessary to add a dollar sign to "anchor" the row. This notation technique works, but it's clumsy and difficult to understand, and it would not translate well to the multidimensional world. If you create the formula by using labels, it looks like this:

	A	B	C
1	**Category**	**Sales**	**% of Total Sales**
2	Bikes	$66,302,382	82%
3	Components	$11,799,077	=Sales/TotalSales
4	Clothing	$1,777,841	2%
5	Accessories	$571,298	1%
6	Grand Total	$80,450,598	100%

The reference *Total Sales* refers to cell B6. (The new formula still needs a dollar sign if you want to copy it, but that's not the important part.) When using labels to refer to a cell that is not on the current row or column, you must include *both* the row and column labels, separated by a space. The result is remarkably readable. MDX, however, cannot simply use member names separated by spaces because an online analytical processing (OLAP) cube typically contains many more than two dimensions. MDX uses a notation and terminology for referring to an explicit cell that can be best understood by seeing how to specify a point on a chart.

Imagine a mathematical line. A line has one dimension. In basic charting, if you want to specify a point on the line, you specify a single number or a single coordinate. On the following line, the coordinate for the marked point is 3:

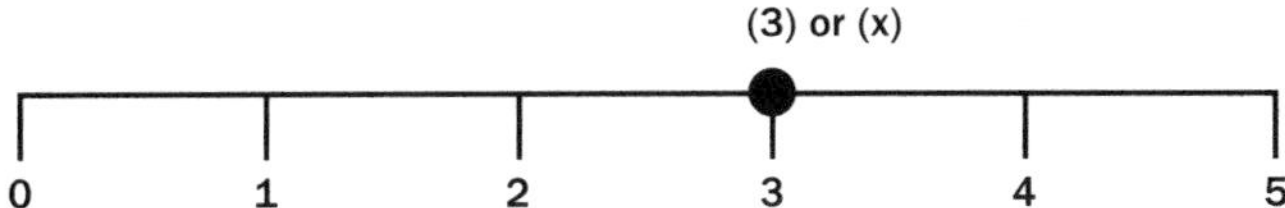

Now imagine a cube with one dimension. If you want to specify a value from the cube, you specify a single member from the dimension. This single value is the coordinate for the cell. In the following hypothetical cube, the coordinate for the marked cell is [February].

January	February	March	April
14	41	33	25

Imagine a mathematical grid. A grid has two dimensions. In basic charting, if you want to specify a point on the grid, you specify a pair of numbers or a double coordinate, typically enclosed in parentheses. On the following grid, the coordinate for the marked point is (3, 4):

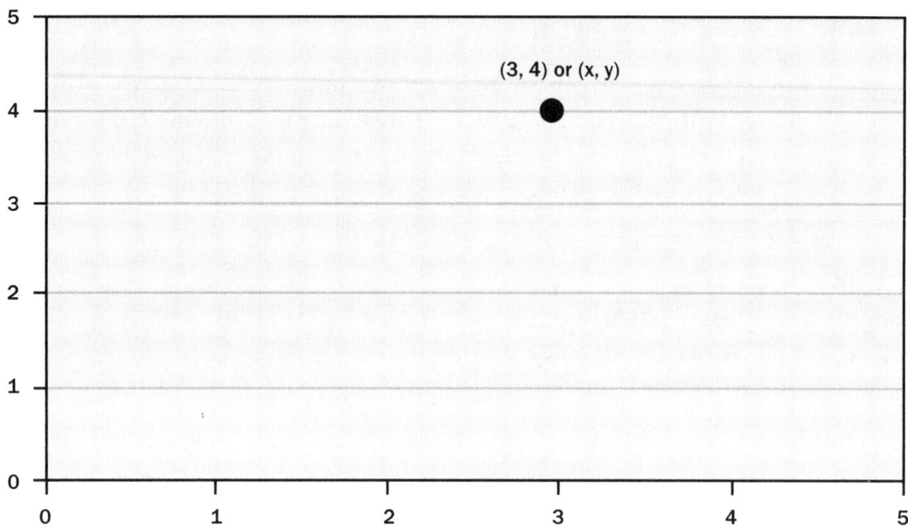

Now imagine a cube with two dimensions. If you want to specify a value from the cube, you specify a single member from each dimension. This double value is the coordinate for the cell. In the following hypothetical cube, the coordinate for the marked cell is (*[January],[Chain]*).

	January	February	March	April
Front Brakes			6	17
Rear Brakes	6	16	6	8
Chain	8	25	21	

Imagine a three-dimensional mathematical space. In charting, to specify a point in the space, you specify three numbers, or a triple coordinate. In the following space, the coordinate for the marked point is (4, 2, 3):

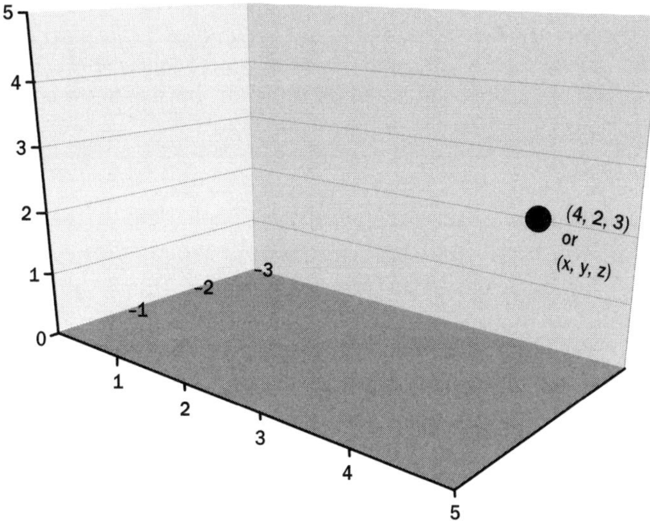

Now imagine a cube with three dimensions. Rather than format the cube as a cube or a rectangle, imagine the three dimensions of the cube as key columns. To specify a member from the cube, you specify a single member from each dimension. In the following hypothetical cube, the coordinate for the marked cell is (*[North America],[Mountain-100 Black, 38],[Time].[All]*).

Sales Territory	Product	Time	Units
All	All	All	113
North America	All	All	64
North America	Bikes	All	38
North America	Mountain-100 Black, 38	All	13
North America	Mountain-100 Black, 38	Qtr1	3
North America	Mountain-100 Black, 38	Mar	3

With more than two or three dimensions, it's usually easier to visualize a cube as a table with dimensions represented by key columns. To retrieve a single value from the cube–that is, to specify a single cell in the cube–you must specify one member from each dimension.

Watch for a pattern in the terminology for a coordinate as it includes more dimensions: A coordinate containing one dimension is a *single* coordinate. A coordinate containing two dimensions is a *double* coordinate. With three dimensions, it is a *triple* coordinate. With four dimensions, it is a *quadruple* coordinate; with five, a *quintuple*; with six, a *sextuple*, with seven, a *septuple*; and with eight, an *octuple*. Once you get past four dimensions in a coordinate, each of the coordinate numbers ends in the suffix *tuple*. The generic term for a coordinate that includes one or more dimensions is a tuple.

> **Note** Some people pronounce the first syllable of *tuple* to rhyme with *cup* (as in the word *quintuple*). Others pronounce it to rhyme with *coop* (as in the word *quadruple*). Each group considers the other to be uncivilized. Since this is a book, you don't have to know how we pronounce it.

As is the case with a mathematical coordinate, a tuple that contains more than a single dimension must be enclosed in parentheses . A tuple that contains one member from each attribute hierarchy of a cube identifies a unique value in the cube. When you extract a value from a cube, the measures are considered to be a dimension, and you must include a measure within a tuple to uniquely identify a value. When you need to refer to a value from a cube, you use a tuple.

Creating an MDX Calculation for Percent of Total

A tuple such as [Sales Amount]–which uses an explicit member name from one dimension–is very common in MDX expressions. A tuple such as *([Sales Amount], [Bikes])*–which uses explicit member names from two or more dimensions–is less common. Usually, when you explicitly include members from more than one dimension in a tuple, you use functions to calculate a member based upon the current member. This gives your MDX expression greater flexibility, like an Excel formula that you create once and copy where you need it.

Suppose you want to calculate what percent each product or product category contributes to the total sales for all products. This expression would have two component values: a numerator value (Sales for the current product) divided by a denominator value (Sales for All Products). The numerator value will change from product to product, but the denominator value always retrieves the member from the All level of the product dimension.

In this procedure, you'll create a calculated member that displays the percent that a category contributes to the total sales for all products.

Add a Percent of Total calculation to a cube

1. Start SQL Server Business Intelligence Development Studio (BIDS), and open the SSAS Step by Step solution that you saved in the C:\Documents and Settings\<username>\My Documents\Microsoft Press\ as2005sbs\Workspace folder.

> **Note** If you skipped Chapter 7, "Designing Aggregations and Hierarchies," open the SSAS Step by Step solution in the C:\Documents and Settings\<username>\My Documents\Microsoft Press\as2005sbs\Answers\chap07\SSAS Step by Step folder.

2. In Solution Explorer, double-click SSAS.cube to open the Cube Designer, and then click the Calculations tab.
3. Click the New Calculated Member button on the Calculations toolbar.

4. In the Name box, type **[Category Percent of Total]**.

   Remember from Chapter 5, "Designing Measure Groups and Measures," that you must enclose a calculation name in brackets when the name of the calculation contains a space or a character other than a letter or number.

5. Expand Measures in the cube metadata tree, on the Metadata tab, located in the Calculation Tools pane, and then expand the Reseller Sales measure group folder.

6. Drag Reseller Sales Amount into the Expression box, click to position the cursor at the end of the expression, and then type , (comma).

7. In the cube metadata tree, expand Product, expand Category, expand Members, and then expand All.

   You'll first start with a constant value for the tuple in the numerator to see how using a constant affects calculations in the cube. This calculation determines the percentage of sales that the Bikes category contributes to all product sales.

8. Drag Bikes into the Expression box and drop it at the end of the expression.

9. Type ((open parenthesis) at the beginning of the expression and) (close parenthesis) at the end of the expression to create a tuple.

   The expression now looks like this:

   ```
   ([Measures].[Reseller Sales Amount],[Product].[Category].&[1])
   ```

   The &[1] is the key value for Bikes. This expression represents the numerator component of the Percent of Total calculation.

10. Type / (forward slash) at the end of the expression and then type (to begin another tuple for the denominator.

11. Drag Reseller Sales Amount into the Expression box, drop it at the end of the current expression, and then type , (comma).

12. Drag the All member of the Category hierarchy to the end of the expression, and then type) to finish the calculation.

Your screen looks like this:

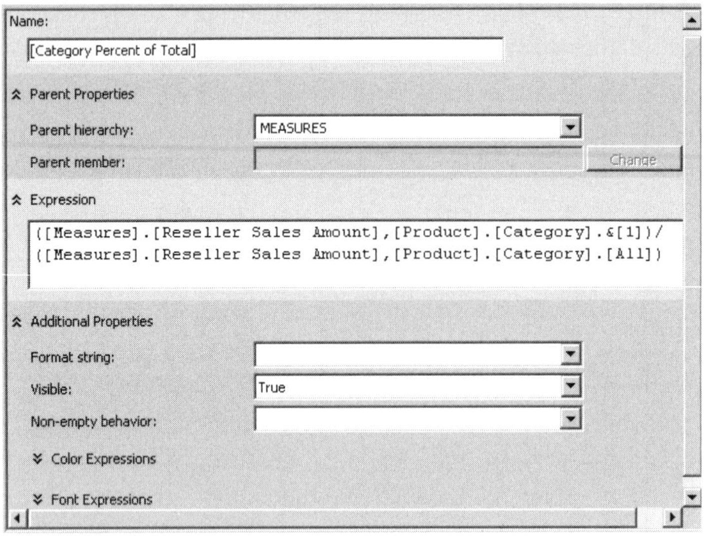

This calculation first computes the Reseller Sales Amount for Bikes and then divides the result by the Reseller Sales Amount for All Products to derive the percentage total.

13. Select "Percent" in the Format String drop-down list.

14. Select Reseller Sales Amount in the Non-Empty Behavior drop-down list.

    As you learned in Chapter 5, you should set this value to make sure that the MDX expression doesn't return an error if the Reseller Sales Amount measure for the All member is empty.

15. To test the calculation, deploy the project. When deployment is complete, click the Browser tab, and then click Reconnect.

16. Expand Measures, drag Category Percent of Total into the grid, expand the Reseller Sales folders, and then drag Reseller Sales Amount into the grid.

17. Expand Product, and then drag the Category attribute to rows.

    The browser grid looks like this:

Category	Category Percent of Total	Reseller Sales Amount
Bikes	82.41%	$66,302,382
Components	82.41%	$11,799,077
Clothing	82.41%	$1,777,841
Accessories	82.41%	$571,298
Grand Total	82.41%	$80,450,597

You can see that while Reseller Sales Amount changes for each category, the value for Category Percent of Sales remains the same. The tuple in the numerator and the tuple in the denominator don't change when you use them in combination with other categories because you specified an *absolute reference* to Bikes sales as *([Measures].[Reseller Sales*

Amount],[Product].[Category].&[1]) and an absolute reference to All products sales as *([Measures].[Reseller Sales Amount], [Product].[Category].[All])*. Using an absolute reference in an MDX expression is just like using an absolute reference in an Excel formula like this:

	A	B	C
1	Category	Sales	% of Total Sales
2	Bikes	$66,302,382	=B2/B6
3	Components	$11,799,077	15%
4	Clothing	$1,777,841	2%
5	Accessories	$571,298	1%
6	Grand Total	$80,450,598	100%

The dollar sign before the cell's coordinates B7 means that you always want B7 to be used as the denominator in the formula, regardless of the position of the cell that will contain this formula.

Next, you'll change the absolute reference in the numerator to a relative reference using the *CurrentMember* function. This allows your formula to reflect the correct percentage of sales regardless of which category is on the current row, even if it is the Category Grand Total.

18. Click the Calculations tab, and then replace &[1] in the Expression box with **CurrentMember**.

    The expression now looks like this:

```
([Measures].[Reseller Sales Amount],[Product].[Category].CurrentMember)/
([Measures].[Reseller Sales Amount],[Product].[Category].[All])
```

    Now the numerator will return the Reseller Sales Amount for the current member of the Category hierarchy and the value for the calculation will show the current category's contributions to total sales.

19. Deploy the project, return to the browser when deployment is finished, and then click Reconnect.

    The grid looks like this:

Category	Category Percent of Total	Reseller Sales Amount
Bikes	82.41%	$66,302,382
Components	14.67%	$11,799,077
Clothing	2.21%	$1,777,841
Accessories	0.71%	$571,298
Grand Total	100.00%	$80,450,597

You can see that the percentages reflect the correct percentage contribution for each category and that the Grand Total is 100%. Your calculation now uses the *CurrentMember* function as a variable to plug the current category into the numerator.

However, there is another way to create the expression to consider the context of the current member—through implicit reference, which you'll do in the next step.

20. Click the Calculations tab, and then change the numerator in the expression so that it contains only the measure.

    The expression now looks like this:

    ```
    ([Measures].[Reseller Sales Amount])/([Measures].[Reseller Sales
    Amount],[Product].[Category].[All])
    ```

    The parentheses that surround the measure in the numerator are optional when it is not included with a dimension member to form a tuple.

21. Deploy the project, open the browser when the project is deployed, and then click Reconnect.

    Notice that the calculation returns the same percentages whether you explicitly use the *CurrentMember* function, as you did earlier in this procedure, or implicitly as you did in this calculation. An MDX expression always calculates using the context of the cell in which it's actually calculated. Each cell has a current member for each dimension. Retrieving a value from a cube requires a member from each dimension of the cube; you can use the current member for most dimensions, but you don't need to explicitly reference it in the tuple. By default, the current member of every attribute hierarchy is implicitly referenced in a tuple, making it easier to build as well as easier to read and understand.

Creating an MDX Calculation for Percent of Parent

Calculating the relative contribution to the total is a comparatively easy calculation to create in a spreadsheet. A spreadsheet, however, has no conception of a hierarchy. In a spreadsheet, it's extremely difficult to create a formula that will calculate the relative contribution of each region to its country or of each state to its region. One of the remarkable strengths of OLAP is the ability of expressions to use the hierarchical relationships in dimensions.

In this procedure, you'll create a calculated member that displays the percent that a member of the Product Category hierarchy contributes to its parent's sales.

Add a Percent of Parent calculation to a cube

1. Click the Calculations tab, and then highlight and copy the text in the Expression box for the Category Percent of Total calculation.

2. Click the New Calculated Member button, and then name the calculation **[Product Percent of Parent]**.

3. Paste the copied expression into the Expression box.

4. Replace [Category].[All] member in the expression with **[Product Category].Parent**.

   The expression now looks like this:

   ```
   ([Measures].[Reseller Sales Amount])/([Measures].[Reseller Sales
   Amount],[Product].[Product Category].Parent)
   ```

The *Parent* function works best when you use it in combination with a user hierarchy. This function returns the member that is the parent of the current member of the specified hierarchy.

5. Select "Percent" in the Format String drop-down list, and select Reseller Sales Amount in the Non-Empty Behavior drop-down list.
6. Deploy the project, open the browser after deployment is finished, and then click Reconnect.
7. Drag Product Percent of Parent into the grid, drag Category off of rows and drop it anywhere in the metadata pane, and then drag the Product Category hierarchy as rows.
8. In the grid, expand Bikes.

   The grid looks like this:

Category	Subcategory	Product Percent of Parent	Category Percent of Total	Reseller Sales Amount
⊟ Bikes	⊞ Mountain Bikes	39.96%	32.93%	$26,492,684
	⊞ Road Bikes	44.28%	36.49%	$29,358,207
	⊞ Touring Bikes	15.76%	12.99%	$10,451,490
	Total	82.41%	82.41%	$66,302,382
⊞ Components		14.67%	14.67%	$11,799,077
⊞ Clothing		2.21%	2.21%	$1,777,841
⊞ Accessories		0.71%	0.71%	$571,298
Grand Total		1.#INF	100.00%	$80,450,597

   Compare the measures Category Percent of Total to Product Percent of Parent at the Category and Subcategory levels. At the category level, the two calculated members return the same percentage, of course, because the category's parent is the total of all products. As you drill down to the subcategory level, however, the calculated members return different percentages. All subcategories of Bikes represent their relative contribution to Bikes and, therefore, their respective percentages sum up to 100%. Notice that the total value you see for Bikes shows the percentage of its parent and not the sum of its subcategory children.

   Another observation to make is the Grand Total for the Product Percent of Parent, which displays as 1.#INF. This is a divide-by-zero error that the browser is attempting to format. The All member for the Product Category attribute hierarchy doesn't have a parent, so the value for that parent is "empty," which is treated as 0. The expression to calculate the percent of parent must behave differently for the top member of a hierarchy than it does for all the other members. To do that, you use the IIF function to check whether the value of the denominator tuple is empty.

9. Click the Calculations tab, and then change the expression to look like this:

```
iif(IsEmpty(([Measures].[Reseller Sales Amount],[Product].[Product
Category].Parent)),1,([Measures].[Reseller Sales Amount])/([Measures].[Reseller Sales
Amount],[Product].[Product Category].Parent)
```

   This expression checks to see if there is a value for the parent of the current member. If the parent value is empty, the expression returns 1. If there is a parent value, then the expression returns the calculated value for the percent of parent.

> **Note** Rather than test for an empty value, you may prefer to test for when the current member is at the All level of the hierarchy. The expression *[Product].[Product Category].CurrentMember.Level.Name* returns the level name of the current product. For the All level, it will be equal to "(All)". Alternatively, the expression *[Product].[Product Category].CurrentMember.Level.Ordinal* returns the level number of the current product. For the All level, it will be equal to 0.

10. Deploy the project, open the browser when the project deploys, and then click Reconnect.

    The grid looks like this:

Category	Subcategory	Product Percent of Parent	Category Percent of Total	Reseller Sales Amount
⊟ Bikes	⊞ Mountain Bikes	39.96%	32.93%	$26,492,684
	⊞ Road Bikes	44.28%	36.49%	$29,358,207
	⊞ Touring Bikes	15.76%	12.99%	$10,451,490
	Total	82.41%	82.41%	$66,302,382
⊞ Components		14.67%	14.67%	$11,799,077
⊞ Clothing		2.21%	2.21%	$1,777,841
⊞ Accessories		0.71%	0.71%	$571,298
Grand Total		100.00%	100.00%	$80,450,597

Querying with MDX

An MDX query statement is different from an MDX expression. An expression is a formula that calculates a single value. A query is a command that populates a report with many values from a cube. The cube browser in the Cube Designer, like many client applications used with Analysis Services, generates MDX queries to retrieve values from the cube. You can use these tools to create reports without writing any MDX queries of your own. Unless you're a developer creating a custom report generator, you'll probably have little occasion to write MDX query statements. So, why should you learn how to create an MDX query statement? The most interesting MDX expressions involve creating a single result based on a large set of values from a cube. Those expressions, in effect, create a subquery behind the scenes. Learning how to create an MDX query will enable you to understand clearly what the subquery is doing when you create complex MDX expressions.

The purpose of an MDX query is to extract values from an OLAP cube into a report. While a cube has dimensions, a report does not. It has axes (typically, a row axis, a column axis, and a filter axis). An axis can include labels from more than one dimension. A cube contains all possible values for all members of all attribute hierarchies of all dimensions. A report contains only selected values from selected levels of selected attribute hierarchies of selected dimensions. An MDX query statement consists of the instructions for extracting a report from a cube.

Executing MDX Queries

SQL Server Management Studio provides an interface for you to type an MDX query, run it, and see the results in a grid. The MDX query window includes a *metadata pane,* which allows you to browse the hierarchies and members of a cube, inserting dimension, attribute, and member names into the MDX expression.

If you write Structured Query Language (SQL) queries, you'll recognize the clauses used to create an MDX query: *SELECT*, *FROM*, and *WHERE*. The *SELECT* clause defines which members to include and where to place them—on rows or columns. The *FROM* clause names the cube, and the optional *WHERE* clause restricts values returned by the query to specific members.

In this procedure, you'll execute MDX queries to become familiar with the SQL Server Management Studio query interface and MDX query syntax.

Use SQL Server Management Studio to execute MDX queries

1. Start SQL Server Management Studio, click Cancel, click the Open File button, navigate to the C:\Documents and Settings\<username>\My Documents\Microsoft Press\as2005sbs\chap08 folder, double-click MDX Queries.mdx, and then click Connect to connect to the Analysis Server.
2. If necessary, select SSAS Step by Step in the Available Databases drop-down list on the toolbar, and click SSAS in the Cube list box in the MDX Query window.

   Your screen looks like this:

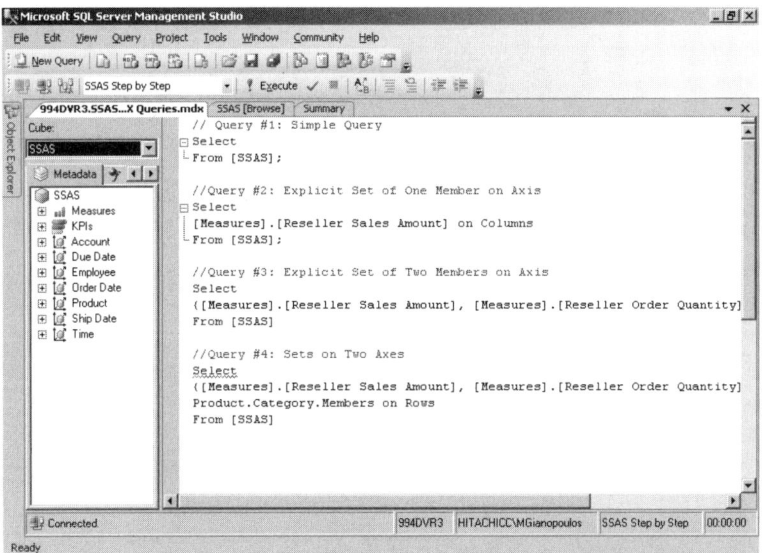

   In the MDX Query window, the SSAS cube metadata displays on the left in the metadata pane, where you inspect information in a selected cube. The MDX queries display on the right in the query pane. Several MDX queries have been saved in this one file for convenience. They can be executed together the way you can execute a series of SQL queries if you insert the GO command between queries. The bottom pane, which will appear after you execute an MDX query, is the results pane, which shows the output of an MDX query.

   Notice that you can add a comment to an MDX query simply by entering two adjacent slash characters (//), and MDX will ignore everything from that point to the end of the line. Comments can appear before or after the text of the query, and can even be inserted between lines of a query. Adding comments is particularly helpful when you have a long query in which the logic can be difficult to follow.

3. Highlight the text of Query #1, Select from SSAS, and then click the Execute button in the toolbar.

   Your screen looks like this:

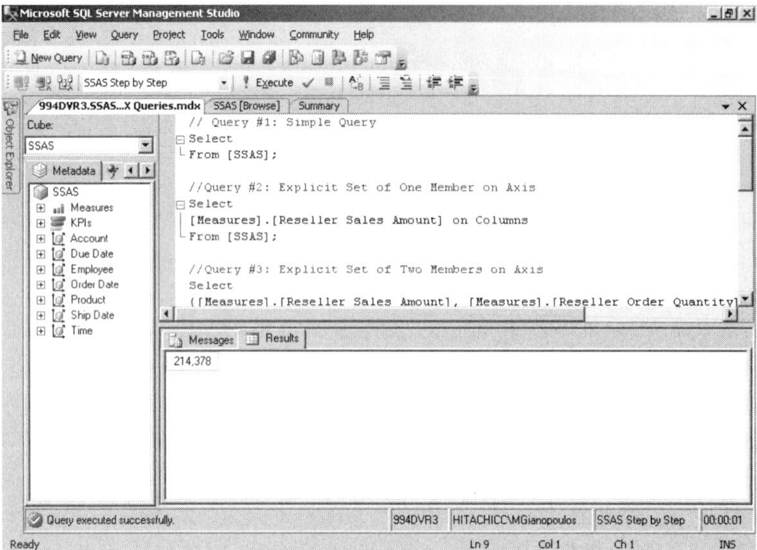

   A single number–214,378–appears in the results pane. This number is the total of Reseller Order Quantity for the entire cube.

   This first query is the simplest possible query you can execute. Since no default measure is specified for the cube, MDX selects the first measure defined in the cube which you can see on the Cube Structure tab in the designer. Additionally, because the query does not specify a member from any dimension, the query uses the default member from each attribute hierarchy in each dimension, which currently is the All member, to create the tuple that retrieves this single value from the cube. A default member exists for every attribute hierarchy in a cube whether or not you explicitly define one. By default, the default member is the All member of an attribute hierarchy, but you can set a different member by providing a value for an attribute's *DefaultMember* property.

   You can create more interesting queries by adding sets of members to the column or row axis. MDX has a number of functions that return sets, which you'll use later in this chapter. But first, take a look the next query, which illustrates how to use a specific measure. This one measure is a set–a set with one member.

4. Highlight the text of Query #2 and then click the Execute button in the toolbar.

Your screen looks like this:

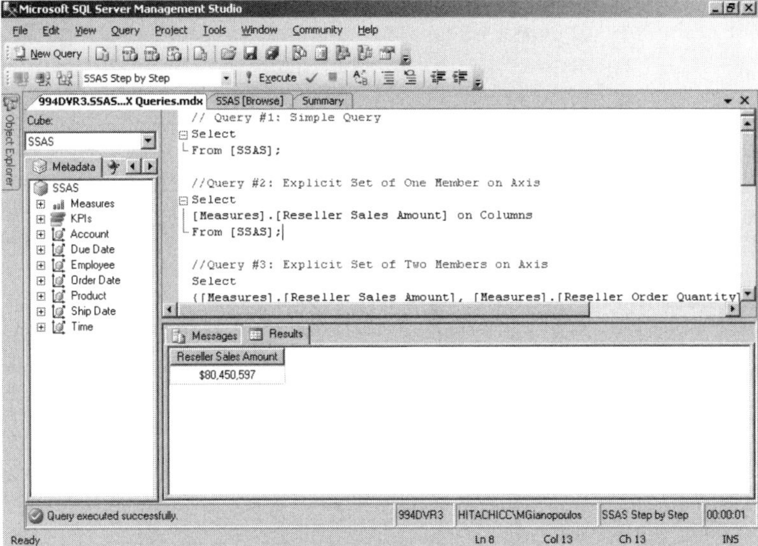

You can add other members from the Measures dimension to this set, but you must enclose the set in braces ({}). The braces aren't necessary when you use set functions, but they become necessary when you create a set that includes more than one member.

5. Highlight the text of Query #3, and then click the Execute button in the toolbar.

   Your screen looks like this:

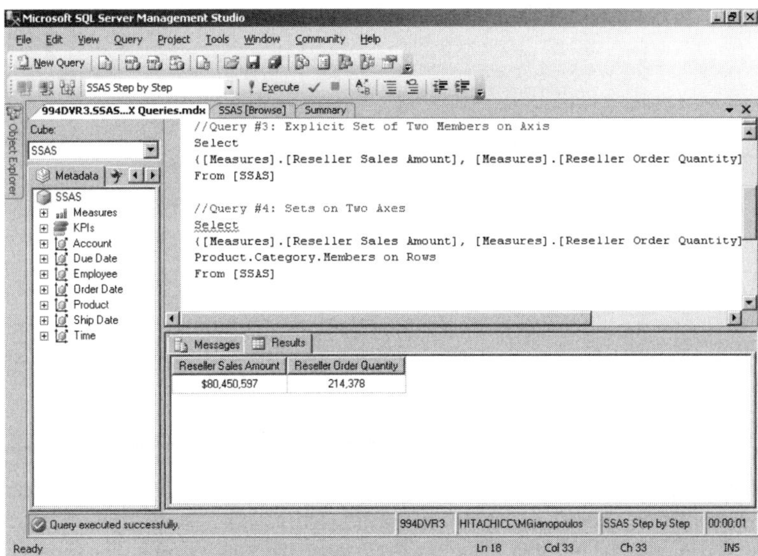

The set on the column axis consists of two positions. Each position corresponds to a tuple, and each tuple contains a single member. If you want, you can add parentheses around each tuple, writing the set as {([Measures].[Reseller Sales Amount]), ([ ] ([Measures].[Reseller Order Quantity])}, to show that each member is a separate tuple within the set. If the first tuple in a set consists of a single member, each subsequent tuple in that set must be a member of the same dimension.

Note You can also manually create a set that includes tuples with multiple members. For example, the following is a legitimate set and could be placed on an axis in an MDX query: *{([Reseller Sales Amount],[Bikes]), ([Reseller Order Quantity], [Clothing])}*. It's unusual, however, to create a set with constant member names in multimember tuples. You're much more likely to use the *CrossJoin* function (described later in this chapter) to create a set with multiple members in each tuple.

You can also add a set to the row axis. In MDX, if you create a query that has only one axis, it must be the column axis. If you create two axes, one must be the column axis and one must be the row axis, although it doesn't matter in which order they appear within the query.

6. Highlight the text of Query #4, and then click the Execute button in the toolbar.

   Your screen looks like this:

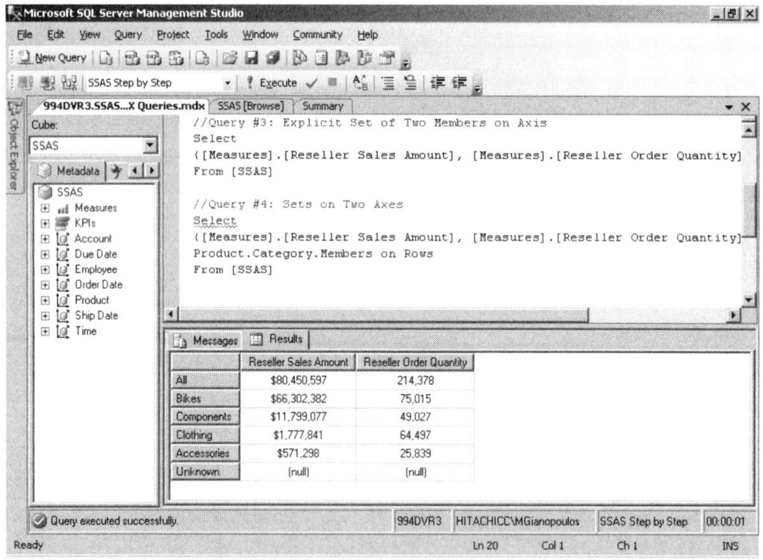

	Reseller Sales Amount	Reseller Order Quantity
All	$80,450,597	214,378
Bikes	$66,302,382	75,015
Components	$11,799,077	49,027
Clothing	$1,777,841	64,497
Accessories	$571,298	25,839
Unknown	(null)	(null)

Note The terms *COLUMNS* and *ROWS* are simply aliases for the true names of the axes, Axis(0), and Axis(1), respectively. The underlying names make it clearer to understand why a single-axis report must include a COLUMNS axis but not a ROWS axis. Technically, an MDX query can have up to 63 axes, with alias names for the first few. There are, however, essentially no situations in which it's necessary to use more than two heading axes for a report.

On the row axis, the *Members* function displays only the members from the Category attribute hierarchy of the Product dimension. Even though the categories are not indented, all the members of the Category hierarchy are in the set, even when there is no value for the intersection with the specified members on the opposite axis.

Because each dimension is composed of one or more attribute hierarchies, you must include both the dimension and hierarchy name when using the *Members* function. The exception is the Measures dimension, which does not contain a hierarchy.

The terminology of an MDX query centers on sets, tuples, and members. A set includes one or more tuples, and a tuple includes one or more members. Sets appear on the axes. Tuples appear either in a set (on a column or row axis), or in the *WHERE* clause to create the filter axis. Aside from the cube name in the *FROM* clause, a member is the only object from a cube that appears directly in an MDX query.

Working with Basic MDX Queries

As you become more proficient with MDX queries, you will discover many useful functions are available to create and manipulate sets. The MDX query window in SQL Server Management Studio includes a list of functions organized by category in the metadata pane. You can drag and drop functions from this list if you need help with the function syntax.

In this procedure, you'll use the *Children* and *CrossJoin* functions to create sets for an MDX query.

Use sets and set functions in MDX queries

1. Highlight the MDX query for Query #4, press Ctrl+C to copy it, click at the end of the query, press Enter twice, and then press Ctrl+V to paste a copy of the query at the bottom of the query window.
2. Move the insertion point to the line above the word Select, and type // **My Query**.

> **Note** In addition to using two sequential slash characters (//) to comment the remainder of the line, you can also use two sequential hyphen characters (--) for the same purpose. If you want to create a comment that either is a partial line or spans multiple lines, you begin the comment with a slash followed by an asterisk (/*) and end it with an asterisk followed by a slash (*/).

3. Replace Category in this new query with **[Product Category]**, highlight the text of the query, and then click Execute.

Your screen looks like this:

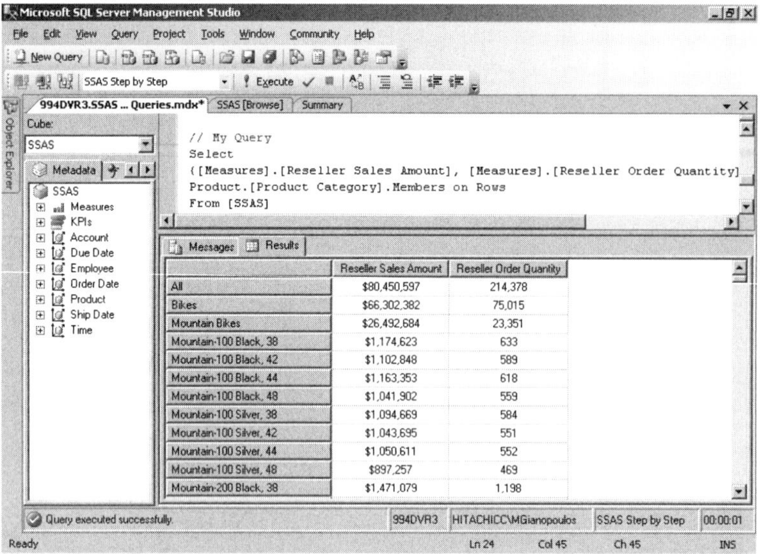

There are more members in the Product Category hierarchy than in the Category hierarchy. Because there are multiple levels within the Product Category hierarchy, you can use hierarchical set functions to reduce the number of members to place on an axis. One such set function is *Children*, which requires you to specify one member, and returns a set of that member's children.

4. In your query, highlight Product.[Product Category].Members, and then press Delete.
5. Click the Functions tab in the metadata pane to the left of the MDX Query window, expand the Navigation folder, and then drag CHILDREN to the position that previously contained the text you just deleted.

   The token that precedes the *Children* function name is *«Member»*. A member has children. You need to name a member explicitly to use this function.

6. Delete the Product.*«Member»* token, click the Metadata tab in the metadata pane, expand the Product dimension object, expand Product Category, expand Category, and then drag Bikes to the position in front of .Children.

   Remember that &[1] is the key value of the Bikes category, which is the preferred syntax in an MDX query when there is a possibility that the name of a member might change later.

7. Highlight the query, and then click the Execute button.

Your screen looks like this:

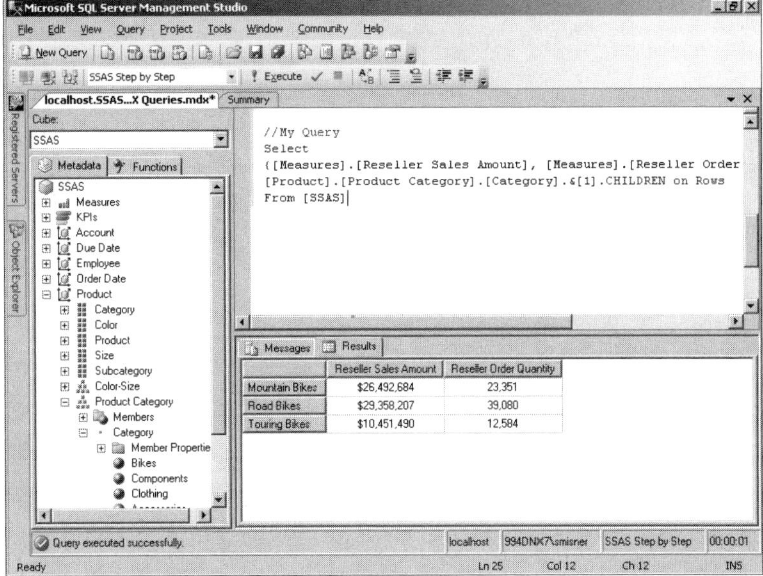

On the row axis, the *Children* function displays only the children of Bikes. If you also want to include the Bikes category, you must add it to the set on the row axis. So far, you've learned how to use tuples, members, and set functions to create a set. Now you will see that you can combine members and set functions to create a single set.

8. Position the cursor in front of [Product].[Product Category].[Category].[&1], and type { (open brace).

   Remember that braces must be used to identify a set when the set contains more than a single member or a single set function.

9. Drag Bikes from the Metadata pane to the position behind the brace ({), and then type , (comma).

10. Position the cursor behind [Product].[Product Category].[Category].[&1].CHILDREN, and then type } (a closing brace).

    The query now looks like this:

```
//My Query
Select
{[Measures].[Reseller Sales Amount], [Measures].[Reseller Order Quantity]} on Columns,
{[Product].[Product Category].[Category].&[1],[Product].[Product
Category].[Category].&[1].CHILDREN} on Rows
From [SSAS]
```

11. Highlight the query and execute it.

Your screen looks like this:

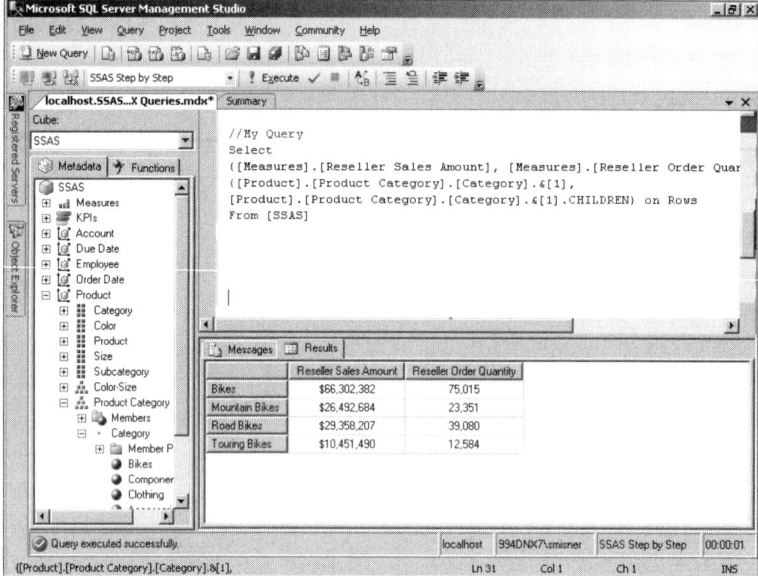

The order of the members that display on the row axis is determined by the order of the members specified in the set. You could place Bikes at the bottom of the set in the results grid by changing the set expression to `{[Product].[Product Category].[Category].&[1].CHILDREN, [Product].[Product Category].[Category].&[1]}`.

Up to this point, you have worked with only one dimension in a set. In an MDX query, you can use the *CrossJoin* function to combine two sets from two dimensions into a single set that you can put onto a single axis.

12. Position the cursor in the first position on the line beneath Select, and then type **CrossJoin(Time.[Calendar Year].[All].Children,**.
13. Position the cursor after the closing brace of the measures set, and then type).

    The query now looks like this:

```
//My Query
Select
CrossJoin([Time].[Calendar Year].[All].Children,{[Measures].[Reseller Sales Amount],
[Measures].[Reseller Order Quantity]}) on Columns,
{[Product].[Product Category].[Category].&[1],[Product].[Product
Category].[Category].&[1].CHILDREN} on Rows
From [SSAS]
```

    The *CrossJoin* function combines two sets into one. In this example, the first set is created by using the *Children* function and the second set consists of explicit members. The new set created by the *CrossJoin* contains a tuple for each combination of members from each of the two sets.

14. Execute the query.

Your screen looks like this:

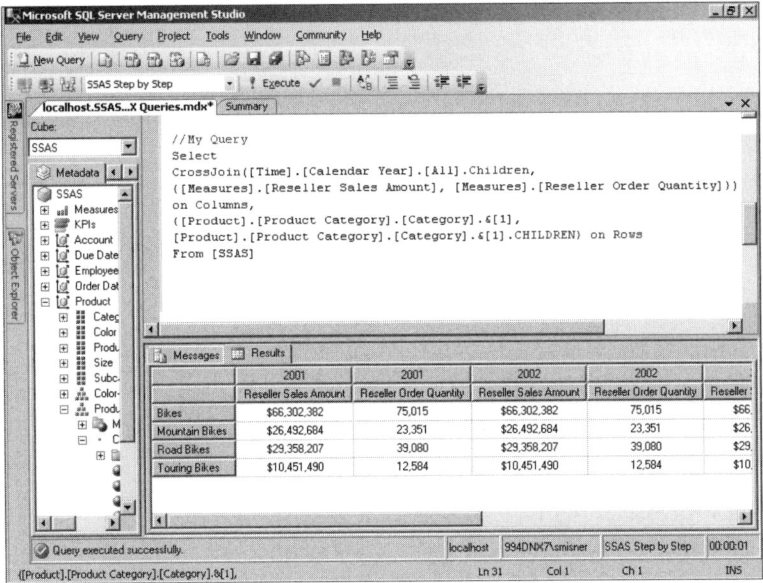

The column axis contains a set with eight positions. Each position is a tuple that includes one member from each of two dimensions. The eight positions correspond to all the possible combinations of the two measures and the four years.

The *CrossJoin* function is a powerful way to create reports that compare multiple dimensions. Because the function is so powerful, it's easy to create sets that are extremely large, particularly when combined with the *Members* function of multiple dimensions.

Designing Custom Members

Earlier in this chapter, you learned how to create a calculated measure–a special type of calculated member that is a member of the Measures dimension. This is the most frequent type of calculated member, but you can also create a calculated member of any dimension. When you create a calculated member of a nonmeasure dimension, you must specify where in the dimension hierarchy you want the new member to go. Suppose, for example, that you want to create a new member that shows the total Reseller Sales Amount for Accessories, Clothing, and Components–that is, the total sales for all categories other than Bikes. You can use the MDX *Sum()* function, one of several aggregate functions available, to create a new value from the sum of these individual categories. You then need to specify a parent for this new calculated member so that it can be properly associated with a dimension and an attribute hierarchy.

Creating a Calculated Member Using a Set-Based Function

The *Sum* (or *Aggregate*) function is frequently used to create a calculated member on a nonmeasure dimension. You can also use the *Sum* function to create a new calculated measure.

This is often done to create a cumulative total. You are not limited to these functions, however. In the Statistical folder on the Functions tab in the metadata pane, you can review the available functions that you can use to aggregate values for a set of members.

In this procedure, you'll add a calculated member that computes an average of the product categories.

Use the *Avg* function

1. In Visual Studio, click the Calculations tab of the SSAS Cube Designer.
2. Click the New Calculated Member button on the toolbar, and type **[Product Category Average]** in the Name box.
3. In the Parent Hierarchy drop-down list, expand Product, click Category, and then click OK.
4. Click the Change button to the right of the Parent Member box, Click All, and then click OK.

> **Note** If you receive an error, close the dialog box, click the Reconnect button, and then retry the step.

Specifying the All member of the Category hierarchy as the parent of the new member puts the new member at the leaf level of the Category hierarchy—the same level as Bikes, Components, Clothing, Accessories, and Unknown.

5. In the Calculation Tools pane, click the Functions tab, expand the Statistical folder, and then drag AVG into the Expressions box.

   The Calculations form looks like this:

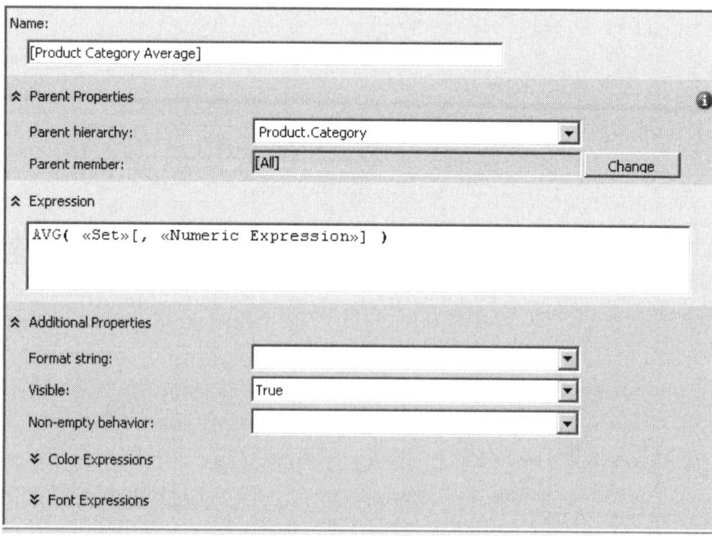

The *Avg* function syntax shows two arguments. The first argument, *«Set»*, is required; this is the argument you use to specify which dimension members to include in a set. You can use any valid set expression, such as explicit members, tuples, or a set function. The second argument, *«Numeric Expression»*, is surrounded by square brackets, indicating that it is optional. If you create a member on a nonmeasure dimension (such as Product Category Average), you'll almost never use the *«Numeric Expression»* argument. If you create a member on the Measures dimension (which you'll do later in this chapter), you'll almost always use the *«Numeric Expression»* argument. The *«Numeric Expression»* argument tells you which measure to use as the base for the new measure.

6. Highlight *«Set», [«Numeric Expression»]*, press Delete, click the Metadata tab in the Calculation Tools pane, drag the All member of the Category attribute to the same position, and then type **.Children** behind [Product].[Category].[All] to create a set expression.

   The expression now looks like this:

```
AVG([Product].[Category].[All].Children)
```

7. Deploy the project, click the Browser tab when deployment finishes, and then click the Reconnect button on the toolbar.

8. Click anywhere in the browser grid, click the Clear Results button in the toolbar, drag Category to the rows axis, and then drag the measures Reseller Order Quantity and Reseller Sales Amount into the grid.

   The grid looks like this:

Category	Reseller Order Quantity	Reseller Sales Amount
Bikes	75,015	$66,302,382
Components	49,027	$11,799,077
Clothing	64,497	$1,777,841
Accessories	25,839	$571,298
Product Category Average	53,595	$20,112,649
Grand Total	214,378	$80,450,597

   Think through the expression that generates the $20,112,649 value for the Product Category Average of Reseller Sales Amount in the grid. The column axis supplies the member from the Measures dimension (Reseller Sales Amount), and the row axis supplies the member from the Category hierarchy (Product Category Average). The Product Category Average member is a calculated member. That calculated member's expression creates a tuple for each leaf member of the Category hierarchy that has a nonempty value: (Bikes, Reseller Sales Amount), (Components, Reseller Sales Amount), (Clothing, Reseller Sales Amount), and (Accessories, Reseller Sales Amount). The values resulting from this set of four tuples are summed together and then divided by the number of members in the set. The Grand Total for the Reseller Sales Amount also represents the sum of the four tuples. Therefore, you can divide this number, $80,450,597, by 4 to verify the Product Category Average for the Reseller Sales Amount is $20,112,649.

   You can use a similar approach to verify the average value calculated for the Reseller Order Quantity measure. When you create a calculated member on a nonmeasure dimension, that member will, by definition, intersect with all the members of the Measures dimension.

Each of those measures already has an aggregation function defined. Using the *Aggregate* function takes advantage of that previously defined aggregation function.

Creating Cumulative Calculations

Almost all OLAP cubes contain a time dimension. That's because almost all business activities take place over time, and it's always useful to compare where one *is* with where one *was*. Not surprisingly, many business reporting requirements involve the use of time, and consequently, MDX supports a large number of functions that facilitate analyzing values with time. Calculating the cumulative values from the beginning of a particular time period, for example, is an extremely common MDX task.

In this procedure, you'll add a calculated measure that computes a cumulative total across a specified range of time for Reseller Order Quantity, first by using the *Sum* function and then by using the *PeriodsToDate* function.

Compare the *Sum* and *PeriodsToDate* functions

1. Click the Calculations tab, and then click New Calculated Member on the toolbar.
2. Name the member **[Cumulative Order Quantity]**.

   Cumulative measures belong in the Measures dimension, so you will leave the default Parent Hierarchy as Measures.
3. In the Calculation Tools pane, click the Functions tab, and from the Statistical Functions list, drag SUM into the Expression box.

   Notice that the syntax for the *Sum* function is similar to the syntax for the *Average* function: SUM(*«Set»*[, *«Numeric Expression»*]).
4. Replace *«Set»* with [Order Date].[Calendar Year].&[2001]:[Order Date].[Calendar Year] .CurrentMember.

   This expression creates a set that begins with the 2001 member of the Order Date dimension and ends with a year for the current position in the results grid. You use a colon (:) between two members to indicate a range of members.
5. Replace [, *«Numeric Expression»*] with **, [Measures].[Reseller Order Quantity]**.
6. Select "#,#" in the Format String drop-down list.

The Calculations form looks like this:

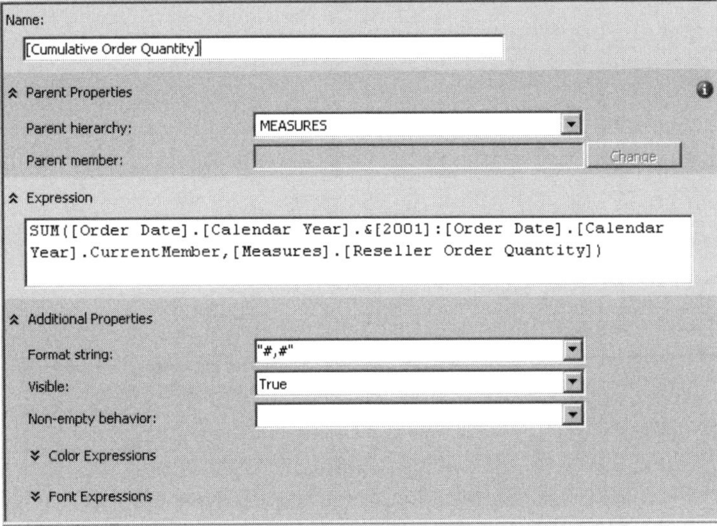

7. Deploy the project. When it is deployed, click the Browser tab, click Reconnect, and then click Clear Results.
8. Drag Reseller Order Quantity and Cumulative Order Quantity from Measures into the grid.
9. From the Order Date dimension, drag the Order Date.Calendar Year attribute into the grid as rows.

   The grid looks like this:

Calendar Year	Reseller Order Quantity	Cumulative Order Quantity
2001	10,835	10,835
2002	58,241	69,076
2003	100,172	169,248
2004	45,130	214,378
Grand Total	214,378	#VALUE!

   You can see the yearly values for Reseller Order Quantity in each row along with the cumulative values. An error displays in the Grand Total cell because there is no CurrentMember for the Order Date dimension related to this cell. For a production database, you should modify the expression to avoid this error condition using an IIF statement, as you learned earlier in this chapter.

   This expression, however, is limited in its usage since it will not work with the Calendar hierarchy, providing you with cumulative values for any level of the hierarchy–year, quarter, or month. To create a more flexible expression, you can use the *PeriodsToDate* function.

10. Click the Calculations tab, and then change the expression to look like this:

```
SUM(
PeriodsToDate([Order Date].[Calendar].CurrentMember.Parent.Level, [Order
Date].[Calendar].CurrentMember),
[Measures].[Reseller Order Quantity] )
```

11. Deploy the project, wait for deployment to finish, click the Browser tab, and then click Reconnect.

12. Drag the Calendar Year hierarchy from the grid, and then drag the Calendar hierarchy from the Order Date dimension to the rows axis of the grid.

    The values computed for the Cumulative Order Quantity are the same because the *PeriodsToDate* function creates a set much like the range you created when using the *Sum* function.

13. Click the Calendar Year caption in the grid to select it, right-click, and then click Expand Items.

    The beginning member of the set created by using the *PeriodsToDate* function is the first member that shares the same parent as the ending member. For example, in the Calendar hierarchy of the Order Date dimension, a current member of quarter 2 in 2002 would produce the set 1:2. (2002 is the comment parent.) A current member of June would produce the set April:June. (The quarter 2 is the common parent.) The level specified in the *PeriodsToDate* function resets the cumulative total to zero when the parent of the current member is different from the parent of the previous member.

    If you want to go back to a different common ancestor, simply specify the level of the ancestor you want. For example, if you replace *[Order Date].[Calendar].CurrentMember.Parent.Level* with *[Order Date].[Calendar].CalendarYear*, then a current member of June produces the range January:August. In this case, a change in the Year member resets the cumulative total to zero.

Working with MDX Scripts

An *MDX script* is not only a collection of MDX expressions or statements that represent cube calculations, but also a definition of how those calculations are processed. Each time you add a calculation to the cube, you are adding a new MDX statement to the cube's MDX script. Rearranging these statements changes the effect of those calculations. In addition, you can add special MDX statements called *script assignments* to deliberately override specified cell values or to modify cell properties such as color.

Managing the Sequence of Calculations

When you have many calculations in a single cube, it is likely that two different calculations can affect the same cell. Sometimes the results of these two calculations will be different, but the result of only one of the calculations displays. Which one gets precedence? You can manually reorganize the cube's MDX script to control which calculation is used when there are competing calculations for the same cell, or you can use the Script Organizer in the Cube Designer to rearrange calculations to produce the correct results.

In this procedure, you'll examine the effect of changing the relative position of the Average Reseller Sales and Product Category Average calculations.

Organize scripts

1. Click the Calculations tab, click the New Calculated Member button, and type **[Average Reseller Sales]** in the Name box.

2. In the Expression box, type **[Measures].[Reseller Sales Amount]/[Measures].[Reseller Order Quantity]**.

3. Type **"$#,#"** in the Format String drop-down list and then select Reseller Order Quantity in the Non-Empty Behavior drop-down list.

4. In the Script Organizer pane, click [Product Category Average], and then click the Move Down button in the toolbar repeatedly until this calculation displays beneath the [Average Reseller Sales] calculation.

5. Deploy the project, click the Browser tab when deployment is complete, and then click Reconnect.

6. Click anywhere in the grid, click the Clear Results button in the toolbar, and then drag objects from the metadata tree to the browser to display the measures Reseller Sales Amount, Reseller Order Quantity, and Average Reseller Sales with the Category attribute of the Product dimension on the row axis.

   Your screen looks like this:

Category	Reseller Sales Amount	Reseller Order Quantity	Average Reseller Sales
Bikes	$66,302,382	75,015	$884
Components	$11,799,077	49,027	$241
Clothing	$1,777,841	64,497	$28
Accessories	$571,298	25,839	$22
Product Category Average	$20,112,649	53,595	$294
Grand Total	$80,450,597	214,378	$375

Notice that the Product Category Average for Average Reseller Sales is 294, but the Average Reseller Sales Grand Total is 375. Why are these numbers different when they both represent averages? How are these averages calculated?

First, consider the Average Reseller Sales expression: *[Measures].[Reseller Sales Amount]/[Measures].[Reseller Order Quantity]*. In the browser, the numerator of the expression is the tuple that combines the current Category member with Reseller Sales Amount and the denominator is the tuple that combines the current Category member with Reseller Order Quantity. Therefore, the expression that computes the Grand Total for the Average Reseller Sales is *([Product].[Category].[All], [Measures].[Reseller Sales Amount)/([Product].[Category].[All], [Measures].[Reseller Order Quantity)*. Replacing these tuples with cell values, the calculation is 80,450,597 / 214,378, which returns a value of 375.

Earlier in this chapter, you verified that the Product Category Average for the Reseller Sales Amount is equal to the Grand Total divided by the number of categories or 80,450,597 / 4 = 20,112,649. This value is returned by the tuple *([Product].[Category].[Product Category Average], [Measures].[Reseller Sales Amount])*. Similarly, the Reseller Order Quantity for Product Category Average, which can be expressed as the tuple *([Product].[Category].[Product Category Average], [Measures].[Order Quantity])*, should be computed by dividing the Grand Total of 214,378 by 4 to get the result of 53,595. You can see these results correctly displayed in the grid.

If you were to apply the same logic described for computing the Average Reseller Sales Grand Total to the Product Category Average of Average Reseller Sales, you would build an expression like this: *([Product].[Category].[Product Category Average], [Measures].[Reseller Sales Amount)/([Product].[Category].[Product Category Average], [Measures].[Reseller Order Quantity)*. This expression evaluates as 20,112,649 / 53,595, which equals 375. Yet this is not the value displayed. Why not?

There is another possible tuple for this cell intersection of Product Category Average and Average Reseller Sales. The expression for Average Reseller Sales at this intersection looks like this: *([Product].[Category].[Product Category Average], [Measures].[Average Reseller Sales]) / ([Product].[Category].[Product Category Average], [Measures].[Average Reseller Sales])*.

Remember that the Product Category Average calculation sums up the tuples for each category and the current measure. When Average Reseller Sales is the current measure, then the expression for Product Category Average looks like this:

([Product].[Category].[Bikes], [Average Reseller Sales]) + ([Product].[Category].[Components], [Average Reseller Sales]) + ([Product].[Category].[Clothing], [Average Reseller Sales]) + ([Product].[Category].[Accessories], [Average Reseller Sales]) / 4.

Looking at the browser, you can see the intersection of each category with Average Reseller Sales to resolve the expression as 884 + 241 + 28 + 22 / 4, which equals 294 when rounded to the whole number. Thus, the value displayed in the intersection of Product Category Average and Average Reseller Sales is using this second expression which computes each category's average sales first and then divides by the number of categories.

When you use calculations that compute average values, you get different results when the average is based on a calculated total as compared to an average based on another average. Which calculation is correct? The answer really depends on what the business users expect the calculation to return when two calculations are possible for a single cell. In this case, if you want to display the average of the average–375–you'll need to change the order of the calculations.

7. Click the Calculations tab. In the Script Organizer pane, drag the Product Category Average calculation and drop it above the Average Reseller Sales calculation.

   The sequence of calculations in the Script Organizer determines the order in which the calculated members are evaluated. For any cell, Analysis Services only evaluates the last calculation in the Script Organizer that affects that cell. Therefore, for the intersection of Product Category Average and Average Reseller Sales, the calculation will now be based on the average sales of all categories divided by the average order quantities of all categories.

8. Deploy the project, and when it's finished, click the Browser tab, then click Reconnect.

The grid looks like this:

Category	Reseller Sales Amount	Reseller Order Quantity	Average Reseller Sales
Bikes	$66,302,382	75,015	$884
Components	$11,799,077	49,027	$241
Clothing	$1,777,841	64,497	$28
Accessories	$571,298	25,839	$22
Product Category Average	$20,112,649	53,595	$375
Grand Total	$80,450,597	214,378	$375

Notice that now the Product Category Average and the Grand Total for Average Reseller Sales both display $375. This scenario illustrates how the use of calculated members can get tricky. You must understand how business users need the data to be calculated when there is an intersection of calculated members, and then ensure that the order of the calculations in the Script Organizer produces correct results.

Adding a Script Assignment

When you first create a cube, a default MDX script that defines calculations in the cube is also created. This script is identified by the Calculate command that appears first on the Calculation tab of the cube designer. You add to this script every time you create a new calculated member or a named set. This script tells the server to calculate the entire cube on the first pass. The MDX expressions and statements that you add to the MDX script then get processed in the order in which they appear in the Script Organizer.

You can use the debugging features in Visual Studio to observe the interaction of calculations during execution of the MDX script. As you step through the script, you use the debugger's cube browser to slice and dice data or to review the calculated members at each step. You can also make changes to the script while debugging to correct problems that you find.

In this procedure, you'll add a script assignment to hide measure values for a group of employees–Abbas and employees managed by Abbas–and then debug the MDX script.

Override cube values with a script assignment

1. Click the Calculations tab, and then click the Script View button on the toolbar.

   Your screen looks like this:

```
/*
The CALCULATE command controls the aggregation of leaf cells in the cube.
If the CALCULATE command is deleted or modified, the data within the cube is affectec
You should edit this command only if you manually specify how the cube is aggregated.
*/
CALCULATE;
CREATE MEMBER CURRENTCUBE.[MEASURES].[Category Percent of Total]
 AS ([Measures].[Reseller Sales Amount])/([Measures].[Reseller Sales Amount],[Product
FORMAT_STRING = "Percent",
NON_EMPTY_BEHAVIOR = ( [Reseller Sales Amount] ),
VISIBLE = 1;
CREATE MEMBER CURRENTCUBE.[MEASURES].[Product Percent of Parent]
 AS iif(IsEmpty(([Measures].[Reseller Sales Amount],[Product].[Product Category].Pare
FORMAT_STRING = "Percent",
NON_EMPTY_BEHAVIOR = ( [Reseller Sales Amount] ),
VISIBLE = 1;
CREATE MEMBER CURRENTCUBE.[MEASURES].[Cumulative Order Quantity]
 AS SUM(
PeriodsToDate([Order Date].[Calendar].CurrentMember.Parent.Level, [Order Date].[Caler
[Measures].[Reseller Order Quantity] ),
FORMAT_STRING = "#,#",
VISIBLE = 1 ;
```

Each calculation that you created in the Form View is a separate MDX statement in the MDX script that you see here. Notice that the sequence of each calculation in the Script Organizer corresponds to the sequence of each calculation in the script.

2. Position your cursor at the end of the *CALCULATE;* command, press Enter to create a new line, and then type **Scope([Measures].Members);**.

   The *Scope* statement is used to define a *subcube*—that is, a specific collection of cube cells. Any MDX statements that you include with the Scope statement will apply only to this subcube.

3. Press Enter, type **Descendants(**, and then navigate through the cube metadata tree from the Employee dimension to the Employees hierarchy to Members, Sanchez, Welcker, and finally to Abbas. Drag Abbas to the right of the parenthesis, and then type **)=NULL;**.

4. Press Enter and type **End Scope;**.

   The complete MDX statement looks like this:

```
Scope([Measures].Members);
Descendants([Employee].[Employees].&[294])=NULL;
End Scope;
```

   The effect of this script assignment is to replace any measure values that would normally display for the Abbas member (with key value 294) and the descendants of this member with a null value. This technique is useful when there are portions of the cube that you *never* want anyone to be able to see.

5. Deploy the project. When this operation is finished, click the Browse tab, click the Reconnect button, clear the grid, and then place all measures in the grid with the Employees hierarchy on rows. Right-click the CEO caption and click Show Empty Cells. Drill down from Sanchez to each lower level until you locate the Abbas member, then drill down one more level.

   The grid looks like this:

CEO	Manager	Supervisor	Individual Contributor	Order Quantity	Reseller Sales Amount	Internet Order Quantity	Internet Sales Amou
⊟ Sánchez	⊞ Bradley					60,398	$29,358,6
	⊞ Bradley					60,398	$29,358,6
	⊞ Duffy					60,398	$29,358,6
	⊞ Hamilton					60,398	$29,358,6
	⊞ Krebs					60,398	$29,358,6
	⊞ Norman					60,398	$29,358,6
	⊞ Norman					60,398	$29,358,6
	⊞ Trenary					60,398	$29,358,6
	⊟ Welcker	⊟ Abbas	⊞ Tsoflias				
			Total				
		⊞ Alberts		49223	15535946.2559	60398	29358677.22069
		⊞ Jiang		160207	63320315.349699	60398	29358677.22069
		Total		209,430	$78,856,262	60,398	$29,358,6
	Total			209,430	$78,856,262	60,398	$29,358,6

You can see that none of the measures for Abbas are visible because the script assignment replaced the cube values with nulls. However, a side effect of this script assignment is that the grand total for each measure is now incorrect because the aggregation of each measure considers the Abbas and descendant members to be nulls. You can step through the script using the debugger to see how this happens.

6. Click the Calculations tab, and then, on the Debug menu, click Start Debugging.

   Your screen looks like this:

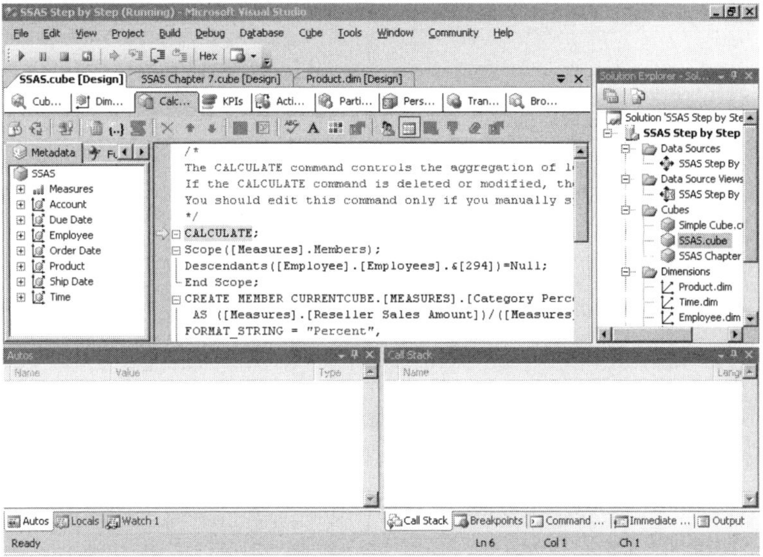

> **Tip** If necessary, autohide the Autos and Call Stack windows so that you can see the debugging browser.

You can now step through the MDX script to view the effect of each statement in the debugging browser. You can even drop objects into the grid on the PivotTable pane at the bottom of the screen to observe the impact on values as you step through the MDX script. You can also work with four different MDX query windows to issue queries that return the current results of the cube based on the current execution status of the MDX script.

7. In the Metadata pane, expand the Employee dimension, drag Employees to the rows axis in the debugging browser, and then drag the Measures object to the totals area.
8. On rows, expand Sanchez, and then expand Welcker.

   Notice that so far, the only calculation available is Unique Customers which, as a distinct count measure, is treated separately. Since you have not executed the MDX script, the calculations defined in this script have not yet affected cube values and aggregated values have not yet been computed.
9. Click the Step Over button in the Debug toolbar. To view the Debug toolbar, click Toolbars from the View menu, and then select Debug.

   The first calculation in the script is highlighted and aggregated values now display in the PivotTable grid.

> **Note** As an alternative to stepping through calculations one by one, you can add a breakpoint to one or more calculations, and then click the Start button to run all calculations between your current position in the script and the next breakpoint.

10. Click the Step Over button twice more.

    The grid looks like this:

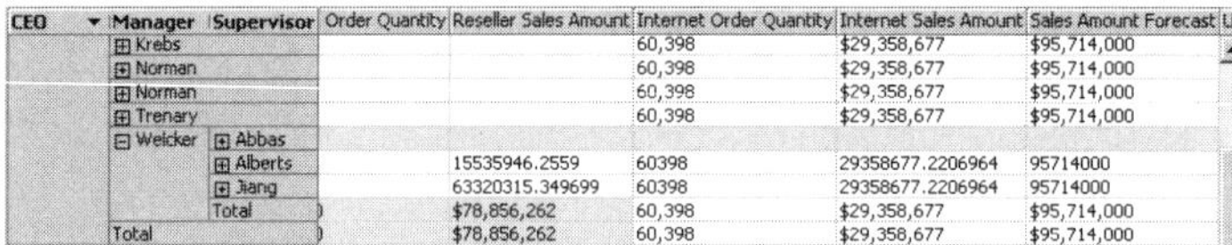

CEO	Manager	Supervisor	Order Quantity	Reseller Sales Amount	Internet Order Quantity	Internet Sales Amount	Sales Amount Forecast
	Krebs				60,398	$29,358,677	$95,714,000
	Norman				60,398	$29,358,677	$95,714,000
	Norman				60,398	$29,358,677	$95,714,000
	Trenary				60,398	$29,358,677	$95,714,000
	Welcker	Abbas					
		Alberts		15535946.2559	60398	29358677.2206964	95714000
		Jiang		63320315.349699	60398	29358677.2206964	95714000
		Total	)	$78,856,262	60,398	$29,358,677	$95,714,000
	Total		)	$78,856,262	60,398	$29,358,677	$95,714,000

    Now the measures for Abbas have been reset to null values.

11. Click the Step Over button until the debugger highlights the Calculate statement.
12. Between the Scope statement and the script assignment, type **Freeze;**.

    The complete MDX statement now looks like this:

```
Scope([Measures].Members);
Freeze;
Descendants([Employee].[Employees].&[294])=NULL;
End Scope;
```

    The *Freeze* statement locks in the results of the other calculations before replacing the values in the subcube. As you saw previously, the aggregated values are computed before the subcube values are set to null.

13. Click the Step Over button four times.

    The grid looks like this:

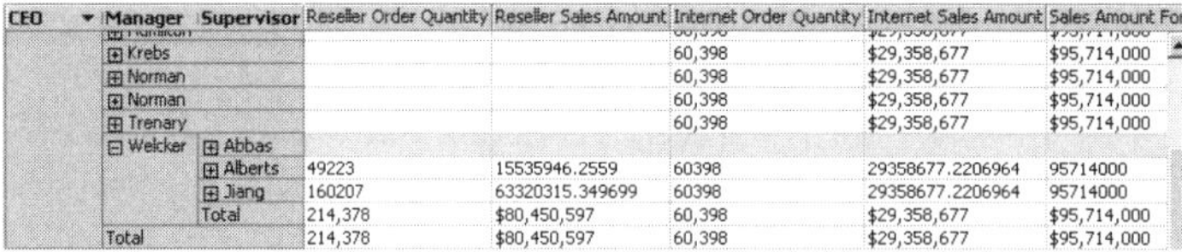

CEO	Manager	Supervisor	Reseller Order Quantity	Reseller Sales Amount	Internet Order Quantity	Internet Sales Amount	Sales Amount For
	Krebs				60,398	$29,358,677	$95,714,000
	Norman				60,398	$29,358,677	$95,714,000
	Norman				60,398	$29,358,677	$95,714,000
	Trenary				60,398	$29,358,677	$95,714,000
	Welcker	Abbas					
		Alberts	49223	15535946.2559	60398	29358677.2206964	95714000
		Jiang	160207	63320315.349699	60398	29358677.2206964	95714000
		Total	214,378	$80,450,597	60,398	$29,358,677	$95,714,000
	Total		214,378	$80,450,597	60,398	$29,358,677	$95,714,000

    This time, the aggregated values are unaffected. The total that you see is the correct aggregated value for all employees, not just the employees whose totals you can see. However, the Abbas values are set to null.

14. Click the Stop Debugging button in the Debug toolbar.
15. Click Yes to save the changes you made during debugging.

Developing Key Performance Indicators

Key performance indicators (KPIs) have captured the attention of the business world in recent years. A KPI measures the progress that a business is making toward meeting its goals. In Analysis Services, a KPI provides a visual representation of these comparative metrics over time, rather than just displaying the numbers. The visual representation is based upon your input and shows whether the progress against goals is positive, neutral, or negative, by using graphical images such as a stoplight with displays a green, yellow, or red light, according to the specified business rules.

Comparing Cube Values to Goals

You create a KPI in the Cube Designer. For each KPI, you develop expressions that calculate the KPI's value, goal, current status, and trend. The Value expression represents where the business is today and is sometimes referred to as actual when comparing it to a goal. The Goal expression defines the business goal, such as a constant value or perhaps a 20% increase in sales from the previous year. The Status expression measures how the Value compares to the Goal. Typically, you associate a visual icon, such as a stoplight or a gauge, to Status value to express whether or not the result is positive or negative. The Trend expression is used to compare the current Status value with the value of Status at a previous point in time. As with Status, you can assign a graphic to illustrate whether the trend is improving, declining, or not changing.

In this procedure, you'll add a KPI to highlight sales performance against a goal.

Create a simple key performance indicator

1. In the cube designer, click the KPIs tab, and then click the New KPI button on the toolbar.
2. In the Name box, type **Simple KPI.**

   Unlike with a calculated member, you can assign a name to a KPI that includes spaces without enclosing the name in square brackets. You cannot, however, include special characters like %, ?, or $ in the KPI name. For a complete list of invalid characters, you can include an invalid character, such as %, in the name. The red asterisk icon to the right of the Name box will flash. If you hover the cursor over the icon, a complete list of invalid characters displays.
3. In the Metadata pane, expand Measures, expand the Reseller Sales folders, and then drag Reseller Sales Amount to the Value Expression box.

   The Value Expression represents the actual state of the business metric. In this example, Reseller Sales Amount represents where sales are for the current time member.
4. Drag Reseller Sales Amount from the Metadata pane to the Goal Expression box, position the cursor at the end of the text, and then type *** 1.2**.

This expression sets the goal at a 20% increase over the current Reseller Sales Amount. Later, you'll see how to create an expression that is based on an increase over a previous period of time. For now, you are setting a fixed amount so that you can study the mechanics of each component of a KPI.

The Goal Expression indicates where the business wants to be–its goal, for sales in this instance. Alternatively, this value could represent an industry benchmark against which a company wants to measure itself.

5. In the Status Indicator drop-down list, select Traffic Light.

6. In the Status Expression box, type **-1**.

   The value of the Status Expression box is ordinarily evaluated from an MDX expression, which you'll do later in this chapter. A valid status expression needs to return a value between -1 and 1. Here, -1 will assign a red traffic light status to the KPI. A value of 0 would result in a yellow traffic light, and a value of 1 would result in a green traffic light.

7. In the Trend Expression box, type **-0.6**.

   Like the status expression, a trend expression is normally defined as an MDX formula and must return a value between -1 and 1. The purpose of the trend expression is to compare a current value, typically defined by the Value expression to the same value at an earlier point in time. You'll work with this type of comparative expression later in this chapter, but for now you'll use a constant so you can see how the value affects the KPI display.

   Your screen looks like this:

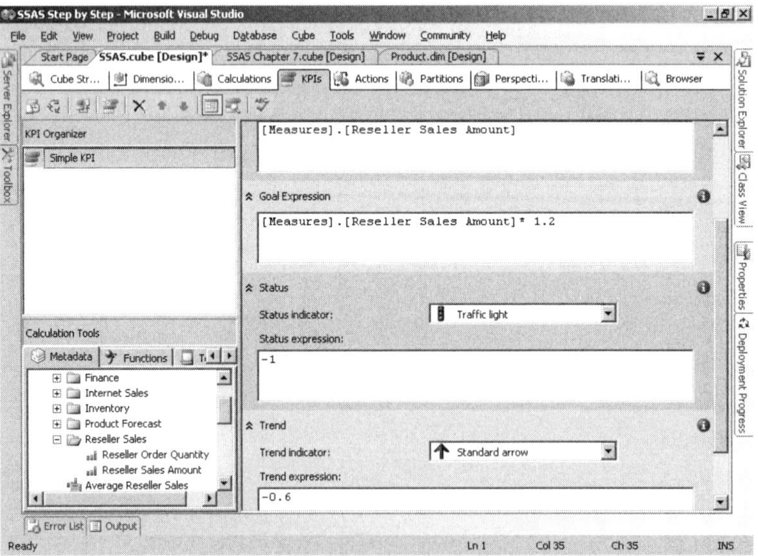

8. Deploy the project, click the Reconnect button in the toolbar when the project is deployed, and then click the Browser View button on the toolbar.

   Your screen looks like this:

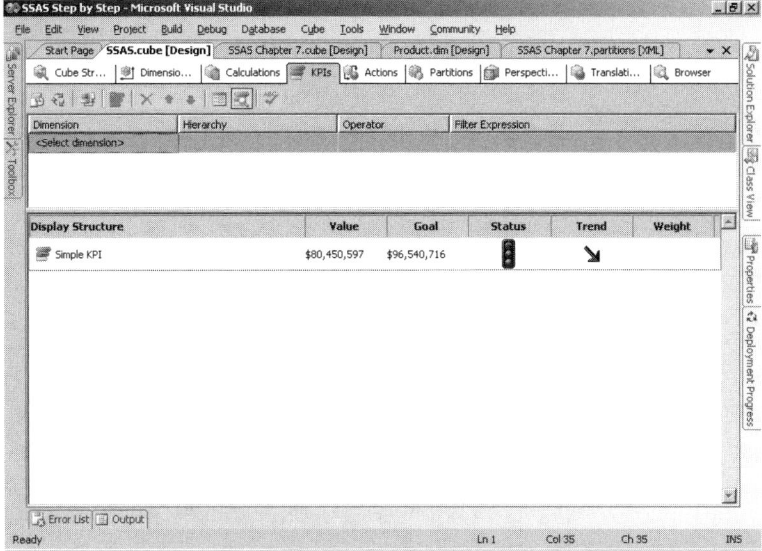

   Like the cube browser, the KPI browser displays KPIs so that you can review the KPI results during development. However, the client application used by business users is likely to provide a different interface for presenting and interacting with KPIs, so you should include a testing phase with the client application before deploying KPIs to a production environment.

   The value of Reseller Sales Amount is the grand total for this measure in the cube. The goal value is the result of multiplying this Reseller Sales Amount by 1.2. The traffic light displays a red light because the Status expression evaluates as -1. The trend arrow points downward because its value is negative and the degree of the angle of this arrow is determined by the numeric value of the Trend expression, which in this case is .6.

9. Click the Form View in the toolbar, change the Status Expression to **0** and the Trend Expression to **0.3**.

10. Deploy the project, and then click the Browser View button in the KPI toolbar.

Your screen looks like this:

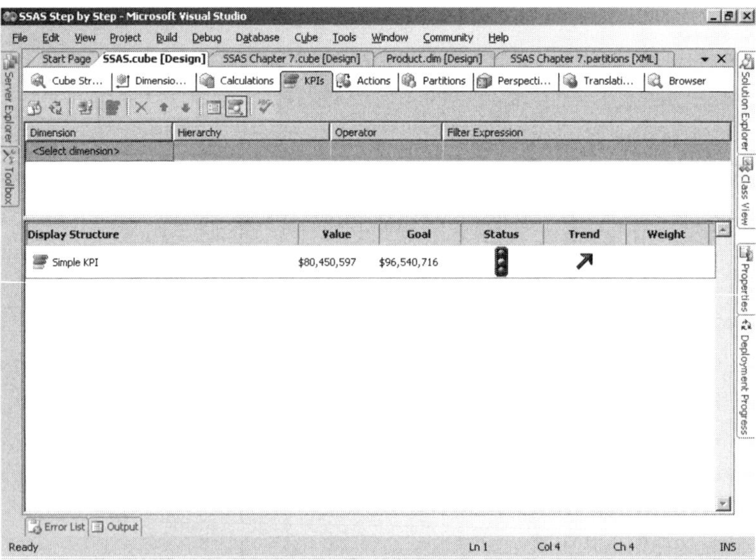

Now the traffic light displays a yellow light and the trend arrow is angled slightly upward.

11. Click the Form View in the toolbar, change the Status Expression to **1** and the Trend Expression to **1**.

12. Deploy the project, and then click the Browser View button in the KPI toolbar.

    You can see that the traffic light now displays a green light and the trend arrow points upward. In the next procedure, you'll see how to construct a complex expression that applies business rules which define the conditions for a red, yellow, or green KPI.

Using MDX Expressions with Key Performance Indicators

In the previous procedure, you hard-coded the results into the Status and Trend Expressions box to see how the graphical representations change. Of course, you would never do this in production. You'll want to plan the expression that you will create for status and trend so that you accurately portray the data. If your actuals compare favorably to the goal, you want the expression to evaluate to 1. If your actuals are not making the desired progress to the goal, you might want the expression to evaluate to 0. If your actuals are unfavorable in relation to the goal, the expression should evaluate to -1. There are only three values for the traffic light corresponding to 1, 0, and -1—green, yellow, and red. A gauge, on the other hand, can use values between 1 and -1 to represent the status.

Likewise, with the Trend, you want the expression to evaluate positively if the trend is good, neutrally if the trend is flat, and negatively if the trend is poor. Any value between 1 and -1 is valid for Trend. The indicator you use for Trend will change accordingly. For example, an arrow will point straight up when Trend is 1 and straight down when it is -1. The arrow is angled upward or downward by degrees depending on whether the Trend is closer to 1 or closer to -1.

In this procedure, you'll create a KPI using complex MDX expressions to compare cube values with business rules.

Create a ratio key performance indicator

1. Click the Form View button in the KPI toolbar, and then click the New KPI button.
2. Name the KPI: **Expenses to Gross Margin Ratio**.
3. Click Finance in the Associated Measure Group list box.
4. In the Value Expression, type the following expression:

   ```
   ([Measures].[Amount],[Account].[Accounts].[Operating Expenses])/
   ([Measures].[Amount],[Account].[Accounts].[Gross Margin])*100
   ```

   This expression calculates the Operating Expenses to Gross Margin ratio.
5. In the Goal Expression, type **30**.

   The desired value of the ratio between Operating Expenses and Gross Margin is 30%.
6. Select Road Signs in the Status Indicator drop-down list.
7. In the Status Expression box, type the following expression:

   ```
   Case
   when
   ([Measures].[Amount],[Account].[Accounts].[Operating Expenses])
   /([Measures].[Amount],[Account].[Accounts].[Gross Margin]) < .50
   then
   1
   when
   ([Measures].[Amount],[Account].[Accounts].[Operating Expenses])
   /([Measures].[Amount],[Account].[Accounts].[Gross Margin]) <= .75
   then 0
   when
   ([Measures].[Amount],[Account].[Accounts].[Operating Expenses])
   /([Measures].[Amount],[Account].[Accounts].[Gross Margin]) > .75
   then -1
   end
   ```

   This statement compares the actual ratio of Operating Expenses to Gross Margin to business rules which define whether the result is good, fair, or poor as defined by the values 1, 0, or -1, respectively. If, for example, the ratio is less than 50%, the KPI status will return a value of 1 and the road sign indicator will display as a green road sign. If the actual ratio is less than or equal to 75%, then the expression will return a zero, and a yellow road sign will be displayed for this KPI. Finally, if the ratio is greater than 75%, then the expression will return -1 and the KPI will be displayed with a red road sign.
8. In the Trend Expression, type the following expression:

   ```
   Case
   When IsEmpty([Time].[Calendar].PrevMember)
   then 1
   when
   ```

```
([Measures].[Amount],[Account].[Accounts].[Operating Expenses])
/([Measures].[Amount],[Account].[Accounts].[Gross Margin]) >
([Measures].[Amount],[Account].[Accounts].[Operating Expenses],
[Time].[Calendar].PrevMember)
/([Measures].[Amount],[Account].[Accounts].[Gross
Margin],[Time].[Calendar].PrevMember)
then 1

when
([Measures].[Amount],[Account].[Accounts].[Operating Expenses])
/([Measures].[Amount],[Account].[Accounts].[Gross Margin]) <
([Measures].[Amount],[Account].[Accounts].[Operating Expenses],
[Time].[Calendar].PrevMember)
/([Measures].[Amount],[Account].[Accounts].[Gross
Margin],[Time].[Calendar].PrevMember)
then -1
end
```

This statement compares the ratio for the current time period to the previous time period in the Calendar hierarchy. The previous time period for January 2004 is December 2003, for example. Likewise, when the current time period is the first quarter of 2003, the previous time period is the fourth quarter of 2002.

9. Deploy the project, and then click the Browser View button in the KPI toolbar.
10. In the Dimension filter at the top of the Browser window, select Time in the Dimension drop-down list, select Calendar in the Hierarchy drop-down list, and then select Equal in the Operator drop-down list.
11. In the Filter Expression drop-down list, expand members in the hierarchy to navigate from 2001 to quarter 4, select November, and then click OK.
12. To get the KPI browser to process this filter, click anywhere on the screen.

    Your screen looks like this:

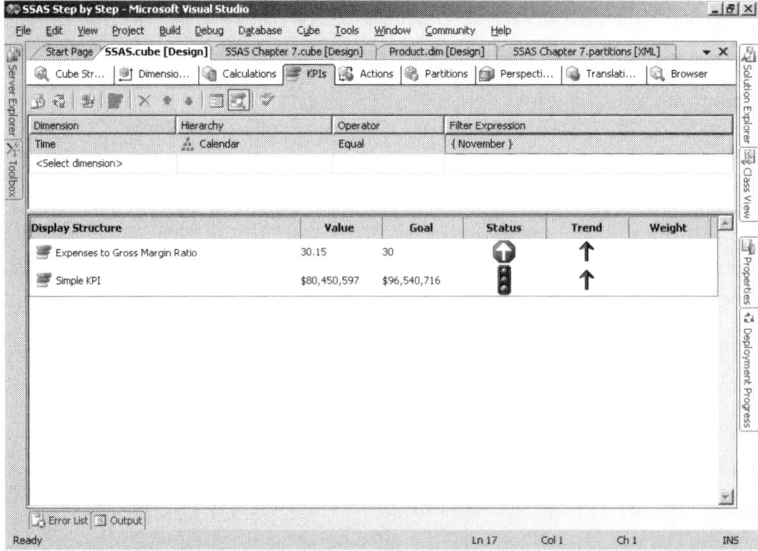

The green road sign signifies that the Status Expression equals 1, which indicates that the Expenses to Gross Margin Ratio was less than 50%. The trend arrow doesn't change because the MDX expression defining the trend compares the CurrentMember of the Time dimension to the PrevMember. However, the KPI Browser doesn't let you specify a CurrentMember for the Time dimension. The selection of November 2001 in the KPI browser is really making a smaller version of the original cube for you to examine and contains the selected member November 2001 as well as the All member for time. The All level remains the Time dimensions' CurrentMember, and has no PrevMember. Therefore, as defined by the MDX expression, when there is no PrevMember, the MDX expression returns a value of 1, and the trend arrow points upward. This may seem counterintuitive, but as you gain more experience with MDX, you'll understand why this behavior occurs here. To test the value of the trend, you need to use a client application that can query the cube, such as Reporting Services, or write a query in the MDX query editor in SQL Server Management Studio. When you include a specific month on rows or columns in the client application or the query editor, you will see the correct trend value calculating because you are explicitly defining the CurrentMember in each of those situations.

13. In the Filter Expression drop-down list, deselect November to remove this member from the filter, expand 2002, and then select 2, click OK, and then click anywhere on the screen.

    Now you see a yellow road sign for the Expenses to Gross Margin KPI because the Status Expression resolved as 0, which occurs when the ratio is between 50% and 75%. The trend arrow points upward since the ratio for the second quarter of 2002 is greater than the value of this ratio for the first quarter of the same year.

14. In the Filter Expression drop-down list, deselect 2 to remove this member from the filter, expand 2004, and then select 1, click OK, and then click anywhere on the screen.

    For this time period, you see a red road sign for the Expenses to Gross Margin KPI because the Status Expression resolved as -1, since the ratio is more than 75%.

    KPIs can be a bit of work to set up, but once you get the business goals, you can use a case statement for the Status expression to make the indicators display the way you want them.

15. Save the solution.

Chapter 8 Quick Reference

To	Do this
Create a contribution calculation	Create an expression using a measure in the numerator and a tuple that includes the All member (or a parent member) of an attribute hierarchy and the measure in the denominator.
Execute an MDX query	In SQL Server Management Studio, connect to the Analysis Server, open the MDX query window, type an MDX query, and then click the Execute button.

To	Do this
Add a comment to an MDX query	Enter double slash characters (//) before the comment.
Include all the members of the Product Category user hierarchy on the column axis	Use the clause *[Product].[Product Category].Members ON COLUMNS*.
Put sets of members on two axes	Use both *ON COLUMNS* and *ON ROWS* in a query.
Create a set from explicit members	Enclose the list of members separated by commas, between opening braces (}) and closing braces (}).
Create a set consisting of all possible combinations of two sets	Use the *CrossJoin* function with the two sets as arguments.
Calculate the average of all members of the Category attribute hierarchy	Use the expression *Avg([Product].[Category].[All].Children)*.
Calculate the cumulative Reseller Sales Amount restarting with each new member of the Year level in the Order Date.Calendar Year user hierarchy	Use the expression *Sum(PeriodsToDate([Order Date].[Calendar].CalendarYear, [Order Date].[Calendar].CurrentMember), [Measures].[Reseller Sales Amount])*
Resolve calculation conflicts that impact the same cells	Position the calculation that should be visible when both calculations are included in the same query below the other calculation using the Script Organizer.

Replace cell values for a member and its descendants with nulls without impacting cube aggregations	Use a collection of statements like this:
	
	`Scope([Measures].Members);`
	`Freeze;`
	`Descendants([Employee].[Employees].&[294])=NULL;`
	`End Scope;`

Create a key performance indicator	On the KPI tab of the Cube Designer, click the New KPI button, type an expression for Value, Goal, Status, and Trend, and select indicators for Status and Trend. Status and Trend must resolve to values between 1 and -1.

Chapter 9

Exploring Special Features

After completing this chapter, you will be able to:

- Use a referenced dimension.
- Define a many-to-many dimension.
- Add and browse translations for attributes and measures.
- Create perspectives for different types of users.

In Chapter 8, "Using MDX," you learned how to customize a cube by adding calculations as new measures and as new dimension members, as well as by manipulating calculations through sequencing and through script assignments. In this chapter, you'll further customize your solution by using advanced dimension design techniques and by addressing the special requirements of businesses working in a global economy. Then you'll learn how to organize a cube so that users can focus on a particular type of analysis without feeling overwhelmed by the array of information accessible in the cube.

Defining Dimension Relationships

In Chapter 5, "Designing Measure Groups and Measures," you were introduced to dimension usage as the definition of the relationship between dimension and each fact table. There are many types of relationships. So far, you've seen that each dimension has a *regular relationship* to one or more measure groups. With a regular relationship, an attribute column in a dimension relates to a column in a fact table for that measure group. There are other special types of relationships that can exist between dimensions and fact tables. In this section, you'll learn how to define dimension usage for a referenced dimension as well as a many-to-many dimension.

Using a Referenced Relationship Type

When you want to use all tables in a snowflake schema as a single dimension, you can create a regular dimension that includes all tables in the snowflake. When you add the dimension to a cube, a regular relationship with the most granular table is automatically created. The Product dimension is an example of a snowflake schema that has a regular relationship with measure groups in the SSAS cube. However, there might be situations when you want to separate the tables in the snowflake and implement them as separate dimensions in a cube. If the non–leaf-level table in a snowflake schema is indirectly related to the fact table through the leaf-level table (that is, the leaf-level that represents the granularity attribute in the fact table), you can create a special dimension usage type known as a *referenced dimension*. With this relationship in place, you can still roll up measure values in the new dimension even though there is no corresponding key column for that dimension in the underlying fact table.

In this procedure, you'll add two dimensions to the project, Reseller and Geography, and specify a referenced dimension usage type for Geography and the Reseller Sales measure group, with Reseller as the intermediate dimension.

Create a referenced dimension

1. Start SQL Server Business Intelligence Development Studio (BIDS), and open the SSAS Step by Step solution that you saved in C:\Documents and Settings\<username>\My Documents\Microsoft Press\as2005sbs\Workspace.

> **Note** If you skipped Chapter 8, open the SSAS Step by Step solution in the C:\Documents and Settings\<username>\My Documents\Microsoft Press\as2005sbs\Answers\chap08\SSAS Step by Step folder.

2. In Solution Explorer, double-click SSAS Step By Step DW.dsv, right-click the background of the Data Source View Diagram pane, click Add/Remove Tables, double-click both dbo.DimGeography and dbo.DimReseller to add them to the Included Objects list, and then click OK.

   Now that there are many tables in the data source view (DSV), you'll need to look carefully and possibly rearrange tables. You should be able to see the relationship between DimReseller and DimGeography based on GeographyKey. Notice also that FactResellerSales has a foreign key relationship with DimReseller, but not with DimGeography. DimReseller is the intermediate dimension that you'll use to create a reference relationship between FactResellerSales and DimGeography.

3. In Solution Explorer, right-click the SSAS Step by Step project, point to Add, and then click Existing Item.

4. Browse to the C:\Documents and Settings\<username>\My Documents\Microsoft Press\as2005sbs\chap09 folder, click Geography.dim, then while pressing the Ctrl key, click Reseller.dim, and then click Add.

   You now have two dimensions added to the project, but they still need to be added to the cube.

5. In Solution Explorer, double-click SSAS.cube to open the cube designer.

6. In the Dimensions pane in the lower left, right-click the background, and then click Add Cube Dimension.

7. Select Geography, select Reseller while pressing the Ctrl key, and then click OK.

8. Deploy the project, and then click the Browser tab, and then click Reconnect. In the cube metadata tree, expand Measures, Reseller Sales, and drag the Reseller Sales Amount measure to the data area of the grid.

   Notice the aggregated value of Reseller Sales Amount is $80,450,597.

9. Expand the Geography dimension and drag the Geography hierarchy to the rows axis.

   Your screen looks like this:

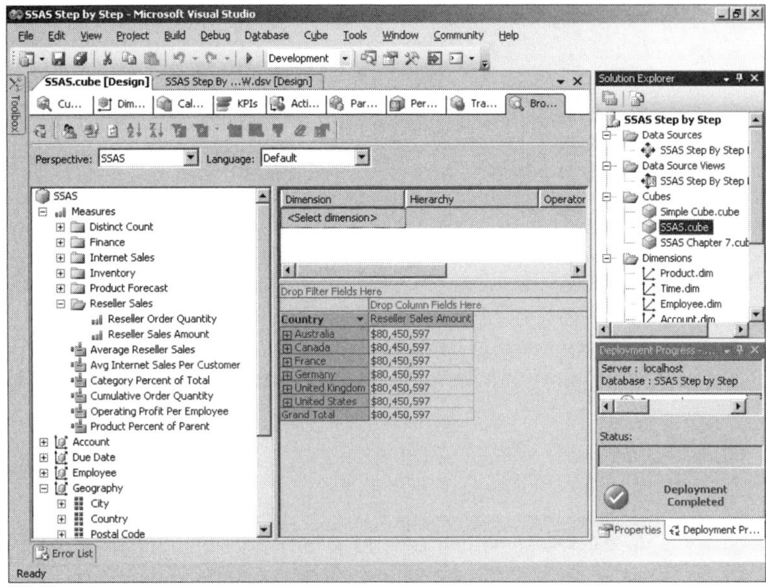

   Here you can see that the All level value of Reseller Sales Amount populates all cells because there is no relationship between the Geography dimension and Reseller Sales Amount.

10. Click the Dimension Usage tab.

    Notice that the dimension usage for the Reseller dimension and the Reseller Sales measure group is already created. This is a standard dimension usage type, in which there is one key in the fact table that corresponds to a primary key in the dimension table. No relationship has been created for Geography because none of the fact tables contain a foreign key to this table. However, the Reseller dimension has a GeographyKey and can be used as a referenced dimension to enable reporting by geography for sales through the reseller channel.

11. Click the ellipsis button in the intersection of Geography and Reseller Sales.

12. Select Referenced in the Select Relationship Type drop-down list, select Reseller in the Intermediate Dimension drop-down list, and then select GeographyKey in both the Reference Dimension Attribute and Intermediate Dimension Attribute drop-down lists.

The Define Relationship dialog box looks like this:

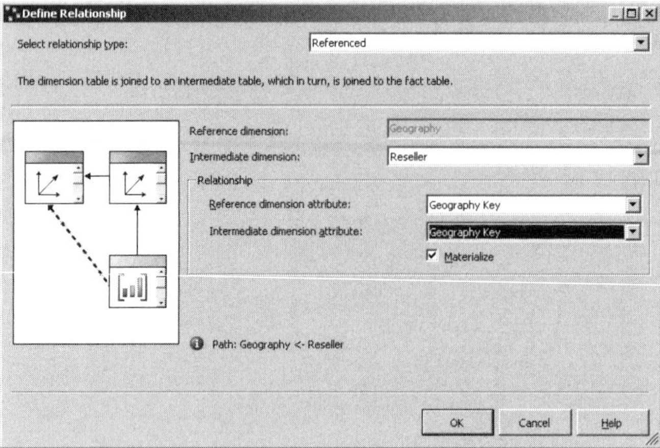

Notice the Materialize check box is selected by default. This means the value of the link between each fact table and referenced dimension row will be stored in multidimensional online analytical processing (MOLAP) during processing. Materializing this value impacts storage and performance in a limited way, but it does improve query performance.

13. Click OK.

Your screen looks like this:

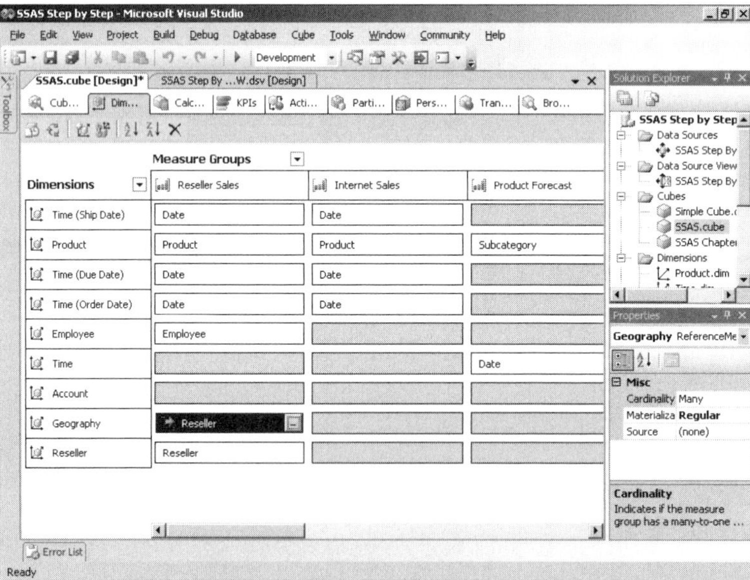

There is now an established relationship between Reseller Sales and the Geography dimension. A referenced dimension icon appears at the intersection of the two items to help you more easily identify this special type of relationship. Now you're ready to test the dimension usage.

14. Deploy the project, click the Browser tab, and then click Reconnect on the toolbar.
15. If the Reseller Sales Amount measure and the Geography Hierarchy are not still in the grid, drag them in now.

    Your screen looks like this:

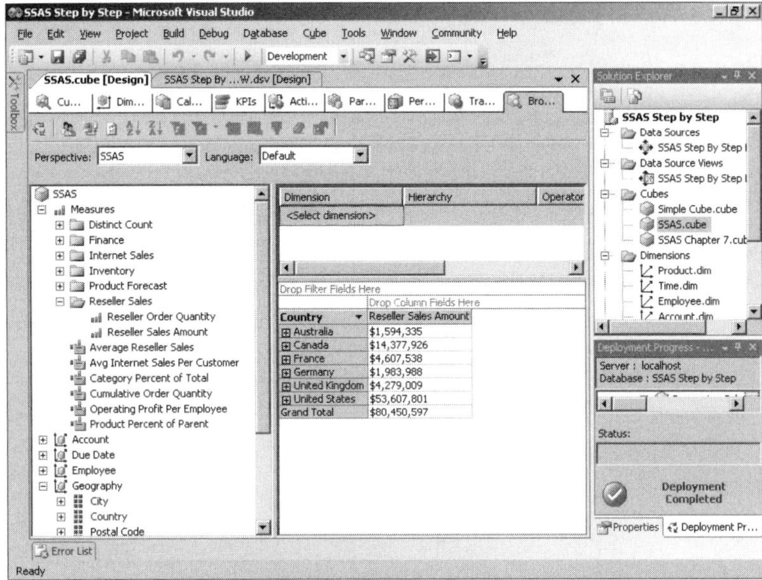

Notice that the cells all contain the correct values, because now there is a relationship between the Geography dimension and the Reseller Sales Amount, even though the tables from the underlying data source do not have a direct relationship.

Using a Many-to-Many Relationship Type

Typically, a single row in the fact table relates to one member in any particular dimension. Conversely, a specific member in a dimension table could relate to many rows in a fact table. This type of relationship is a one-to-many relationship and is the most common relationship between dimensions and fact tables.

There are certain types of analysis, however, that require a *many-to-many relationship* between fact table rows and dimension members. If you've ever had a joint checking account, this scenario should sound familiar. In a banking data warehouse, the transactions that increase or decrease your account balance are each represented individually in a fact table. These transactions each share a common dimension key which links them to your checking account, which would represent a single member in an Account dimension. You and your checking account partner are two members of a Customer dimension. There needs to be a way to summarize transactions for the account using either your name or your partner's name. If both names appear in a report, the summarized transactions by individual customer should reflect the same total but should not be counted twice.

If the Account dimension is established as a many-to-many dimension, then this type of summarization is easily performed by Analysis Services. In this scenario, a single checking account can have many transactions, but can also have multiple customers associated with the same account. An intermediate fact table is needed to map each account to one or more customers. It doesn't contain any measures—just keys to the dimensions that it is linking together.

The SSAS Step By Step DW database contains data for an analogous situation. The combination of SalesOrderNumber and SalesOrderLineNumber in the fact table uniquely identifies sales transactions. Due to the highly detailed nature of transactions like sales orders, there's no need to physically create separate dimension tables to analyze transactions by SalesOrderNumber. Nonetheless, SalesOrderNumber remains important and does uniquely identify members of a dimension. When dimension members are stored like this in a fact table, they form a *degenerate dimension*. In the next procedure, you'll be creating a cube dimension from these columns. Then, you'll use a many-to-many relationship to aggregate these sales orders by account manager. More than one account manager might be given credit for a sale for incentive compensation purposes, but you don't want to reflect this allocation to multiple account managers in the grand total for the dimension. In other words, the same sale could be added into the total sales for multiple sales managers, but this doesn't change the total sales for the company.

In this procedure, you'll add the Account Manager dimension and the Fact Account Manager measure group to the cube, and specify a many-to-many dimension usage type.

Build a many-to-many dimension relationship

1. Open the SSAS Step by Step DSV, right-click the FactResellerSales table name in the Data Source View Diagram pane, and then click New Named Calculation.
2. Type a Column Name, **SalesOrderDescription**. Type this expression into the Expression box:

   ```
   CONVERT ( CHAR ( 10 ), SalesOrderNumber )  + 'Line '  + CONVERT ( CHAR ( 4 ),
   SalesOrderLineNumber )
   ```

   Then click OK.

   The new column that you just added combines the SalesOrderNumber with the SalesOrderLineNumber. When you view this column in the DSV, notice the Named Calculation icon.

3. Right-click the Data Source View Diagram pane, click Add/Remove tables, and add dbo.DimAccountManager and dbo.FactAccountManager, and then click OK.

   Notice that FactAccountManager doesn't have any relationships to the other tables in the DSV. However, it does contain columns for SalesOrderNumber and SalesOrderLine-Number (keys for the degenerate dimension in FactResellerSales) and a column for AccountManagerKey, a new dimension that you'll add in the next step. FactAccount-Manager has no measures of its own, but serves as an intermediate fact table between sales transactions by sales order and account managers by sales order. It is the center-piece of the many-to-many relationship that you're building in the cube.

4. Right-click the project, point to Add, click Existing Item, browse to the C:\Documents and Settings\<username>\My Documents\Microsoft Press\as2005sbs\chap09 folder, click AccountManager.dim, and then click Add.

   The Account Manager dimension is a standard dimension that contains names of account managers. It is the dimension that will be used to aggregate sales, with some sales being shared equally by more than one account manager.

   Next, you need to create a cube dimension for the sales orders. By creating a separate dimension, you'll be able to filter data by sales order number so that you can see how the same sales order is allocated to multiple account managers.

5. In Solution Explorer, right-click the Dimensions folder, and click New Dimension. Click Next on the Welcome page if necessary. Select Build The Dimension Using A Data Source, but clear the Auto Build check box. Click Next.

6. Accept the default DSV, and then click Next.

7. Select Standard Dimension on the Select The Dimension Table page of the Dimension wizard. Click Next.

8. Select dbo.FactResellerSales in the Main Table drop-down list, select the check box for both SalesOrderNumber and SalesOrderLineNumber in the Key Columns list, and select SalesOrderDescription for the Member Name.

The Select The Main Dimension Table page of the wizard looks like this:

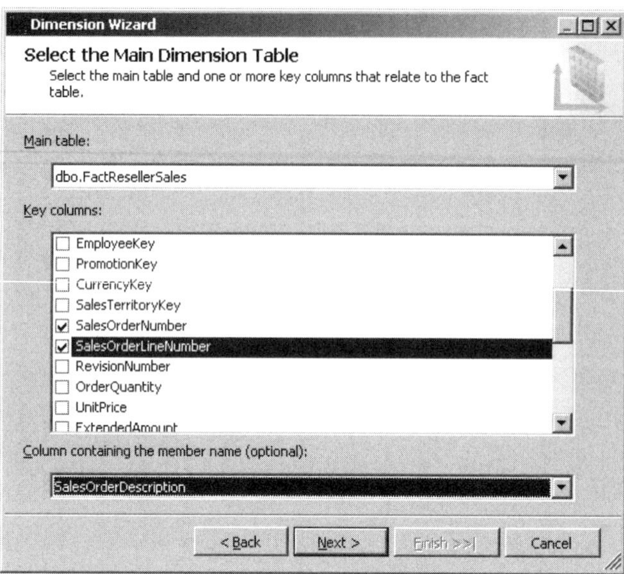

You can use multiple keys, referred to as a *composite key*, when creating a dimension to uniquely identify each dimension member. Even though the source data is in a fact table, you can still build a dimension because you have columns available to create unique members.

9. Click Next four times to reach the last page of the wizard, type a name for the dimension, **Reseller Sales Order Details**, and then click Finish.
10. In the Dimension Designer for Reseller Sales Order Details, rename the Fact Reseller Sales key attribute to **Reseller Sales Order** to avoid confusion with the Measure Group or the Fact table.
11. Drag the SalesOrderNumber from the Data Source View pane into the Attributes pane to add a new attribute to the dimension.

Your screen looks like this:

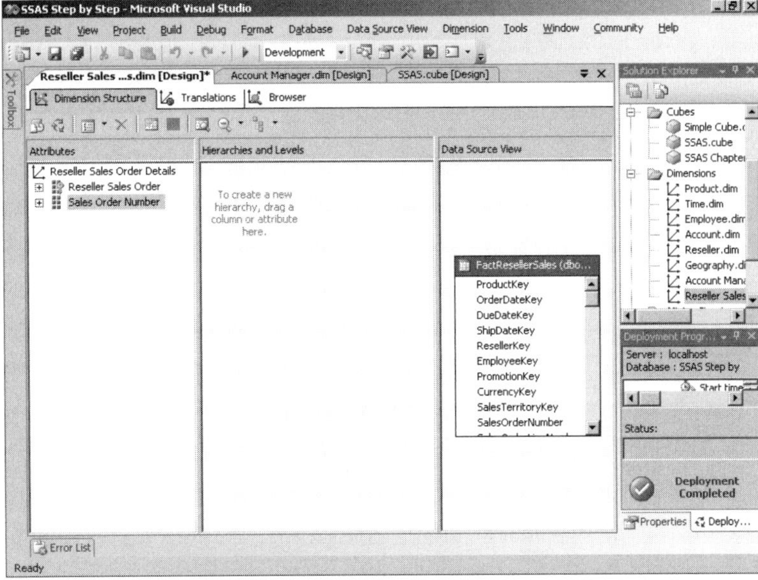

12. Click the Cube Structure tab of the Cube Designer, right-click the background of the Dimensions pane, click Add Cube Dimension, click AccountManager, pressing Ctrl, click Reseller Sales Order Details, and then click OK.

    Now the dimensions needed to support the many-to-many relationship are in place, but the DSV needs to be updated to reflect the foreign key relationship between the intermediate fact table, FactAccountManager, to the Reseller Sales Order Details dimension.

13. In the Data Source View Designer, find the FactAccountManager table, click SalesOrderNumber and, while pressing the Ctrl key, click SalesOrderLineNumber. Without releasing the mouse button, point to one of the same column names in the FactResellerSales table, and then release the mouse button.

14. In the Create Relationship dialog box, confirm that the Source Columns match up with the Destination Columns, and then click OK.

15. Click Yes when prompted by the Create Logical Primary Key? message box.

    A foreign key relationship is now defined in the DSV, even though this relationship does not exist in the physical tables. This feature is particularly useful when you need to define relationships, but do not have permissions to make changes to the data structures at the source.

    In this case, it's important to keep separate the concepts of fact tables and dimensions. By defining the relationship between FactAccountManager and FactResellerSales using SalesOrderNumber and SalesOrderLineNumber, you are really defining a relationship between the FactAccountManager table as a *fact table* and the Reseller Sales Order

Details *degenerate dimension*. Because the degenerate dimension is inside the fact table, it's easy to get confused by the relationships.

Now you're ready to add FactAccountManager as a measure group so that it can be used as an intermediate table, defining relationships between the Reseller Sales Order dimension and the Account Manager dimension.

16. Switch to the Cube Structure tab of the Cube Designer, right-click the Measures pane, click New Measure Group, and then double-click FactAccountManager.
17. Expand Fact Account Manager to view the measures added to this measure group.

    You need at least one measure for the measure group to be valid in the cube, and Fact Account Manager Count can serve that purpose. To prevent users from accessing to the required (but otherwise not useful) count measure, you'll change its Visible property.
18. Right-click Fact Account Manager Count, click Properties, locate the Visible property in the Properties window, and then select False in the Visible property's drop-down list.
19. Click the Dimension Usage tab to review relationships.

    Notice that the Reseller Sales Order Details dimension has a relationship to Reseller Sales (by way of the Reseller Sales Order key column).
20. Scroll to the right to locate the Fact Account Manager measure group.

    Your screen looks like this:

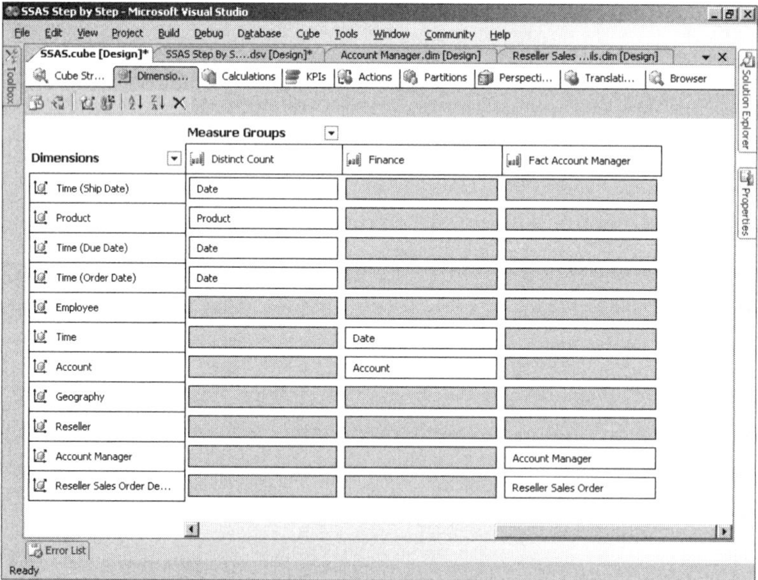

Account Manager has a relationship to Fact Account Manager via AccountManagerKey. ResellerSalesOrderDetails also has a relationship to FactAccountManager based on the SalesOrderNumber and SalesOrderLineNumber relationship that you added to the DSV.

21. Scroll to the left, click in the intersection of Account Manager and Reseller Sales, click the ellipsis button, and then select Many-To-Many in the Select Relationship Type drop-down list.

22. Select Fact Account Manager in the Intermediate Measure Group drop-down list.

    The Define Relationship list box looks like this:

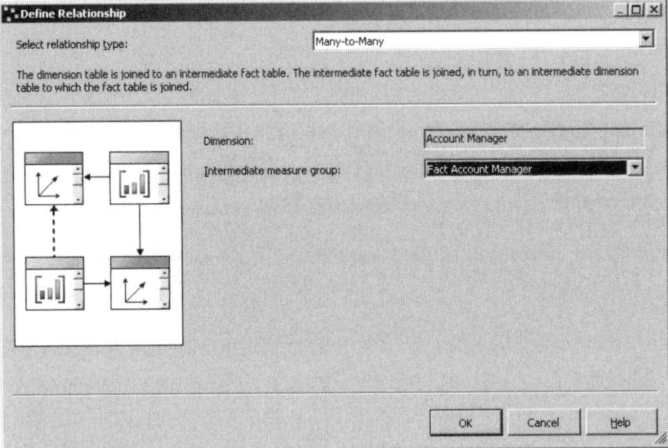

23. Click OK.

    Your screen looks like this:

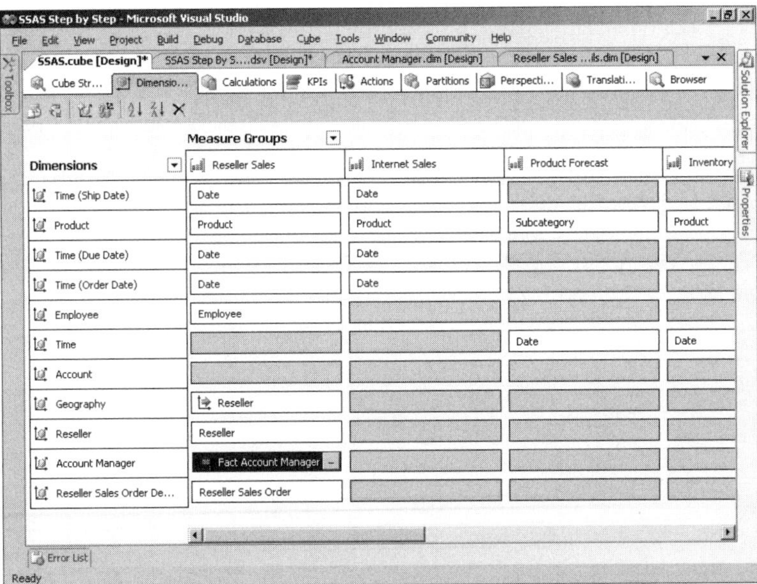

Notice the icon at the intersection of Account Manager and Reseller Sales.

24. Deploy the project, click the Browser tab, and then click Reconnect.
25. Expand the Reseller Sales Order Details dimension and drag the Sales Order Number into the area labeled Drop Filter Fields Here. Click the arrow to the right of Sales Order Number to view the list of dimension members, clear the check box for (All), click S043661, and then click OK.
26. On the rows, remove Country and replace it with the Reseller Sales Order attribute onto rows.

    Your screen looks like this:

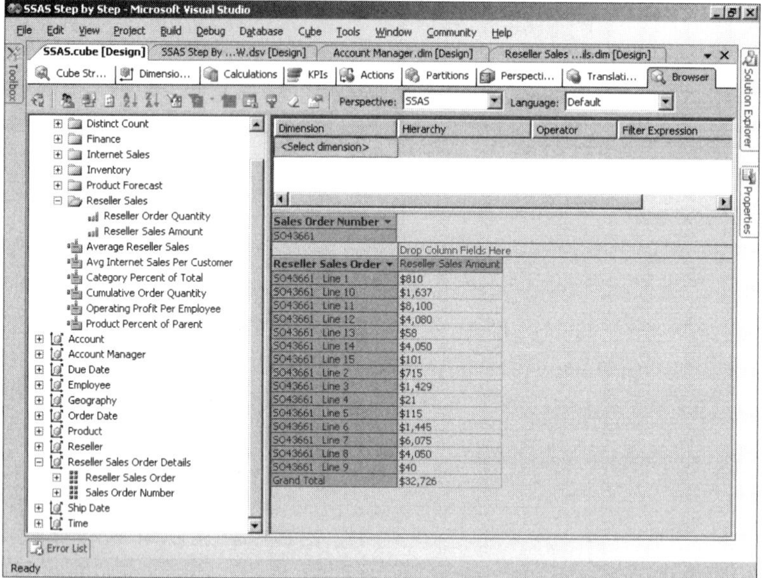

Here you can see how a single sales order breaks down by line number. Note the total of the sale, $32,726.

27. Now drag the Account Manager dimension into the grid to the left of the Reseller Sales Order Details Dimension.

Your screen looks like this:

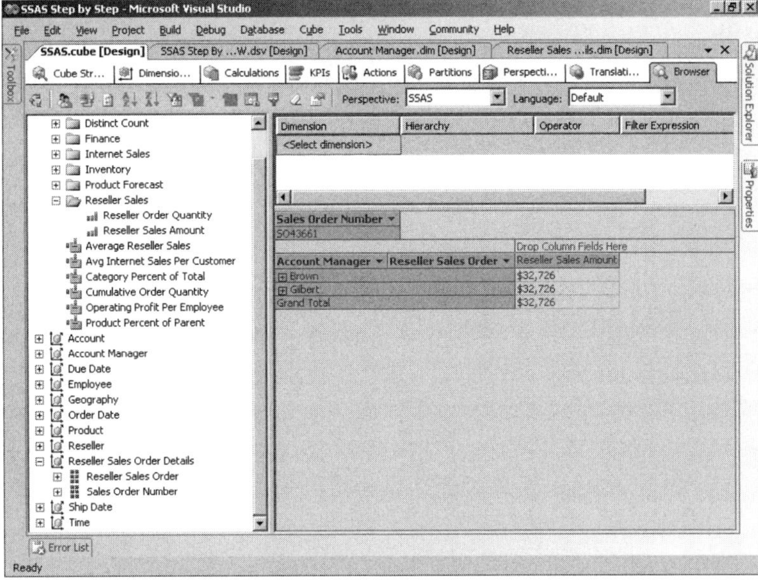

28. Now you can see how the sale is equally allocated to two Account Managers, but the total does not aggregate the sale twice for Sales Order Number S043661.

Supporting Currency Conversions

Many companies that do business in two or more countries analyze or convert data in multiple currencies. Currency conversion can have a broad-reaching effect on many parts of the business; sales, salaries, and financial statements are just a few examples where a company may need to consider exchange rates. In addition to tracking multiple currencies, a company needs to consider how frequently exchange rates change, how to capture that information, and whether to include the Currency ISO Codes to be standards-compliant. ISO is the International Standards Organization that has created a set of three character codes to represent each type of currency.

To support currency conversion, your data warehouse needs to include some additional tables. You need a currency dimension that lists multiple currencies and a fact table that tracks exchange rates for each currency over time. You then add these tables to your cube as a dimension and measure group, respectively. There are special properties that you need to set for dimensions and measures to identify them for use in currency conversions. The last step is to create multidimensional expressions (MDX) scripts for the cube to perform the calculations that convert currencies on demand. Fortunately, Analysis Services includes a wizard to create the necessary MDX scripts for you.

There are three types of currency measures that can be used in currency conversion. You might only use two of these currency types, or you might use all three depending on your business requirements:

- The *pivot currency* is the standard against which all other exchange rates are measured. Its value is always 1. For example, if you establish the US Dollar (USD) as the pivot currency, you define exchange rates as .549 AUD per 1 USD, .630 CAD per 1 USD, and .972 EUR per 1 USD. You will always have a pivot currency in a currency conversion.
- The *local currency* is the currency used when adding transactions to the fact table. If you have a European subsidiary, the local currency for the European transactions might be Euros, while local currency might be pesos for transactions generated by your Mexican subsidiary. When you store transactions of multiple currencies in a fact table, the cube must be able to identify which currency is associated with each record. You can either include the currency identifier in the transaction itself as a dimension key column, or you can associate a currency with a dimension used in the transaction. For example, you include a subsidiary identifier as a key column in the fact table and store the currency identifier in the subsidiary dimension table.
- The *reporting currency* is used when you analyze or report results. To analyze and compare sales data across locations, you need to convert all sales measures into a common currency if you store local currency in the fact table. If you want the flexibility to convert transactions into any currency, you use a many-to-many relationship. For example, the analysts in your Japanese subsidiary could choose a different reporting currency than analysts in the Bolivian subsidiary. Alternatively, you could convert all local currencies in the fact table to a single, common currency using a many-to-one relationship. In this case, the reporting currency is the same as the pivot currency.

Working with Currency Conversions

Because the measures in the sales fact tables are associated with a certain day, their converted values must reflect the exchange rate that was current on that day. You use a special fact table, such as FactCurrencyRate in the SSAS Step by Step DW relational database, to store exchange rates by currency and by time. These rates are used to convert the local currency in the fact tables to the pivot currency and then again to convert the pivot currency to the reporting currency. The FactCurrencyRate should have a relationship to a time dimension and a currency dimension, such as DimTime and DimCurrency, as shown in the SSAS Step by Step DW database. When you create a measure group for the currency fact table, you need to set the measure group's *Type* property to ExchangeRate. This property identifies this measure group for Analysis Services to use when building the MDX scripts required to support currency conversion.

In addition to the special exchange rate measure group, your cube also needs a currency dimension to store the names of each currency and their ISO codes. This dimension has special requirements in order for Analysis Services to correctly use this dimension for currency conversions. The best way to make sure the required properties are set correctly is to change the Dimension Type setting to Currency when you are building the dimension using the Dimension Wizard. When you work with a Currency dimension type, you can specify the dimension table column uniquely identifying each currency and, optionally, the dimension table column identifying the ISO code for each currency. Your cube also must contain a dimension with *Type* set to Time.

To finalize support for currency conversion in your cube, you can use the Business Intelligence Wizard. This wizard simplifies the remaining tasks to set up a reporting currency and MDX scripts that apply the correct calculations to measures according to your business requirements. You can even execute the wizard as many times as necessary if you have multiple conversion requirements. For example, you might need one type of conversion for sales results, a different conversion for cost of goods sold, and yet another conversion affecting financial accounts for international regulatory reporting.

The simplest type of currency conversion is to apply an exchange rate to a measure, but you have two other options. You can develop currency conversions that apply to individual members of an Account dimension by name by using the Account Hierarchy option. Use the Account Hierarchy Based On Type option if you need to apply exchange rates to specific account types (such as Assets or Revenues, for example).

For more information about currency conversions, refer to the topic, "Working with Currency Conversions (SSAS)" in SQL Server Books Online.

Localizing Cubes

In the previous procedures, you implemented currency conversion to accommodate multiple currency valuations for Adventure Works, a global company. You can also apply translations to a cube to display the labels on rows and columns in different languages. You can even implement translations to reflect members of a dimension by language. Together, currency conversion and translation enable you to provide users with an analytical solution that displays their local currency and language.

Adding Translations

Member captions are the labels for attributes that appear as headers in rows and columns when you browse a cube. By default, these captions correspond to the name that you assign to an attribute, but you can replace the default caption with a translated caption. Additionally, you can store translated names for dimension members as attributes in a dimension table. For example, you can have an English Product Name attribute, a Spanish Product Name attribute, and any number of other attributes with product names in different languages. The Translations feature in Analysis Services allows you to display captions and attribute names that correspond to a specific language.

In this procedure, you'll add French translations to the Time dimension and to folder captions.

Add translated captions and attribute values

1. In Solution Explorer, double-click the Time dimension to open the Dimension Designer.
2. Click the Translations tab, and then click the New Translation button on the Translations toolbar:

   Your screen looks like this:

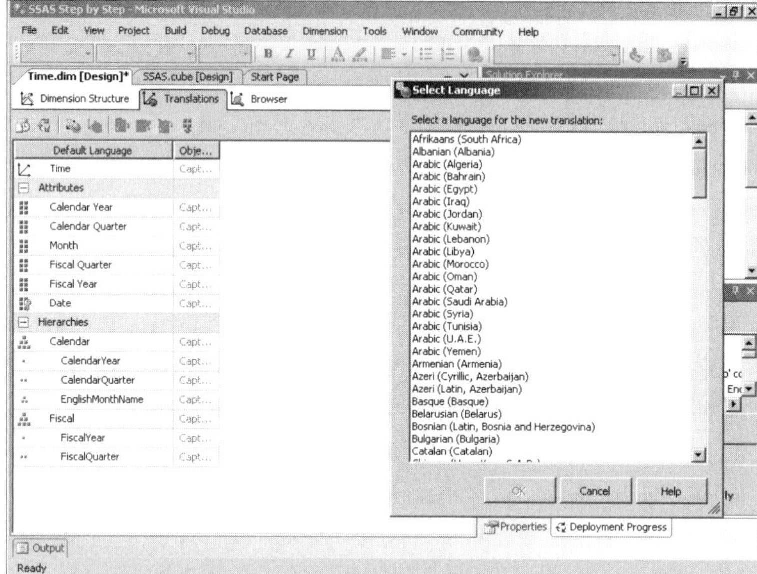

   The Select Language dialog box shows all the available languages.

3. Click French (France) in the list box, and then click OK.

   Notice that a new column, named French (France), appears in the Translation page.

4. At the intersection of the Time dimension and the French (France), type a caption: **Date**.
5. Continue changing member captions as shown in the table below:

For this caption	Add this translation
CalendarYear	Année Civile
Calendar Quarter	Quart de Civile
Fiscal Quarter	Quart Fiscal
Fiscal Year	Exercice Budgétaire

Your screen looks like this:

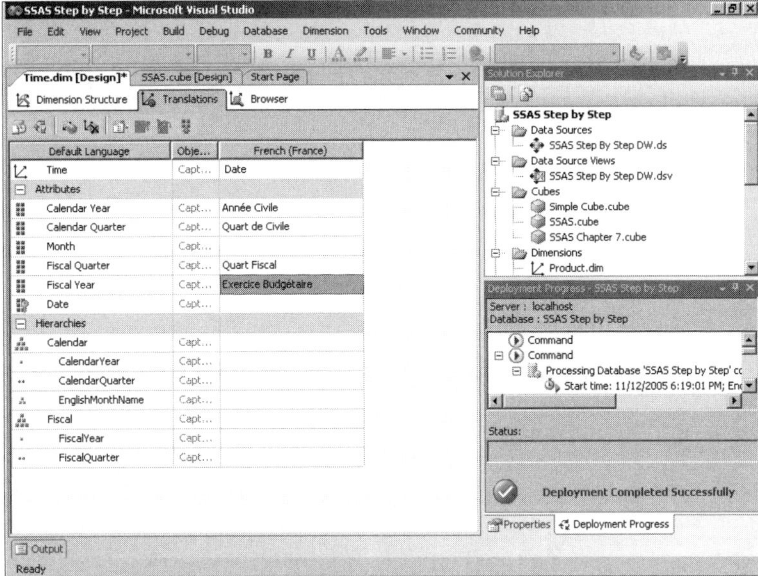

Note Don't worry if you don't know how to type letters with accents. This is just an example for you to understand how to add translations to a dimension.

6. In the Month row, click in the box in the French (France) column, and click the ellipsis button. Type **Mois** in the Translated Caption box, and click FrenchMonthName in the Translation Columns pane.

   Your screen looks like this:

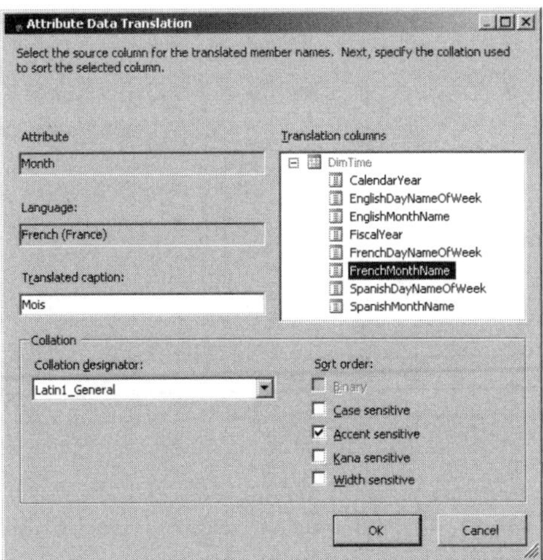

Here you not only assign a translated caption for an attribute, but you also reference a column in the dimension table that contains the names of the members.

7. Click OK.

   Notice that translations for attribute names stored in a table are identified with a special icon next to the translated caption.

8. Open the Cube Designer for the SSAS cube, and then click the Translations tab.

   There are two translations here already because the Geography and Reseller dimensions have translations defined.

9. Update the French translations on this tab as shown in the following table:

For this caption or DisplayFolder	Add this translation
Reseller Sales	Ventes de Revendeur
Reseller Sales Amount	Quantité De Ventes De Revendeur
Internet Sales	Ventes d'Internet
Internet Sales Amount	Quantité de Ventes d'Internet
Product	Produit
Time	Date
Account	Compte

Your screen looks like this:

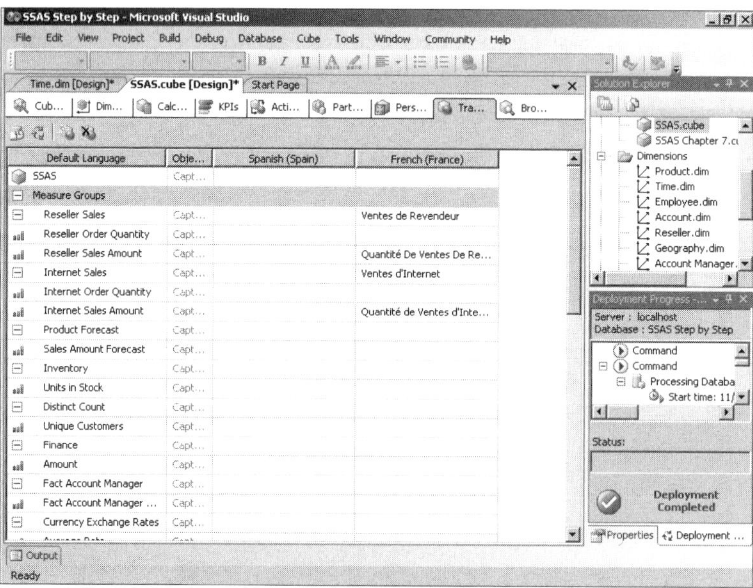

Because this cube is for learning purposes only, you won't enter a translation for every caption. This set of translations is sufficient to illustrate the process you should follow to localize cubes for your own production environment.

10. Deploy the project, click the Browser tab, and then click Reconnect.

    You'll test the translations in the next procedure.

Browsing Translations

In Visual Studio, you can test the translations in the browsers available in the Dimension Designer as well as the Cube Designer. Your end users' browsing experience, however, will depend on the client application they use to connect to the cube. Not all tools offer translation capabilities, so be sure to verify support for translations in the client applications used in your organization before adding them to the cube or dimension structures.

In this procedure, you'll review the effect of changing language in a browser when translations are available.

Change language in the cube browser

1. In the Language list box on the browser toolbar, click French (France).

   Your screen looks like this:

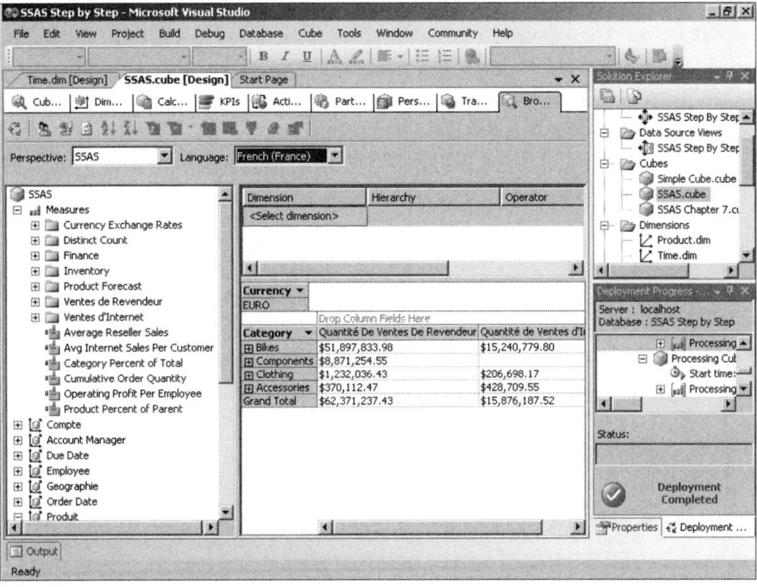

Notice that all the captions for the measures currently displayed in the grid are French. Also, in the cube metadata tree, you can see that folder names for measures as well as names for dimensions are French. Of course, in a production system, you would make much more extensive changes to completely localize the cube.

2. In the Language drop-down list on the browser toolbar, click Default to return the browser to its original language setting.

Organizing Information with Folders and Perspectives

By now, you should recognize that a single cube can be multifunctional. In effect, it can serve as the single source information for multiple workgroups or departments across your organization. While this centralization of information is beneficial for users, application developers, and IT administrators alike, it might be difficult for users to find their way to the information they need. Some might even feel overwhelmed by all the measures and dimensions built into a single cube. Analysis Services provides two features to better organize information for users–Display Folders and Perspectives. You can use Display Folders to organize Measures into common groupings so that users do not have to look in every measure group to find the measures they need to analyze. The addition of Perspectives to a cube is another option for customizing the user's navigation experience by limiting the view of dimensions and measures to specific subject areas.

Organizing Measures

A cube browser lists the available measures by measure group. Because measures in the same measure group come from the same fact table, they are naturally related and often used together for analysis. However, for users who need to use measures from several different measure groups, the default organization of measures by measure group might not be convenient. You can create display folders to help users navigate measures just like a user hierarchy helps them navigate attributes. Before you spend a lot of time reorganizing measures by display folder, be sure this feature is supported by your client applications.

In this procedure, you'll organize measures into display folders.

Use display folders for measures and calculations

1. Click the Cube Structure tab, and then, in the Measure Groups pane, expand Reseller Sales.
2. Click Reseller Order Quantity, and then type **Sales** in the *DisplayFolder* property box.
3. Click Reseller Sales Amount, and then select Sales in the *DisplayFolder* property's drop-down list.

   Notice the folder name becomes an available value in the list box after you assign the first measure to this folder.

4. Repeat the previous step for the following measures in the Internet Sales measure group: Internet Sales Amount, Internet Order Quantity. Similarly, add Unique Customers (in the Distinct Count folder) to the Sales display folder.

5. Click the Calculations tab, and then click the Calculation Properties button on the Calculations toolbar.

6. In the Calculation Name list box, click [MEASURES].[Category Percent of Total], type **Sales** in the Display Folder box for this calculation, and then click Reseller Sales in the Associated Measure Group drop-down list.

7. Next, assign [MEASURES].[Average Reseller Sales] to the Sales display folder and the Reseller Sales measure group.

   The Calculation Properties dialog box looks like this:

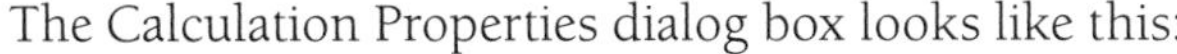

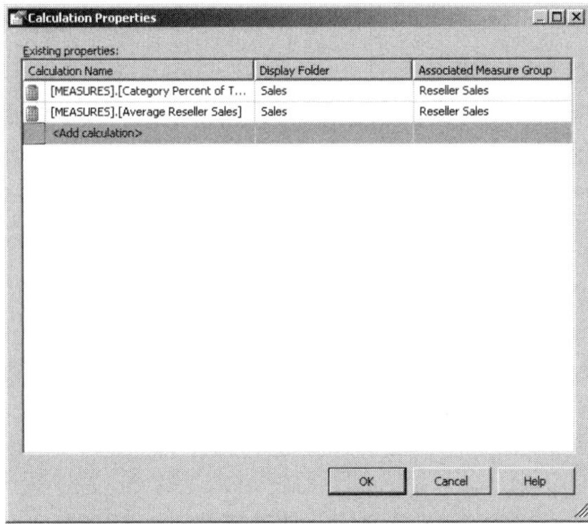

   In a production system, you should associate each calculation with a measure group or display folder to group the calculations logically, but for now you can leave the remaining calculations unassigned.

8. Click OK to close the dialog box, deploy the project, click the Browser tab, and then click Reconnect.

9. Expand Measures, expand Reseller Sales, and then expand the Sales folder.

The cube metadata tree looks like this:

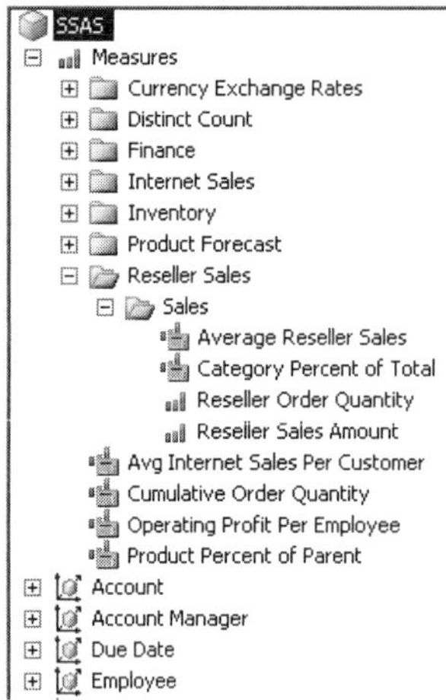

In Visual Studio, the display folder appears in the tree beneath the measure group, but client applications will use the display folder differently. However, you can see here that the calculations are now included with the measures that come directly from the underlying fact table.

Using Perspectives

Perspectives are another way to help users navigate a cube easily. When you create a perspective, you select specific objects from the cube–measures, dimensions, attributes, and calculations. To a client application, a perspective looks just like another cube. However, it's important to note that security does not apply to perspectives. As you learn in Chapter 11, "Implementing Security," you can secure databases, cubes, and dimensions only. If a user has access to a cube, the user also has access to any perspective added to that cube.

In this procedure, you'll create and review a perspective.

Create and browse a perspective

1. In the Cube Designer, click the Perspectives tab, and then click the New Perspective button in the Designer toolbar.

   By default, when you first create a perspective, all objects in the cube are selected. However, if you accept the default selections, the perspective would be identical to the cube.

2. Click the Perspective Name box, and then type **Sales**.
3. Clear the check box for each of the following measure groups: Product Forecast, Inventory, and Finance.

Your screen looks like this:

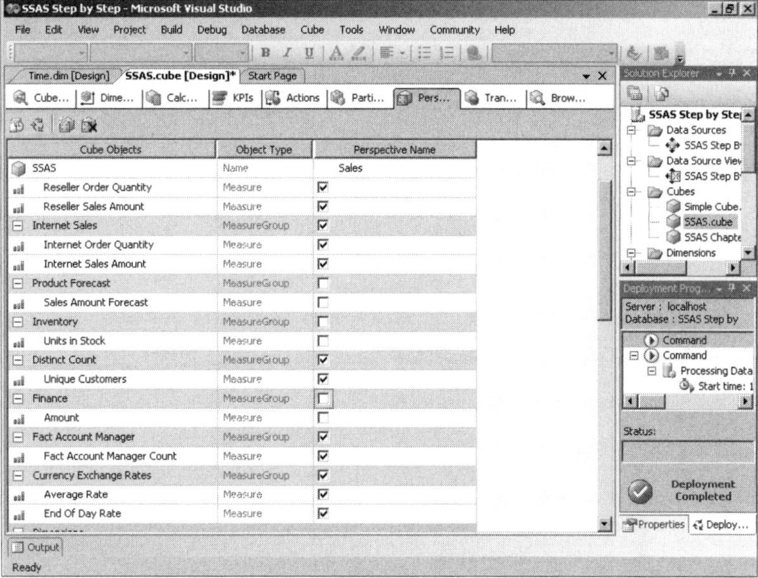

Removing a measure group from a perspective removes all measures associated with that measure group from the perspective as well. You can also remove an individual measure by clearing its check box.

4. Clear the check box for each dimension *except* the following dimensions which should remain selected: Product, Order Date, and Reporting Currency.

   Your screen looks like this:

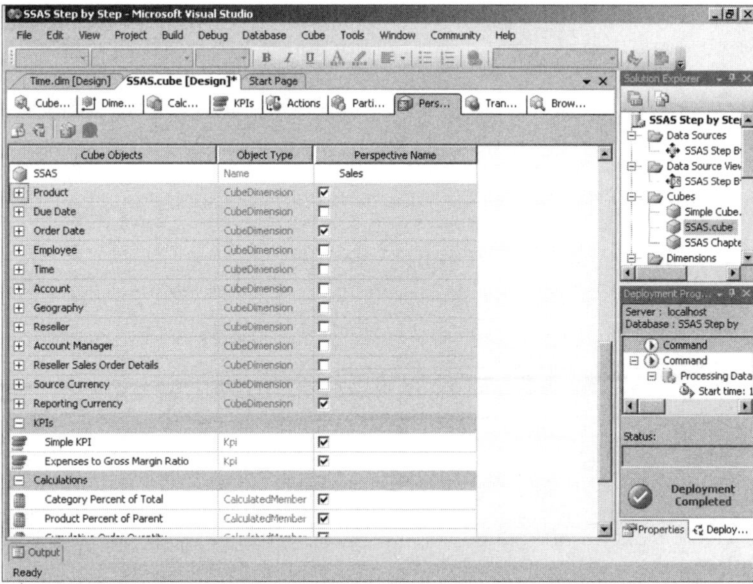

5. Expand Product, and then clear the check box for each attribute.

   Your screen looks like this:

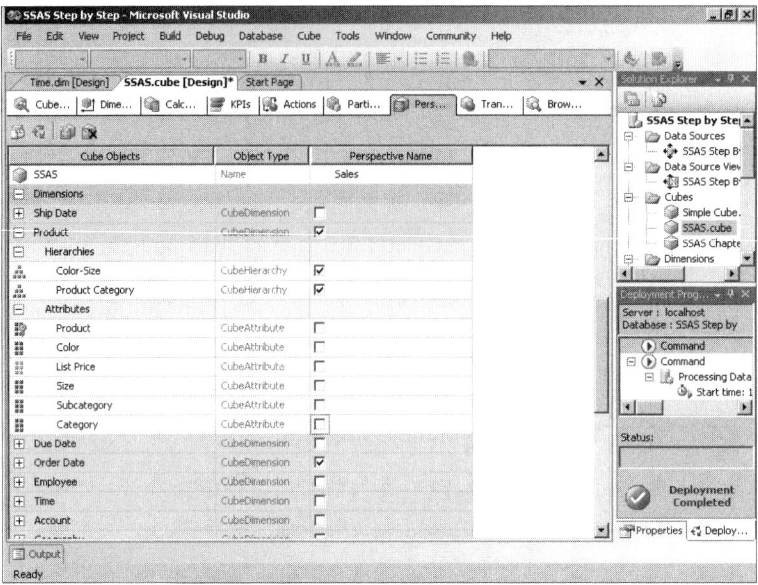

   As you can see, you can be selective about which attributes or hierarchies from a dimension to include in a perspective. Removing an attribute that is part of a user hierarchy doesn't remove that attribute from the hierarchy. It simply isn't available to place independently on an axis in a cube browser.

6. Clear the check box for each key performance indicator (KPI) and for Operating Profit per Employee.

Your screen looks like this:

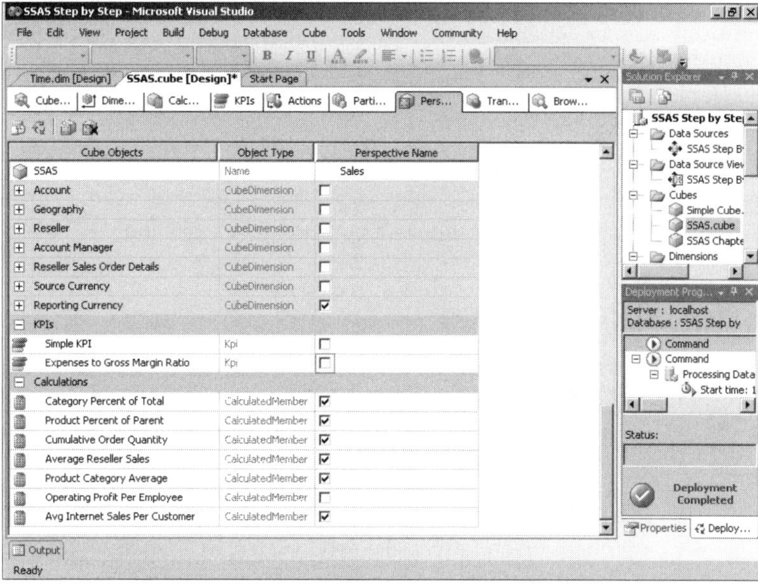

7. Deploy the project, click the Browser tab, and then click Reconnect.
8. In the Perspective list box below the Designer toolbar, click Sales.
9. In the cube metadata tree, expand Measures and Product, and then in the grid, expand Bikes.

   Your screen looks like this:

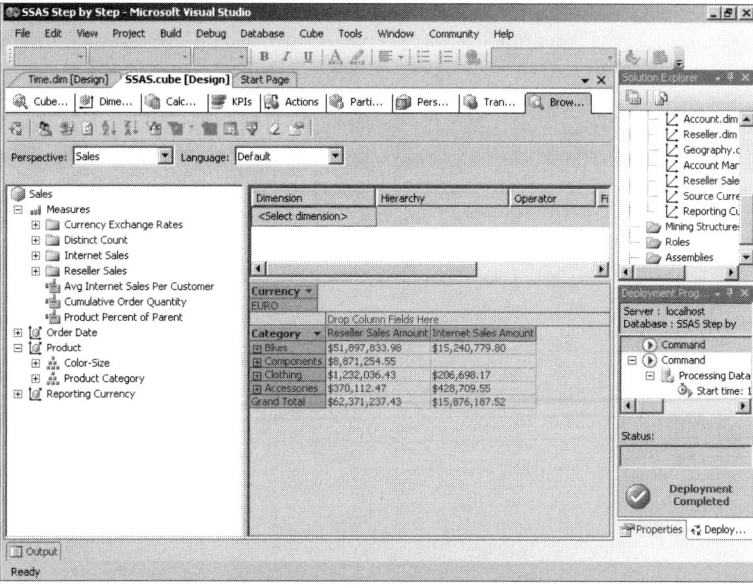

Notice that the list of available objects available in the cube metadata tree is greatly simplified. Also, the Subcategory attribute is still available for browsing even though it does not appear separately in the cube metadata tree. To see subcategories with categories in the browser, you can drag the Category off the grid.

10. Drag Category from rows.

You should work closely with users to determine how many perspectives would be useful and which objects to include in each perspective. This feature is invaluable for customizing the appearance of a cube to meet specific user needs.

Chapter 9 Quick Reference

To	Do this
Create a referenced dimension	Use the Dimension Wizard to create a new dimension. This dimension must be related to another dimension table that is related to a fact table. On the Cube Structure tab of the Cube Designer, add the new dimension. On the Dimension Usage tab of the Cube Designer, click the intersection of the new dimension and a measure group, select Referenced in the Select Relationship Type drop-down list box, click the related dimension in the Dimension list box, and then click the applicable key values in the Reference Dimension Attribute and Intermediate Dimension Attribute drop-down lists.
Define a many-to-many relationship	Use the Dimension Wizard to create two dimensions that each relate to an intermediate fact table that maps many members of the first dimension to many members of the second dimension. One of the dimensions should relate to a main fact table. On the Cube Structure tab, add a measure group for each fact table and add the two new dimensions. On the Dimension Usage tab of the Cube Designer, click the intersection of the dimension relating to the main fact table and the measure group for that table, select Regular in the Select Relationship Type drop-down list, and then click the applicable key value in the Measure Group Column list box. On the Dimension Usage tab, click the intersection of the other dimension and the intermediate measure group, select Regular in the Select Relationship Type drop-down list, and then click the applicable key value in the Measure Group Column list box. On the Dimension Usage tab, click the intersection of the main measure group and the dimension related to the intermediate measure group, select Many-To-Many in the Select Relationship Type drop-down list, and then click the intermediate measure group in the Intermediate Measure Group list box.

To	Do this
Implement a many-to-many currency conversion	On the Cube Structure tab of the Cube Designer, add a measure group containing exchange rates and set its *Type* property to ExchangeRate and its *AggregateFunction* property to AverageOfChildren or LastNonEmpty as applicable. Use the Dimension Wizard to create a dimension with Dimension Type of Currency to map the currency key column to the CurrencySource attribute type and the ISO code column (if one exists) to the Currency ISO Code. Right-click the cube in Solution Explorer, and click Add Business Intelligence, click Define Currency Conversion, specify the exchange rate measure group, the pivot currency, the exchange rate direction, and the dimension objects to be modified by the conversion. Select the conversion type many-to-many, specify the location of the currency identifier, and select the reporting currencies. In the Data Source View Designer, add a logical primary key to the named query for reporting currencies and relate the named query to applicable fact tables. On the Dimension Usage tab of the Cube Designer, add a regular relationship between the reporting currency dimension and the exchange rate measure group, and then add a many-to-many relationship between the reporting currency dimension and applicable measure groups.
Support translations in a cube	On the Translations tab of the Cube Designer, click the New Translation button on the designer toolbar, and then select a language.
Add a translated caption for a dimension object to a cube	On the Translations tab of the Cube Designer, type the translation in the box at the intersection of the dimension object and the translation language.
Add translated attribute values to a cube	On the Translations tab of the Cube Designer, click the ellipsis button in the box at the intersection of the dimension object and the translation language, type a translation for the caption in the Translated Caption box, and then click the column that contains the translated attribute values in the Translation Columns pane.
Test translations in the Cube Designer	Deploy the project after adding translations, and then select the applicable language in the Language drop-down list in the browser toolbar.
Use display folders for measures	On the Cube Structure tab of the Cube Designer, click a measure, and then set its *DisplayFolder* property.
Use display folders for calculations	On the Calculations tab of the Cube Designer, click the Calculation Properties button on the Calculations toolbar, select a calculation in the Calculation Name drop-down list, type a folder name in the Display folder box, and then, optionally, select a measure group in the Associated Measure Group drop-down list.
Create and browse a perspective	In the Cube Designer, click the Perspectives tab, click the New Perspective button in the designer toolbar, and then clear the check box of each dimension object to remove from the perspective.
Test a perspective in the Cube Designer	Deploy the project after adding a perspective, and then select the perspective in the Perspective list box in the browser toolbar.

Chapter 10
Interacting with Cubes

After completing this chapter, you will be able to:

- Use actions to view reports associated with selected attributes.
- Add drillthrough capabilities to a cube.
- Prepare dimensions and cubes to allow dynamic changes.

Throughout the preceding chapters of this book, you have been making changes to the structure of cubes and dimensions to support particular analytical requirements. Now you're ready to explore the features that increase the functionality of your analysis applications even more—actions and writeback. In this chapter, you'll learn how to use actions to integrate reporting applications with your cube so that users can access the detailed information associated with their current focus of analysis. Additionally, you'll learn how to implement writeback. *Writeback* allows users to add values to a cube temporarily to support what-if analysis or permanently to support forecasting or budgeting applications.

Implementing Actions

You already know that the purpose of an online analytical processing (OLAP) application is to provide users with valuable information to drive business decisions. *Actions* provide another mechanism by which users can gather information and take steps based on the information they find in cubes. You can add actions to a cube that will later be executed by users. An action is always initiated by a user and relates to an object in a cube. That object might be a dimension member or a particular cell, which is then used as a parameter for the action. Actions only work with some client applications, however, so be sure actions are supported before adding them to cubes.

There are several types of actions that you can add to a cube. A URL action is useful for navigating to a particular Web site based on cube data. For example, you might want to visit a customer's Web site after viewing that customer's data in a cube, or you might want to access information from an internal reporting Web server to get more information about a particular product you're analyzing. If you're using Microsoft SQL Server 2005 Reporting Services, you can use the Reporting action to link a report to a cube object. This method is much easier to implement than URL access if all of your reports are accessed through Reporting Services. Another popular action type is drillthrough, which you can implement to provide access to detailed data that you don't want to store in the cube. The action generates an HTML page to contain the drillthrough data rather than using a predefined reporting template that might be used with URL or Reporting actions.

Using Standard Actions

The Cube Designer in Visual Studio includes a tab for Actions. You use the form on this tab to define an action by specifying the action target, the action type, and the action expression that generates a string used to run the action. An action target is the portion of the cube to which the action relates and is the object that the user clicks to launch the action. The action expression is a multidimensional expression (MDX) that evaluates as a string relevant to the action type. Each action type has its own syntax requirements, but generally you include the MDX *CurrentMember* function in the action expression to link the object to the current cube context.

In this procedure, you'll add a new URL action to open a Web page that contains a report for a selected product.

Create a URL action

1. Run PublishReports.cmd in the folder C:\Documents and Settings\<username>\My Documents\Microsoft Press\as2005sbs\chap10 folder to publish the reports that you need so that you can follow the procedures in this chapter.

> **Important** This procedure requires installation of Reporting Services before you begin.

2. Start SQL Server Business Intelligence Development Studio (BIDS), and open the SSAS Step by Step solution that you saved in C:\Documents and Settings\<username>\My Documents\Microsoft Press\as2005sbs\Workspace.

> **Note** If you skipped Chapter 9, "Exploring Special Features," open the SSAS Step by Step solution in the C:\Documents and Settings\<username>\My Documents\Microsoft Press\as2005sbs\Answers\chap09\SSAS Step by Step folder.

3. Open the Cube Designer for the SSAS cube, and then click on the Actions tab.
4. Click the New Action button on the toolbar, and then name the action **Product Detail**.
5. In the Target Type drop-down list, select Attribute Members.

   There are several target types from which to choose. If you select Cube, the action will relate to the entire cube and you do not need to provide any more detail about the target. In the client application, the action will be available for all cube objects–every member, every cell, every dimension, and every level.

Alternatively, you can limit an action to certain members within a dimension. If you select Dimension Members as the target type, then the action is available for all members of the dimension that you specify as the target object. Similarly, you can select Hierarchy or Level to limit the availability of the action to members of the specified hierarchy or level. You can limit the action even further if you select a target type of Attribute Members.

Another option is to use Cells as the target type. Unlike the Cube target type, Cells does not include members of a dimension. When a user clicks on a cell in a client application, the action passes the value of the cell as a parameter.

6. In the Target Object drop-down list, expand Product, select the Product attribute, and then click OK.

   Your screen looks like this:

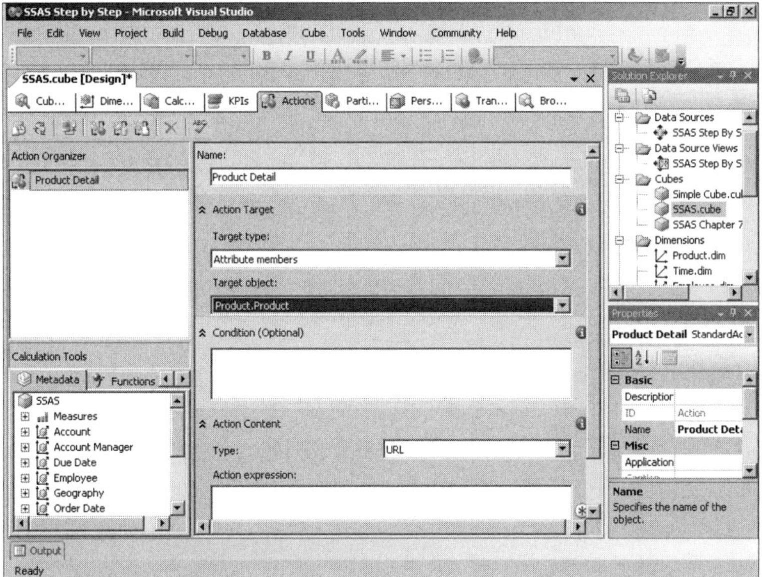

   You won't create a Condition expression for this action. You only use this option when you want to limit the scope of the target, such as when you want an action to apply only to a subset of members of the Product attribute rather than all its members. Just like the MDX expressions that you created in Chapter 8, "Using MDX," you can either type the MDX expression directly in the Condition box or you can drag and drop objects from the Metadata and Function tabs in the Calculation Tools pane.

7. In the Type drop-down list box, select URL.

8. In the Action Expression box, type this expression:

```
"http://localhost/ReportServer?/Sample SSAS Reports/Product Detail&Product=" +
Product.Product.CurrentMember.Name +
"&rs:Command=Render&rc:Toolbar=false&rc:Parameters=false"
```

   In this example, you use the syntax for Reporting Services URL access to generate a report. This URL is composed of a fixed string that specifies a report server, a folder path for the report to display, and the name of that report which is concatenated with an MDX expression that represents the name of the product that is clicked to trigger the action. The URL is completed by concatenating another fixed string that tells the report server to render the report without the standard Reporting Services toolbar and without the parameter list box that allows the user to change the report to view a different product.

   While this example illustrates how to construct a URL that displays a Reporting Services report, you can certainly use a similar approach to build a URL that references a specific page on your corporate Web site related to the product that is selected to launch the action. The key to a dynamic URL is the use of an MDX expression which returns a key value, a name, or other attribute related to the attribute member. To return the name of the selected attribute member, you use the syntax `Dimension.Hierarchy.CurrentMember`, where `Dimension.Hierarchy` represents the names of the dimension and hierarchy specified as the Target Object.

9. Deploy the project, click the Browser tab, and then, if necessary, click Reconnect.

10. Expand Product, and drag Product to rows. Then expand Measures, expand the Reseller Sales folder, expand the Sales folder, and then drag Reseller Order Quantity to the center of the grid.

11. Click the Cable Lock caption to select this attribute member, right-click Cable Lock to display the context menu, and then click Product Detail.

Your screen looks like this:

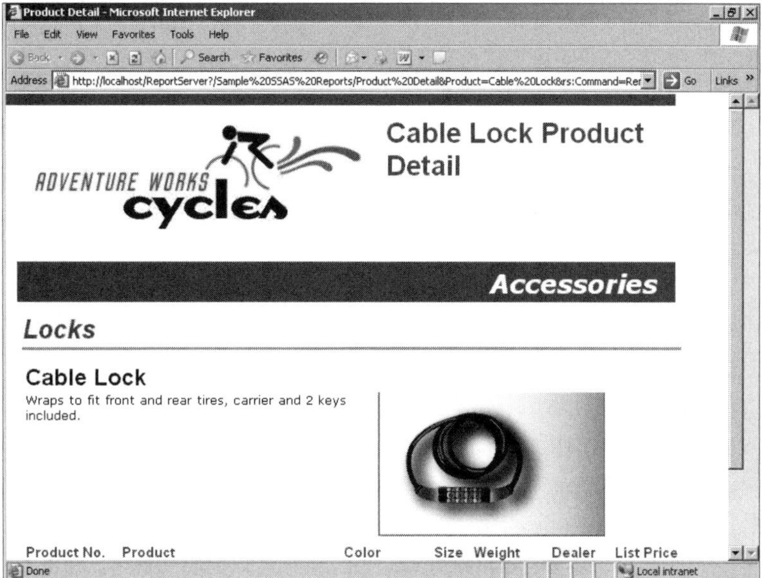

In this example, by using URL access to get a report specific to the selected product, you are taking advantage of the Reporting Services delivery features. However, you can certainly access any Web application that allows you to pass a parameter, such as the product name in this example, to locate a particular page on your corporate Web site. In the next section, you'll learn how to access reports through linking.

Linking to Reports

When Reporting Services is part of your business intelligence (BI) infrastructure, you can easily create actions that execute these reports without having to build URLs by using an MDX expression. Of course, your client application is still required to support actions for this approach to work. When you create a Reporting action, you can simply specify the host server for Reporting Services and the path to the report.

In this procedure, you'll add a new Reporting action to open the Reporting Services Web application and then display a report for a selected reseller.

Create a reporting action

1. Switch to Visual Studio, click the Actions tab in the Cube Designer, click the New Reporting Action button on the Actions toolbar, and then name the action **Reseller Sales Order Details**.
2. In the Target Type drop-down list, select Attribute Members.

3. In the Target Object drop-down list, expand Reseller, select the Reseller attribute (that is, the attribute named Reseller), and then click OK. The Target Object is now Reseller.Reseller.
4. In the Server Name box, type **localhost**.
5. In the Report Path box, type **ReportServer?/Sample SSAS Reports/Order Details**.

   This Report Path string will be concatenated with the server name to build the URL to the Order Details report on the report server, much like you did with the expression in the previous procedure. However, this time, you don't need to include any of the report server commands or a parameter in the string.

   Notice that you can specify a format for the report. The default is HTML5, but you can change this value to HTML3, Excel, or PDF.
6. Expand the Parameters section, type **Reseller** in the first box in the Parameter Name column, and then type **[Reseller].[Reseller].CurrentMember.Name** in the Parameter Value column of the same row.

   In the previous procedure, you embedded the parameter name and the expression used to derive the parameter value in the URL. Here you are using the Actions graphical interface to specify the parameter and assign an expression to that parameter, which at run time will be used to construct a URL when the user launches this action. You can also click the ellipsis button in the Parameter Value box to access the MDX Builder if you prefer to use a graphical interface when creating an expression for the parameter value.
7. Deploy the project, click the Browser tab, and then click Reconnect.
8. Drag Product off the grid, expand Reseller, and then drag the Reseller attribute to rows.
9. Click Active Cycling to select this single attribute, right-click it to display the context menu, and then click Reseller Sales Order Details.

   Notice that Product Detail is not an option. An action is only available when you right-click on a target object for which an action is defined. Since Product Detail only applies to members of the Product attribute hierarchy of the Product dimensions, the associated action is not available when you right-click on members of the Reseller hierarchy.

Your screen looks like this:

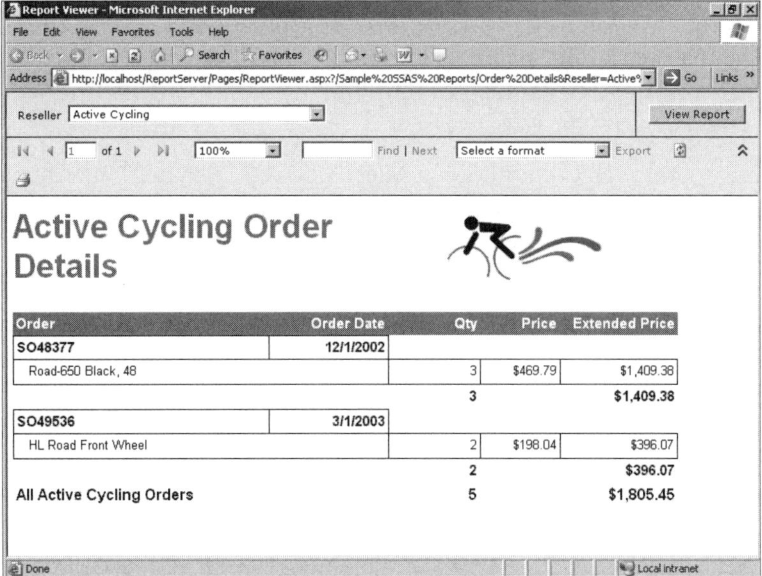

With this type of report link, you can scroll through multiple pages of a report, export the report to another file format, or change the current reseller for which details are displayed. You can disable features by using Reporting Services commands just as you did in the previous procedure, by adding the command to the Report Path. For example, if you want to remove the ability for the user to change the Reseller on this report, use this Report Path:

```
ReportServer?/Sample SSAS Reports/Order Details&rc:Parameters=false
```

Adding Drillthrough

Another popular action type is drillthrough, which you can implement to provide access to detailed data that you don't want to store in the cube. A drillthrough action retrieves specific rows from that fact table that created a specific value in the cube. Enabling drillthrough does not provide access to original source data, such as the transaction tables used to populate the fact table–only to the fact table. Even though drillthrough only goes to the fact table, it can be extremely useful in many situations and it's very easy to implement.

In this procedure, you'll add a new drillthrough action to display detail records for Internet sales orders.

Create a drillthrough action

1. Switch to Visual Studio, click the Actions tab of the Cube Designer, and then click the New Drillthrough Action button on the Actions toolbar.

2. Type **Internet Sales Order Details** in the Name box.
3. Select Internet Sales in the Measure Group Members drop-down list.

   Notice that, unlike a standard action, a drillthrough action doesn't use target objects. Instead, you associate a measure group with the drillthrough action, which in turn links the action to a specific fact table.
4. In the Drillthrough Columns table, select MEASURES in the Dimension drop-down list, select both Internet Order Quantity and Internet Sales Amount in the Return Columns drop-down list, and then click OK.
5. On the next row, select Product in the Dimension drop-down list, and then, in the Return Columns drop-down list, select Product, Subcategory, and Category, and then click OK.
6. On the next row, select Order Date in the Dimension Columns drop-down list, select Date in the Return Columns drop-down list, and then click OK.
7. Scroll down, if necessary, to view the bottom of the Actions form, expand the Additional Properties section, and then type **100** in the Maximum Rows box.

   The bottom of the form in your screen looks like this:

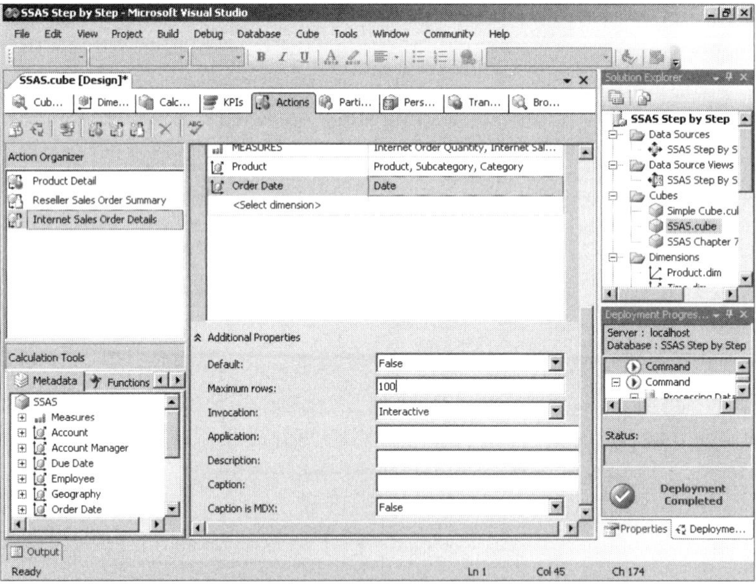

8. Deploy the project, click the Browser tab, click Reconnect, click anywhere in the grid, and then click the Clear Results button in the toolbar.
9. Expand the Internet Sales measure group, expand the Sales folder, and then drag the Internet Order Quantity measure into the center of the grid.

10. Drag the Product.Category hierarchy to the rows axis of the grid, expand Order Date, and then drag the Order Date.Calendar hierarchy to the columns axis.

11. In the grid, expand the Bikes category to display the subcategories, click on the cell intersection of Mountain Bikes and 2001 to select the cell, right-click the selected cell, and then click Internet Sales Order Details.

    The Data Sample Viewer looks like this:

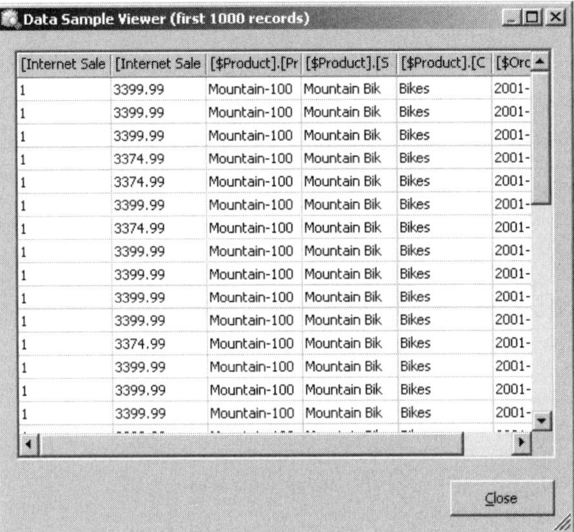

    The client application used to browse a cube placed into production will likely use a different interface to display drillthrough actions. Note that even though the caption of the Data Sample Viewer indicates the first 1,000 records are displayed, the list of records is actually limited to the maximum number of rows that you specified in the Action form.

12. Close the Data Sample Viewer dialog box.

Using Writeback

One important analytical activity is planning. Planning is an opportunity to anticipate the future and also to look back and see the truth of the parable that "life is what happens while you are making other plans." Planning has interesting challenges because it's an interactive process. Rather than simply looking at historical values generated by business systems, humans typically enter planning values. To effectively use the planning capabilities of Analysis Services, you need a client application that supports interactivity. In this section, you'll learn how to create and administer a cube that supports interactive forecasting. This cube will allow you to create a high-level forecast—at the quarter level, for product categories. You'll be able to create multiple scenarios of forecasts and even dynamically add new scenarios as needed. In the process, you'll get a taste of how a client application could make interactive changes to the cube, and you'll understand what to look for when acquiring or creating a client application to support planning activities.

Write-Enabling a Dimension

Typically, creating a forecast requires more than one iteration. You create a first-pass forecast and have meetings to discuss the ramifications. Then you create a second-pass forecast and have meetings to discuss that one. Often, it's important to keep track of each interim stage of the process. A Scenario dimension allows you to give a name to each pass of the forecast. You often need to add additional Scenario dimensions during the course of the planning cycle. Analysis Services allows you to create a dimension that you can modify dynamically—that is, you can *write-enable* a dimension.

In this procedure, you'll create a write-enabled Scenario dimension.

Create a write-enabled dimension

1. In Solution Explorer, double-click SSAS Step by Step DW.dsv, right-click the background of the Data Source View Diagram pane, and then click Add/Remove Tables.
2. In the Add/Remove tables dialog box, double-click dbo.DimScenario in the Available Objects list to move it to the Included Objects list, and then click OK.
3. In Solution Explorer, right-click the Dimensions folder, click New Dimension, and then, if displayed, click the Next button on the Welcome page of the wizard.
4. Clear the Auto Build check box, and then click Next.
5. Select the SSAS Step by Step DW data source view (DSV), and then click Next.
6. Keep Standard Dimension selected, and then click Next.
7. Select dbo.DimScenario in the Main Table drop-down list, select the ScenarioKey check box in the Key Columns list, select ScenarioName in the Column Containing The Member Name (Optional) drop-down list, and then click Next.
8. Keep Regular selected as the Dimension Type, and then click Next.
9. Type **Scenario** as the name of the dimension, and then click Finish.
10. Rename the Dim Scenario attribute as **Scenario**.
11. In the Properties window, change the *IsAggregatable* property value to False.

    In a Scenario dimension, you do not want an All level. Summing the values of the scenarios is never appropriate.
12. Click the Scenario dimension object in the Attributes tree, and then, in the Properties window, change the *WriteEnabled* property to True.

Your screen looks like this:

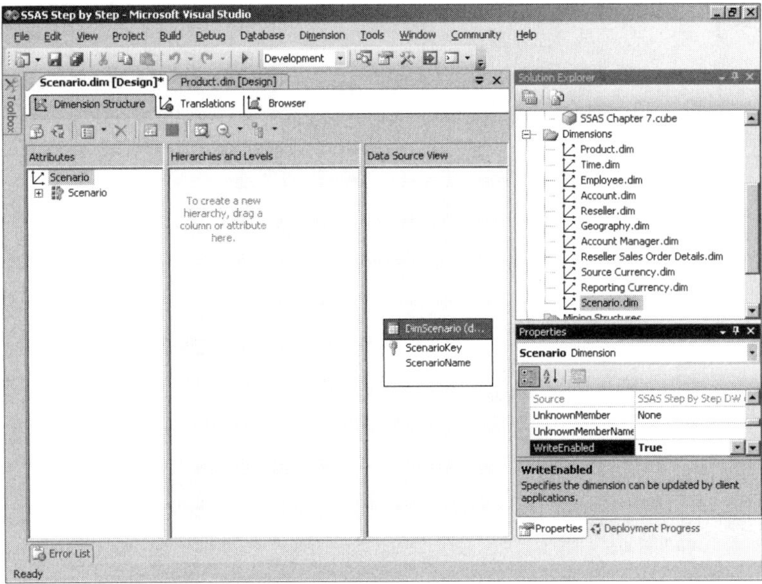

13. Deploy the project.

    You now have a shared, single-level, write-enabled Scenario dimension that you can use in creating a sales forecast cube. In order to add members to this dimension, you need a client application that can accept user input for a new dimension member.

Dynamically Adding Members to a Dimension

In the course of a planning cycle, it's often necessary to add one more round than originally planned–preferably without disrupting the use of the data. Because you write-enabled the Scenario dimension, you can easily add a new scenario. Typically, writing new values into a dimension is something that a client application would help you do. Fortunately, the dimension browser in Visual Studio will allow you to test writing new values to a dimension.

In this procedure, you'll add a new member to the Scenario dimension.

Write back a new dimension member

1. Click the Browser tab in the Scenario dimension designer.
2. Click the Writeback button on the dimension designer toolbar.

Your screen looks like this:

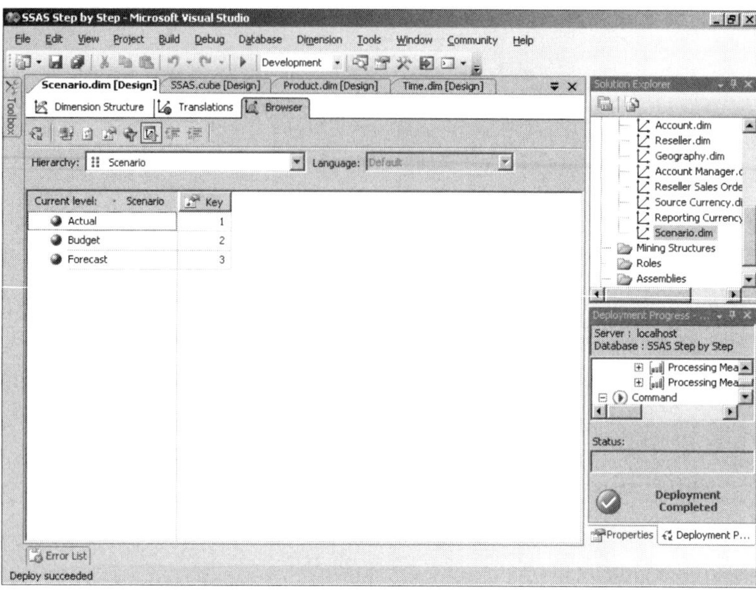

3. Right-click Forecast in the Current Level column, click Create Sibling, and then type **Forecast Second Pass**.

4. Click in the Key column next to Forecast Second Pass, type **4**, and then press Enter.

   Your screen looks like this:

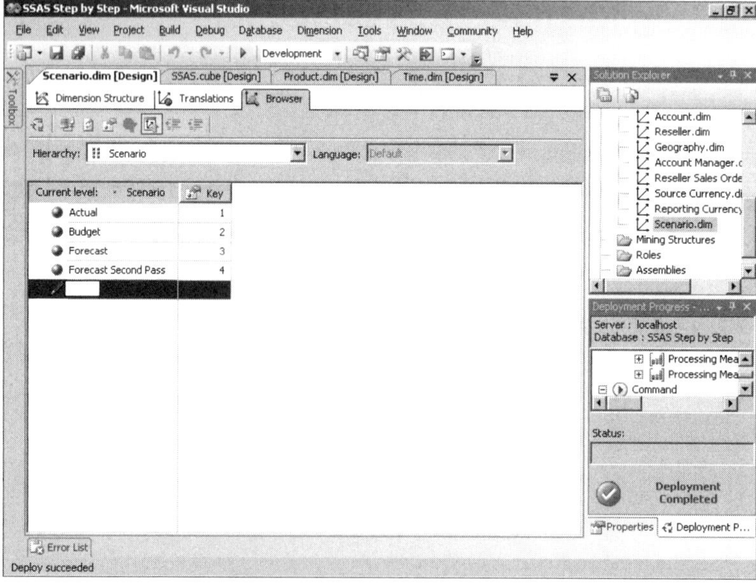

Unlike writing back values to a cube—where values are stored in a special writeback table—when you add a new member to a dimension, the member is added directly to the original dimension table. You must have permission to add rows to the dimension table in order to use dimension writeback. You don't need to process the cube or the dimension in order for new dimension members to take effect. The process is remarkably seamless.

It's even easy to write back data values that use the new dimension member. You do not need to stop the planning process. You do not need to process anything. The new member is instantly available and usable. The ability to dynamically create new members—particularly for a Scenario dimension—is critical for a planning application.

Modifying the Cube Structure for Writeback

Logically, since all the values in the sales forecast cube will be hand-entered by you, the cube should not require a fact table. As you'll soon learn, that's because when you write values back to a cube, they're not stored in the fact table. Physically, however, you cannot create a measure group in a cube without a fact table. If for no other reason, the columns of the fact table determine the potential dimensions and measures for the cube. You can add an empty fact table to a data source view by using a Named Query. The fact table is purely a logical object and will remain completely empty. You must have a fact table to create a measure group, but nobody said the fact table had to contain facts.

In this procedure, you'll create a measure group from an empty fact table.

Create a unit forecast measure group

1. In Solution Explorer, double-click SSAS Step by Step DW.dsv, right-click the background of the Data Source View Diagram pane, and then click New Named Query.
2. Type a name for the named query, **Units Forecast**, and then type the following query in the SQL Pane of the Query Definition box:

```
Select null as ScenarioKey, null as CategoryKey, null as FiscalQuarter, null as [Sales
Units]
```

The Create Named Query dialog box looks like this:

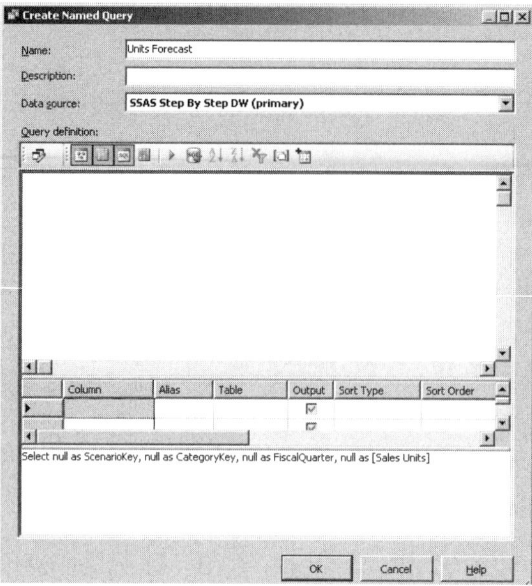

3. Click OK.
4. Right-click the Unit Forecast named query, and then click Explore Data.

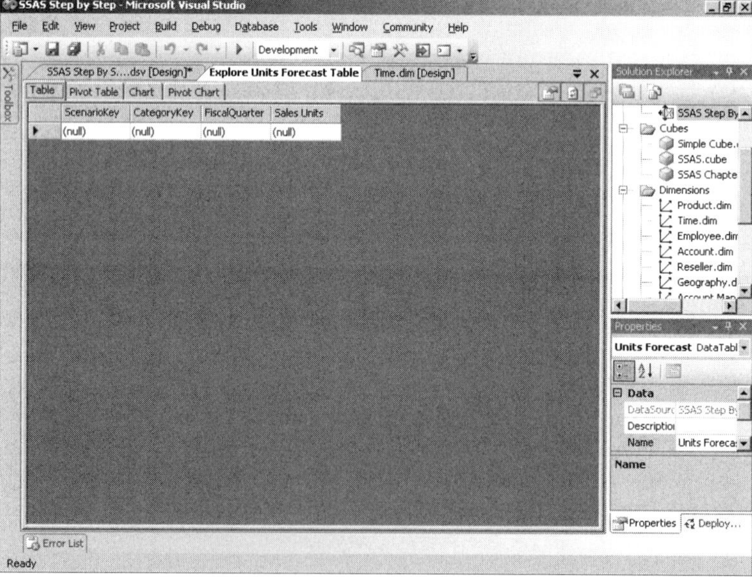

You can see the columns for the fact table, and confirm the fact that it has only a single row which is completely empty.

5. Close the Explore Data window, and then open the SSAS cube.

6. On the Cube Structure tab right-click anywhere in the Measures pane, click New Measure, select Units Forecast in the Source Table drop-down list, select Sales Units in the Source Column list, and then click OK.

   Because the new measure group is not yet associated with any dimensions, a red wavy line appears beneath the measure group name to indicate an error exists. You'll fix this error later in this procedure by defining dimension relationships on the Dimension Usage tab.

7. Right-click anywhere in the Dimensions pane, click Add Cube Dimension, select Scenario, and then click OK.

8. Click the Dimension Usage tab, scroll horizontally to the right to locate the Units Forecast measure group, and then click the intersection of Units Forecast and Product, and then click the ellipsis button.

9. Select Regular in the Select Relationship Type drop-down list, select Category in the Granularity Attribute drop-down list, select CategoryKey in the MeasureGroupColumns drop-down list, and then click OK.

   You'll forecast sales units by product category and by quarter. Product categories are found in the Product dimension, but they're not at the lowest level of the dimension. Likewise, calendar quarters are found in the Time.Calendar dimension, but, again, they're not at the lowest level of the dimension. When you define the relationship between a dimension and a measure group, you can choose any attribute in the dimension as long as a corresponding key column is available in the measure group's fact table.

10. Click the intersection of Units Forecast and Time, and then click the ellipsis button.

11. Select Regular in the Select Relationship Type drop-down list, select Fiscal Quarter in the Granularity Attribute drop-down list, select FiscalQuarter in the MeasureGroupColumns drop-down list, and then click OK.

12. Click the intersection of Units Forecast and Scenario, and then click the ellipsis button.

13. Select Regular in the Select Relationship Type drop-down list, select Scenario in the Granularity Attribute drop-down list, select ScenarioKey in the MeasureGroupColumns drop-down list, and then click OK.

With one measure and all relationships to pertinent dimensions defined, you should now have all you need to save and process the cube. If you were to try, however, you would see a message informing you that key attributes in the fact table cannot be found in the related dimension tables. Before processing a cube from a fact table with no data, you must manually reconfigure the error processing for the corresponding measure group in the cube.

14. Click the Cube Structure tab, click Units Forecast in the Measures pane, and then, in the Properties window, select (custom) in the *ErrorConfiguration* property's drop-down list.

15. Click the plus sign to expand the *ErrorConfiguration* property, and then select IgnoreError in the *KeyNotFound* property's drop-down list.

    Your screen looks like this:

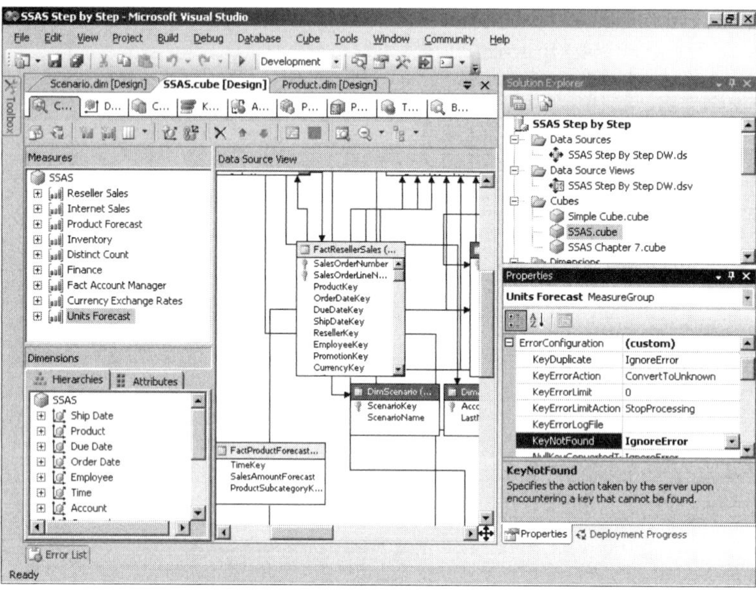

16. Deploy the project, click the Browser tab, click Reconnect, click anywhere in the grid, and then click the Clear Results button in the toolbar.

17. Expand the Units Forecast measure group, drag the Sales Units measure into the center of the grid, expand the Scenario dimension, and then drag the Scenario attribute to the rows axis.

Your screen looks like this:

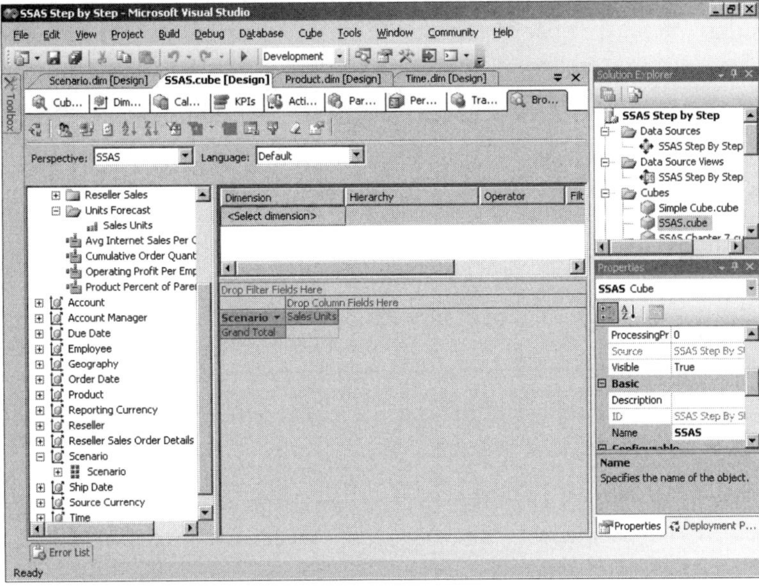

Not surprisingly, the browser is empty. The important points are that the measure group exists and that it has placeholders where you can add forecast values.

Writing Values Back to a Cube

In Analysis Services, you can write values only to the lowest level of a cube. In other words, you cannot change the value of an aggregation. If you could change the value of an aggregation, you would be able to make the cube internally inconsistent. Technically, Analysis Services writes incremental change values to a special writeback table in a relational database. Analysis Services then dynamically combines the writeback values with any values from the fact table.

Note For application developers, Analysis Services includes a tool—the Update Cube MDX statement—that will allocate a given high-level input value to create the necessary lowest-level values. A client application can thus appear to write back at a high level. In reality, however, the values being written back to the cube are always at the lowest level of the cube.

To write values back to a cube, you must have a client application that includes writeback capabilities. None of the browsers included with Analysis Services or with Microsoft Office 2003 includes writeback capability. Included on the companion CD for this book is a Microsoft Excel 2003 workbook that includes macros that demonstrate how to write values back to the Unit Forecast measure group of the SSAS cube.

To write values back so that they'll be retained for future use, the cube must be *write-enabled*. When you write-enable a cube, you specify the location of a relational table where the write-back values will be stored.

In this procedure, you'll write-enable a partition, use Excel to enter new values for the measure group, and review the relational table where the writeback values are stored.

Write back values

1. Click the Partitions tab, expand Units Forecast, right-click the Units Forecast partition, and then click Writeback Settings.

   The Enable Writeback – Units Forecast dialog box looks like this:

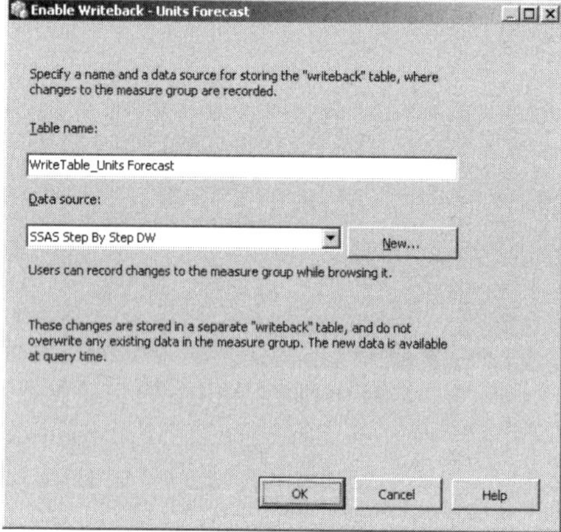

> **Note** You don't need to write the data back to the same data source as the one containing the fact table. For example, if the fact table for the cube is in a corporate data warehouse that you don't have permission to write to, you can create a Microsoft SQL Server database that you can use for the writeback table. The Enable Writeback dialog box even allows you to define a new data source dynamically.

2. Click OK.

Your screen looks like this:

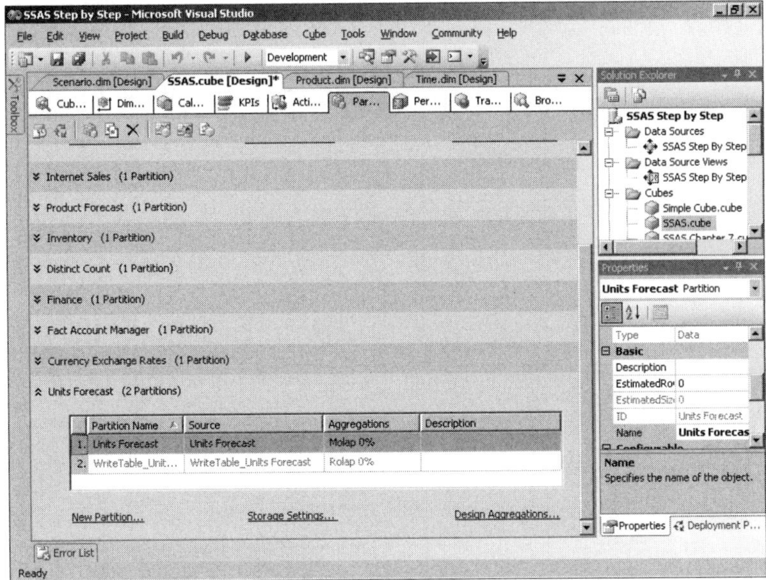

Notice there is a new relational OLAP (ROLAP) partition added for this measure group that you cannot edit. You'll learn more about ROLAP partitions in Chapter 12, "Managing Partitions and Database Processing."

3. Deploy the project to add the new partition to the server.
4. When deployment is complete, start Microsoft Excel. On the File menu, click Open, navigate to C:\Documents and Settings\<username>\My Documents\Microsoft Press\as2005sbs\chap10, and open the Writeback workbook.

> **Note** You must have macro security set to Medium before using this workbook. When the Security Warning displays upon opening the workbook, click Enable Macros.

5. Click Retrieve Values From Cube.

Your screen looks like this:

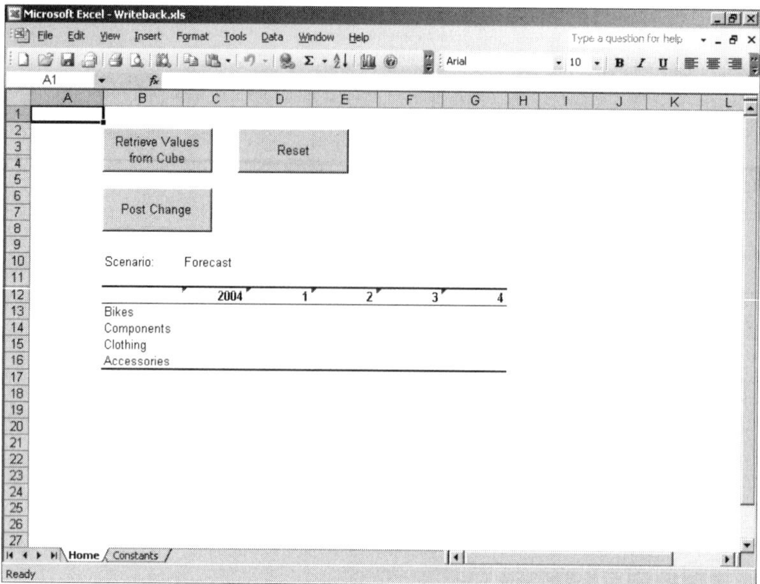

The labels from the Product and Time dimensions appear. The Category and Quarter values represent the detail levels within the Unit Forecast measure group. The 2004 values are aggregations. Because no data is in the fact table, and no writeback data has been stored yet either, the cell intersections of Category and Quarter are empty.

6. In the Bikes row, type **3,000** for quarter 1 (D13), **4,000** for quarter 2 (E13), **5,000** for quarter 3 (F13), and **6,000** for quarter 4 (G13). Then click Post Change.
7. Click Reset, which clears the data range and resets the connection to the server, and then click Retrieve Values From Cube.

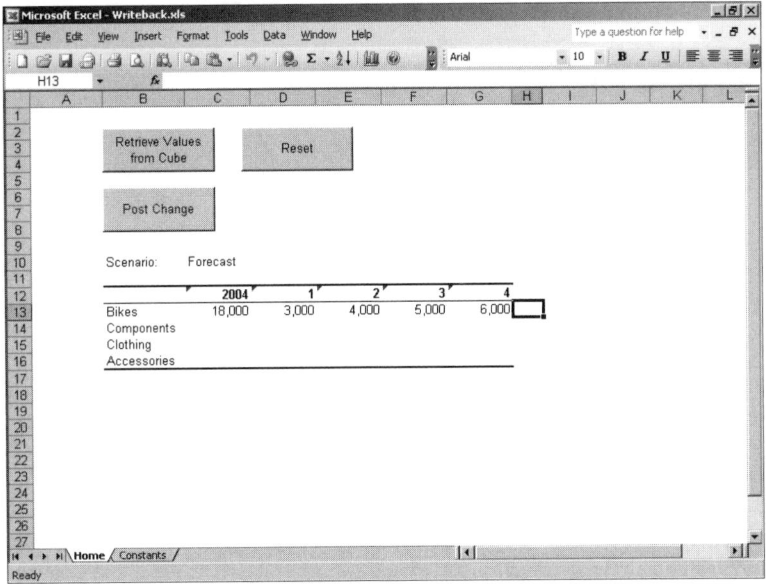

The values reappear—along with the total for 2004. The values are stored in the write-back table and are now visible to anyone who accesses the cube. You can also write back values for a different scenario.

Note You can find out more about how to use security to determine who can write values back to a cube in Chapter 11, "Implementing Security."

Note If you know Microsoft Visual Basic and want to create your own application that can write values to a cube, look at the macros in the Writeback workbook for some useful sample code.

Because the values written back to a cube are stored in a relational table, you can browse them. You can use the native tool for the data source that contains the writeback table, or you can browse the values from within SQL Server Management Studio.

8. In SQL Server Management Studio, connect to the Database Engine, and then expand the following items in the tree: Databases, SSAS Step by Step DW, and Tables.
9. Right-click dbo.WriteTable_Units Forecast, and then click Open Table.

Your screen looks like this:

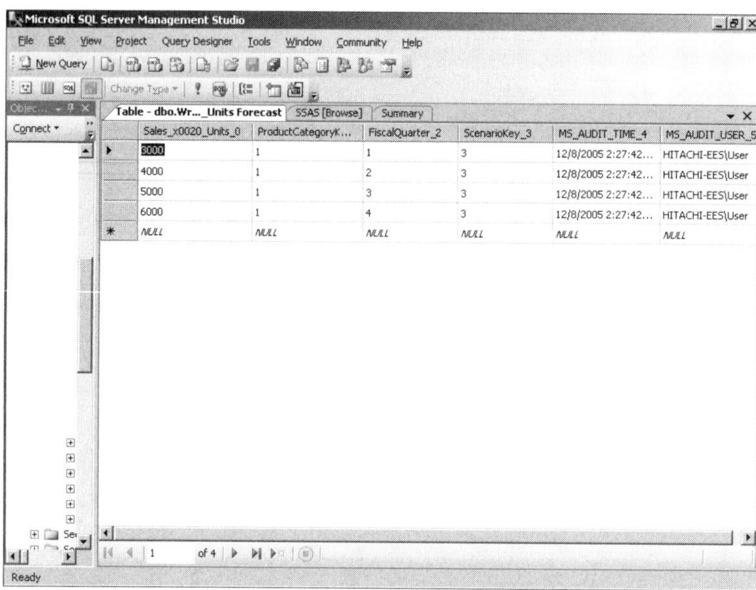

You can now see the rows contained in the writeback table. You can resize the window as necessary to see all the columns.

The MS_AUDIT_TIME and MS_AUDIT_USER columns on the right contain audit-trail information: the name of the user who made the changes, and the time the changes were made. The Sales_x0020_Units_0 column on the left contains the measure for the cube. (The table includes one column for each measure in the cube.) The remaining columns contain the member keys for each level of each dimension in the cube for which data has been entered.

The writeback table stores incremental values. If you were to change the value of Sales Units for Bikes in quarter 1 of 2004 to *4,000* and write the value back to the cube again, you would get an additional row with new audit information and the value *1,000*.

10. Close SQL Server Management Studio and Excel.

> **Note** Because the writeback values are stored in a relational table, you could use tools of your relational database system to append the values to the original fact table. Then, using SQL Server Management Studio, process the cube and delete the write-back partition.

In this section, you've seen how the writeback process works, but only with limited tools. If planning will be a part of your work with Analysis Services, you'll need to obtain or create a client application that supports writeback—at least for cube data.

Chapter 10 Quick Reference

To	Do this
Create a URL action	In the Cube Designer, click the Actions tab, click the New Action button, name the action, select a target type and target object, specify the type of action as URL, and then type an expression that resolves as a URL.
Create a Reporting action	In the Cube Designer, click the Actions tab, click the New Reporting Action button, name the action, select a target type and target object, type the report server name, type a report path, and then, optionally, type a report parameter name and an MDX expression as the parameter value.
Create a drillthrough action	In the Cube Designer, click the Actions tab, click the New Drillthrough Action button, name the action, select a measure group, and then specify drillthrough columns.
Write-enable a dimension	On the Dimension Structure tab of the Dimension Designer, select the dimension, and then, in the Properties window, change the *Write-Enabled* property to True.
Add a member to a write-enabled dimension	On the Browser tab of the Dimension Designer, click the Writeback button, right-click a dimension member, click Create Sibling, and then type a name and a key value for the new member.
Create a single-measure measure group from an empty fact table	In the Data Source View, create a named query with columns for the measure and for each dimension to which the measure group will be related. On the Cube Structure tab of the Cube Designer, right-click in the Measures pane, click New Measure, click the named query in the Source Table list box, and then select the measure in the Source Column drop-down list. In the Properties window, change the measure group's *ErrorConfiguration* property to (custom), and then change the *KeyNotFound* property to IgnoreError. On the Dimension Usage tab of the Cube Designer, create a regular relationship between the measure group and any related dimensions.
Write-enable a partition	On the Partitions tab of the Cube Designer, right-click the partition, click Writeback Settings, and then specify a data source for the write-back table.

Part IV
Production Management

In this part:

Chapter 11: Implementing Security 271
Chapter 12: Managing Partitions and Database Processing 295
Chapter 13: Managing Deployment 335

In Part II, "Design Fundamentals," and Part III, "Advanced Design," you explored many techniques that you can use to build flexible and powerful analytical solutions. However, implementing these solutions is not limited to the design and construction of database objects. You need to secure access to data, synchronize updates to the data warehouse with the dimensions and cubes, and perform routine administrative tasks. The chapters of Part IV show you how to manage your analytical solutions in a production environment.

Chapter 11

Implementing Security

After completing this chapter, you will be able to:

- Create security roles in an OLAP database.
- Manage security roles at the database and cube levels.
- Restrict access to dimensions and parts of dimensions.
- Create a custom calculated member for different roles.
- Create MDX expressions to apply cell-level security.

In most real-world applications, online analytical processing (OLAP) databases are designed to answer many different questions that diverse groups of individuals might ask. For example, a sales representative might be interested in his or her sales in a particular region by product by customer. A district manager might be interested in the total sales in one region by product by customer. And a technical support representative might be interested in the number of telephone inquiries by product by customer. In many cases, a series of cubes will provide these answers. In certain circumstances, all of this information could reside in one cube. If you'd like the sales rep to be able to see only his or her own sales information and *not* another sales rep's data, you must implement security. In this chapter, you'll learn about how security works in Microsoft SQL Server 2005 Analysis Services.

Using Role-Based Security

Analysis Services security is based on and integrated with Microsoft Windows security. When you define security in Analysis Services, you create roles in the OLAP database. Each *role* can contain one or more specific user accounts or user groups as defined in the operating system. Once you've created a database role, you can associate that role with cubes in the OLAP database. In addition, you can fine-tune security within a cube by restricting access to metadata (the members on dimensions) as well as access to data (the values stored in the cubes).

Note Analysis Services has a fixed server role that automatically includes members of the local Administrators group on the host server. To perform any administrative task within an Analysis Services instance, the active user must be a member of the local Administrators group. Any member of this group has complete access to every cube and database on the server. As an alternative, you use database roles to grant administrative permissions such that a user can administer one database but can be excluded from administering a different database.

Creating Security Roles

Security in Analysis Services depends on operating system User and Group accounts. When a new person is granted the right to use a Windows server, a server administrator must first create a user account for that person. That user account should be assigned to one or more appropriate user groups. In this chapter, you'll create security by using Windows users and groups. If you have only default users and groups, you should create some sample ones to use as a test. If you already have your own users and groups available in your Windows server, you can use them.

When you create a new database or cube, the server role gives access to members of the local Administrators. A client cube browser application can browse the cube, provided that the user belongs to the local Administrators group. Any user who does not belong to the local Administrators group has no permission at all—either to administer or to browse the cubes. If you create a cube and make it available to other users in your organization, they will not be able to see anything in the cube. In many situations, you want to allow all users to browse a cube but not to administer the cube using Visual Studio or SQL Server Management Studio. To do that, you must create a new role.

In this procedure, you'll create sample users and groups in preparation for implementing role-based security.

Create sample users and groups

1. In Windows 2003, click the Start menu, point to All Programs, Administrative Tools, and then click Computer Management.

> **Note** Although the general principles don't change, the detailed steps for adding a new user or group vary depending on which Windows operating system you're using. Refer to Help for your operating system if you're not familiar with creating users and groups.

2. Under the System Tools folder, expand the Local Users And Groups node, right-click the Users folder and then click New User.

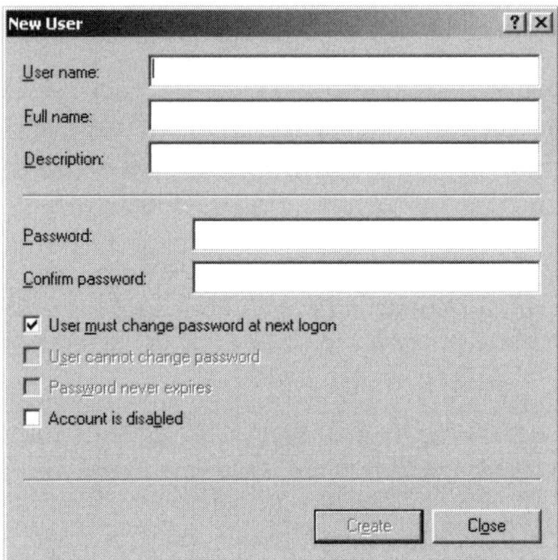

3. Type **_jdoe** in the User Name box. (The underscore at the beginning of the name will make it easy to find and remove the sample users and groups.) Type **John Doe** in the Full Name box, type **salesCube1** in the Password box, clear the User Must Change Password At Next Logon check box, and then click Create.

   The boxes in the New User dialog box clear when the user has been created.

4. To create a second sample user, type **_mjturner** in the User Name box, type **Mary Jane Turner** in the Full Name box, type **salesCube2** in the Password box, clear the User Must Change Password At Next Logon check box, and then click Create.
5. To create a third sample user, type **_jsmith** in the User Name box, type **Jeni Smith** in the Full Name box, type **salesAdmin** in the Password box, clear the User Must Change Password At Next Logon check box, and then click Close.
6. Right-click the Groups folder, click New Group, type **_FinancialAnalysts** in the Group Name box, and then click Add.
7. In the Enter The Object Names To Select box, type **_jdoe**, and then click OK.
8. Click Create, type **_FinancialReviewers** in the Group Name box, click the Add button, type **_jdoe;_mjturner**, click OK, and then click Close.
9. Close the Computer Management console.

> **Important** After completing this chapter, be sure to delete the sample users and groups from your computer.

Creating a new user or a new group has no effect on Analysis Services until you explicitly add the user or group to a specific database. Of course, adding a user account to the existing Administrators group would change who could run the SQL Server Management Studio or Visual Studio applications to browse cubes with no security applied.

In this procedure, you'll create a standard user security role.

Create an Analysis Services role for all users

1. Start SQL Server Business Intelligence Development Studio (BIDS), and open the SSAS Step by Step solution that you saved in the C:\Documents and Settings\<username>\My Documents\Microsoft Press\as2005sbs\Workspace folder.

> **Note** If you skipped Chapter 10, "Interacting with Cubes," open the SSAS Step by Step solution in the C:\Documents and Settings\<username>\My Documents\Microsoft Press\as2005sbs\Answers\chap10\SSAS Step by Step folder.

2. In the Solution Explorer window, right-click Roles, and then click New Role.
3. In Solution Explorer, right-click Role.Role, click Rename, then type **All Users.role**, press Enter, and then click Yes when prompted to change the object.

> **Important** As with all objects within an Analysis Services project, you must be sure that the file extension, which in this case is .role, is preserved when you rename the object.

Your screen looks like this:

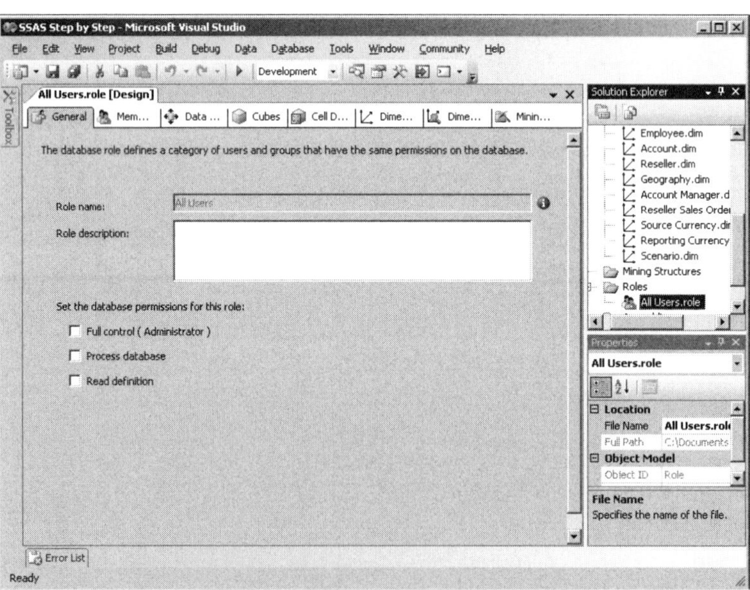

4. Click the Membership tab, click Add, click Advanced, click Find Now, select Everyone in the Search Results list, and then click OK twice to close all dialog boxes.

Your screen looks like this:

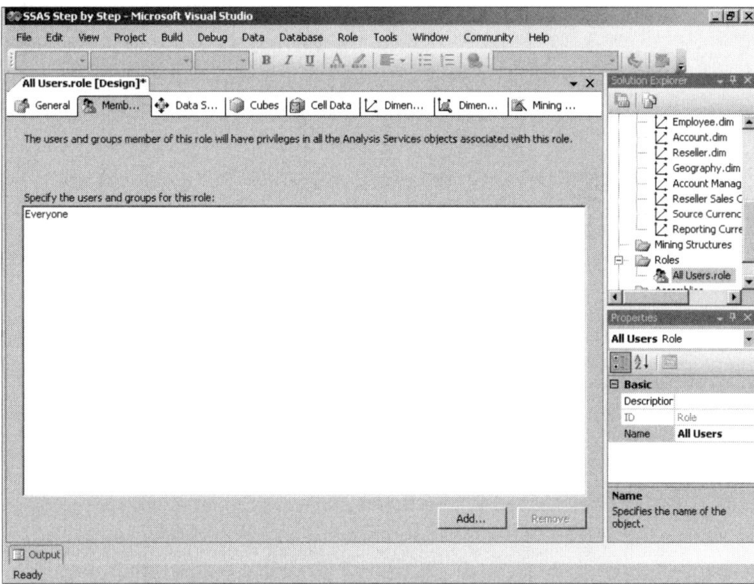

Although the database role now includes all users that have access to the server, only members of the server role can read Analysis Services data at this point. You must explicitly grant permissions to cubes and dimensions in order for all users to browse data.

5. Click the Data Sources tab.

   Your screen looks like this:

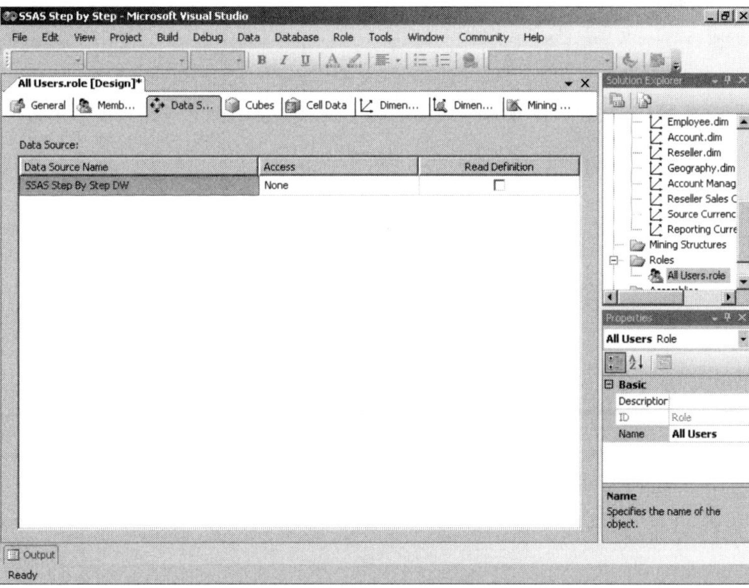

Access to the SSAS Step by Step DW data source object is not available, by default, since users query the data in the cube and do not query the data source directly.

6. Click the Cubes tab, and then select Read in the Access drop-down list for the SSAS cube.

   Your screen looks like this:

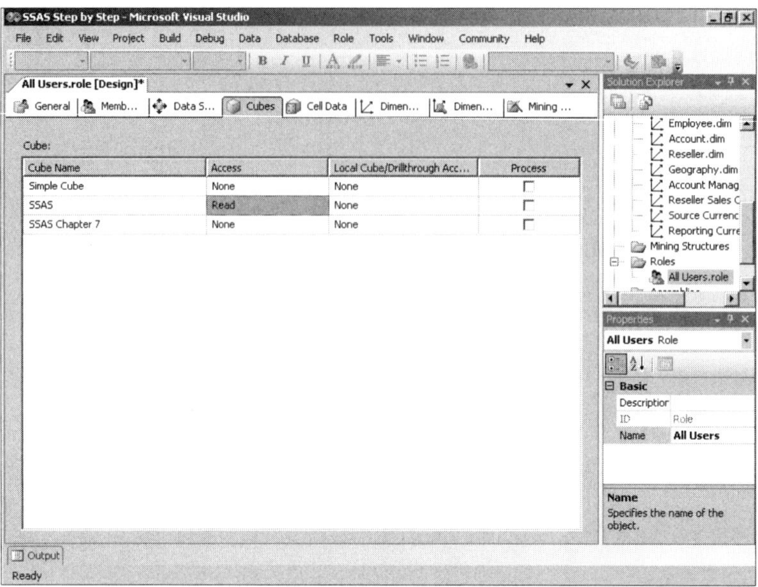

   By default, a new role has no access to the cubes in the database. If you decide to grant a role access to a cube, you need to decide whether access will be read-only or, to accommodate writeback, read/write. Additionally, you can grant permissions to allow the role to use drillthrough and, optionally, to create a local cube for offline analysis. Finally, you can grant the role permissions to process the cube, but generally you choose this option only when creating a database role that is limited to those users to whom you want to give administrative responsibilities.

7. Click the Dimensions tab.

Your screen looks like this:

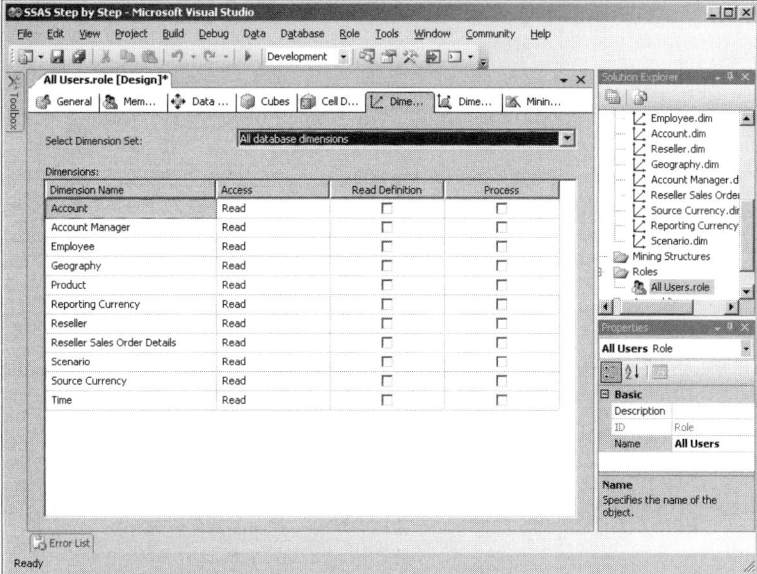

Once you grant a role Read or Read/Write access to a cube, then the role by default has Read access to each dimension in the cube. You can modify a role to prevent access to certain dimensions, which will be covered in more detail later in this chapter. Even if you grant read permissions for one or more dimensions, users assigned to this role cannot view data until the role is granted permission to access the cube.

A role's dimension access does not have to be universal across all cubes within the database. For example, if a role has access to more than one cube in the same database, you can separately specify which dimensions are accessible in each cube by first changing the selection in the Select Dimension Set drop-down list to limit the scope of the dimension permissions to a particular cube.

8. In Solution Explorer, right-click the project, and then click Deploy.

The SSAS cube is now available for browsing by any user who can connect to the server. If you intend to make all your OLAP cubes freely available in the organization, this completes all that you need to know about user security in Analysis Services.

Managing Roles

When different users should have different permissions to access data from cubes, you need to create multiple roles. You can create each new role individually without reusing security definitions created for other roles, or you can copy an existing role and make any necessary changes to the new role. For example, if you need a new role that's only slightly different from an existing role, you can make a duplicate copy of the existing role and then modify it.

In this procedure, you'll create two roles, one for financial analysts and another for financial reviewers.

Copy roles

1. In Solution Explorer, right-click All Users.role, click Copy, right-click the Roles folder, click Paste, type **Financial Analysts** in the Name box, and then click OK.
2. Copy All Users.role again, and then right-click the Roles folder again, click Paste, type **Financial Reviewers** in the Name box, and then click OK.

   You now have a total of three roles created for this project, which will all be associated with the corresponding Analysis Services database on the server once the project is deployed. Right now, each role is identical, but as you progress through this chapter, you will modify each role to set different permissions that control what users can see in the database and whether they can use the drillthrough or writeback features of Analysis Services.

Applying Security to a Dimension

When you apply security at the cube level, you simply allow or disallow access to the entire cube. That is often appropriate, but it gives you no flexibility. Often, you want managers to see information unavailable to individual contributors, or you don't want individuals in the marketing department to see budget details from the manufacturing department. Dimension-level security provides a powerful, but simple, mechanism for granting partial access to a cube.

Restricting Access to a Dimension

The simplest–and most useful–option for restricting access to a dimension is to prevent all access to its attribute hierarchies. Earlier in this chapter, you gave complete access to the SSAS cube to all users. Perhaps you don't want all users to be able to see values broken out by certain attributes within a dimension.

In this procedure, you'll modify the permissions for the All Users role to prevent all access to any member of the Account Manager dimension.

Fully restrict a dimension

1. Double-click the All Users role in the Solution Explorer to open the Role Designer, if it's not already open.
2. Click the Dimensions tab, and then select SSAS Cube Dimensions in the Select Dimensions Set drop-down list.
3. Clear the check box in the Inherit column for Account Manager.

Your screen looks like this:

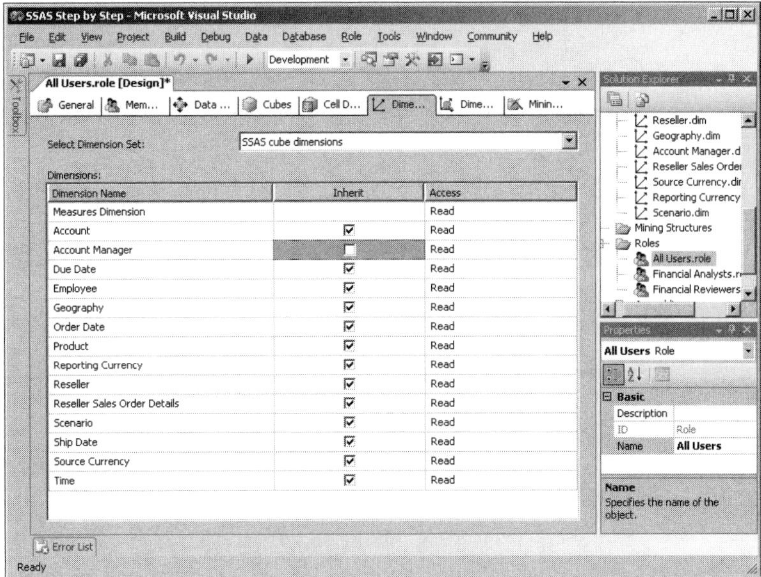

Security at the cube level is inherited from the permissions defined at the database level for each dimension, unless you override these permissions on this tab and on the Dimension Data tab.

4. Click the Dimension Data tab.
5. In the Dimension drop-down list, select Account Manager (the one listed below the SSAS cube, which controls the dimension access for this cube only), click OK, and then select Deselect All Members in the Attribute Hierarchy section.

Important It's very important to select the correct dimension object in this Dimension drop-down list. For example, if you selected the Account Manager object listed below the SSAS Step by Step database, you would be deselecting members at the database level. However, you disabled inheritance on the Dimension tab of the Role Designer so changes to the dimension security at the database level will not affect dimension security at the cube level. If you were to deploy the database now, this role would still have access to all members of the Account Manager dimension.

Your screen looks like this:

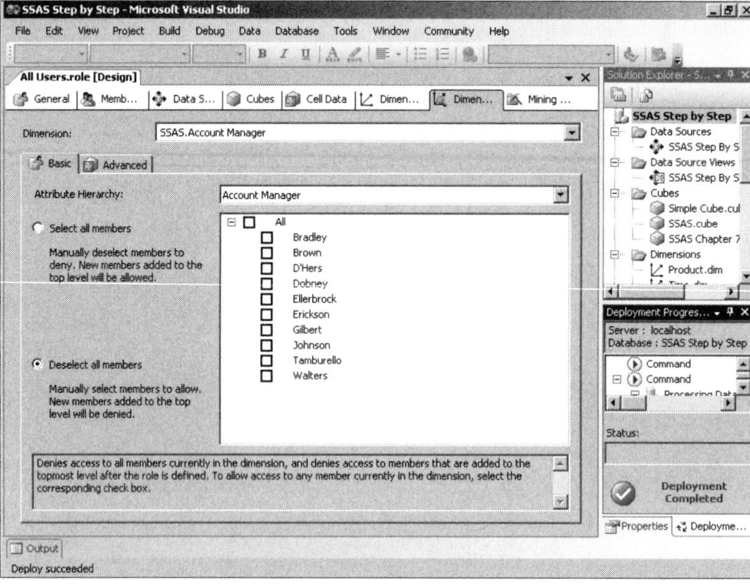

6. Deploy the project to apply the change to the security permissions for the All Users role.
7. In Solution Explorer, double-click SSAS.cube to open the cube designer, click the Browser tab, and then click the Change User button in the toolbar.
8. Select Roles, select All Users in the Roles drop-down list, and then click OK.

   The Security Context – SSAS dialog box looks like this:

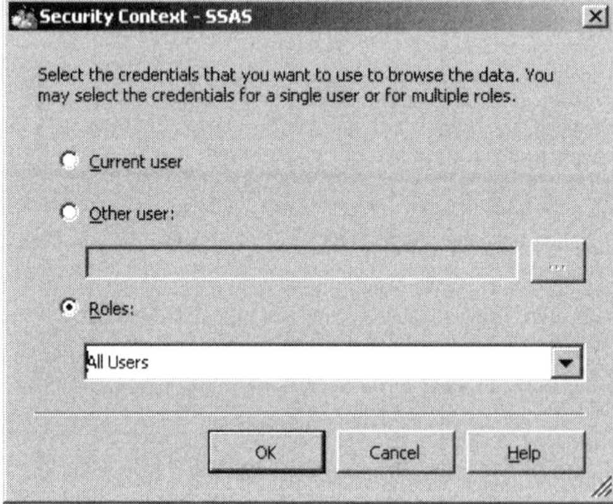

9. Click OK.

   Notice the message below the toolbar that indicates that you are browsing the cube with the credentials of All Users.

10. Drag the Measures object to the center of the grid, and then drag the Account Manager dimension object to the rows axis of the grid.

11. In the metadata tree, expand the Account Manager dimension object, expand the Account Manager attribute hierarchy, expand the Members folder, and then try to expand the All member.

    Your screen looks like this:

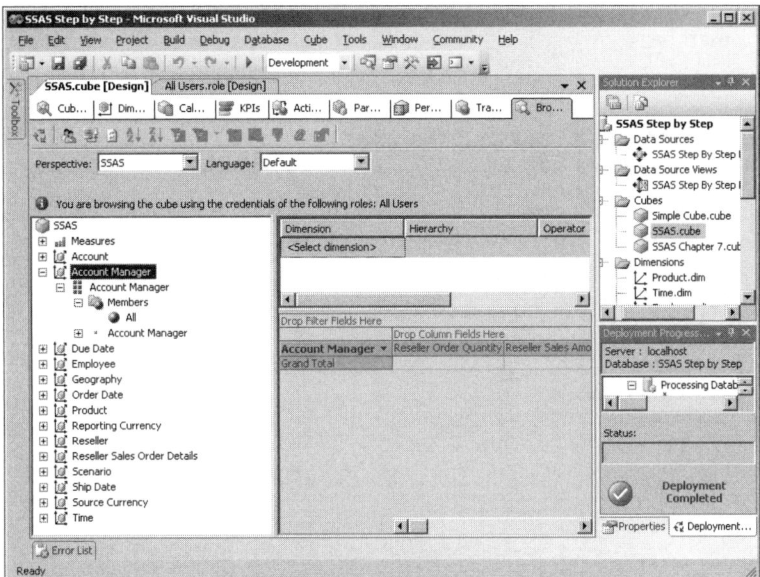

When you deselect all members of an attribute hierarchy, you cannot view those members in the cube browser, and you cannot browse the members in the cube metadata tree view. Note that restricting access to a dimension doesn't make it invisible to users. Dimension security simply hides the members of the specified attribute hierarchy.

> **Tip** You need to explicitly restrict access for *each* attribute hierarchy of a dimension to restrict access for the entire dimension.

Restricting Access to Specific Members of a Dimension

You might want to allow a group of users to see some parts of a dimension but not all of it. The dimensions of a role allow you to do that. Suppose, for example, that you want all users to be able to see the sales figures only for product categories and subcategories, but not for individual products.

In this procedure, you'll limit the All Users role to viewing specific members of the Category and Subcategory attribute hierarchies of the Product dimension.

Restrict the members of a dimension

1. If the Role Designer for All Users is not currently open, double-click All Users.role in Solution Explorer.
2. Click the Dimension Data tab, select Product in the Dimension drop-down list (under SSAS), and then click OK.
3. Select Category in the Attribute Hierarchy drop-down list, and then click each of the following categories–Components, Clothing, Accessories, and Unknown–to deselect these members.

   Your screen looks like this:

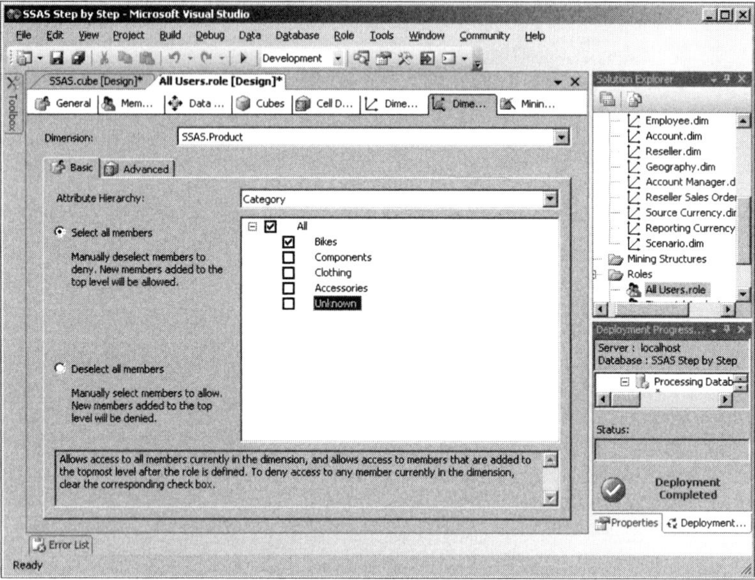

4. Deploy the project to apply the change to the security permissions for the All Users role.
5. Switch to the Browser tab of the Cube Designer, and then click Reconnect.
6. Expand Product, and then drag Subcategory to the rows axis.

Your screen looks like this:

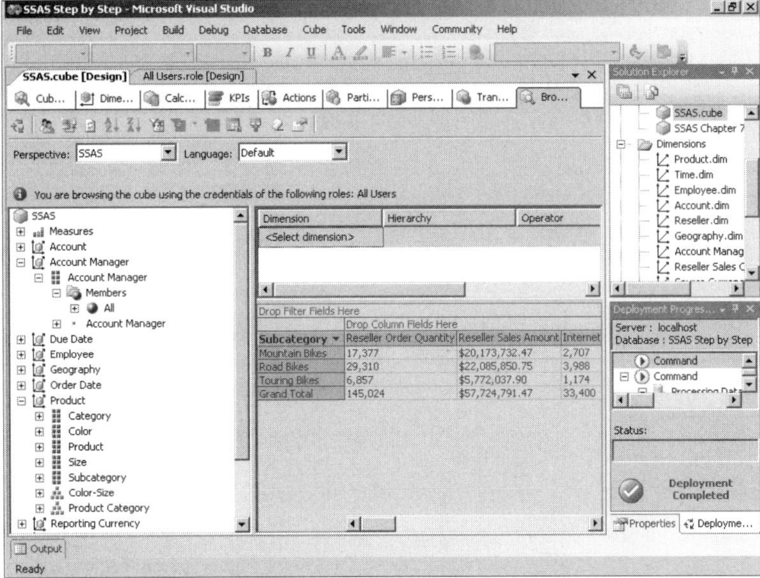

Notice that only Mountain Bikes, Road Bikes, and Touring Bikes are visible. Because of the relationship between Category and Subcategory, the security which limited Category members to Bikes also affected the Subcategory members. Also notice that the Grand Total still includes all product sales and is not affected by dimension security, making the report appear to be inaccurate.

Controlling Visual Totals for a Dimension

In addition to excluding specific members from dimensions, you can also filter the aggregate values for a dimension so that the Grand Total only displays the aggregate for the visible members. By controlling *visual totals* for a dimension, the difference between the values displayed and the actual Grand Total for the dimension cannot be deduced.

In this procedure, you'll enable visual totals for the Subcategory attribute hierarchy.

Enable visual totals

1. Open the role designer for All Users, click the Dimension Data tab, select Subcategory in the Attribute Hierarchy drop-down list, and then click the Advanced tab.
2. At the bottom of the screen, select the Enable Visual Total check box.

   Default settings for the cube's access return all values directly from the cube. The Grand Total for Subcategory is an aggregated value from the cube, not a calculation based on visible members in the browser. By changing the setting for this attribute hierarchy to Enable Visual Total, the cube will now display the total of the visible members instead of returning the aggregated value for the hierarchy.

3. Deploy the project to apply the change to the attribute hierarchy.
4. Click Reconnect in the Cube Designer's Browser.

   Your screen looks like this:

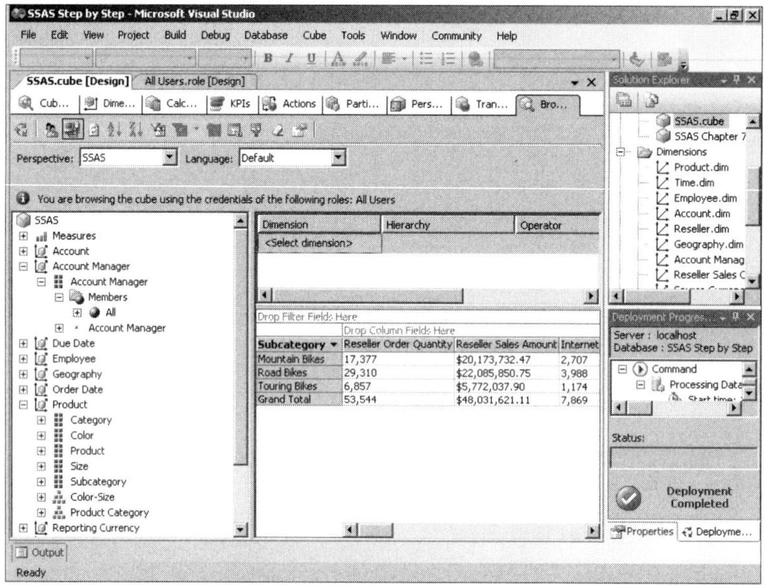

The Grand Total now appears as the sum of Mountain Bikes, Road Bikes, and Touring Bikes. It's as if the other Subcategories don't exist, and no one–at least no one who is viewing the cube as a member of the All Users role–has access to the information necessary to figure out all product sales.

Defining a Default Member for a Dimension

The default member is used for any filter attribute hierarchy that does not have an explicit value selected. By default, the default member for an attribute hierarchy is the member of the All level. You can manually set the default member of an attribute hierarchy by specifying a member as the value for its *DefaultMember* property. But what if you need a different default member for different groups of users? For example, suppose that for the Time.Calendar dimension, most users want to see the most recent year, but budget analysts want to see the most recent month. By defining the default member in a role, you can give each group the appropriate default member.

> **Note** Adding a default member to a role is independent of using an expression to calculate the default member. You can add a constant default member to a role, and you can put a calculated default member directly in the dimension. The only reason for putting a default member into a role is if you want different default members (constants or expressions) for different groups of users.

In this procedure, you'll assign a default member to the Time.Calendar hierarchy for the All Users role.

Create a default dimension member for a role

1. Switch to the Role Designer for All Users.
2. In the Dimension drop-down list on the Dimension Data tab, select Time (under SSAS), and then click OK.
3. In the Attribute Hierarchy drop-down list, select Calendar Year.
4. In the Default Member box on the Advanced tab, click the Edit MDX button.

   Alternatively, you can type a multidimensional expression (MDX) directly in the Default Member box. The MDX Builder, however, allows you to use drag-and-drop with functions and cube metadata to aid the construction of an expression.
5. Expand the Set folder in the Functions pane, scroll down to locate the TAIL function, and then drag TAIL into the Expression box.

   The syntax for the *Tail* function is *TAIL(«Set»[, «Count»])*. The *Tail* function returns a specified number of members at the end of a set. Since you want the default member to be the most recent year in the Time dimension, you will create a set of members from the Calendar Year attribute hierarchy of the Time dimension and use the *Tail* function to retrieve the most recent, or last, member in that set.
6. In the Expression box, highlight *«Set»*, and then drag Calendar Year from the Metadata pane and drop on *«Set»*.
7. Highlight *[, «Count»]*, and then type **.Members, 1**. After the closing parenthesis of the *Tail* function, type **.Item(0)**.

   The MDX Builder dialog box looks like this:

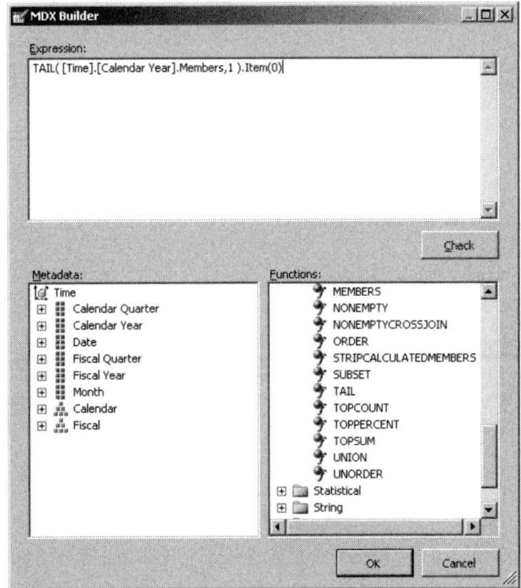

The *Members* function retrieves a set of all the members of the Calendar Year level. The *Item* function then extracts the first (and only!) member of that set. The result of the expression is thus the last member of the Calendar Year attribute hierarchy.

8. Click OK, and then deploy the project to apply the change to the attribute hierarchy, and then click Reconnect on the Browser tab of the Cube Designer.
9. Click anywhere in the grid, click the Clear Results button on the Browser toolbar, and then drag the Amount measure from the Finance folder into the Totals area.

   Your screen looks like this:

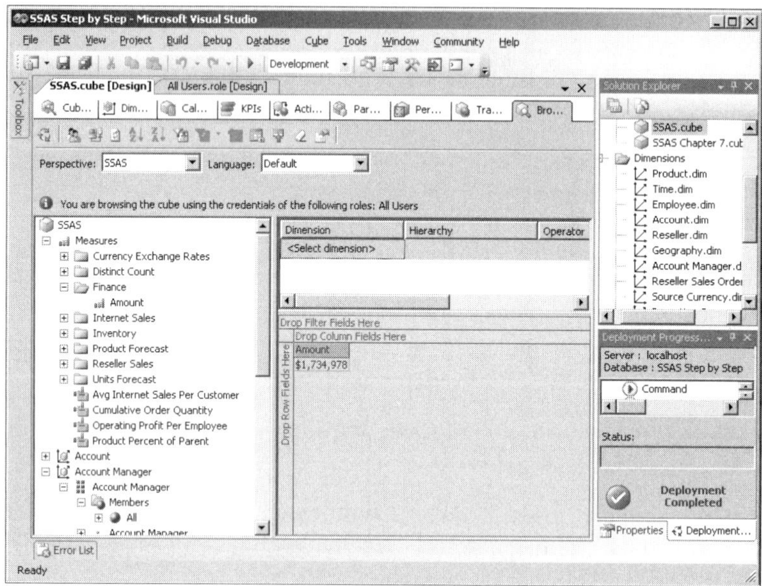

   The amount, $1,734,978, represents the amount for the Calendar Year 2004, which is the last year in the set of members in the Calendar Year attribute hierarchy. Since this attribute hierarchy is not on a row or column axis and is not used as a filter, the default member is automatically applied.

10. Drag the Time.CalendarYear attribute hierarchy onto rows.

Your screen looks like this:

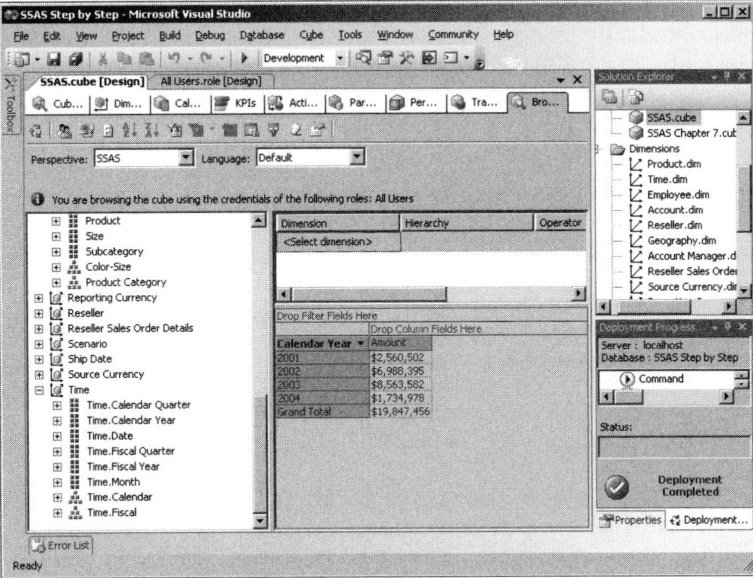

Here you can verify that the amount you saw in the previous step does in fact belong to the year 2004.

Securing Data at the Cell Level

Dimension-level security prevents the user from seeing certain members. Such security does not directly prevent viewing of cell values, but, clearly, if a member does not appear, the values for that member will not be visible either. In short, in most situations, dimension-level security is all you'll ever need. In some situations, however, you might want reports to display all the members but block the values for some of the cells. When you need to secure specific cells without removing members, you need to apply cell-level security to a cube.

Preventing Values in Cells from Being Read

The Finance measure group contains, among other things, expense information. It includes information related to payroll, such as Salaries and Employee Benefits. Salary information is typically very sensitive within a company. You might want to change a cube so that financial reviewers can see the higher level financial information, but not the detailed financial information. You can use cell-level security to do this.

In this procedure, you'll secure detailed Labor data in the SSAS cube.

Add an MDX expression to enable read permissions for specific cube cells

1. In the Browser, replace the Time.Calendar attribute hierarchy on rows with the Accounts hierarchy, and then expand the following members in the grid: Net Income, Operating Profit, Operating Expenses, and Labor Expenses. You might need to resize windows in Visual Studio to see the full grid as it expands horizontally.

   Your screen looks like this:

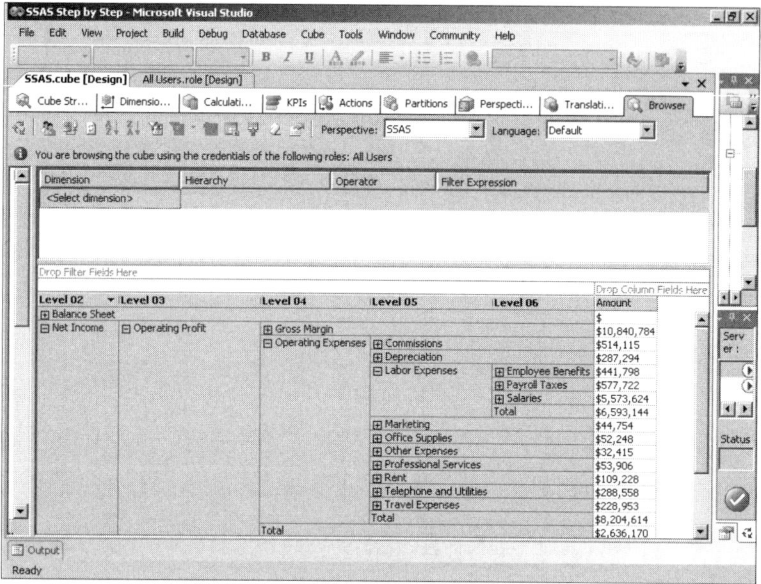

   With no security applied to this dimension or to particular cell values, you can view the dollar amounts for Employee Benefits, Payroll Taxes, and Salaries.

2. In Solution Explorer, double-click Financial Reviewers.role to open the Role Designer.
3. Click the Membership tab, click Add, click Advanced, click Object Types, select the Groups check box, click OK, click Find Now, select _FinancialReviewers, and then click OK twice.
4. Click the Cubes tab, and then select Read in the Access drop-down list for the SSAS cube.
5. Click the Cell Data tab, select SSAS in the Cube drop-down list if necessary, and then select the Enable Read Permissions check box.
6. Type the following MDX expression in the Allow Reading of Cube Content box: **[Account].[Accounts].Parent.Name<>"Labor Expenses"**.

Your screen looks like this:

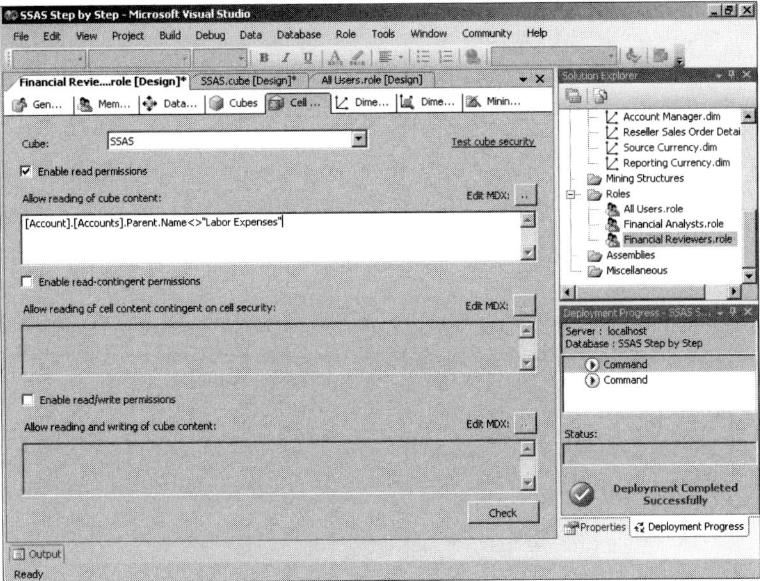

For cell-level security, you need an MDX expression that can be calculated for each cell of a grid. For each cell, before the value is displayed, the expression is evaluated. If, in the context of that one cell, the expression returns the value 1 (*True*), the value is displayed. If the expression returns 0 (*False*), the value is not displayed.

7. Deploy the project to apply the change, switch to the cube Browser, and then click Reconnect.

8. Click the Change Users button on the toolbar, select Financial Reviewers in the Roles drop-down list, clear the All Users check box, and then click OK twice.

9. Drag the Accounts hierarchy to rows, and then expand Measures, Finance and drag Amount to the totals area, and then expand the following members in the grid: Net Income, Operating Profit, Operating Expenses, and Labor Expenses.

Your screen looks like this:

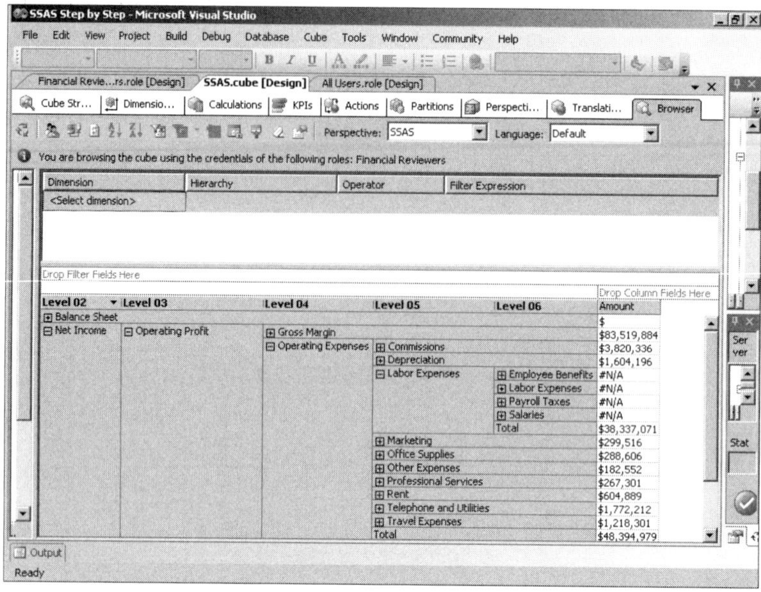

The detailed Labor members still appear, but #N/A appears in all the cells.

10. Close the Browse Window.

Allowing Users to Write to Cells

Cell-level security is particularly important in write-enabled cubes because you might want different groups of people to be able to modify different cell values. The Units Forecast partition in the SSAS cube has been write-enabled if you successfully completed Chapter 10. As a default, a role gives unrestricted read permission but no write permission, even if a partition in the cube is write-enabled. To allow the members of a role to write to a cube, the cube must be write-enabled and then the role must be given read/write permission.

In this procedure, you'll grant permissions to the Financial Analysts role to use writeback with the SSAS cube.

Enable user writeback

1. Open the Role Designer for the Financial Analysts role.
2. Click the Membership tab, click Add, click Advanced, click Object Types, select the Groups check box, click OK, click Find Now, click _FinancialAnalysts, and then click OK twice.
3. Click the Cubes tab, and then select Read/Write in the Access drop-down list of the SSAS cube.

4. Click the Cell Data tab, and then click the checkbox to Enable Read/Write Permissions.

   This will enable this user to have unrestricted read and write access on this cube. If you prefer to restrict some access, you can type or build an MDX expression.

5. Save the project, and then close Visual Studio.

Setting Administration Security

Members of the local Administrators group are automatically members of the Analysis Services server role, and consequently have permissions to perform any task and view any data in all databases deployed on the server. You must be a member of this role in order to grant other users administrative, read, or read/write permissions. When granting administrative permissions to users who are not members of the local Administrators group, you must first decide whether to provide permissions at the server level or at the database level. When granted permissions at the server level, a user can change server properties, create a database, create database roles, and run traces on the Analysis Server. To add a user or group to the server role, you can access the Security page of the Properties dialog box for the Analysis Services instance in SQL Server Management Studio. If you want to grant administrative permissions at the database level, then you can either create a database role in SQL Server Management Studio or add a role to the project in Visual Studio and deploy the project.

Creating Security Roles for Processing

At the server level, an Analysis Services administrator has full access to every database, but you can create database roles to limit the administrative rights for an individual or a group. When you decide to limit administrative permissions by using a database role, you can also choose to limit permissions to specific cubes or dimensions. You can even prevent administrators of a database from viewing the data in that database.

In this procedure, you'll create a database role to grant permissions to process the SSAS cube.

Create a database role with cube processing permissions

1. Start SQL Server Management Studio, connect to Analysis Services, expand the Databases folder, expand the SSAS Step by Step database, right-click the Roles folder, and then click New Role.

> **Note** To complete the remaining procedures in this chapter, you must have successfully completed the procedures in each of the preceding chapters. If you skipped the previous chapters, you can use Visual Studio to open the SSAS Step by Step solution in the C:\Documents and Settings\<username>\My Documents\Microsoft Press\as2005sbs\Answers\chap10\SSAS Step by Step folder and then deploy the project to the Analysis Server to create and process the database.

The Create Role dialog box looks like this:

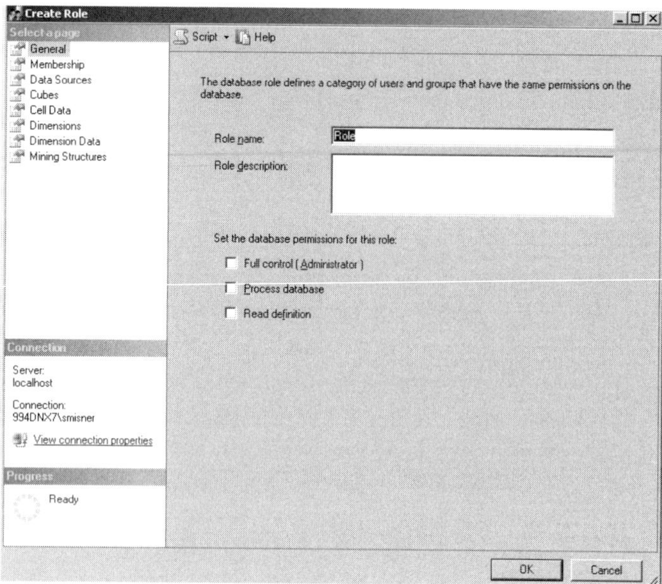

While the interface is slightly different from the Role Designer in Visual Studio, the Create Role dialog box in SQL Server Management Studio allows you to specify the same settings.

2. In the Role Name box, type **SSAS Cube Processing**.

   Selecting the Process Database check box on this page of the dialog box would grant permissions at the database level. Leave this check box cleared when you want processing rights to apply only at the cube level.

3. Click Membership in the Select A Page list, click Add, click Advanced, click Find Now, click _jsmith in the Search Results list, and then click OK twice.

4. Click Cubes in the Select A Page list, and then select the Process check box for the SSAS cube.

The Create Role dialog box looks like this:

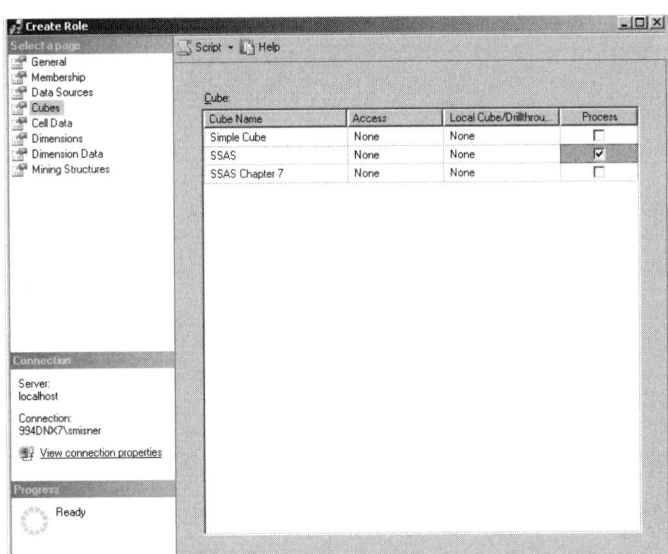

Members of this role can process the cube, but will not be able to use any client application (including SQL Server Management Studio) to view the cube unless they belong to another role granting read access. When a user belongs to more than one role and each role grants different permissions, all permissions from each role are granted to the user.

5. Click Dimensions in the Select A Page list, and then select the Process check box for each dimension, and then click OK.

   Now this role can also process all dimensions in the database. As you've learned in this chapter, you have a lot of flexibility to create roles to suit your security requirements.

Chapter 11 Quick Reference

To	Do this
Allow all network users to see the contents of a cube	In the Role Designer, right-click the Roles folder, click New Role, type a name for the role, click the Membership tab, click Add, click Advanced, click Find Now, click the Everyone group, and then click OK twice. Click the cubes tab, and then click Read in the Access list box. Deploy the project.
Duplicate an existing role	Right-click the role object in Solution Explorer, click Copy, right-click the Roles folder, click Paste, type a name for the role, and click OK.

To	Do this
Restrict access to a dimension of a cube	Right-click the cube, and click Manage Roles. Select a role, and click the ellipsis button in the Restricted Dimensions column. Select a dimension, and in the Rule column, select Fully Restricted from the drop-down list.
Restrict access to specific members of a dimension	After selecting an attribute hierarchy on the Dimension Data tab of the Role Designer, clear or select the appropriate members of the attribute hierarchy.
See how a cube would appear if you were logged in as a member of a specific group	On the Browser tab of the Cube Designer, click the Change User button on the Browser toolbar, and then select a user or role.
Add cell-level security to a cube	On the Cell Data tab of the Role Designer, click the Enable Read Permissions box, and then, in the Allow Reading Of Cube Content box, type an MDX expression that returns a 1 or 0 for each cell in the cube.
Add a database-level administrator role that can process a cube and its dimensions, but not view the cube data	On the Cube tab of the Role Designer, click the Process box for the cube, and leave the Access setting as None. On the Dimensions tab, click the Process box for each dimension.

Chapter 12

Managing Partitions and Database Processing

After completing this chapter, you will be able to:

- Use partitions to manage large cubes.
- Avoid problems with cubes stored using HOLAP or ROLAP storage.
- Compare full and incremental updates of a dimension.
- Avoid problems when incrementally updating a cube.
- Configure proactive caching.
- Use performance tools to monitor Analysis Services activity.

Conceptually, the Analysis server is a black box, mysteriously converting the values in a data warehouse into a miraculous object called a cube. And, for the most part, you can simply ignore what goes on inside that black box and let the Analysis server work its magic. Knowledge is, however, power, and that adage certainly holds true in the domain of Microsoft SQL Server 2005 Analysis Services. The more you know about what goes on within the black box of the Analysis server, the better you'll be able to troubleshoot unusual situations and find solutions to difficult problems. This chapter explains in broad terms what goes on inside the black box. The explanations are simplified, but they encompass some of the most complex topics in this book. If nothing else, this chapter can give you an appreciation for the sophistication and elegance of the Analysis server design.

Managing Very Large Databases

Partitions make it possible for you to create extremely large cubes. You can effectively create small, medium-sized, and even remarkably large cubes without using partitions. But partitions are useful when you need to create very large, enterprise-wide applications. For that reason, the ability to manage multiple partitions is available only with Microsoft SQL Server 2005 Enterprise Edition.

Understanding Partition Strategies

Each online analytical processing (OLAP) cube consists of at least one *partition*. You design the measures and dimensions for an entire cube, but you design storage modes and aggregations at the partition level. Whether a cube contains only a single partition or many partitions, the process of designing storage is the same.

One of the benefits of creating multiple partitions is that you can design different storage for different portions of the cube. For example, say you have one partition that contains information for the current and previous years. You access this information frequently, so you specify multidimensional OLAP (MOLAP) storage with aggregations to provide a 50% performance boost. A second partition contains values for the third, fourth, and fifth years. These years are usually accessed only at a summary level (if at all), and the relational warehouse is also occasionally accessed, so you specify hybrid OLAP (HOLAP) storage, with aggregations to the 30% performance level. A third partition contains several previous years. Those years are infrequently accessed—the relational warehouse is never used—so you specify MOLAP storage with aggregations to the 5% performance level and then archive the relational warehouse to tape.

A second major benefit of creating partitions is that you can process a partition independently of the rest of the cube. As a fairly extreme example, suppose that you have an OLAP cube used to monitor manufacturing activities and you want to update the information in that cube every 10 minutes. You don't have time to completely process the database every 10 minutes. By putting the current day into a separate partition, you can process that partition every 10 minutes, without having to process the rest of the cube. In effect, creating a partition for the current day is like performing an incremental update on the cube, except that you can completely replace the values in that one partition every 10 minutes, guaranteeing consistency with the relational data source.

A client application has no awareness of—let alone control over—partitions used on the server. You can modify the design of partitions without affecting any client application. The most important task when creating partitions is to make sure that each appropriate value from the fact table (or fact tables) makes it into *one and only one* partition.

Creating Partitions

When you're creating partitions, make sure each partition gets unique data. Otherwise, it's easy to double-count values in multiple partitions. The dangers of creating partitions are similar to the dangers of executing an incremental update on a cube. This similarity is not coincidental. In fact, when you perform an incremental update on a cube, the Analysis server creates a new partition, loads values into the new partition, and then merges the two partitions. Analysis Services provides two techniques to avoid double-counting:

- Create a separate fact table for each partition.
- Specify a filter (a SQL WHERE clause) to restrict rows from the fact table.

In this procedure, you delete the default partition, and then create three new partitions by using partition queries that filter data by date.

Create partitions based on fact table filters

1. Start SQL Server Business Intelligence Development Studio (BIDS), and open the SSAS Step by Step solution that you saved in the C:\Documents and Settings\<username>\My Documents\Microsoft Press\as2005sbs\Workspace folder.

> **Note** To complete this procedure, you must be using either Enterprise Edition or Developer Edition. If you skipped Chapter 11, "Implementing Security," open the SSAS Step by Step solution in the C:\Documents and Settings\<username>\My Documents\Microsoft Press\as2005sbs\Answers\chap11\SSAS Step by Step folder.

2. In Solution Explorer, double-click SSAS.cube to open the Cube Designer, and then click the Partitions tab.

   As you learned in Chapter 7, "Designing Aggregations and Hierarchies," every cube has at least one partition by default. A new partition is created every time that you create another measure group. In the SSAS cube, you can see there are eight partitions—Reseller Sales, Internet Sales, Product Forecast, Inventory, Distinct Count, Finance, Fact Account Manager, and Units Forecast. The first partition of the cube is always expanded when you first open the Partitions tab, and all other partitions are collapsed.

   For this procedure, you're creating new partitions that are differentiated by date, but use the same fact table as a source. The first new partition will contain historical transactions with order dates up to and including 2002, the second partition will contain transactions from 2003, and the third partition will contain data for 2004 and later. You can't change the existing default partition by adding the WHERE clause; instead, you must delete that partition and then add a new one that includes the applicable filter.

3. Right-click the first row of the table for the Reseller Sales partition, click Delete, and then click OK.

   Deleting the partition does not delete the Reseller Sales partition section of the designer, but you must define a new partition for this measure group before you process the cube. If you plan to maintain separate fact tables for each partition, then you can simply create each new partition with a SELECT statement that includes all data from the assigned fact table. On the other hand, if you plan to create multiple partitions from a single fact table, you need to add a WHERE clause to the SELECT statement to control which data goes into which partition.

4. Click the New Partition link to launch the Partition Wizard, and then click Next.

The dialog box looks like this:

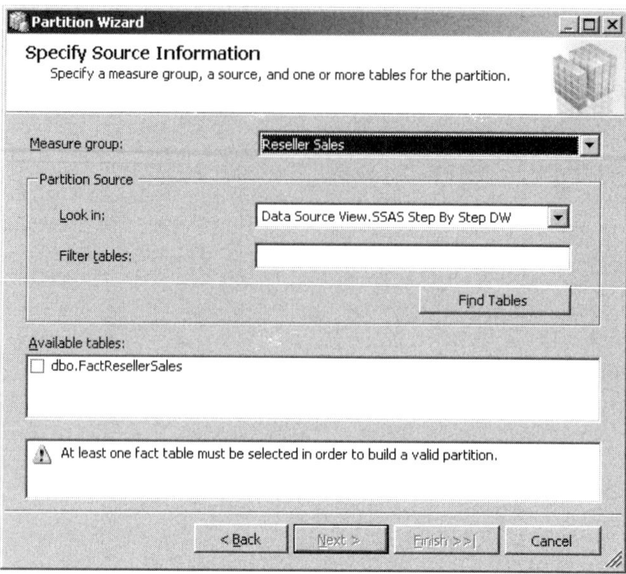

Because you clicked the New Partition link in the Reseller Sales section, the default measure group is set to Reseller Sales.

5. Select dbo.FactResellerSales in the Available Tables list, and then click Next.

   If you were to use one fact table per partition, you could finish the wizard at this point as long as you select a fact table that isn't already assigned to a partition. Otherwise, you'll get an error if you don't include a WHERE clause in the SELECT statement because the Cube Designer keeps track of the fact table assignments. To define which rows in a fact table will be associated with this partition, you need to specify a query. Notice the warning at the bottom of the dialog box that this query cannot use table rows that are included in any other partition.

6. Select the Specify A Query To Restrict Rows check box.

   Notice the Query box is automatically populated with a SELECT statement. This default select statement includes all of the table's columns as defined in the Data Source View.

   The first partition should include only data prior to January 1, 2003. If you were to review the contents of the DimTime table, you would find that the key value for this date–January 1, 2003–is 550.

7. Change the query to **select * from FactResellerSales where orderdatekey < 550**.

The dialog box looks like this:

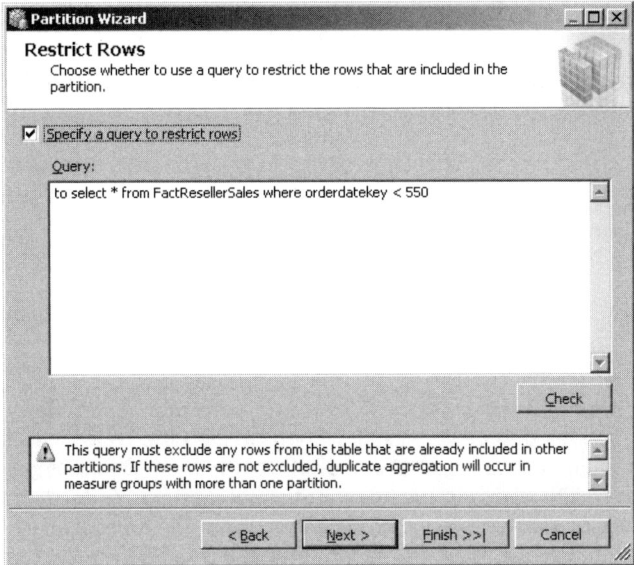

Tip When you use a single table, you should change the query to select all columns by replacing the default query with Select * From <table>. By eliminating the use of specific column names in the query, you will not be required to change the partition query later if you add columns to the table schema in the future.

8. Click Next.

   The Processing and Storage Locations page of the Partition Wizard looks like this:

You can locate partitions on different servers. There are some requirements to meet before you can use this option, however. To learn more, refer to "Creating and Managing a Remote Partition" in SQL Server Books Online.

9. Click Next, change the name of the partition to **Reseller Sales through 2002**, select Design Aggregations Later, and then click Finish.

   Now you're ready to create another new partition to store data with order dates from January 1, 2003 through December 31, 2003. The key for January 1, 2003, is 550 and the key for December 31, 2003, is 914. You'll need these keys to define the WHERE clause for the partition query.

10. Repeat steps 4 through 6, and then modify the partition query to **select * from FactResellerSales where orderdatekey between 550 and 914**.

> **Important** You need to be very careful when creating the WHERE clause in the partition query to avoid duplicating rows in the cube by creating overlapping partitions. For example, if the WHERE clause in the first partition were `where orderdatekey <= 500` instead of `where orderdatekey < 500`, then rows with the orderdatekey = 500 would be included in the first and second partitions that you created. There will be no warning when you have duplicated rows.

11. Click Next twice, change the partition name to **Reseller Sales 2003**, click Design Aggregations Later, and then click Finish.

12. Repeat steps 4 through 6 one more time, and then modify the partition query to **Select * from FactResellerSales where orderdatekey > 914**.

13. Click Next twice, change the partition name to **Reseller Sales 2004**, click Design Aggregations Later, click Deploy And Process Now, and then click Finish.

The Process Partition – Reseller Sales 2004 dialog box looks like this:

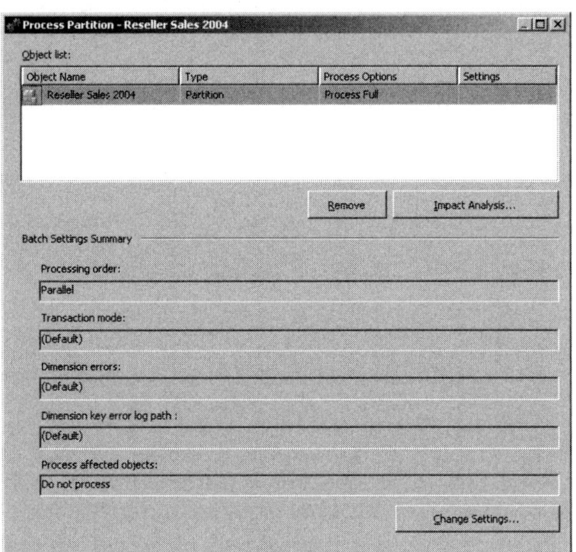

Notice the object to be processed now is only the current partition. Processing this one partition without processing the other partitions for this measure group is possible, but the cube won't be available for browsing until all partitions are processed. Because you want all partitions processed, you won't proceed with processing using this method.

14. Click Close, and then, in Solution Explorer, right-click the project, and then click Deploy.

    By default, deployment of the project processes only those objects that need to be fully processed. You'll learn more about processing individual objects later in this chapter.

15. When deployment is complete, click the Browser tab of the Cube Designer, click the Reconnect button, place Order Date.Calendar Year on rows and place the Reseller Sales Amount measure in the totals area of the grid.

    The Reseller Sales Amount Grand Total is $80,450,597, which is the correct value. You can see there are values for each calendar year from 2001 to 2004, which indicates that each partition is loaded with data. There is no way to know in this cube browser, or in any client application, how the data has been partitioned.

Merging Partitions

Consider the situation described earlier in "Understanding Partition Strategies," where you create a new partition each day for a manufacturing cube. Each month you would create up to 31 additional partitions in the cube. Simply keeping the partitions straight would be extraordinarily confusing. One solution is to use only two partitions: one for the current day and one for all previous time. Each night, merge the current day partition with the previous time partition, and then create a new current day partition for the next day. Merged partitions don't run significantly faster than separate partitions, but they can be much easier to manage.

In this procedure, you'll merge the partition that contains data up to and including 2002 with the partition that contains data for 2003.

Merge two partitions

1. Start SQL Server Management Studio, click Analysis Services in the Server Type list box, type **localhost** in the Server Name box, and then click Connect.
2. Expand the following items in the tree: Databases, SSAS Step by Step, Cubes, SSAS, Measure Groups, Reseller Sales, and Partitions.
3. Right-click the Reseller Sales through 2002 partition, and then click Merge Partitions.

> **Important** The partition you select before opening the Merge Partition dialog box is the partition that will be retained *after* the merge.

4. In the Source Partitions section, select the Merge check box for Reseller Sales 2003.

   Your screen looks like this:

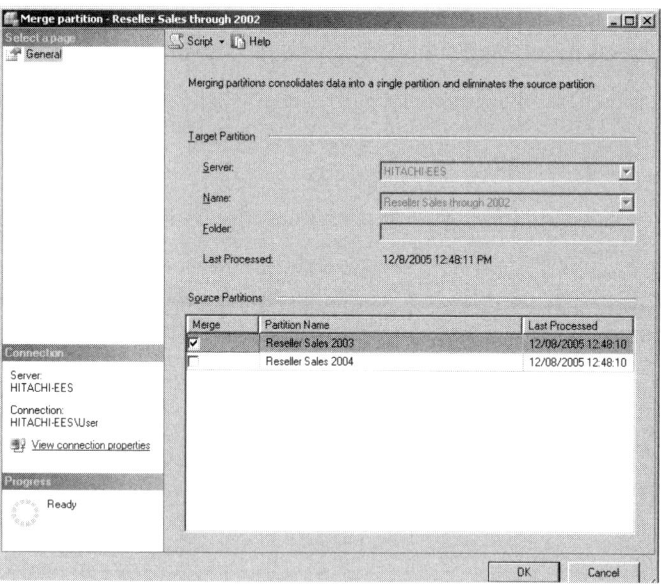

5. Click OK, right-click the Partitions folder, and then click Refresh.

Now the Reseller Sales 2003 partition is no longer available because the data in that partition has been merged into the partition that previously contained data for 2002 and earlier.

> **Important** Merging partitions does not update the partition query, nor does it combine fact tables. You need to make changes to the partition properties or the fact table contents, depending on how you have defined your partitions.

6. Right-click Reseller Sales through 2002, and then click Properties.
7. Select the Source box (under the Source category), click the ellipsis button in the Source box, and then change the query in the Source box to **Select * from FactResellerSales where orderdatekey <= 914**.

   Your screen looks like this:

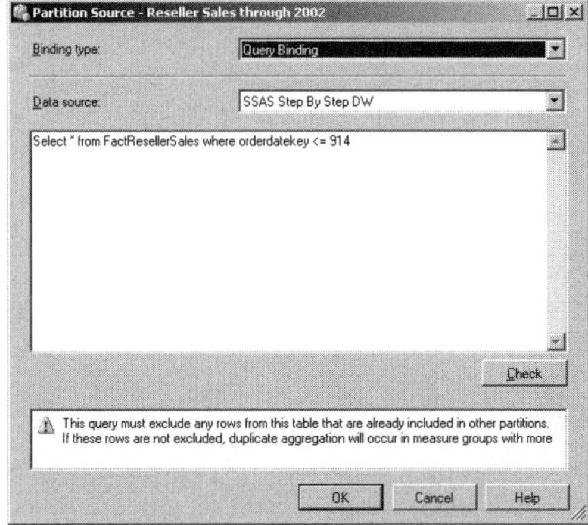

8. Click OK twice to close all dialog boxes.
9. Right-click Reseller Sales through 2002, click Rename, and then change 2002 to **2003** to reflect the current contents of the partition.

> **Caution** By merging partitions in SQL Server Management Studio, the SSAS Step by Step database is no longer synchronized with the solution that is currently open in Visual Studio. If you attempt to deploy the solution, you will see a warning message that deployment will overwrite the database on the server. Consequently, to continue making design changes to SSAS Step by Step, you should create a new project in Visual Studio that imports the database from the server any time there is a possibility that administrators have modified the database directly on the server.

10. In Visual Studio, on the File menu, click Close Project, and then, on the File menu, click New, and then Project.
11. In the New Project dialog box, click Import Analysis Services 9.0 Database, type **SSAS** in the Name box, type **C:\Documents and Settings\<username>\My Documents \Microsoft Press\as2005sbs\Workspace** in the Location box (replacing <username> with your login name), and then click OK.
12. Click Next on the Welcome page of the Import Analysis Services 9.0 Wizard, select SSAS Step by Step in the Database drop-down list, click Next, and then click Finish when the import is complete.
13. Open the SSAS cube, and then click the Partitions tab.

    Your screen looks like this:

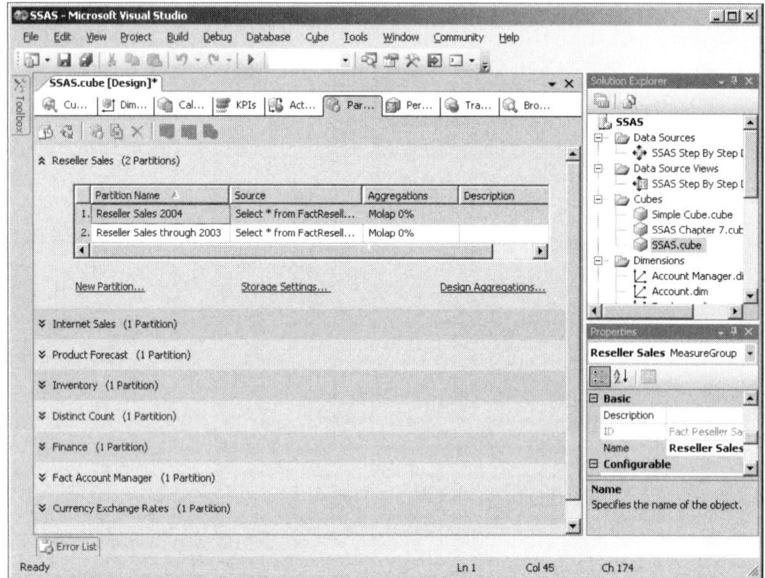

You can see that there are only two partitions–Reseller Sales through 2003 and Reseller Sales 2004–defined for the Reseller Sales measure group.

Working with Storage

Analysis Services always stores information about database objects–cubes, partitions, dimensions, for example–in data files on the server. You can think of this layer of information as a map. For each partition in a cube, though, you decide where to store the detail and aggregated values. You can choose from three physical storage options: ROLAP, HOLAP, and MOLAP.

- ROLAP, for *relational OLAP*, leaves detail values in the relational fact table and stores aggregated values in the relational database as well.

- HOLAP, for *hybrid OLAP*, leaves the detail values in the relational fact table but stores the aggregated values in the cube.
- MOLAP, for *multidimensional OLAP*, stores both detail and aggregated values within the cube.

All three storage modes include the cube map within Analysis Services. It's the cube map that makes the data appear as a cube to a person running a query. That means the storage mode is invisible to client applications—that is, applications that query the cube. The client application always sees the cube. The storage option you choose affects only performance.

Because a client application can't tell which storage mode you have chosen, you can change the storage mode without affecting any client applications. Once you specify storage and start using the cube, you can change your mind later and switch to a different storage type. Because a cube appears to the client application as a single, logical entity, you can use different storage modes for different portions of a cube. In order to do that, you must use multiple partitions.

> **Note** Regardless of which storage option you choose, Analysis Services will never allocate storage for missing values. For example, if you have a database that shows you didn't start selling products in Australia until 2003, Analysis Services will use no storage space for detail or aggregated values for Australia in 2003.

Understanding Analysis Services Storage Modes

Choosing a storage mode is not as difficult as it might seem. In the first place, using Analysis Services to store aggregations in a relational database never makes any sense, so you should *never* choose the ROLAP with aggregations option. Aggregations in a relational database are both bulky and slow. The purpose of creating aggregations is to improve performance, and relational aggregations defeat the purpose. The only reason you might choose the ROLAP option is if you're learning about aggregations and want to physically look at aggregations or if your analytical solution requires near real-time data. ROLAP aggregations are completely unusable by any application other than Analysis Services.

Aggregations in both MOLAP and HOLAP are identical, so the only difference is where the detail-level values are stored. If you count the space required by the original warehouse as well as the space needed for the OLAP cubes, MOLAP does consume more storage space than HOLAP because the MOLAP storage option does duplicate the values from the fact table. Analysis Services, however, is efficient in how it stores data. For example, the SSAS Step by Step DW database requires approximately 37 MB of storage space. A cube containing the same level of detail (with no aggregations) takes only 14 MB of storage space! With a very large warehouse database, you could process the data into a MOLAP cube and then archive and remove the original warehouse. By using the MOLAP storage option, you could actually end up using a fraction of the original storage space.

If you have a large, permanent warehouse, and if using aggregations can satisfy most queries, HOLAP storage is an excellent option. Queries that must go to the detail data will be slower than if the cube used MOLAP storage, but if they're infrequent, the performance gain might not be worth the incremental storage requirements. In addition, processing a MOLAP cube can take more time than processing a HOLAP cube. While developing an OLAP cube–during the time that you might process frequently–you may want to use HOLAP storage simply to speed up processing. Once you have completed the database design, you can switch to MOLAP storage to maximize query performance.

Note In the Analysis Services documentation and in many presentations about Analysis Services, you might see arguments in defense of ROLAP storage. These arguments actually apply to HOLAP storage, where you leave the detail values in the relational database and store only aggregations in the physical cube files.

Some descriptions of warehouse technology use the term ROLAP to refer to a relational data warehouse that has a fact table and dimensional tables. This is a different meaning of the term than is used within Analysis Services and corresponds most closely to a HOLAP (or ROLAP) cube with no aggregations.

Setting Storage Options

So far, you've learned how to design aggregations by partition (in Chapter 7) and how to define the source of a partition when you add a new partition. When you work with aggregations, you are also prompted to specify a storage option, which you've left as MOLAP, the default storage mode. You can use the Aggregation Design Wizard or the Partition Storage Settings dialog box, both accessible from the Partitions tab of the Cube Designer, to assign a different storage mode to a partition.

In this procedure, you'll set different storage options for two identical cubes.

Set storage options for sample cubes

1. In Visual Studio, open the Working with Storage solution in the C:\Documents and Settings\<username>\My Documents\Microsoft Press\as2005sbs\chap12\Working with Storage folder.

   The Working with Storage solution contains two identical cubes. For each of these cubes, the storage option is set to the default MOLAP with no aggregations. Before updating the data source, you'll assign a different type of data storage to one of the cubes to see the effect that changing data in the warehouse has when you use different data storage methods.

2. In Solution Explorer, double-click ROLAP.cube, click the Partitions tab of the Cube Designer, right-click Reseller Sales in the partition table, and then click Storage Settings.

Note If you click the Storage Settings link without selecting a partition in the partitions table, then the changes you make won't affect existing partitions. The storage settings that you specify will instead become the default settings for new partitions.

3. Move the slider to Real-time ROLAP.

   Your screen looks like this:

   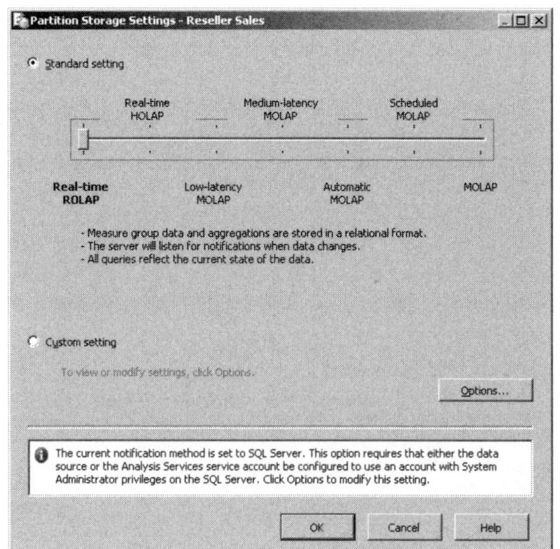

   Notice the information message about the requirement that the Analysis Services service account must have System Administrator privileges on the SQL Server when using the SQL Server notification method. (You learn more about the different notification methods later in this chapter.) If you used the default installation settings during installation of Analysis Services, then the NT AUTHORITY\SYSTEM account is used as the Analysis Services service account. This account has SQL Server System Administrator privileges by default.

Important If you create a separate service account for Analysis Services, you will need to grant System Administrator privileges to that service account in SQL Server Management Studio.

4. Click OK to return to the Partitions window.
5. In Solution Explorer, right-click the Working with Storage project, and then click Deploy.

Each cube will be processed with the applicable storage settings. When processing is complete, you have two cubes. One cube uses MOLAP storage and the other cube uses ROLAP storage.

Before you insert records into the data source, you should look at the values in the cubes so that you can observe the changes later. Each cube has identical contents now, so you can arbitrarily browse the ROLAP cube as an example and check for key values from that one cube.

6. In the Cube Designer for the ROLAP cube, click the Browser tab, drag the Measures object to the Totals area of the grid, expand Sales Territory and drag Sales Territory Country to the rows axis, and then expand Order Date and drag Order Date.Year to the columns axis.

7. On rows, drill down by clicking 2004 and then 2 to see that the last month with data is June.

Your screen looks like this:

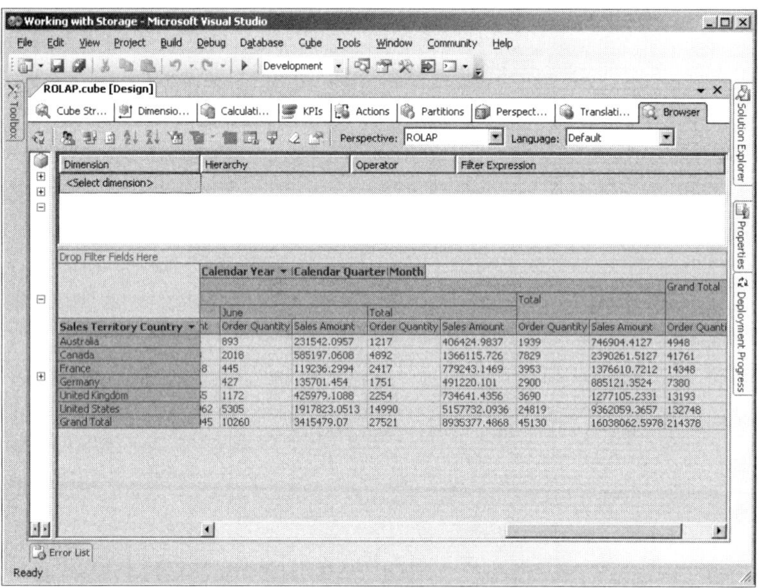

Before changing data in the warehouse, the grand total for Order Quantity for all countries is 214,378 and the total order quantity for Australia in June 2004 is 893. After changing the data source, you'll see the effect that changing values in the data warehouse has on cubes using MOLAP and ROLAP storage modes.

Changing Data in a Warehouse

When you process an OLAP database, you make information in the cube and dimensions match the information stored in the data warehouse, using the rules, or schema, you created when you designed the database. If you change the schema—for example, if you add a measure or a dimension to a cube—you must process at least the affected portions of the database. You also need to process at least a portion of the database if the information in the data warehouse changes, as it inevitably will.

The information in a data warehouse is almost always time-dependent. That means that, at the very least, you'll continually add new time periods to your data warehouse. In time, you might also add additional products or additional sales regions. When the data warehouse changes, you need to process the database to resynchronize the OLAP database with the relational data warehouse.

The FactResellerSales table in the SSAS Step by Step DW database contains data for six countries through June 2004. In the SSAS Step by Step database, the DimSalesTerritory dimension table includes only the six countries that appear in the fact table. The DimTime dimension table, however, includes months through August 2004. It is not uncommon in a warehouse to include months in the time dimension through the end of the current quarter or year, but to add members to other dimensions only as they are needed.

Included in the as2005sbs\chap12 folder is a SQL script named Update Warehouse.sql. This script adds one new entry to the DimSalesTerritory table (Mexico) and additional rows in the fact table for sales in Mexico and in Australia for June 2004. Inserting these records into the source database for the cubes simulates, on a very small scale, the load operations that occur regularly in a production data warehouse.

In this procedure, you'll execute queries that change data in the warehouse and observe the effect of changed data on the cubes.

Browse data after updating the warehouse

1. In SQL Server Management Studio, click the Open File button on the toolbar, navigate to the C:\Documents and Settings\<username>\My Documents\Microsoft Press \as2005sbs\chap12 folder, double-click the Update Warehouse.sql file, and then click Connect.

   This set of SQL queries will update the relational database that is the source for the cubes in the Working with Storage project. One query adds a new record to the Sales Territory dimension table and another query adds two records to the FactResellerSales table.

2. Click the Execute button on the toolbar.

   Now that you have changed the data in the data warehouse, the cubes in the Working with Storage database no longer match the data in the warehouse. The way a cube behaves depends on the storage mode of the cube. To see which values changed, start by browsing the data in the MOLAP cube.

3. In the Object Explorer window of SQL Server Management Studio, click the Connect button, click Analysis Services, click Connect in the Connect To Server dialog box,

expand the following items in the tree—Databases, Working with Storage, and Cubes, right-click the MOLAP cube, and then click Browse.

4. Drag the Measures object to the Totals area of the grid, expand Sales Territory, and then drag Sales Territory Country to the rows axis.

   Your screen looks like this:

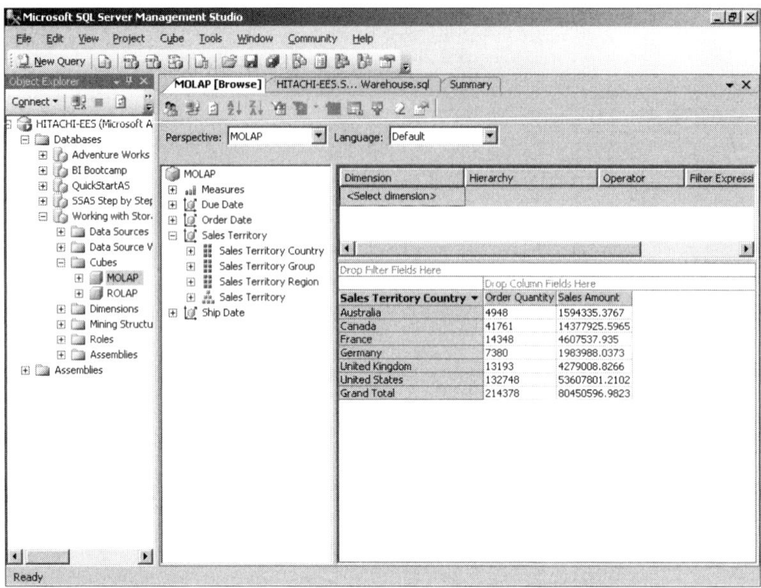

   The grand total for Order Quantity for all countries is still 214,378, and Mexico doesn't appear in the list of countries. All these values are unchanged from before the warehouse changed.

   The MOLAP cube uses MOLAP storage, and it behaves as if you had not changed the data source. When you use MOLAP storage, with or without aggregates, the cube is completely detached from the data warehouse. You can even delete the warehouse database without affecting the OLAP database.

5. Close the browser window. In Object Explorer, right-click the ROLAP cube, click Browse, place Measures in the totals area of the grid, and then place Order Date.Year on rows.

Your screen looks like this:

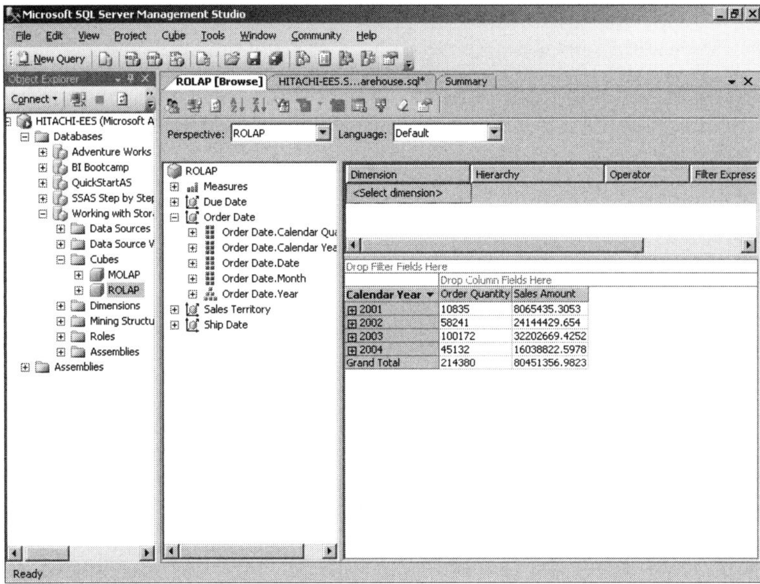

The grand total for Order Quantity for all countries is now 214,380, which is different from the previous 214,378 total. Because there are no aggregations designed for the cube, all the values are aggregated from the relational data store immediately. Problems arise, however, when you attempt to browse to an area where new members exist in the fact table that aren't represented in the dimension.

6. Expand Sales Territory and place Sales Territory Country on columns.

   Your screen looks like this:

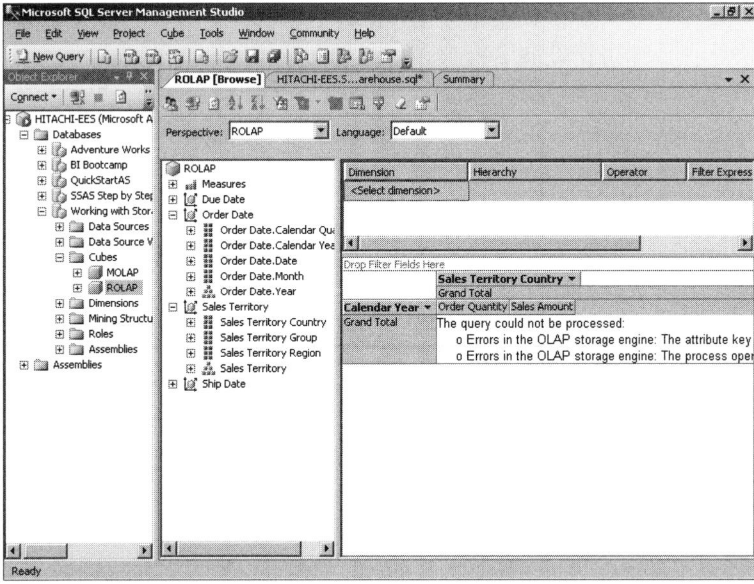

An error message displays because the server has recognized a discrepancy in the Sales Territory Country attribute.

7. Close the browser window.

   Cubes that use HOLAP or ROLAP data storage will compute aggregated values correctly from the relational source. But if dimension data has changed, these cubes are still unable to display the detail values related to new dimension members. This fact makes HOLAP and ROLAP storage modes vulnerable to changes in cell values. You should always process databases containing HOLAP or ROLAP cubes as soon as the data warehouse changes. In MOLAP storage mode, all cell values–detail and aggregated alike–are oblivious to the data warehouse unless you explicitly process the database. You can even delete the data warehouse without affecting the cube. One way to ensure the detail data in HOLAP and ROLAP cubes is accessible is to use proactive caching, which you'll learn how to do later in this chapter.

Managing OLAP Processing

The easiest way to make sure that an OLAP database is completely consistent with the data warehouse–and with itself–is to process the entire database. When you process the database, you completely discard all the dimensions and cubes within the database and create new ones. This takes place as a single transaction, which means that client applications can continue to use the existing cubes until processing is complete. It also means that if an error occurs at any point during the processing, the entire change is rolled back, again ensuring that the database is internally consistent.

Processing the entire database is the simplest, cleanest, and best option, provided that you have sufficient time and storage space available. Although processing a large database can consume a considerable amount of time, users can continue to access the existing database while data is being updated in a new version of the database. As an example, suppose you have an OLAP database that you update every day and that requires 10 hours to fully process. Assuming you have sufficient disk space, you could still choose to process the entire database–perhaps by starting the nightly processing after 19:00 or as soon as new data is available. Users would then have access to the updated database by the next morning. You would not have to exclude users from the system or wait for them to leave for the day.

Processing a large database can also consume a considerable amount of disk space. The Analysis server not only creates a second copy of all the dimension and cube files created during the transaction, but it also uses additional temporary files to accumulate aggregations, particularly when creating aggregations from a large fact table.

Consequently, some databases are simply too large to process as a single transaction. Analysis Services provides several options for processing individual components of a database. These options allow you to create and manage extremely large databases, but they also require much more work to avoid preventing users from accessing the cubes or, worse, to avoid including invalid or inconsistent values in the cubes.

Processing a Dimension

When you process a dimension, the server creates a map that includes the path for each member of that dimension. Every cube that includes the dimension uses that map. When you process an existing dimension, the map is destroyed and a new map is created. Destroying the dimension map invalidates all the cubes that use the dimension. When you process an entire database, new dimensions are processed first and then all the cubes are processed as well. But when you process a single dimension, you make all the cubes that use that dimension inaccessible to client applications.

Fortunately, you can make certain changes to a dimension without destroying the existing map. If you don't destroy the existing map, you don't invalidate existing cubes. Analysis Services allows you to *incrementally update* a dimension to make changes that don't destroy the dimension map. The most useful change you can then make is adding new members to a dimension. You can also delete members or change attribute values.

To enable you to perform an incremental update on a dimension when you delete or rename an existing member, or change the attribute relationships for a member, the default value of *RelationshipType* property for each attribute relationship is Flexible. If this property is set instead to Rigid and you try to run an incremental update, Analysis Services will fail the operation if it detects changes in the dimension table that aren't allowed. Deleting or changing members of a rigid relationship requires the dimension to be fully reprocessed, which in turn forces each cube using the dimension to be reprocessed.

In this procedure, you'll compare the Process Full and Process Update processing options for updates to the Sales Territory dimension.

Update a dimension

1. In the Object Explorer of SQL Server Management Studio, expand the Dimensions folder for the Working with Storage database, right-click Sales Territory, and then click Process.

Your screen looks like this:

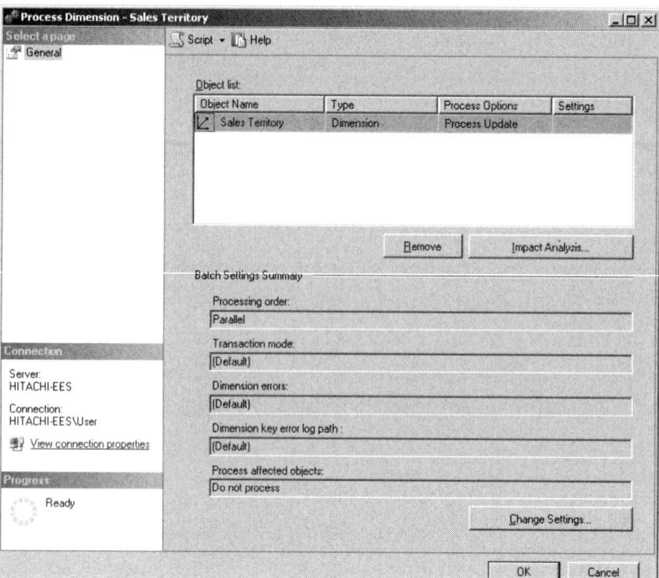

Notice the Process Options value is Process Update. Analysis Services selects the processing option that brings the dimension object up-to-date. In this case, because no structural changes are detected in the dimension design, Analysis Services determines that full processing is not required, and suggests an incremental update instead.

The processing option for incremental updates, Process Update, is appropriate when you make changes to the dimension table. However, you will change this value to Process Full to observe the impact on cubes by using this option instead. Notice the current setting for Process Affected Objects, visible at the bottom of the dialog box, is Do Not Process. Thus, any objects dependent on this dimension, such as partitions in the cube, will not be processed. Before you begin processing, you can review the impact of processing the Sales Territory dimension on other objects in the database by using the Impact Analysis feature.

2. Select Process Full in the Process Options drop-down list, and then click Impact Analysis.

Your screen looks like this:

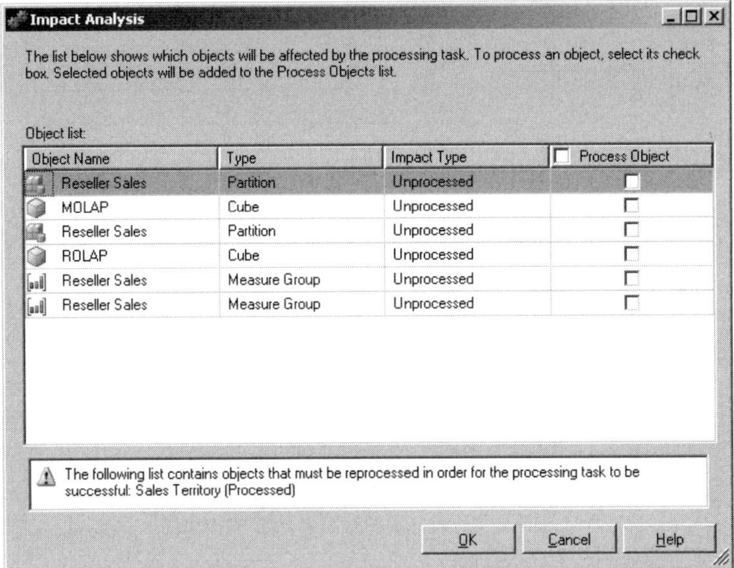

The information on this screen tells you that if you proceed with a full process of the Sales Territory, all measure groups, partitions, and cubes in the database will also need to be processed. You can be selective about which objects to process after processing Sales Territory. For this procedure, you won't select any of these objects to process.

3. Click OK twice, and then click Close when processing is complete.
4. Browse the MOLAP cube in SQL Server Management Studio.

   You see an error message indicating that the cube cannot be browsed. By performing a full process of the Sales Territory dimension, the MOLAP cube was placed in an unprocessed state and now requires processing.
5. Browse the ROLAP cube.

   Even though the ROLAP cube always reads fact data from the relational table, it is still dependent on dimension maps. When the dimension map for Sales Territory is rebuilt, the ROLAP cube must be reprocessed in order to reference the new dimension map.

6. Close both browser windows. In Object Explorer, right-click the Working with Storage database, and then click Process.

   The default processing option for the database is Process Full. Performing a full process of the database rebuilds all objects, even though the Process Affected Objects value is currently Do Not Process. That setting doesn't apply to this situation.

7. Click OK to process the database, and then click Close when processing is complete.

8. Browse the MOLAP cube, placing Measures in the totals area and Sales Territory Country on rows.

   The MOLAP cube (with MOLAP storage) now recognizes the new member of the Sales Territory dimension as well as the changes in the fact table because a full process of the dimension and the cube was performed.

   Now take a look at what happens when you have new dimension and fact table records, but only perform an incremental update of the dimension.

9. Click the Open File button on the toolbar, navigate to the C:\Documents and Settings\<username>\My Documents\Microsoft Press\as2005sbs\chap12 folder, double-click the Incremental Update Warehouse.sql file, and then click Connect.

   This SQL script adds one new record to the Sales Territory dimension table for Japan and another query adds another record to the FactResellerSales table to record a sale in Japan.

10. Click the Execute button on the toolbar.

    Now you're ready to see what happens when you incrementally update the Sales Territory dimension.

11. In Object Explorer, right-click Sales Territory, click Process, click OK, and then click Close when processing is complete.

    The Process Update option is an incremental update. Analysis Services reads the dimension table and adds new members that it finds to the dimension map, deletes members that are no longer found in the table, and applies any other changes that it detects.

12. Switch to the MOLAP cube browser, and then click the Reconnect button.

    The MOLAP cube does not recognize the new fact table record. You don't see Japan listed on rows because the browser, by default, excludes members for which there is no related fact table data.

13. Right-click anywhere in the Sales Territory Country column in the grid, and then click Show Empty Cells.

Your screen looks like this:

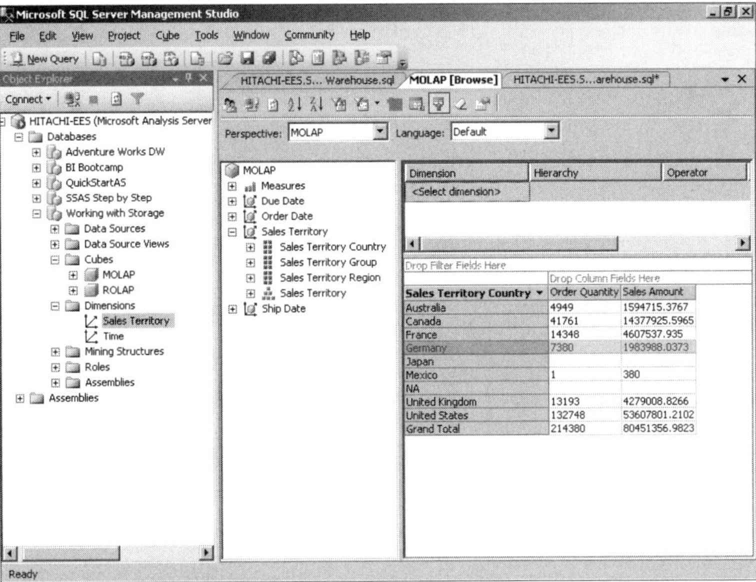

Here you can see that Japan is in fact recognized as a new member, but the new fact table record for the sale in Japan has not been processed into the cube yet.

14. Browse the ROLAP cube, with Measures in the totals area and Sales Territory Country on rows.

    Your screen looks like this:

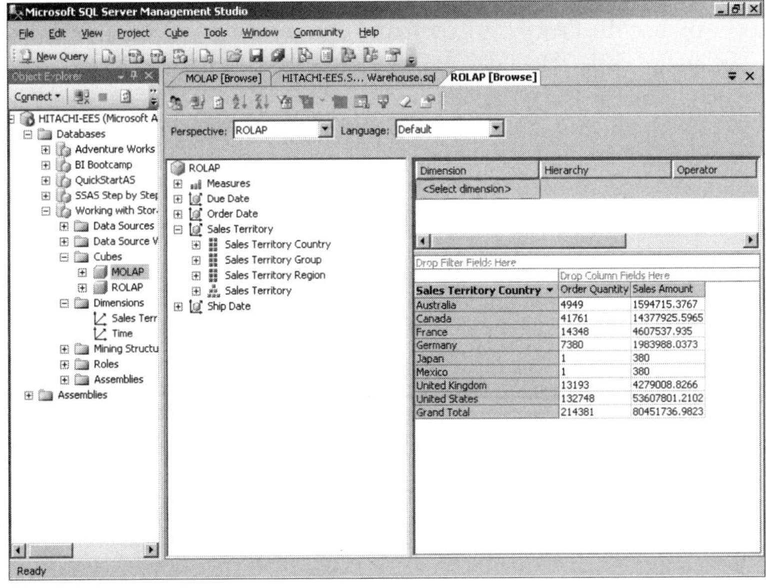

The ROLAP cube, by contrast, recognizes both the new member of the Sales Territory dimension and includes the new value from the fact table. The ROLAP cube does not require any further processing to reflect the current state of the warehouse.

Processing a Cube

When you click the Process command for a cube that has already been processed, the default processing option is always Process Full. When you fully process a cube, the Analysis server checks to see whether any changes have been made to any of the dimension schemas used by the cube. If changes have been made, the server processes the dimension before processing the cube. The server then generates a set of temporary files containing replacement data for the cube. Once processing has completed successfully, the server deletes the current files for the cube and renames the temporary files to the permanent names.

The Process Data option for a cube is virtually identical to the Full Process option. In both cases, the server generates all the files for a new cube, swapping the files into place when the processing is complete. The only real difference is that the Process Data option doesn't check to see whether you have made any changes to the dimension schema. It processes the cube using the existing dimension files, period.

One option, Process Incremental, is both powerful and dangerous. It creates new cube files, precisely as if you were using the Process Full option. When the processing is complete, however, the server doesn't replace the old files with the new ones. Rather, it *merges* the two sets of files, creating a third set of cube files. Finally, it deletes all but the third set of files and renames those files to become the final cube files. One implication of this operation is that for a single cube, the Process Incremental option might actually require *more* disk space than the Process Full option, since it creates three sets of files, rather than just two. A more important implication is that if you use the Process Incremental option using a fact table that includes values already stored in the cube, those values will be double-counted after you process the cube. An alternate option, Process Data, simply clears out the data in the cube structure, and reloads data from the fact table as defined for each partition.

In this procedure, you'll use the Process Incremental processing option to update the MOLAP cube, and then you'll fix the resulting errors by using the Process Data processing option.

Update data in a cube incrementally

1. In the Object Explorer of SQL Server Management Studio, expand the following items in the tree–Working with Storage, MOLAP, Measure Groups, Reseller Sales, and Partitions, right-click the Reseller Sales partition, and then click Process.
2. Select Process Incremental in the Processing Options drop-down list, and then click the Configure link.
3. In the Data Source Or View drop-down list, select SSAS Step by Step DW in the Data Source folder, and then click OK.

4. Type **FactResellerSales** in the Table Schema and Name box.

   Your screen looks like this:

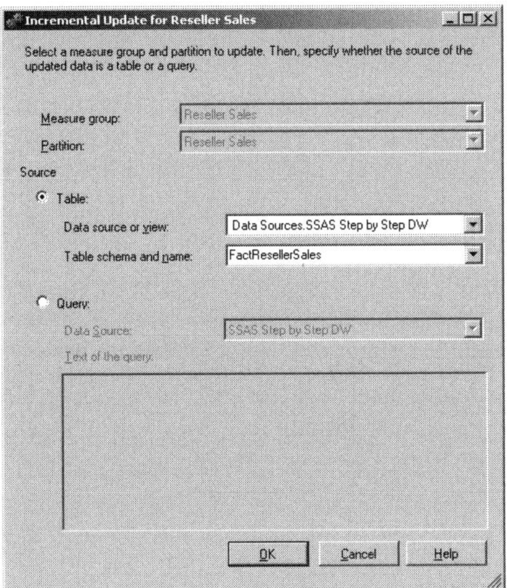

5. Click OK twice, and then click the Close button when processing is complete.
6. Switch to the MOLAP cube browser, click Reconnect, and drag Measures to the Totals area and Sales Territory Country to rows.

   Your screen looks like this:

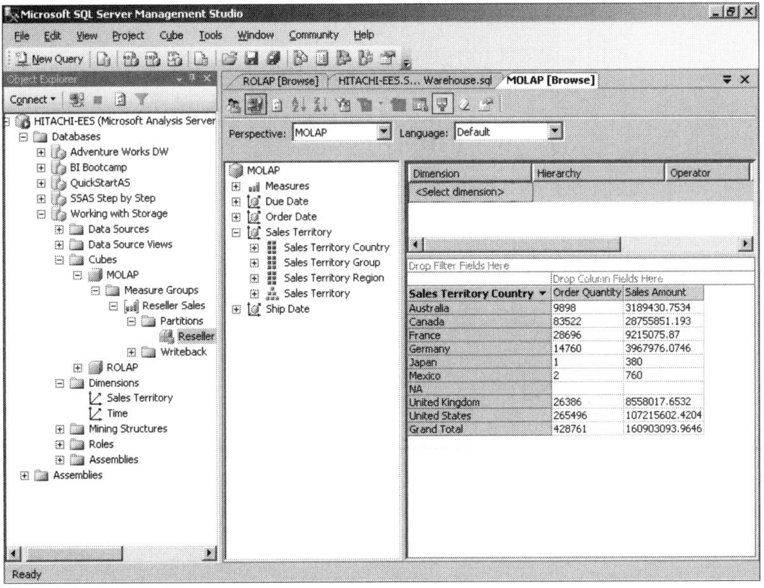

The total for Order Quantity is now 428,761. (The original grand total in the fact table was 214,378. This grand total was increased to 214,380 when you executed the Update Warehouse query and processed the cube. After executing the Incremental Update Warehouse query, the fact table total for Order Quantity is now 214,381. The current values in the fact table–214,381–are added to the current values in the cube–214,380–which results in a new grand total in the cube, 428,761.) This problem only affects the MOLAP cube; the ROLAP cube continues to read only the values in the fact table at the time of the query.

With a dimension, when you perform an incremental update, the Analysis server adds a member only if the unique path is not already in the dimension. With a dimension, you can never double-count member names. With a cube, it's easy to double-count values because the server adds the values of the measure for each row as it processes the fact table data. The server typically adds any one row from the fact table to multiple aggregation cells, and any cell in the cube typically contains values from multiple rows in the fact table.

To avoid loading the same values into a MOLAP cube more than once, you need to perform one of two tasks before using Process Incremental:

- Retrieve values from a different table.
- Filter the fact table to retrieve only specific values.

You're most likely to choose to update data in a cube by using the Process Incremental option when you're simply adding new values, such as sales for a new time period, to the cube. You might find it convenient in the warehouse to store those new values in a separate fact table. In Chapter 13, "Managing Deployment," you'll learn how to use an XML for Analysis (XMLA) script to filter a partition.

7. Right-click the Reseller Sales partition, click Process, and then select Process Data in the Processing Options drop-down list.
8. Click Close when processing is finished, switch to the MOLAP cube browser window, and then click the Reconnect button.

   The total for Order Quantity is now correctly 214,381.
9. Close the MOLAP and ROLAP cube browsers in SQL Server Management Studio.

Configuring Proactive Caching

As you've learned in this chapter, keeping an Analysis Services database up-to-date can be challenging. You have to consider when to process changes to database objects relative to changes in the data warehouse, how processing one object impacts other objects, and how the processing option you use will affect user queries. Proactive caching is an Analysis Services feature that simplifies database processing by managing the details for you.

To configure proactive caching, you need to consider the following options:

- Should processing of the cube occur in fixed intervals of time or only when data in the underlying source has changed?
- While the cube is being processed, how should user queries be resolved–from the most recent version of the cube (which might contain old data) or from the underlying relational source (new data)?
- If processing will be triggered by changes in the data warehouse, how should Analysis Services be notified of a change?

In this procedure, you'll enable proactive caching.

Set caching and latency options

1. In the Object Explorer of SQL Server Management Studio, right-click the Reseller Sales partition of the MOLAP cube in the Working with Storage database, and then click Properties.

   Your screen looks like this:

   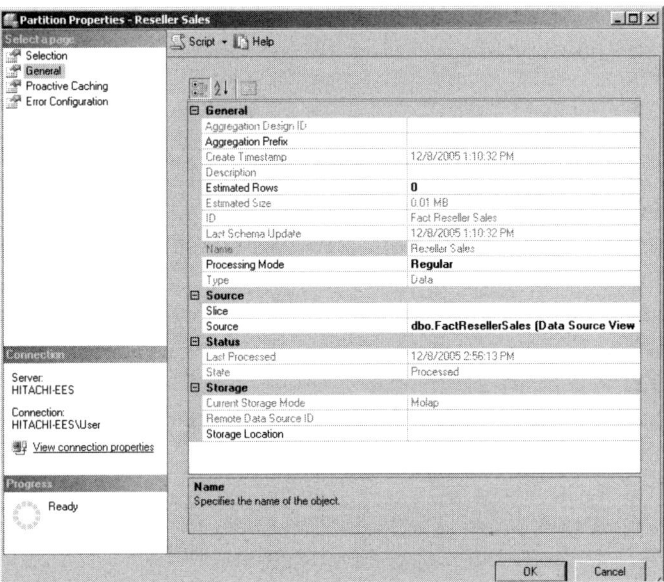

2. Click Proactive Caching in the Select a Page list.

Your screen looks like this:

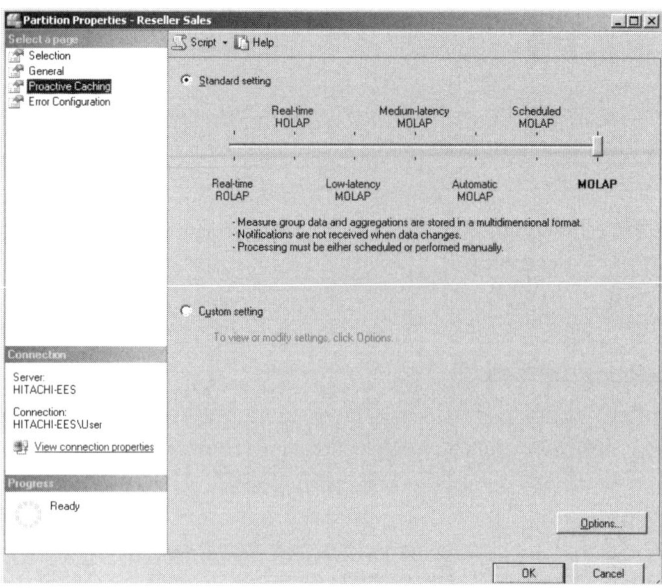

3. Move the slider to Scheduled MOLAP, and then click Options.

   The Storage Options dialog box looks like this:

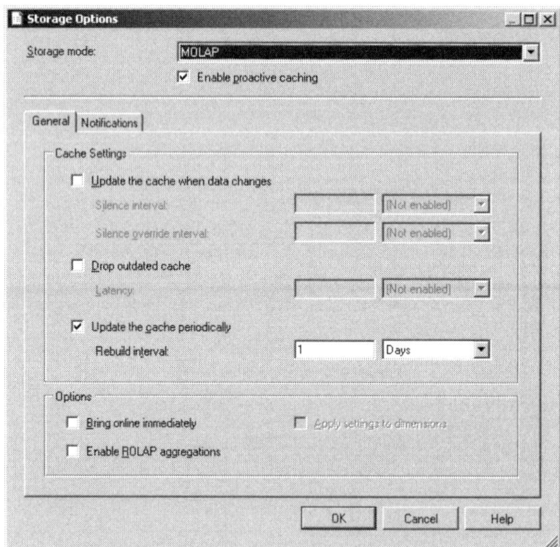

Notice Proactive Caching is enabled, and the cache is configured to rebuild in one-day intervals. In this case, the MOLAP storage for this partition will automatically update once every day, unless you change the setting to a shorter interval. Unfortunately, you can change only the frequency of the rebuild, but not the time of day that the rebuild takes place. The Rebuild Interval can be as often as every second or it can be set as an interval of many days.

By using Scheduled MOLAP, you will force a periodic update of the MOLAP cache, whether or not new data has appeared in the warehouse. This may result in more frequent processing of the partition than is necessary if data is not regularly added to the warehouse. On the other hand, the partition may not be processed frequently enough if the intervals are too long relative to the frequency of updates to the warehouse.

4. Click Cancel to return to the Specify Storage and Caching Options page, move the slider to Automatic MOLAP, and then click Options.

   The Storage Options dialog box looks like this:

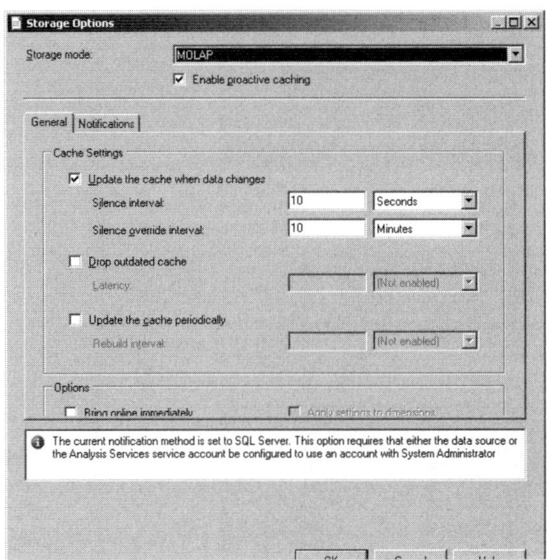

Automatic MOLAP also enables proactive caching, but updates the cache only when the data changes instead of on a periodic basis. The default settings start cache processing after a 10-second Silence Interval, with a Silence Override Interval of 10 minutes. The Silence Interval setting prevents processing from starting until data updates in the warehouse have completely stopped for the specified interval. This situation is analogous to waiting for rush hour traffic to end. If your warehouse is routinely updated during the first 10 minutes of every hour, that period of time is the rush period. Once 10 seconds (or the amount of time specified by the Silence Interval) have elapsed, the cache is processed.

But what if there are so many updates to the fact table during the rush period that processing cannot start after the expected 10-minute duration? This Silence Override Interval setting tells the Analysis server to go ahead and start processing the cache if 10 minutes have elapsed and data is still being added to the warehouse. The server uses a snapshot to isolate the records that it will include in the update process from the records that are added to the warehouse after processing has begun.

5. Click Cancel, move the slider to Medium-Latency MOLAP, and then click Options.

   The Storage Options dialog box looks like this:

   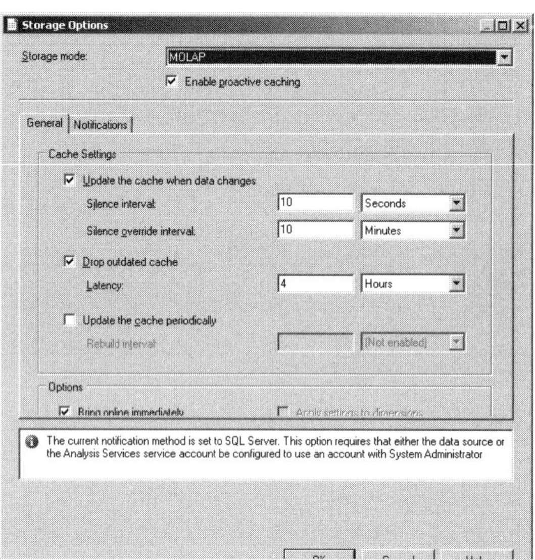

   The settings on this page are similar to the Automatic MOLAP settings, but now the Drop Outdated Cache option is enabled with a default value for Latency of 4 hours. With medium-latency MOLAP, the Analysis server will eliminate the cache if it hasn't been processed within the past four hours (or the period that you specify if you change the default value).

   When the cache is dropped by the server, any queries can be answered from the relational data source until a new cache is created. Notice the Bring Online Immediately option is enabled for medium-latency MOLAP. This option tells the Analysis server that as soon as it drops the outdated cache, queries should be resolved from the relational tables until the new cache is available. This setting is useful when processing has started, but not completed within a desired period of time, in order to provide users with relatively current data in response to queries. If you disable this option and you have the Drop Outdated Cache option enabled, then queries cannot be answered until the new MOLAP cache is created. If you prefer to continue answering queries with the old cache while a new cache is being built, you must disable the Drop Outdated Cache option.

6. Click Cancel, move the slider to Low-Latency MOLAP, and then click Options.

The Storage Options dialog box looks like this:

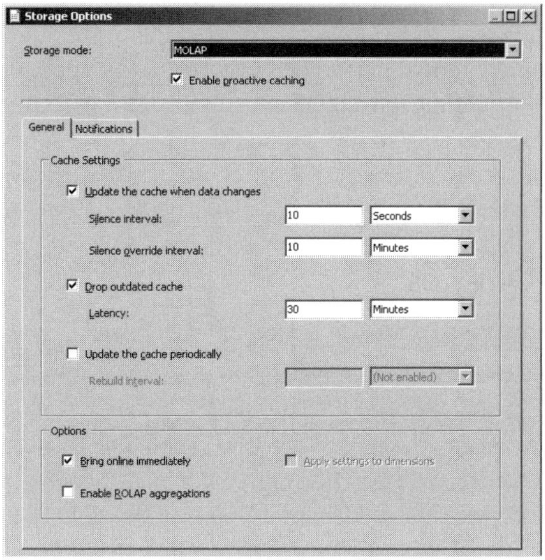

The key difference between low-latency MOLAP and medium-latency MOLAP is that, with low-latency, the default Latency setting is 30 minutes. To test latency, you will reduce this value to two minutes—which is likely to be too frequent for a production database but makes a shorter interval for you to test. You will also change the Silence Interval setting to a longer interval to make sure that any change to the data source doesn't trigger processing an update of the cache.

7. Change the Silence Interval to **10 minutes**, change the Latency setting to **2 minutes**.

   You'll observe proactive caching in action later in this chapter by using SQL Server Profiler to monitor how Analysis Services responds to queries after the fact table is updated.

8. Click the Notifications tab.

   You use the notification options to specify the conditions which indicate that data has changed in the warehouse. The default value is SQL Server. Any dimension and fact tables used for the current partition are monitored for changes, but you can also specifically identify tables to be monitored.

   Alternatively, you can choose to have a client application send notification of changes by using the Client Initiated option, or you can choose to poll specific tables by using the Scheduled Polling option. Scheduled Polling is useful if your warehouse is stored in a relational database that is not in SQL Server. For more information about polling queries, refer to SQL Server Books Online.

9. Click OK twice to close all dialog boxes.

Monitoring Cube Activity

Generally, you'll find few performance problems with small databases. As you work with large databases, you can address many potential performance problems by applying one or more strategies designed specifically for coping with large cubes. Partitioning a cube is only a first step. Through trial and error, you will have to determine the appropriate storage mode, aggregation design, and processing options. SQL Server Profiler and the Performance Monitor are useful tools you can use to see what's happening behind the scenes on the Analysis server.

Profiling Analysis Services Queries

SQL Server Profiler can capture events from Analysis Services to help you monitor and troubleshoot performance. Not only can you spot operations that are running slowly, but you can also view the actual MDX and Structured Query Language (SQL) statements that are executed and you can save events for playback later. In order to use SQL Server Profiler, you must be a member of the Analysis Server server role. (For more information about assigning a user or group to the Analysis Server server role, see Chapter 11.) By default, local administrators are members of this role.

In this procedure, you'll update the relational source for the MOLAP cube, and then monitor the impact of proactive caching on the execution of queries to the cube.

Use SQL Server Profiler to monitor queries

1. Click Start, point to All Programs, point to Microsoft SQL Server 2005, point to Performance Tools, and then click SQL Server Profiler.
2. On the File menu, click New Trace.
3. In the Server Type drop-down list, click Analysis Services, and then click Connect.
4. Type **Analysis Services Trace** in the Trace Name box, and then click Run.

Your screen looks like this:

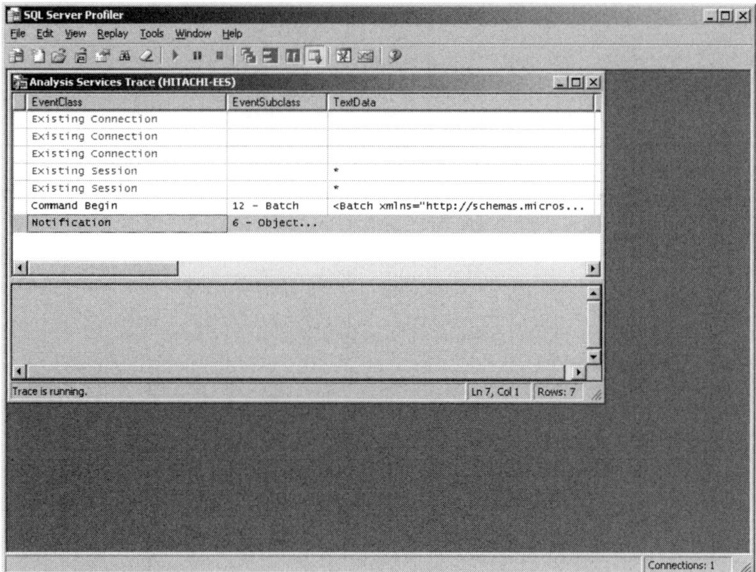

5. In SQL Server Management Studio, click the Open File button on the toolbar, navigate to the C:\Documents and Settings\<username>\My Documents\Microsoft Press \as2005sbs\chap12 folder, double-click the Test Latency.sql file, and then click Connect.

   This SQL script adds one more to the FactResellerSales table to record a sale in Mexico.

6. Click the Execute button on the toolbar.

   Now you're ready to see what happens when you incrementally update the Sales Territory dimension.

7. In SQL Server Management Studio, browse the MOLAP cube in the Working with Storage database by placing Sales Territory on rows and Measures in the totals area.

   The total for Order Quantity is still 214,381 which does not include the newly added fact table.

8. Switch to SQL Server Profiler, and then click the Pause Selected Trace button. Maximize the trace window, scroll to find the first Query Begin event class and 0 – MDXQuery event subclass, and then click that row.

Your screen looks like this:

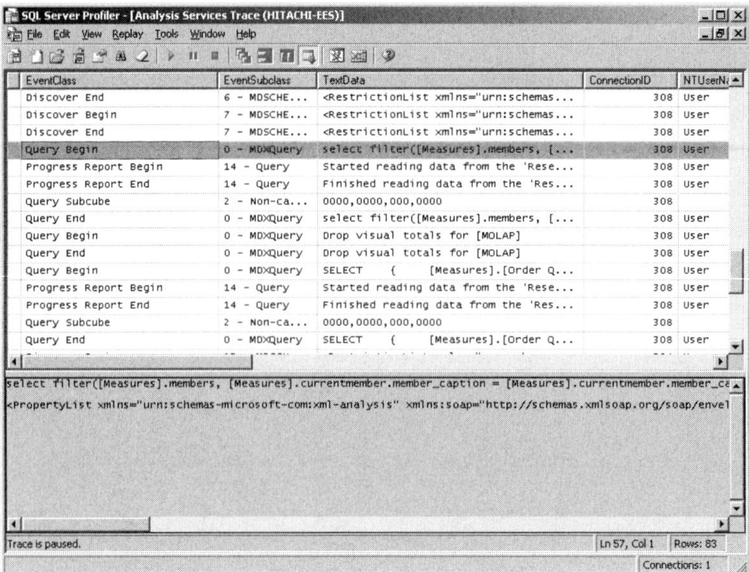

You can see here the text of the MDX query that is sent to the server. In fact, you should notice there are multiple queries logged in the trace. Each time you drag an object on or off the grid in the browser, a new query is executed.

The trace lines between Query Begin and Query End provide the details related to the execution of this query. In this case, you can see the 14 – Query subclass which indicates that partition data for Reseller Sales is being read. In addition, you might see the 1 – Cache data or 2 – Noncache data event subclasses, or even both. These event subclasses let you know whether the data to answer the query is found in the server's memory (placed there as a result of a previous query) or if the partition data had to be read from disk. In either case, you can see that the values in the browser—which currently do not include the additional fact record—are provided from the cube.

9. After two minutes have passed, click the Start Selected Trace button in the SQL Server Profiler toolbar, switch to SQL Server Management Studio, and then click the Reconnect button.

   Reconnecting to the cube executes the last query in the browser, which currently shows each measure by Sales Territory Country on rows. Now the order quantity for Mexico is 2 and the total order quantity is 214,382.

10. Click the Pause Selected Trace button, scroll to find the most recent Query Begin event class, which is followed by a 25 – Execute SQL event subclass, and then click that row.

Your screen looks like this:

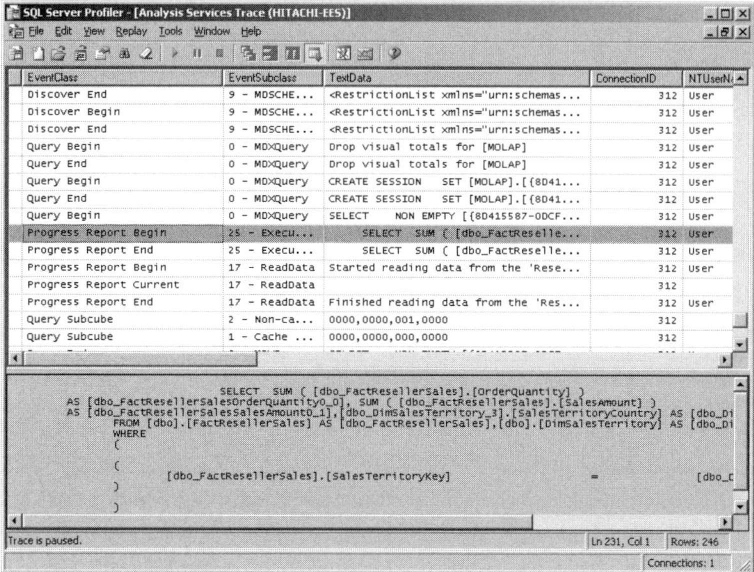

This time, the latency configuration of proactive caching redirected the query from the cube browser to the underlying source. However, reprocessing of the cube has yet to start because the 10-minute Silence Interval has not yet expired.

11. Click the Start Selected Trace button in the SQL Server Profiler toolbar and wait. Approximately 10 minutes after you updated the fact table using the Test Latency query, you will see a series of trace lines related to processing. Your screen looks like this:

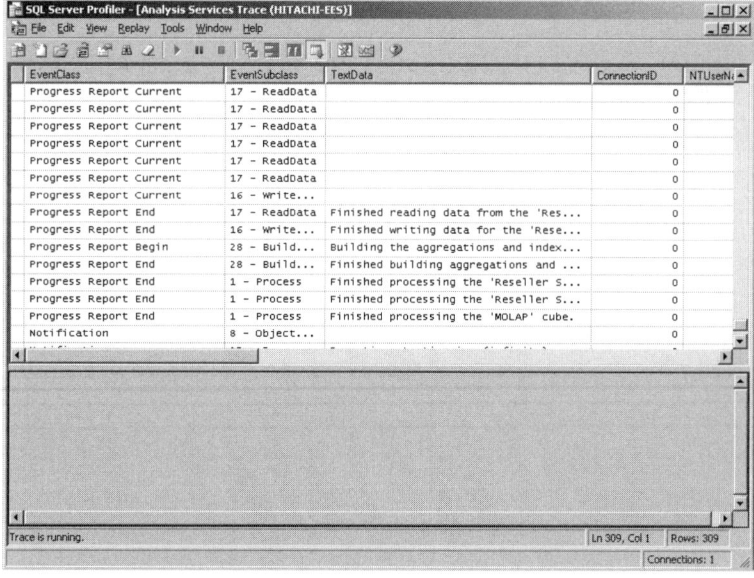

Here you can see the activity related to processing database objects that are part of the MOLAP cube. You can review the SQL statements used to load the cube's partitions with data by clicking on any row with EventSubclass 25 – ExecuteSQL. (You might have to scroll through the trace window to locate these rows.) In addition, you can see how long each stage of the processing operation lasts by scrolling horizontally to locate the Duration column.

Now that the cube is processed, any subsequent queries will be answered from the cube itself. The Analysis server only issues SQL queries when it has been notified that the underlying data source has changed, the latency period has expired, and an updated cube is not yet available.

12. Click the Pause Selected Trace button.

Using the Performance Monitor

There are several Analysis Services performance counters available that you can use to track performance. These performance tools are organized by object, such as *MSAS2005:Cache,* which represent server resources. You can monitor the current value of counters interactively through the Windows Performance tool, or you can create performance logs that capture statistics over a period of time. To find instructions for using the Windows Performance tool, search the help file for your operating system. You can find more information about the Analysis Services performance counters by searching SQL Server Books Online.

In this procedure, you'll use the Direct Hit Ratio performance counter to monitor queries.

Monitor a performance counter

1. In SQL Server Profiler, click the Performance Monitor button.

> **Note** Alternatively, in Windows 2003, click Start, point to Administrative Tools, and then click Performance.

2. Click the New Counter Set button in the toolbar.
3. Right-click anywhere in the graph, and then click Add Counters.

The Add Counters dialog box looks like this:

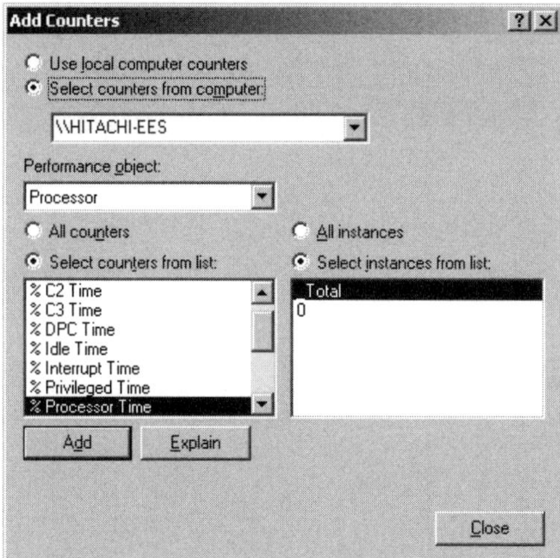

4. Click Use Local Computer Counters, and then, in the Performance Object drop-down list, select MSAS 2005: Cache.
5. In the Select Counters From List, select Direct Hit Ratio, and then click Add.

> **Tip** When you click a counter in the list, you can click Explain to view a description of the selected counter. You can leave the message box open and click on other counters to view the respective explanations.

This counter measures the ratio between the number of hits to the in-memory cache and the number of lookups when an answer is not found in memory. When this ratio is high, the query is resolved primarily from data in memory. Conversely, when this ratio is low, the query must be resolved by a lookup to the partition and dimension files on disk.

6. Click Close to close the Add Counters dialog box.
7. Open SQL Server Management Studio, expand the Databases folder for the Analysis Server, expand the SSAS Step by Step folder, expand the Cubes folder, right-click SSAS, and then click Browse. Drag Measures to the totals area of the grid and place the Category hierarchy of the Product.dimension on rows.
8. Switch to the Performance window.

Your screen looks similar to this:

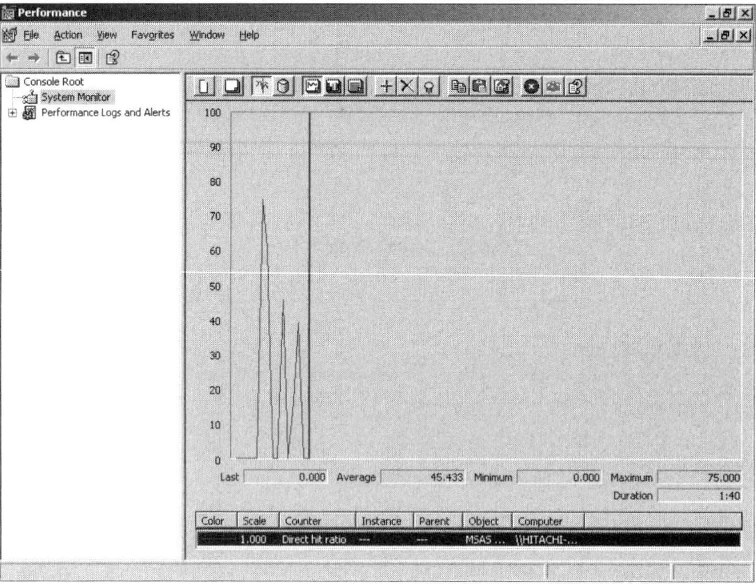

If you have recently browsed this cube, then some data is in memory and raises the value of the ratio. Otherwise, you may see a lower ratio in your graph.

9. Switch to SQL Server Management Studio, drag the Category hierarchy off the grid, drag the Subcategory hierarchy to rows, wait a moment, then remove the Subcategory hierarchy and return the Category hierarchy to rows.
10. Switch to the Performance window.

    Your screen looks similar to this:

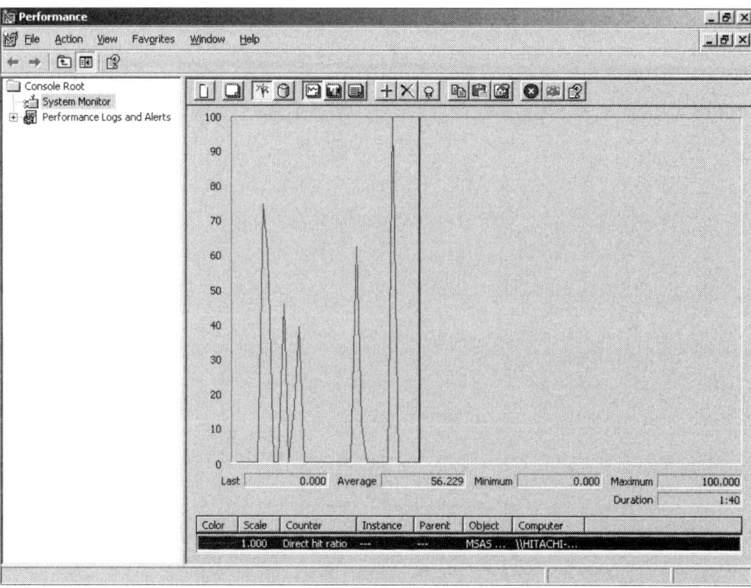

When you restore the Category hierarchy, the query can be answered directly from the cache, and accordingly, the ratio spikes to 100 percent, which you can see as the final spike in this graph.

You can, of course, also create performance logs to monitor Analysis Services activity over longer periods of time. By monitoring performance, you can identify bottlenecks in processing or querying as well as measure the impact of designing more or fewer aggregations, to name only a few situations. If you're responsible for maintaining and tuning an Analysis Services implementation, you'll find the available performance counters invaluable.

Chapter 12 Quick Reference

To	Do this
Create a new partition for a cube	On the Partitions tab of the Cube Designer, click the New Partition link, assign a fact table, and, optionally, specify a query to limit the partition to specific fact table rows.
Merge one partition with another	In SQL Server Management Studio, right-click the partition, click Merge, and then select a partition to be merged into the first partition.
Specify a storage mode for a partition	On the Partitions tab of the Cube Designer, right-click the partition, click Storage Settings, and then move the slider to the desired storage setting.
Synchronize an Analysis Services database with a warehouse database	In SQL Server Management Studio, right-click the Analysis Services database, and then click Process. Choose an applicable Processing Option.
Add new members to a dimension without invalidating existing cubes	In SQL Server Management Studio, right-click the dimension, click Process, and change the Processing Option to Process Update.
Avoid double-counting values when incrementally updating a cube	Either put new incremental values into a separate fact table or create a query limited to fact table rows that have not yet been loaded into the cube. In SQL Server Management Studio, right-click a partition, click Process, change the Processing Option to Process Incremental, click Configure, and specify the new fact table or the query.
Configure proactive caching for a partition	On the Partitions tab of the Cube Designer, right-click a partition, click Storage Settings, select a storage mode, click Options, and select Enable Proactive Caching. *or* In SQL Server Management Studio, right-click a partition, click Properties, click Proactive Caching, select a storage mode, click Options, and select Enable Proactive Caching.
Monitor Analysis Services	Create an Analysis Services trace in SQL Server Profiler or add performance counters to the monitor or log in Performance Monitor.

Chapter 13
Managing Deployment

After completing this chapter, you will be able to:

- Use the Deployment Wizard to deploy a database to an Analysis Server.
- Process a database manually.
- Automate database processing with SQL Server Integration Services.
- Use SQL Server Management Studio to back up and restore a database.

Building an analytical solution is usually an iterative process, requiring several cycles of design, development, and testing to be certain that requirements have been met satisfactorily. Often these iterative cycles are performed on a test server. When at last the solution is ready to release into production, you'll need to reproduce the database objects on the production server and then process the database to load data into the dimensions and cubes. You'll also need to perform routine administrative tasks to keep the data current by processing updates to the data warehouse. Finally, you'll need to keep the data protected from disaster by making regular backups. This chapter shows you how to deploy a database to a production environment and how to maintain the database once it is deployed.

Reviewing Deployment Options

Before you can view the results of design changes that you make to database objects in Visual Studio, you must use the Deploy command to move these objects to an Analysis Server where they are processed as necessary. When the development cycle is complete, you can change the project properties in Visual Studio to specify the target production server. Then you can use the Deploy command to deploy and process the database in the new location.

There are several other deployment methods you can use to place a database on an Analysis Server. For instance, you can create an XML file that defines all database objects by using Visual Studio's Build command and then use the build output file with the Analysis Services Deployment Wizard. This wizard creates a deployment script that you can run interactively or save for execution at a later time. Another option is simply to back up the database on one server and restore it to another server. Alternatively, you can use SQL Server Management Studio's Synchronize Database Wizard. Any of these options is a good choice when you only need to deploy a database once.

When your analytical solution requires multiple copies of the same database, a programmatic approach makes the task of deploying many databases much easier. One option is to build an

XML for Analysis (XMLA) script to run independently or to embed in a custom application that interacts with Analysis Services. Another programmatic option is to use *Analysis Management Objects* (AMO), the application program interface for Analysis Services, to create a deployment application for frequent usage.

Building a Database

When creating and maintaining an analytical solution involves a team of people, the responsibility for developing the database is often separate from the responsibility for deploying the database. If you're the database developer, you might need to hand off the final database files to an administrator who will copy the files to the production server and process the database. The Analysis Services Deployment Wizard is a good tool for the administrator to use in this situation, but first you need to create an *asdatabase* file, an XML file to contain the definitions of the database and its objects. These definitions are organized as a collection of special XML elements that conform to the object definition syntax of Analysis Services Scripting Language (ASSL), a type of XML used with Analysis Services. You use Visual Studio's Build command to create this file from your project.

In this procedure, you'll use the Build command to create an asdatabase file.

Use the Build command

1. Start SQL Server Business Intelligence Development Studio, and then open the Managing Deployment solution located in the C:\Documents and Settings\<username>\My Documents\Microsoft Press\as2005sbs\chap13\Managing Deployment folder.
2. In Solution Explorer, right-click the Managing Deployment project, and then click Build.

   During the build process, Visual Studio performs a syntax check of the XML definitions of each object in the project, and then generates a set of files which are stored in the solution's bin folder. One of these files is the asdatabase file, which is the consolidation of all the individual object definition files. When the build is complete, you will see "Build succeeded" in the status bar of Visual Studio.
3. Using Windows Explorer, navigate to C:\Documents and settings\<username>\My Documents\Microsoft Press\as2005sbs\chap13\Managing Deployment\Managing Deployment.

Your screen looks like this:

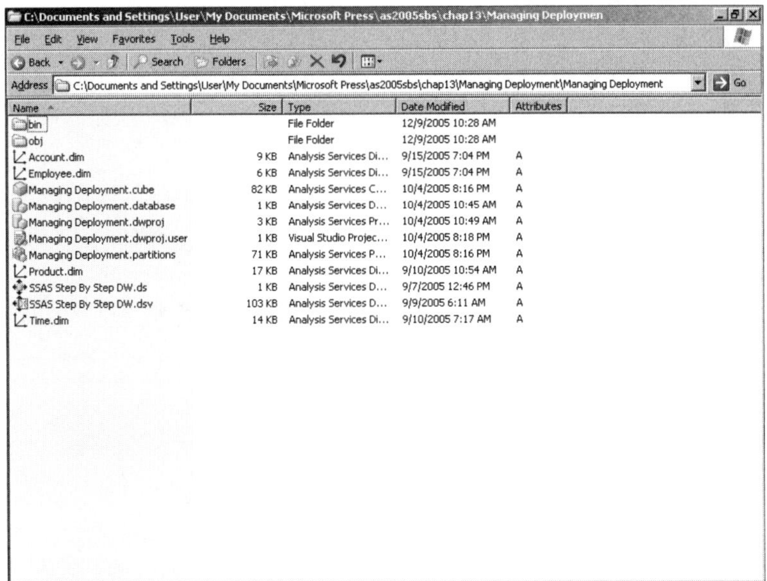

You should see one cube file, one data source file, one data source view file, one database file, four dimension files, one partitions file, one Analysis Services project file, and one Visual Studio user options file. All of these files, with the exception of the project and user options files, are visible in Solution Explorer when you use the Show All Files option.

The Build process created the two folders you see here–bin and obj. You'll examine the contents of the bin folder later. First, review the contents of a dimension file.

4. Right-click Product.dim and click Open With. Click Open Width if you receive a Caution dialog box.
5. Select the Select The Program From A List option, click OK, select Internet Explorer, and then click OK.

Your screen looks similar to this:

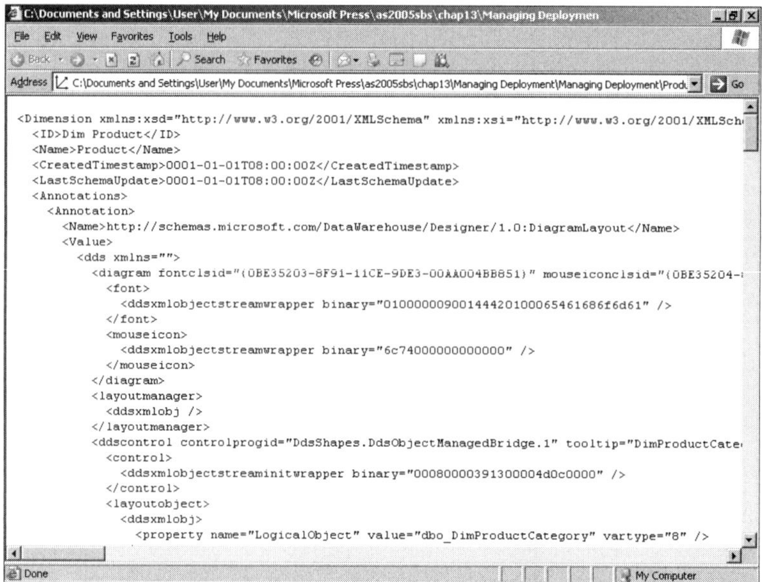

The product dimension is described in this file using ASSL. The subelements and attributes of the *<Annotations>* element are used only by the Dimension Designer in Visual Studio. The remainder of the file is used by Analysis Services to instantiate the physical dimension structure on the server.

6. Scroll through the file in Internet Explorer to locate the *<Attribute>* elements and the *<Hierarchy>* elements.

   You should recognize several element values defined for this dimension if you successfully completed Chapter 4, "Designing Dimensions."

7. Switch to Windows Explorer and open the bin folder.

Your screen looks like this:

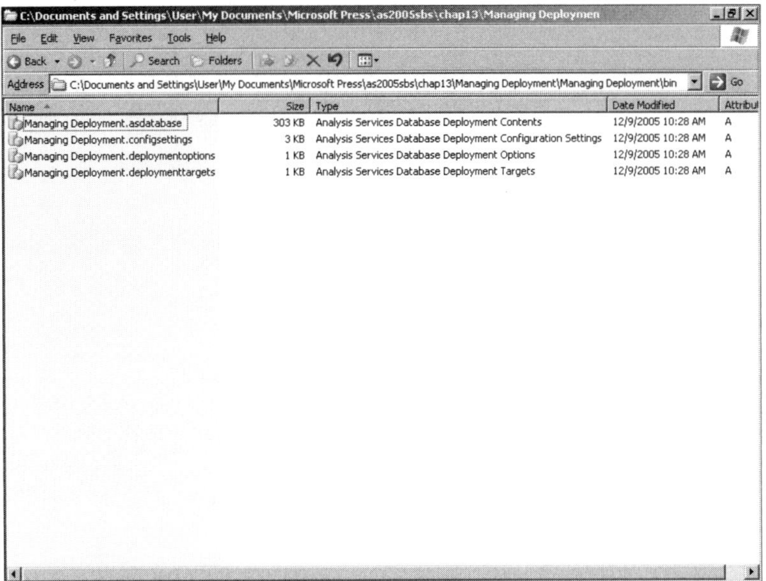

You should see four files—one Analysis Services Database Deployment Contents file, one Analysis Services Database Deployment Configuration Settings file, one Analysis Services Database Deployment Options file, and one Analysis Services Database Deployment Targets file. Each of these files is an XML file created by the Build process.

8. Right-click Managing Deployment.asdatabase and click Open With. Click Open Width if you receive a Caution dialog box.

9. Select the Select The Program From A List option, click OK, click Internet Explorer, and then click OK.

Your screen looks similar to this:

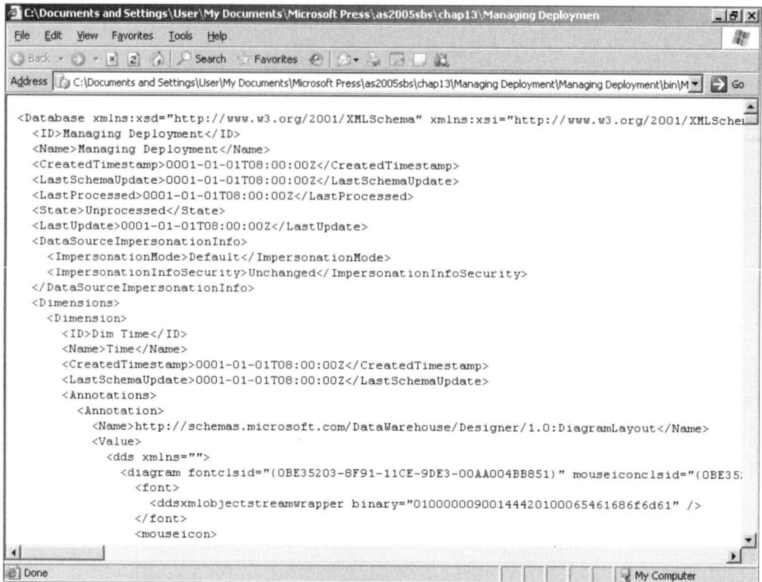

This XML file consolidates all of the object definitions into a single file in preparation for deployment to the Analysis server.

> **Tip** If you're trying to find all the occurrences of an object ID, or if you know you set a property but can't remember what object it belonged to, the asdatabase file is a great place to search.

10. Scroll through the file in Internet Explorer to locate the elements of the Product dimension.

    The definition of the Product dimension in the asdatabase file matches the definition that you reviewed in the Product.dim file. In addition, you'll find definitions for the data source, the data source view, the remaining dimensions, the cube, and the partition in the Managing Deployment.asdatabase file.

11. Close the Internet Explorer windows.

    At this point, you could give access to the Managing Deployment.asdatabase file to the administrator of the production server. The administrator could in turn use Copy and Paste commands to move the file from the development server to the production server, but the file can't be used directly by the Analysis server. The file must be deployed to make the contents usable, which you'll learn how to do in the next procedure.

Deploying a Database

If you're an administrator of an Analysis Server, you will likely be responsible for deploying databases to that server. When you're asked to place a new database on the server, you can obtain the asdatabase file from the database developer to use as an input file for the Analysis Services Deployment Wizard. The wizard reproduces the database object files on the target server and optionally processes the resulting database afterwards. Alternatively, you could use the wizard to produce an XMLA script to perform these same tasks, and then schedule the script to execute later.

In this procedure, you'll deploy a database using the Analysis Services Deployment Wizard.

Use the Analysis Services Deployment Wizard

1. Click Start, point to All Programs, point to Microsoft SQL Server 2005, point to Analysis Services, and then click Deployment Wizard.
2. Click Next to skip the Welcome page, click the ellipsis button next to the Database File box, navigate to the C:\Documents and Settings\<username>\My Documents\Microsoft Press\as2005sbs\chap13\Managing Deployment\Managing Deployment\bin folder, double-click the Managing Deployment.asdatabase file, and then click Next.

   The Installation Target page of the Analysis Services Deployment Wizard looks like this:

   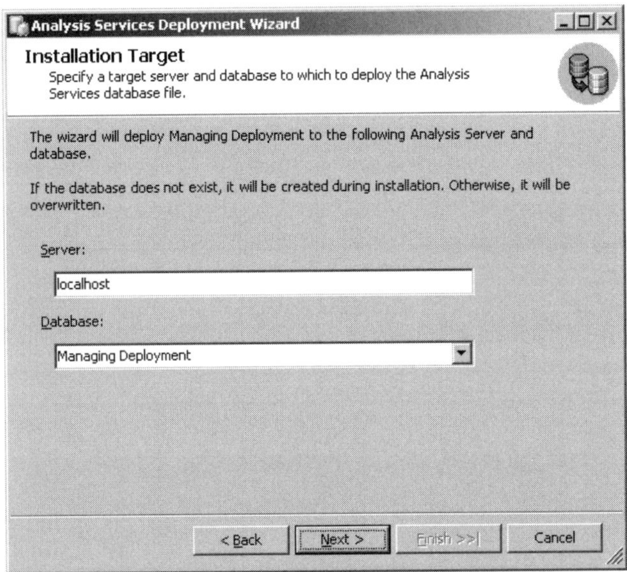

   You have the option to target a different Analysis server if you have access to multiple servers, such as when you have both a development and a production server in your network. You can also change the name of the database at this time. For this procedure, you'll accept the defaults.

3. Click Next.

The Specify Options for Partitions and Roles page of the Analysis Services Deployment Wizard looks like this:

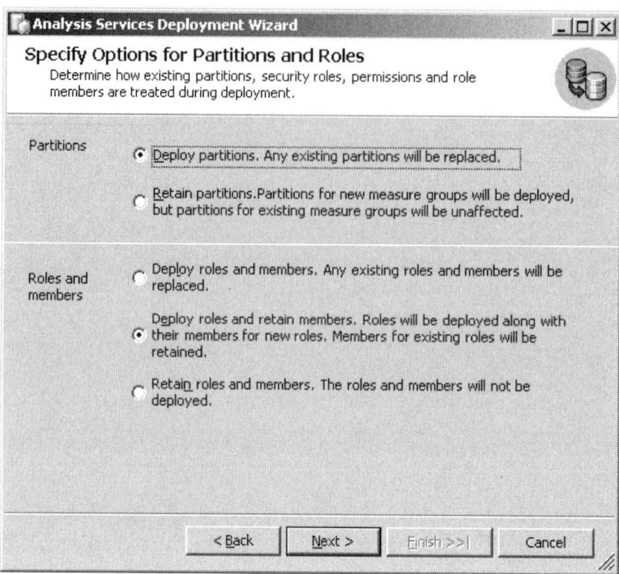

If you are redeploying a database to an Analysis server, you can choose whether to overwrite existing partitions and roles. Since this database has never been deployed, you'll accept the defaults.

4. Click Next.

   If you resize the dialog box, the Specify Configuration Properties page of the Analysis Services Deployment Wizard looks like this:

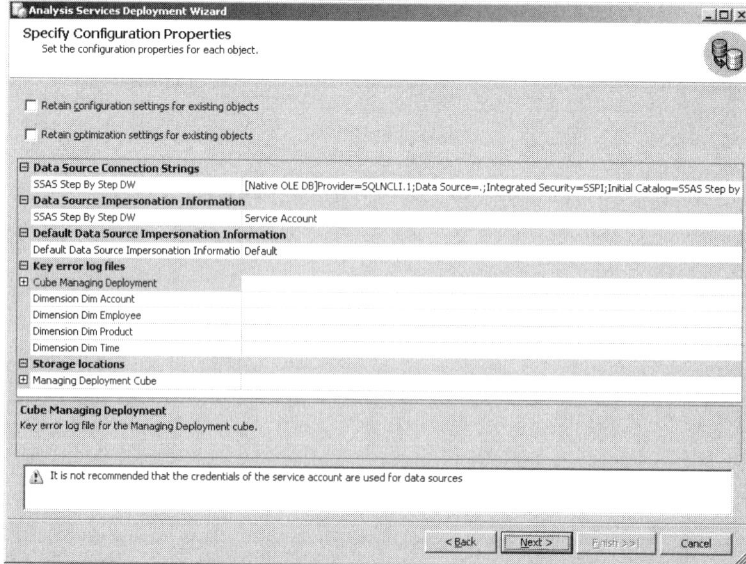

> **Important** Microsoft does not recommend that you configure Analysis Services to use the service account credentials for access to the data source during processing. In a production environment, you should change the Data Source Impersonation Information on this page of the wizard to more suitable credentials.

Not only can you protect existing partitions and roles, but you can also preserve the configuration settings for any objects that are already deployed to the server. For new objects, you can specify a different data source connection string, data source impersonation information, locations for log files, and locations for partition storage. Using the deployment wizard allows you to easily revise configuration properties when moving a database from one server to another, such as placing a database into production after development and testing. As with previous steps, accept the defaults on this page.

5. Click Next, and then select the None option for Processing Method.

   The Select Processing Options page of the Analysis Services Deployment Wizard looks like this:

   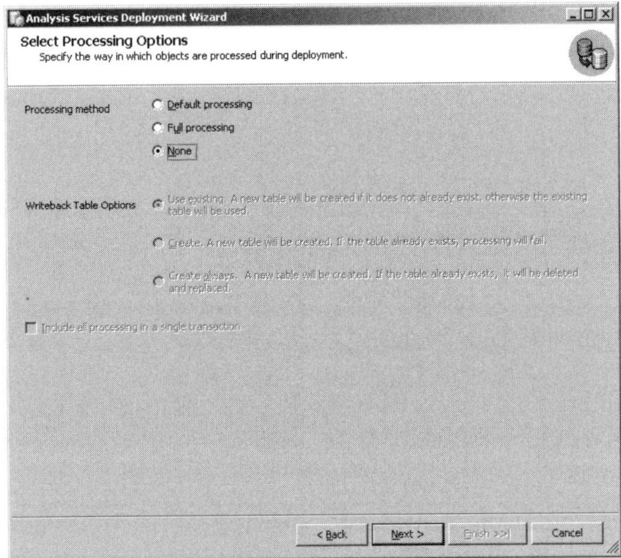

   On this page, you specify a processing option for all database objects—Default, Full, or None. By changing the processing option to None, you will be able to see the difference between deploying a database, which you'll do in a later step of this procedure, and processing a database, which you'll do in the next procedure.

Another option on this page helps you manage writeback tables. If a cube is enabled for writeback, you can specify what should happen with an existing writeback table, if one exists. Finally, you can opt to manage processing of the database as one single transaction, instead of handling the processing of each database object as a separate transaction.

6. Click Next.

   The Confirm Deployment page of the Analysis Services Deployment Wizard looks like this:

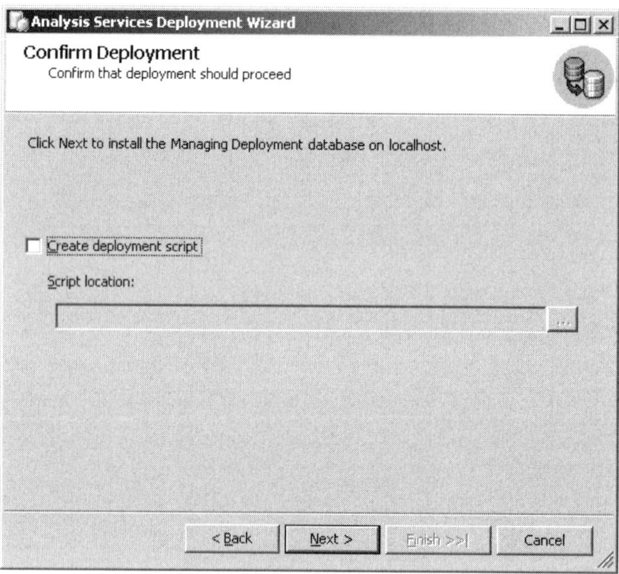

The Create Deployment Script option is disabled by default, which results in deployment of the database when you complete the wizard. Processing will also be performed after deployment unless you selected None for the processing option on a previous page of the wizard. Deployment extracts the object definitions from the asdatabase file into separate files stored in the data folder of the Analysis server. This set of files is very similar to the files that you reviewed in the Visual Studio project folder.

If you enable the Create Deployment Script option, then the Deployment Wizard will create an XMLA script that you can use to deploy the database later. However, by creating the script, deployment will not take place when you finish the wizard.

7. Click Next.

The Deploying Database page of the Analysis Services Deployment Wizard looks like this:

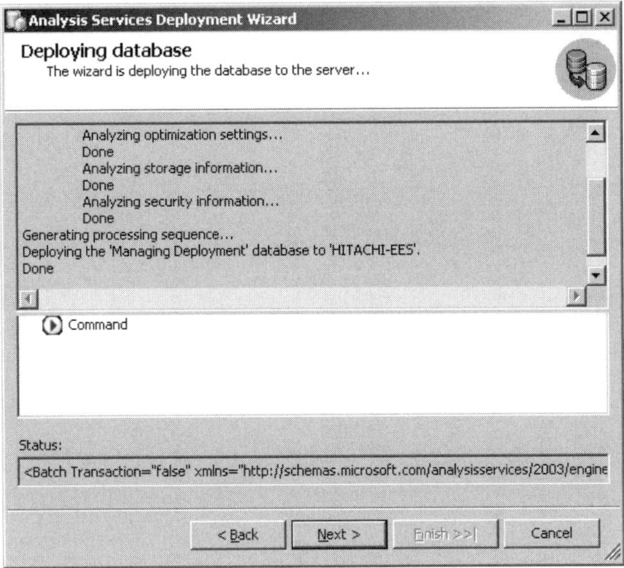

Now the contents of the asdatabase file have been extracted to the server, but the partitions and dimensions have not yet been processed.

8. Click Next, and then click Finish to close the wizard.
9. In Windows Explorer, navigate to the C:\Program Files\Microsoft SQL Server\MSSQL.2 \OLAP\Data folder.

> **Note** The actual folder on your computer may be different. Microsoft SQL Server components are installed in the Program Files\Microsoft SQL Server folder using the naming convention MSSQL.n, where n is a number assigned uniquely to a component. If you don't see the OLAP folder in MSSQL.2, explore the other folders until you locate it.

Your screen looks like this:

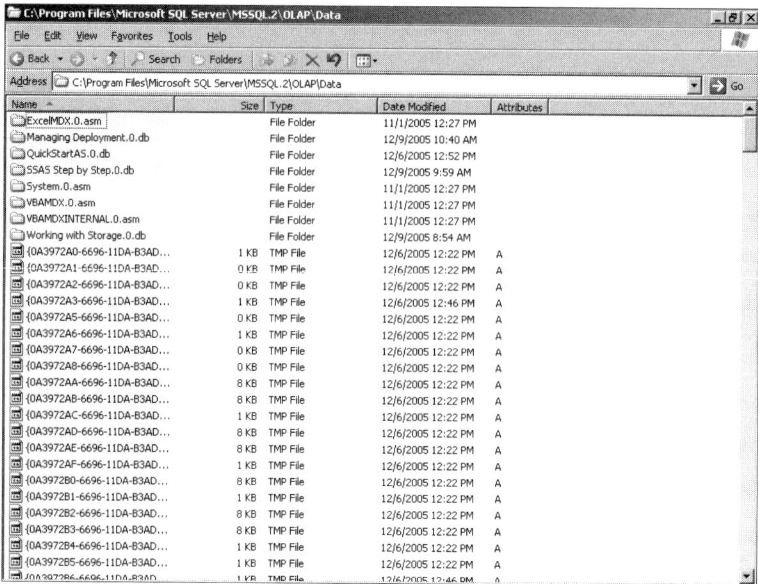

You specify the location of the OLAP Data folder when you install Analysis Services. By default, this folder is under Program Files\Microsoft SQL Server\MSSQL.2\OLAP\Data on the Windows drive, but may be located in a similarly named folder depending on your specific installation.

In this folder, you can see all the databases that have been deployed to the Analysis server. There is an XML file and a corresponding folder for each database. The name of these files and folders includes a version number that is automatically incremented. This naming system allows the server to process database objects in a new folder, and then redirect future queries to the new folder without the need to delete or rename the old one.

10. Open the file Managing Deployment.0.db.xml with Internet Explorer.

Your screen looks like this:

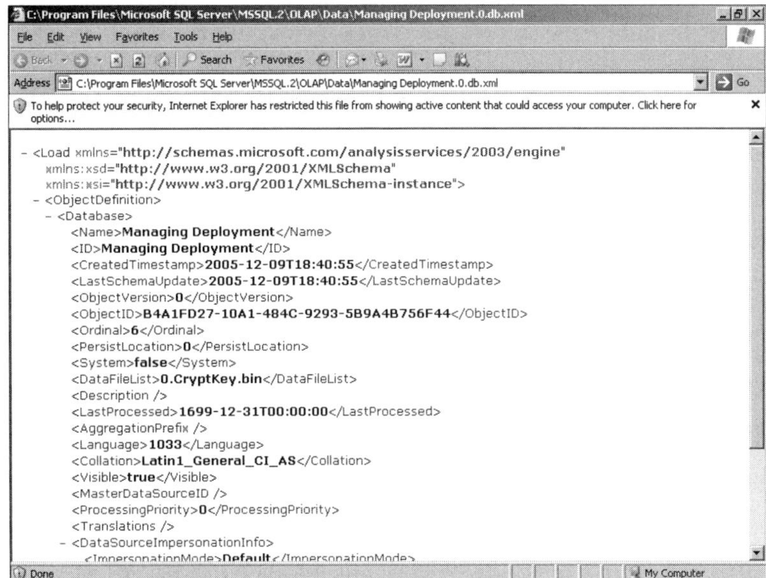

The Deployment Wizard extracts the database definition from the asdatabase file and inserts the applicable ASSL into the database file.

11. Close Internet Explorer, and then open the Managing Deployment.0.db folder in Windows Explorer.

    Your screen looks like this:

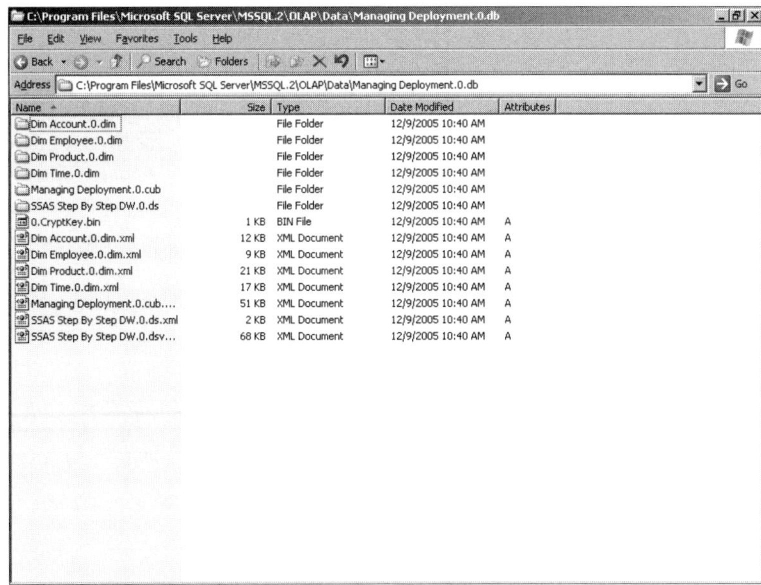

The XML files in this folder represent the separate database objects. The difference between these XML files and the files in your Visual Studio project folder is that these XML files include values for all properties of the object, while the project files contain only property values that are not default values. In both cases, the XML files define the metadata for the database object, but do not contain data themselves. When a database object is processed, data is stored in the folder that corresponds to the XML file.

12. Open the Dim Product.0.dim folder.

    This folder is currently empty because the dimension has not been processed. Deploying a database simply creates the XML metadata files and creates the folders in the Data folder of the Analysis server in preparation for processing.

> **Note** When you deploy a project from Visual Studio, processing automatically takes place for each new or changed object. If you don't want processing to occur right away, you can use the Build command to create an asdatabase file and then use the Deployment Wizard to set up the metadata files and folders on the target server.

Processing a Database

Analysis Services uses the concept of a *transaction* when processing a database. By default, when the server begins processing the database, it begins a new transaction. When it completes processing, it *commits* the transaction. If, for some reason, processing isn't completed successfully, the server *rolls back* the transaction and the database looks like it did before the transaction started. During the course of the transaction, all changes are made to temporary files so that applications retrieving values from the server are not aware that a transaction is taking place.

When you process a database, all the dimensions and all the cubes are processed within a single transaction. This means that all users can continue to use any cube or dimension with the database—seeing no changes—until the entire database has processed. Also, if anything should go wrong during the processing, all the temporary files are deleted—or *rolled back*—and the database remains as if nothing had happened. You can watch the server create and rename temporary files by looking at the data folder while processing the database.

In this procedure, you'll process the Managing Deployment database and observe the changes to the file system.

Use SQL Server Management Studio to process a database

1. In Windows Explorer, open the Managing Deployment.0.db folder within the C:\Program Files\Microsoft SQL Server\MSSQL.2\OLAP\Data folder. If necessary, on the View menu, select Details. Make a note of the date and time each file was last modified.

2. Open SQL Server Management Studio, connect to Analysis Services, expand the Databases folder, right-click Managing Deployment, and then click Process. (You might want to tile the SQL Server Management Studio and Windows Explorer windows vertically so you can see both at the same time.)

   Your screen looks similar to this:

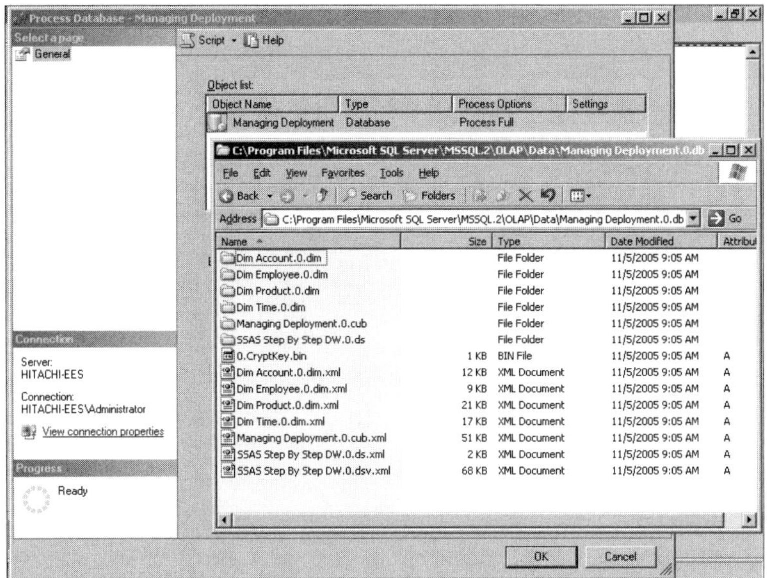

   You can see that the default processing option for this database is currently Process Full because it has never been processed. This dialog box is the same dialog box that you used in Chapter 12, "Managing Partitions and Database Processing." You can process objects in parallel or sequentially, set writeback table options, force a process of objects dependent on this database, and set error configuration properties each time you manually process an object.

3. Click OK to start processing, and then, as soon as the Process log window opens, switch to the Windows Explorer window that displays the database files. Press the F5 key to refresh the window.

Your screen looks similar to this:

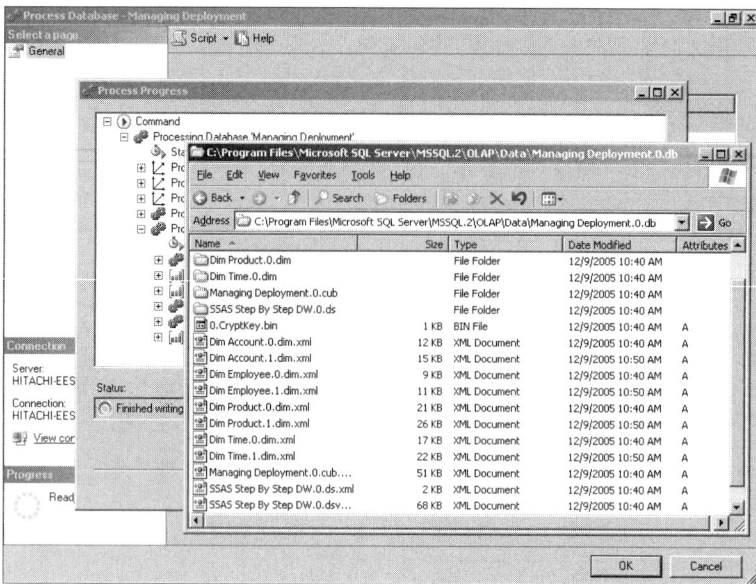

You'll see new files and folders appear, each with a different version number included in the name.

As soon as the database completes processing, you can refresh the window to see the temporary files disappear and you again see single names for the files in the database. The date and time for these files, however, does indicate that they're the new versions of the files.

When processing is complete, your screen looks similar to this:

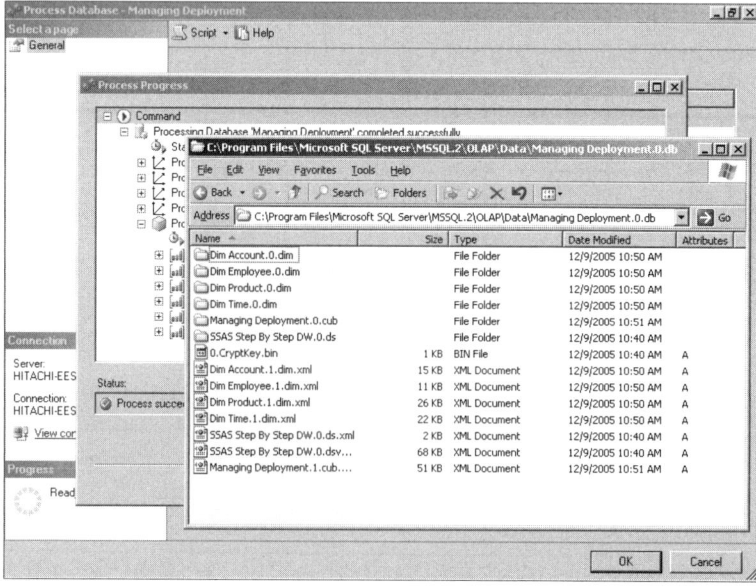

4. Switch back to SQL Server Management Studio.

   You can see in the Process Database dialog box, the dimensions are processed first, followed by the partitions for each measure group. If you expand the objects in the dialog box, you can review the SQL queries that were used to load data into dimensions and partitions.

5. Click Close, and then switch to Windows explorer to open the Dim Product 0.dim folder in the C:\Program Files\Microsoft SQL Server\MSSQL.2\OLAP\Data\Managing Deployment.0.db folder.

   Your screen looks similar to this:

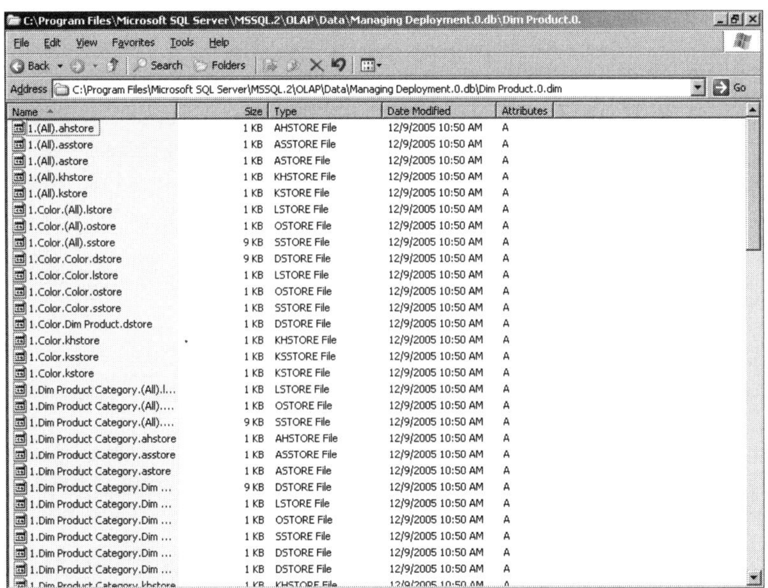

   Once you process the database, the folders contain actual data files. These are not XML files, but compressed data files that you can't browse from Windows Explorer.

Managing Database Objects Programmatically

For many organizations, deploying and managing databases by using Analysis Services wizards and SQL Server Management Studio is sufficient. When you have a large number of databases to manage or you need to schedule maintenance activities to occur at specific times, you might prefer to use XMLA scripts or custom applications to perform deployment and management tasks. Anything you can do in the user interface can be done programmatically through scripting or by using AMO.

Working with XMLA Scripts

You can easily create XMLA scripts to capture object definitions or commands for executing actions on the Analysis Server by using the Script command in SQL Server Management Studio. You can also execute an XMLA script in this environment, much like you can execute (Transact) T-SQL or multidimensional expressions (MDX) queries. A script can be scheduled as a SQL Server Agent job if you want the script to run unattended. It's also possible to embed a script in a custom application to automate Analysis Services management activities as part of a larger solution.

In this procedure, you'll create an XMLA script to add a new partition to the Managing Deployment cube, and then process the partition.

Create and execute a processing script

1. In SQL Server Management Studio, expand the Managing Deployment database, expand the Cubes folder, right-click the Managing Deployment cube, and then click Browse. Click Reconnect if necessary.
2. Drag the Reseller Order Quantity measure from the Reseller Sales folder to the totals area of the grid, and then drag Order Date.Calendar Year from the Order Date dimension to the rows axis.

   Your screen looks like this:

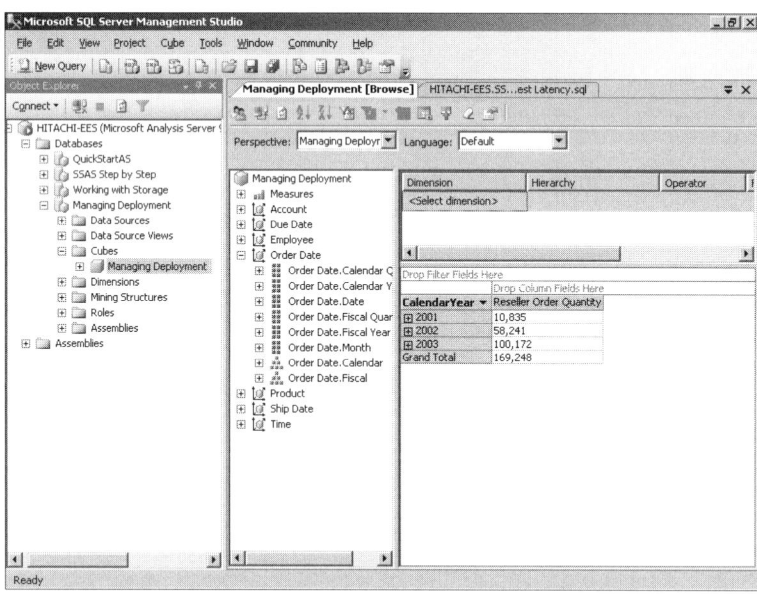

   Right now, only data from 2001 through 2003 is in the processed cube.

3. In Object Explorer, expand the following items: Managing Deployment cube, Measure Groups, Reseller Sales, and Partitions folder. Right-click Reseller Sales 2003, point to Script Partition As, point to CREATE To, and then click New Query Editor Window.

   Your screen looks like this:

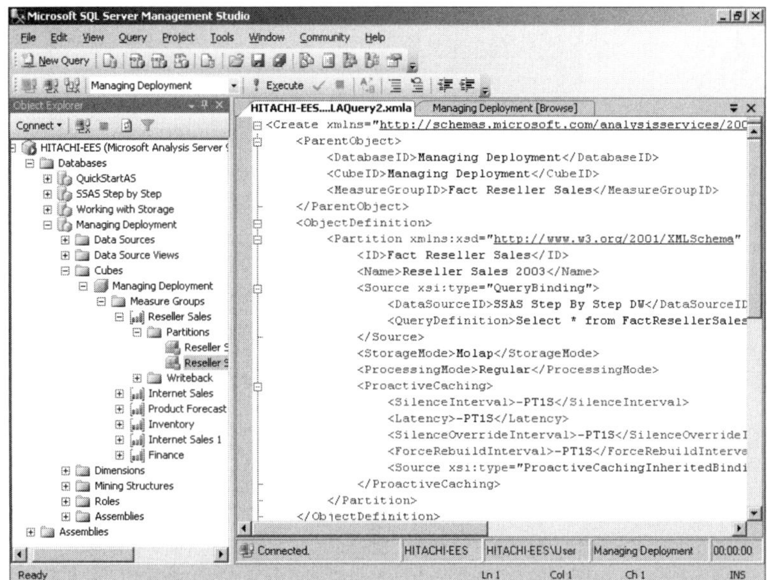

   You can script any database object to recreate that object, or use the selected object as a basis for building a new object. For example, you can make changes to a script for an existing partition to create a new partition, which you'll do in the next step.

4. Change subelements of the *Partition* element in the script, as shown below:

```
<ID>Fact Reseller Sales 2004</ID>|
        <Name>Reseller Sales 2004</Name>
        <Source xsi:type="QueryBinding">
          <DataSourceID>SSAS Step By Step DW</DataSourceID>
          <QueryDefinition>Select * from FactResellerSales where orderdatekey &gt;
914</QueryDefinition>
        </Source>
```

   To create a new partition, you must take care to provide a unique ID and name for the partition as well as a unique query definition so that you don't overwrite an existing partition or create a partition that includes fact table rows that are already in another partition.

5. Right-click Reseller Sales 2003, click Process, click the Script button at the top of the dialog box, and then click Cancel.

Your screen looks like this:

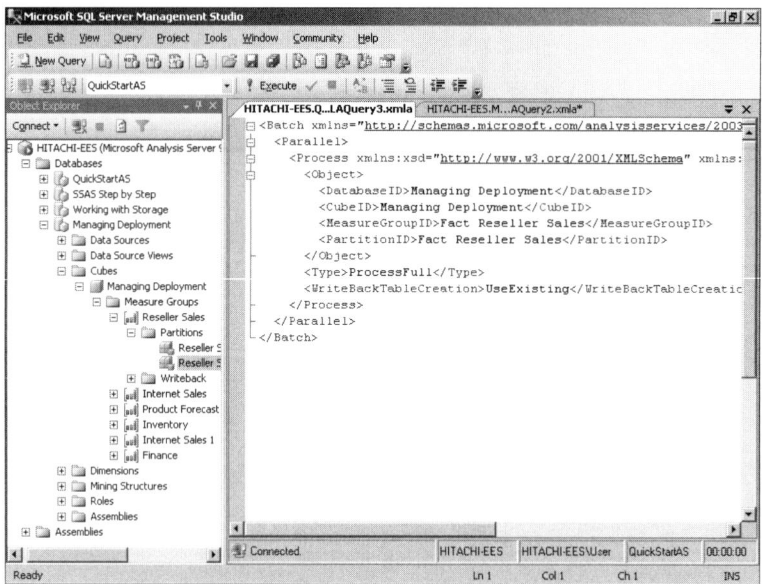

All server actions—such as processing—can be scripted for later execution. You can combine the *Process* script here with the *Create* script in the other XMLA query window to perform both commands in a single script. Just as you can modify the script of an object to create a new object, you can also modify the script of a command for use with another object. You'll make this type of modification in the next step.

6. Change the Partition ID to **Fact Reseller Sales 2004**.

7. Highlight the entire *Process* script, press Ctrl+C, switch to the XMLA query window that contains the *Create* script, position the cursor at the bottom of the script, and then press Ctrl+V.

   Now the two commands are combined into a single script, but the structure of this script is invalid. If you want to send multiple commands to the server in one XMLA script, you need to enclose both the *Create* and *Process* commands within the *Batch* command.

8. Use copy and paste to move the *Batch* command line to the first line of the script.

The final XMLA script looks like this:

```
<Batch xmlns="http://schemas.microsoft.com/analysisservices/2003/engine">
  <Create xmlns="http://schemas.microsoft.com/analysisservices/2003/engine">
    <ParentObject>
      <DatabaseID>Managing Deployment</DatabaseID>
      <CubeID>Managing Deployment</CubeID>
      <MeasureGroupID>Fact Reseller Sales</MeasureGroupID>
    </ParentObject>
    <ObjectDefinition>
      <Partition xmlns:xsd="http://www.w3.org/2001/XMLSchema" xmlns:xsi="http://
www.w3.org/2001/XMLSchema-instance">
        <ID>Fact Reseller Sales 2004</ID>
        <Name>Reseller Sales 2004</Name>
        <Source xsi:type="QueryBinding">
          <DataSourceID>SSAS Step By Step DW</DataSourceID>
          <QueryDefinition>Select * from FactResellerSales where orderdatekey &gt;
914</QueryDefinition>
        </Source>
        <StorageMode>Molap</StorageMode>
        <ProcessingMode>Regular</ProcessingMode>
        <ProactiveCaching>
          <SilenceInterval>-PT1S</SilenceInterval>
          <Latency>-PT1S</Latency>
          <SilenceOverrideInterval>-PT1S</SilenceOverrideInterval>
          <ForceRebuildInterval>-PT1S</ForceRebuildInterval>
          <Source xsi:type="ProactiveCachingInheritedBinding"/>
        </ProactiveCaching>
      </Partition>
    </ObjectDefinition>
  </Create>
  <Parallel>
    <Process xmlns:xsd="http://www.w3.org/2001/XMLSchema" xmlns:xsi="http://
www.w3.org/2001/XMLSchema-instance">
      <Object>
        <DatabaseID>Managing Deployment</DatabaseID>
        <CubeID>Managing Deployment</CubeID>
        <MeasureGroupID>Fact Reseller Sales</MeasureGroupID>
        <PartitionID>Fact Reseller Sales 2004</PartitionID>
      </Object>
      <Type>ProcessFull</Type>
      <WriteBackTableCreation>UseExisting</WriteBackTableCreation>
    </Process>
  </Parallel>
</Batch>
Click the Execute button in the query window.
```

9. When the query has executed successfully, switch to the cube browser, and then click Reconnect.

Your screen looks like this:

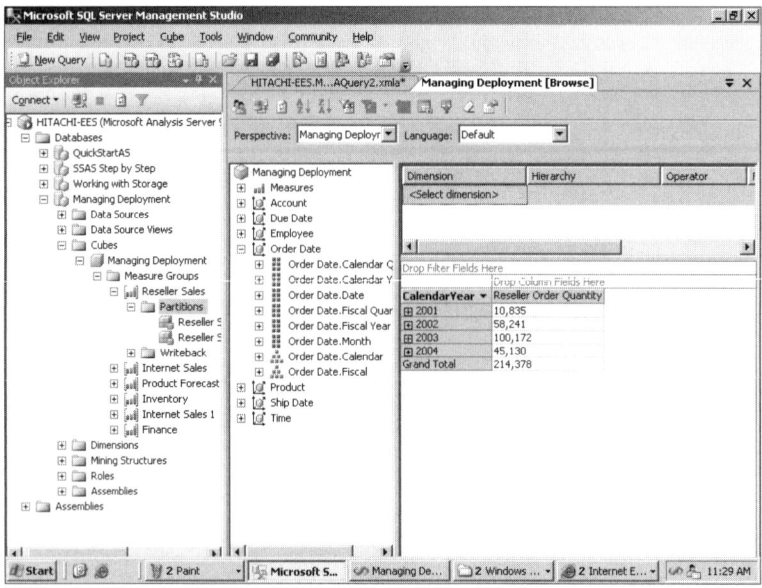

The data for the 2004 partition is now available in the cube.

> **Working with Analysis Management Objects**
>
> AMO is the .NET library that you can use in your Microsoft Visual Basic .NET or Microsoft C# .NET applications. You can use AMO to create any database object, apply security, or process objects. When you are building a solution, you could start building objects by using the designers in Visual Studio, fine-tune the definitions of these objects by modifying the ASSL directly in the object files, and then you can finalize the design, deploy, and process the database by using AMO. Of course, you could build an application with AMO that does nothing but process databases.
>
> The code to create database objects in AMO is very similar to ASSL. This similarity is very useful for learning how to use properties in AMO. You can build an example dimension in Visual Studio, and then reference the dim file as you learn to build the same dimension using AMO. For more information about AMO, refer to the topic "AMO Managed Programming Reference Documentation" in SQL Server Books Online.

Automating Database Processing

For most OLAP databases, updating the cubes with new values is a routine process that must be performed on a regular basis–monthly, weekly, nightly, or even hourly. Analysis Services doesn't provide any direct tools for automating the processing of databases. Manually carrying out routine tasks–particularly if you'll be incrementally updating dimensions and cubes–can be an extremely tedious assignment.

Fortunately, Microsoft SQL Server 2005 has a facility for automating many different types of data manipulation activities, including processing OLAP components, called SQL Server Integration Services (SSIS). While you can use Analysis Services without using SQL Server, to use SISS, you must first install it from the SQL Server media.

Creating a SQL Server Integration Services Package

SSIS is a general-purpose application designed to move and manipulate data. SSIS can use many different data sources and many different data targets. It can group multiple processing tasks into a *package*, which you can reuse and schedule.

In this procedure, you'll create an SSIS package.

Create a package

1. In Visual Studio, click the File menu, point to New, and then click Project.
2. Click Integration Services Project in the Templates list, type **OLAP Update** in the Name box, change the Location to C:\Documents and Settings\<username>\My Documents \Microsoft Press\as2005sbs\Workspace, and then click OK.

   Your screen looks like this:

   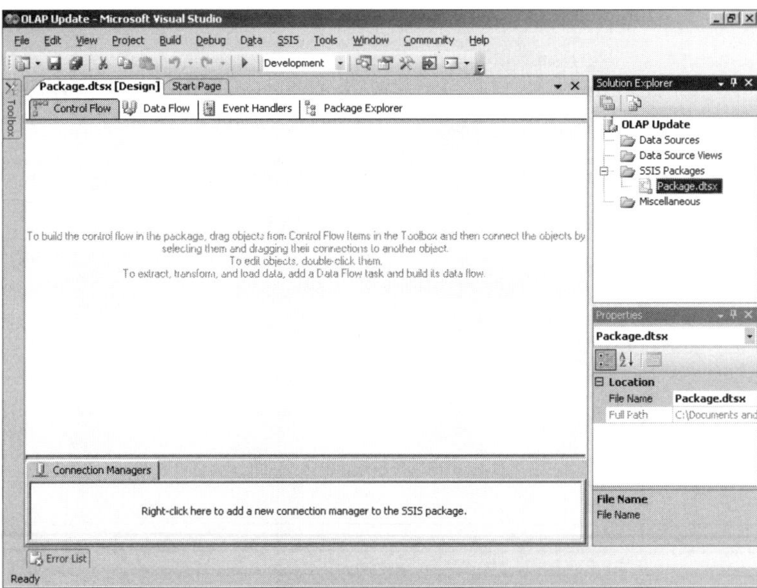

   Notice in Solution Explorer that a default package has already been created called Package.dtsx. In the main window of Visual Studio, you see the package designer which provides the workspace in which you design the tasks that you want to automate.

3. Right-click Package.dtsx, click Rename, and then type **OLAP Update Package.dtsx**, and then click Yes to confirm the name change.

   You can now add tasks to the package

Using the Analysis Services Processing Task

The Toolbox window to the left of the package designer window contains icons for various types of tasks that you can automate in a package. The Analysis Services Processing Task appears as a cube in the Toolbox. This task allows you to process Analysis server objects as part of the package. Suppose that you want to process the Managing Deployment database each night. You can add that task to the package.

In this procedure, you'll add an Analysis Services Processing Task to the OLAP Update Package to process the Managing Deployment database.

Create an Analysis Services Processing Task

1. Drag the Analysis Services Processing Task cube icon from the Toolbox window onto the Control Flow workspace.
2. Double-click the Analysis Services Processing Task.

   The Analysis Services Processing Task Editor dialog box appears.
3. In the Name box, type **Process OLAP Database**.
4. Click Analysis Services in the page list on the left side of the dialog box, click New, click Edit, select Use Windows NT Integrated Security, select Managing Deployment in the Initial Catalog drop-down list, and then click OK twice to return to the Analysis Services Processing Task Editor dialog box.
5. Click Add, and then select the check box to the left of Managing Deployment.

   The Add Analysis Services Object dialog box looks like this:

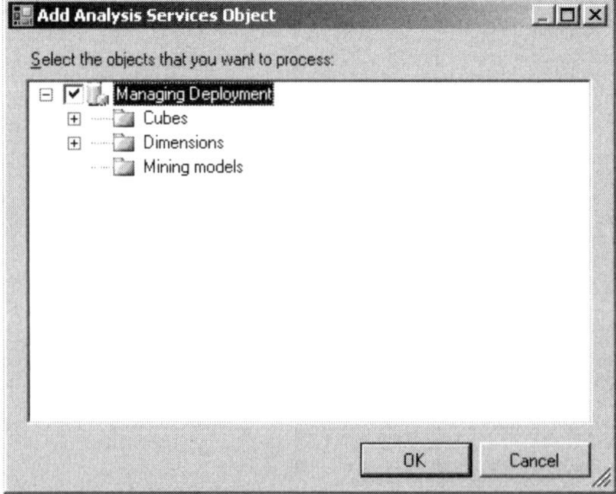

Alternatively, you can select one or more specific objects, such as measure groups, partitions, or dimensions to be processed by this task.

6. Click OK.

   Your screen looks like this:

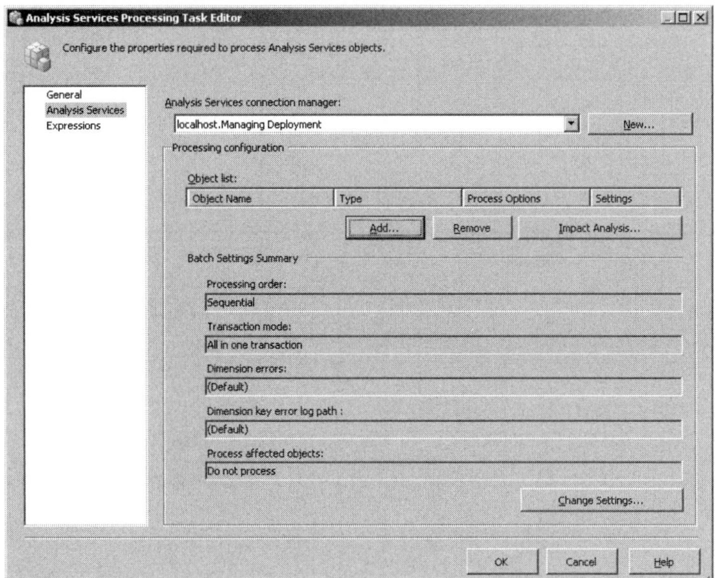

   If you understand how to process an object using the available commands in SQL Server Management Studio, Visual Studio, or the Deployment Wizard, you can easily create an SSIS task to automate that processing.

7. Click OK.

Handling Task Failures

An SSIS package can contain multiple tasks. You can control the *workflow* between various tasks. For example, you can create a task to send yourself an e-mail message. You can then create a workflow connection that will execute the e-mail task only if the processing task fails. SSIS provides three workflow options: Completion, Success, and Failure.

In this procedure, you'll create an e-mail task and then create a Failure workflow connection between the Analysis Services Processing task and the e-mail task.

Send an e-mail message if the task fails

1. Drag the Send Mail Task icon from the Toolbox window onto the Control Flow workspace.
2. Double-click the Send Mail Task Properties, click Mail in the page list on the left side of the dialog box, select New Connection in the SmtpConnection drop-down list, and then type the name of your Simple Mail Transfer Protocol (SMTP) server in the SMTP Server

box. You may need to click the Use Windows Authentication check box if your SMTP requires Windows credentials.

The SMTP Connection Manager Editor looks similar to this:

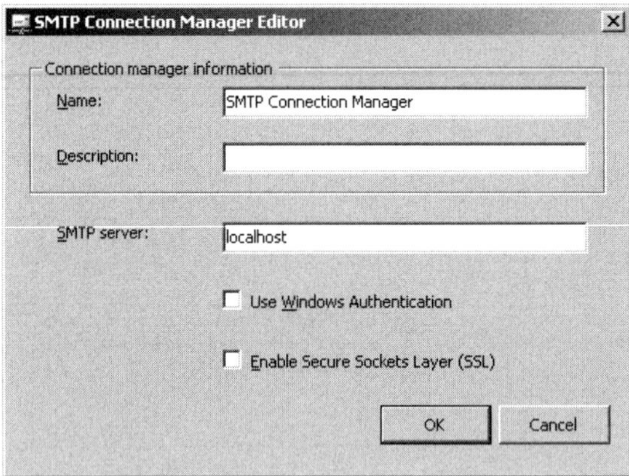

3. Click OK to return to the Send Mail Task Editor dialog box, type your e-mail address in the From box and in the To box, type **OLAP Process failed** in the Subject box, and type **The OLAP task to update the Managing Deployment database did not complete successfully** in the MessageSource box.

   The Send Mail Task Editor looks similar to this:

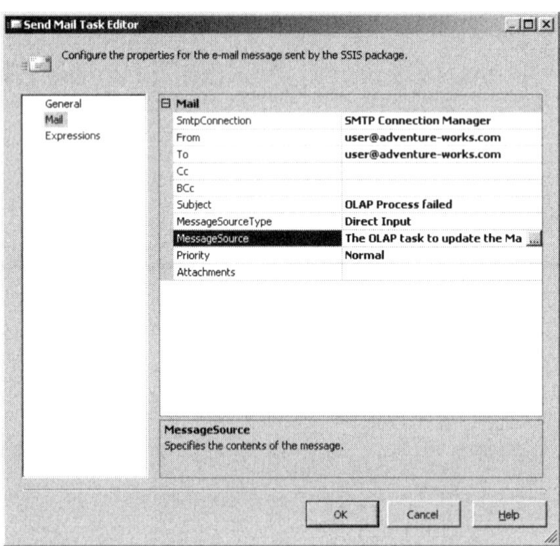

4. Click OK, click the Process OLAP Database task, and then drag the green line from that task to the Send Mail task.
5. Right-click the green arrow, and then click Failure.

Your screen looks like this:

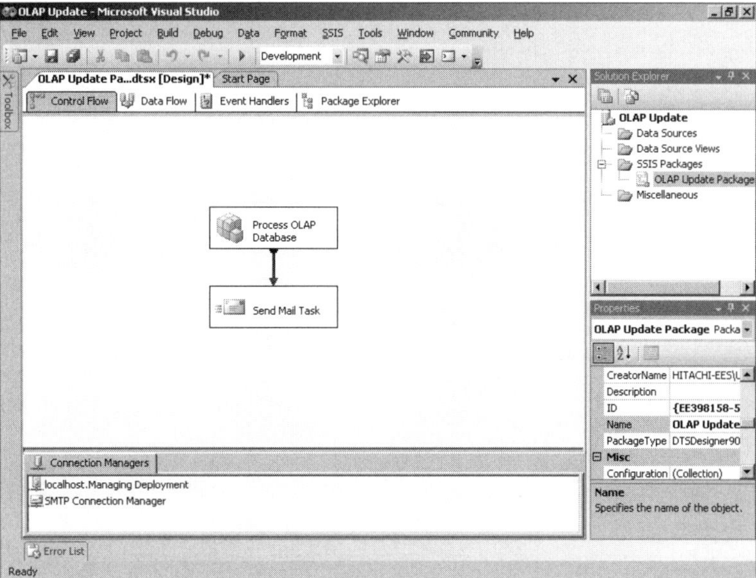

Workflow connections allow you to create sophisticated packages. If you need to create a package that incrementally updates all the dimensions and cubes of a database, you create a single task for each OLAP action and then join them together with Success workflow connections. From each task, you also create a Failure workflow connection to the error e-mail message.

Scheduling a SQL Server Integration Services Package

Once you have created a package, you can choose to execute it immediately, or you can schedule the task to run at a specific time. Suppose that you want to process the Managing Deployment database each day at 19:00. You can create that schedule for the package.

In this procedure, you'll save the OLAP Update package to the server and create a schedule for periodic execution of the package.

Create a package schedule

1. Close Visual Studio, clicking Yes when asked whether you want to save the project files.
2. In SQL Server Management Studio, connect to Integration Services.
3. Expand the Stored Packages folder, right-click the File System folder, and then click Import Package.
4. Select File System in the Package Location drop-down list, click the button to the right of the Package Path box, navigate to the C:\Documents and Settings\<username>\My Documents\Microsoft Press\as2005sbs\Workspace\OLAP Update\OLAP Update

folder, double-click Update OLAP Package.dtsx, and then click the Package Name box to force the name of the package to be read.

Your screen looks like this:

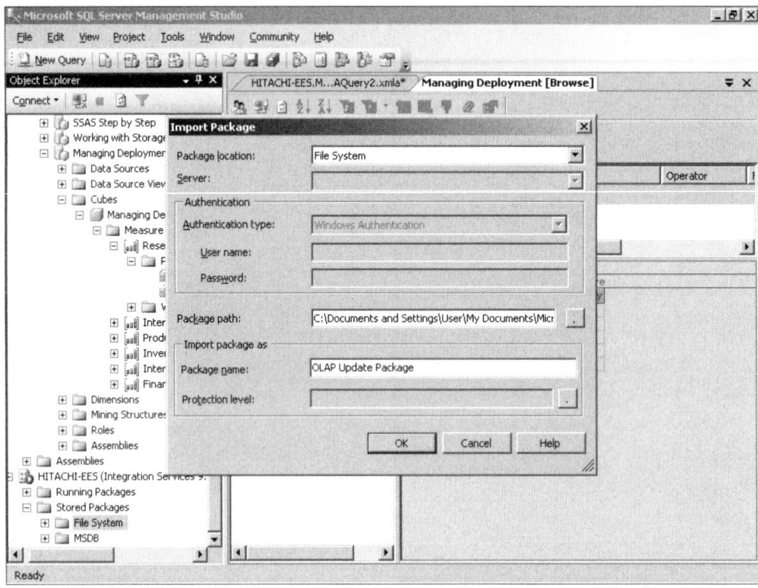

5. Click OK.

   The package is now available to the Integration server where it can be executed on demand or on a schedule.

6. Right-click Update OLAP Package.dtsx, click Run Package, and then click Command Line in the page list on the left side of the Execute Package Utility dialog box.

   The Execute Package Utility dialog box looks like this:

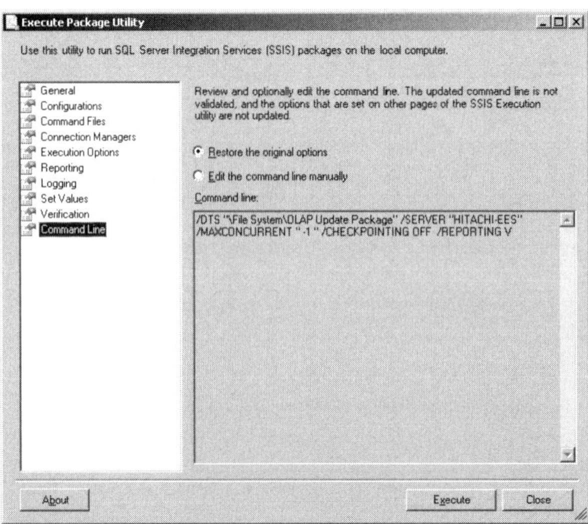

7. Highlight the command line text `/DTS "\File System\OLAP Update Package" /SERVER <servername> /MAXCONCURRENT " -1 " /CHECKPOINTING OFF /REPORTING V`, press Ctrl+C to copy the text to the clipboard, and then click Close.
8. In the Object Explorer window, connect to the Database Engine, expand SQL Server Agent, right-click the Jobs folder, and then click New Job.
9. Type **Update OLAP** in the Name box, click Steps in the Select A Page list, click New, type **Execute package** in the Step Name box, select Operating System (CmdExec) in the Type drop-down list, position the cursor in the Command box, and then press Ctrl+V to paste the contents of the clipboard into the Command box.
10. Position the cursor at the beginning of the command string, type **dtexec**, and press the spacebar.

    The New Job Step dialog box looks like this:

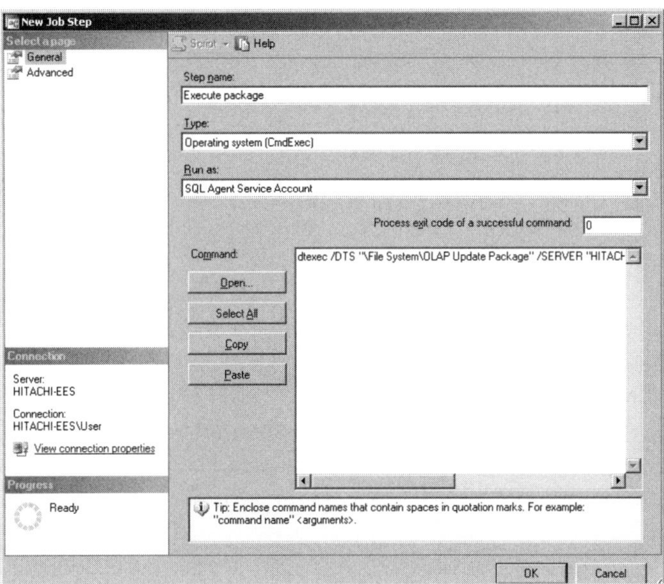

11. Click OK, click Schedules in the Select A Page list, click New, type **OLAP Update** in the Name box, select One Time in the Schedule Type drop-down list. Change the time box to **7:00:00 PM**.

The New Job Schedule dialog box looks like this:

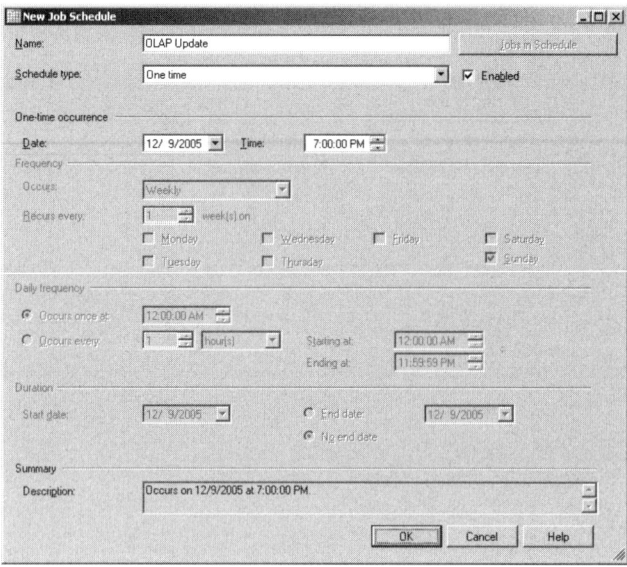

12. Click OK twice to schedule the task.

    The scheduled task becomes a SQL Server Agent job. To edit or delete the schedule, you must go into the SQL Server Agent folder.

13. Expand the Jobs folder, right-click the OLAP Update job in the Object Explorer window. Click Delete, and click OK to confirm the deletion.

    The SSIS component of SQL Server 2005 is a powerful tool. It's capable of simplifying and facilitating all types of data management tasks, particularly those associated with creating and maintaining a data warehouse. The Analysis Services Processing Task opens SSIS capabilities to Analysis Services, but it's only a small part of SSIS.

Planning for Disaster and Recovery

Best practices for any technology infrastructure always include a plan for disaster and recovery. Of course, your Analysis Services environment should be included in this plan. To effectively recover from a problem that compromises the data on the Analysis Server, you should make regular backups of all databases on the Analysis Server. SQL Server Management Studio includes commands to back up and restore your Analysis Services databases. Additionally, you can use XMLA scripts or AMO to automate these processes.

Backing Up an Analysis Services Database

To manually back up Analysis Services databases, you use the Backup command in SQL Server Management Studio. You select a location where you want the backup saved and you must provide a name for the backup file created. Each database backup is saved as a *.abf file. For batch processing, you can script the backup definition for each database, and then create a batch script to consolidate the backup process for all databases in your environment. To perform a backup, you must have both server administrator and database administrator permissions.

The contents of a backup file will depend on the storage mode used for database objects. As you learned in Chapter 12, hybrid OLAP (HOLAP) and relational OLAP (ROLAP) use data from the relational source. Therefore, the backup file will contain only metadata for the database, although if you've designed aggregations for a HOLAP partition, the aggregations will, in fact, be saved in the backup file. On the other hand, because a multidimensioanl OLAP (MOLAP) partition is totally self-contained and uses the relational source only for processing (and proactive caching, if enabled), a MOLAP backup file will contain metadata, aggregations, and all data in the database cubes and dimension.

In this procedure, you'll create a backup of the Managing Deployment using the Backup command in SQL Server Management Studio.

Back up a database

1. In SQL Server Management Studio, connect to Analysis Services, expand the Databases folder, right-click Managing Deployment, and then click Back up.

   The Backup Database – Managing Deployment dialog box looks like this:

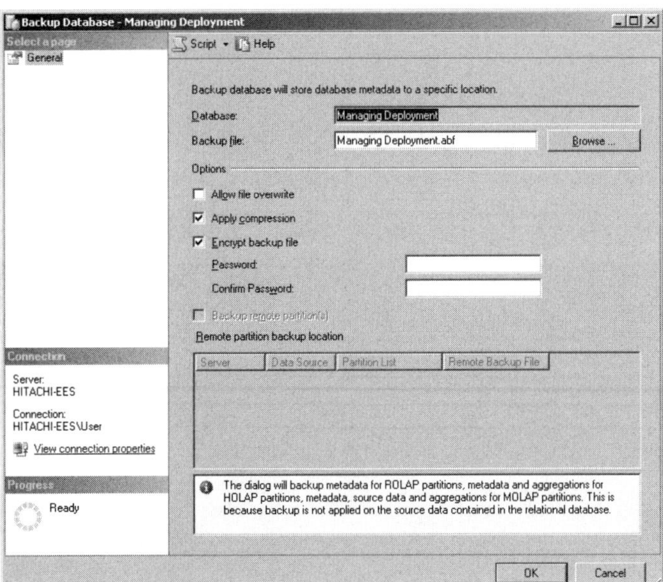

> **Note** The default path for an .abf file is C:\Program Files\Microsoft SQL Server \MSSQL.2\OLAP\Backup folder if you specified the default folders for data and backup files when installing Analysis Services.

2. Type a strong password in the Password box, retype the same password in the Confirm Password box, and then click OK.

   The Managing Deployment.abf file is now available in the \Backup folder and can be included in regular backup procedures of the server's file system. Because this file is encrypted, no one who obtains a copy of this file can view its contents after restoring the database unless he or she knows the encryption password.

Restoring an Analysis Services Database

Hopefully, you'll more often use the Restore command to migrate a database from one server to another than to recover from a disaster. If you need to restore a database, you will need to be a server administrator. Additionally, if the backup file was created with a password, you'll need to provide that password to successfully restore the file.

In this procedure, you'll restore the backup of the SSAS Step by Step database.

Restore a database

1. Right-click the Databases folder (in the Analysis Services tree), and then click Restore.

   Your screen looks like this:

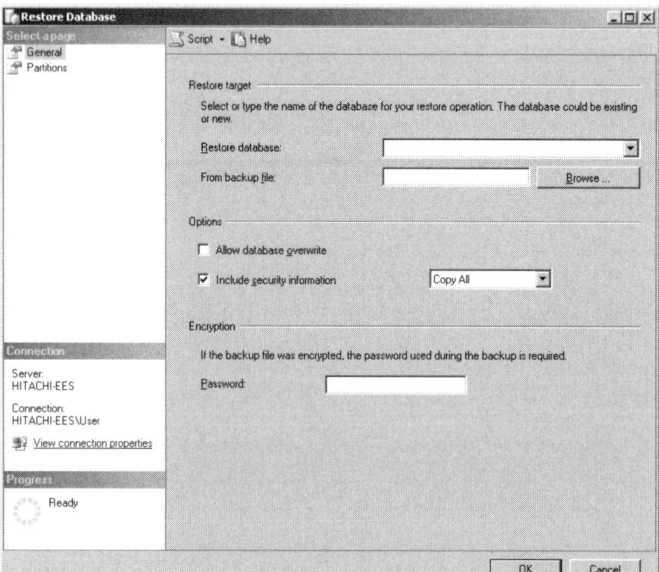

You have the option to restore the database using a different name. If the database already exists on the server, you need to explicitly select the option to Allow Database Overwrite. Also, you can choose whether to keep or discard security information associated with the database.

2. In the Restore Database box, type **My Restored Database**.
3. Click the Browse button, expand the C:\Program Files\Microsoft SQL Server \MSSQL.2\OLAP\Backup folder, select Managing Deployment.abf, and then click OK.
4. In the Password box, type the password that you used when you archived the database in the previous procedure, and then click OK.
5. In Object Explorer, right-click the Databases folder for the Analysis server, and click Refresh.

   Your screen looks similar to this:

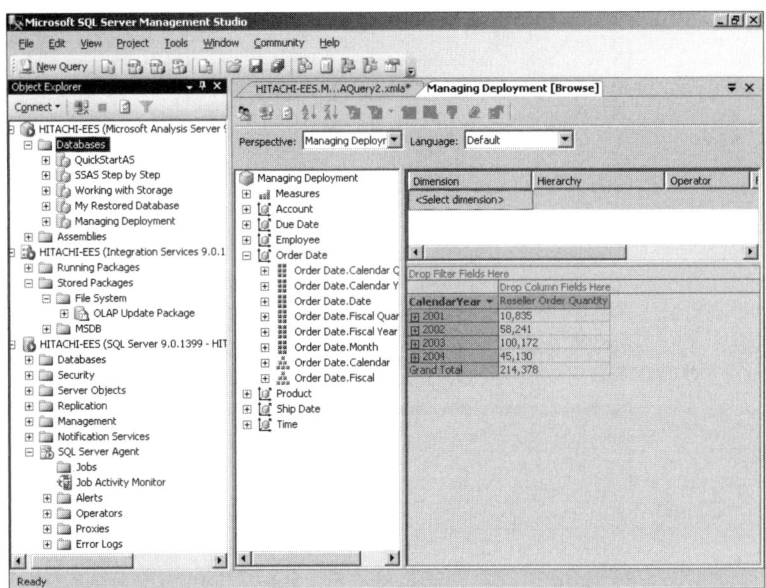

   You should see the new database, My Restored Database, appear in the list of available databases in addition to the original database, SSAS Step by Step.

If you've successfully completed the procedures in each chapter of this book, you should now have a good grasp of the design considerations for building practical and powerful analytical solutions using Analysis Services. You have also learned how to secure databases, how to work with partitioning for large databases, and how to deploy and maintain production databases. The next step is to launch a prototype project so that you can apply the principles you've learned here and introduce your organization to the benefits of Microsoft SQL Server 2005 Analysis Services.

Chapter 13 Quick Reference

To	Do this
Build an asdatabase file	In Solution Explorer in Visual Studio, right-click an Analysis Services project, and then click Build.
Use the Analysis Services Deployment Wizard to deploy an asdatabase file to a server	Click Start, point to All Programs, point to Microsoft SQL Server 2005, point to Analysis Services, click Deployment Wizard, click Next to bypass the Welcome page, specify the path and file name of the asdatabase file in the Database File box, click Next on each page of the wizard until the last page is reached, and then click Finish.
Use SQL Server Management Studio to process an Analysis Services database	In SQL Server Management Studio, connect to Analysis Services, expand the Databases folder, right-click the database to process, click Process, and then click OK to start processing.
Create an XMLA script to create an object based on another object	In SQL Server Management Studio, right-click the object to copy, point to Script Partition As, point to CREATE To, click New Query Editor Window, and then, at minimum, modify the script to assign a unique ID and name.
Create an XMLA script to process an object by modifying a processing script for a similar object	In SQL Server Management Studio, right-click the object to use as a model, click Process, click the Script button at the top of the dialog box, click Cancel, and then modify the script as necessary in the Query Editor window.
Execute an XMLA script in the Query Editor window	Click the Execute button on the SQL Server Management Studio toolbar.
Automate the processing of an OLAP database	In Visual Studio, create an Integration Services project, add an Analysis Services Processing Task, double-click the task, and then specify the OLAP database in the task editor. Save the project.
Schedule an Integration Services package	In SQL Server Management Studio, connect to Integration Services, expand the Stored Packages folder, right-click the File System folder, click Import Package, select File System in the Package Location drop-down list, specify the path and package file name as well as the package name, right-click the package, click Run Package, click Command Line, copy the command line text to the clipboard, connect to the Database Engine, expand SQL Server Agent, right-click the Jobs folder, click New Job, specify a name for the job, click Steps, specify a name for the step, select Operating System (CmdExec) in the Type drop-down list, paste the contents of the clipboard into the Command box, and then type **dtexec** in front of the command line text.
Delete a scheduled Integrated Services package	In SQL Server Management Studio, connect to the Database Engine, expand SQL Server Agent, expand the Jobs folder, right-click the job, and then click OK to confirm.
Back up an OLAP database	In SQL Server Management Studio, connect to Analysis Services, expand the Databases folder, right-click the database, click Backup, provide a password, and then click OK.
Restore an OLAP database	In SQL Server Management Studio, connect to Analysis Services, right-click the Databases folder, click Restore, specify a name for the database, click the Browse button, navigate to the abf file, type the password used to back up the database, and then click OK.

Glossary

action A command stored in a cube and used by a client application to start a new application or to retrieve detailed information about an item selected by the user.

aggregated value A single, summary value, retrieved from a cube, which is derived from multiple rows in a fact table.

aggregation Summarized values of a measure.

Analysis Management Objects (AMO) The application program interface (API) for Analysis Services.

analytical reports Dynamic, interactive reports that allow a user to drill down to detailed information or drill up to high-level summaries; they are typically used by analysts or managers who need deeper insights into a situation.

application key A key column for a record that is created and maintained in a source application.

asdatabase file An XML file used to prepare an Analysis Services database for deployment to a server.

attribute Information about a specific dimension member.

attribute hierarchy A single-level groupable attribute within a dimension.

business intelligence (BI) An approach to management that allows an organization to define what information is useful and relevant to its corporate decision making. Business intelligence helps decision makers make better decisions faster by converting data into information.

cache Server-based storage locations both in memory (automatic) or on disk (designed) that enhance query performance.

calculated measure A calculation created using MDX that is added as a new member to the Measures dimension in a cube.

calculated member A mechanism for aggregating measures using formulas more complex than those stored in a cube.

composite key Multiple key columns used to uniquely identify a record.

cube A multidimensional data structure that represents the intersections of each unique combination of dimensions. At each intersection there is a cell that contains a data value.

dashboard reports Highly summarized, often graphical, representations of the state of the business that are often used by executives and strategic decision makers.

data explosion The geometric growth in the number of values that must be stored in a cube to support fast retrieval.

data source A file that contains the connection string that Analysis Services uses to connect to the database that hosts the data as well as any necessary authentication credentials.

data source view (DSV) A collection of tables that may be a subset of the data warehouse tables to which logical keys and logical relationships can be added.

data warehouse A relational database used as a repository for storing and analyzing numerical information that has been cleansed and verified.

degenerate dimension A dimension whose members are stored in a fact table instead of a dimension table.

denormalization Organization of data by minimizing joins between tables and storing redundant values in a single table to reduce query time.

derived measure An expression which performs arithmetic operations on measures in a fact table to produce values for a new logical column in the fact table.

dimension A list of labels that can be used to cross-tabulate values from other dimensions.

dimension table The relational database table that contains information about each member of a dimension, such as its name, as well as other specific characteristics of each member.

dimension usage The type of relationship between a fact table and a dimension.

direct attribute relationship The relationship between a target attribute and a source attribute, which is required for computing aggregated values for attributes not represented by a foreign key in the fact table.

fact A summarizable numerical value used to monitor business activity; it is also known as a measure.

fact table The relational database table that contains values for one or more measures at the lowest level of detail for one or more dimensions.

foreign key column A column in a database table that contains many values for each value in the primary key column of another database table.

granularity attribute The dimension attribute that corresponds to the foreign key column for that dimension in a fact table.

hierarchy A navigation path that allows the user to move from summarized to detailed information with each level of the hierarchy represented by a different attribute.

hybrid OLAP (HOLAP) An OLAP storage mode that can store data in both multidimensional databases and relational databases.

indirect attribute relationship A relationship between two attributes in which each is directly related to a common attribute but which are not directly related to each other.

join The matching of a record from one relational database table with a record in a second relational database table using a common column.

key performance indicator (KPI) A measurement of business operations that compares a value at a specified point in time to a predetermined goal and, optionally, determines a trend direction. Often, a KPI is displayed using a graphical image such as a stoplight or a gauge using colors and relative indicators according to predetermined business rules.

linked dimension A dimension based on a dimension that is stored in a separate Analysis Services database which may or may not be on the same server.

local currency The currency that applies to the value of a transaction stored in a fact table.

MDX script A collection of MDX expressions or statements that represent cube calculations for which the sequence of these calculations determines how (or whether) each calculation is resolved.

measure A summarizable numerical value used to monitor business activity; it is also known as a fact.

measure group The conceptual container of detail values from a single fact table, along with all possible aggregations for one or more dimension hierarchies.

member A single item within a dimension.

member property An attribute of a member that is not meaningful when grouping values for a report, but contains valuable information about a different attribute.

metadata Information about how data is stored and structured as well as what the data means.

multidimensional database A data warehouse design that uses fact tables and dimension tables to organize data efficiently for summarizing large groups of records.

multidimensional expressions (MDX) A query language for creating reports from an OLAP cube, as well as an expression language used to retrieve values from an OLAP cube.

multidimensional OLAP (MOLAP) An OLAP storage mode in which data is stored in a proprietary structure that allows for extremely fast retrieval.

named calculation A SQL expression added to a table as a logical column.

named query A SQL query used in place of a table either to limit the columns available from a single table or to construct a logical view by combining columns from multiple tables.

natural hierarchy A collection of attributes in which a member of one level of the hierarchy is associated with only one member on the next higher level of the hierarchy. For example, in a Time dimension that contains Year, Quarter, and Month attributes, January 2006, a month, is associated with only one quarter, Q1 2006, and that quarter is associated with only one year, 2006.

nonadditive measure A measure for which its component calculations must be summed separately before multiplication or division of the components can be performed.

normalization The organization of data to reduce redundancy by creating many linked tables so that a value is stored in only one place.

one-to-many relationship The use of one key value from a dimension table in many rows of a fact table.

online analytical processing (OLAP) A database designed to support analysis for decision making in an organization.

online transaction processing (OLTP) A relational database system used to manage the day-to-day operations of an organization.

package A container of tasks used by Microsoft SQL Server 2005 Integration Services (SSIS) that can be organized into a specific sequence for processing

Analysis Services commands, to name just one capability of SSIS.

parent-child dimension A dimension table that contains a primary key column, as well as a foreign key column that relates to the primary key column as a self-referential join.

partition A cube structure used to optimize physical storage, aggregations, and processing.

perspective A subset of the measures and dimensions in a cube.

pivot currency The currency to which all other currencies will be converted by using exchange rates. The value of the pivot currency is always 1, while an exchange rate is used to convert another currency to 1 unit of the pivot currency.

primary key column A column in a database dimension table that contains values that uniquely identify each row.

production reports Typically large, detailed reports that show operational information about a company and are often used by administrators and tactical decision makers.

relational OLAP (ROLAP) An OLAP storage mode in which data is stored in a relational database.

reporting currency The currency to which values are converted for reporting purposes when the fact table stores values using a local currency.

role A definition of security permissions for one or more user accounts or user groups defined in the operating system and applied to an OLAP database or cube.

role-playing dimension A dimension for which multiple foreign key columns exist in a single fact table to represent different contexts for the same dimension. For example, time is a common role-playing dimension with each date in the fact table associated with a different event, such as order date, ship date, and delivery date.

schema When created using the Schema Generation Wizard, a schema is a denormalized relational database containing tables for the measure groups and dimensions defined for a cube.

script assignment An MDX statement that overrides specified cell values or cell properties.

self-referential join A join between a record with a foreign key value that matches the primary key value of another record in the same table.

semiadditive measure A measure that can be summed along some, but not all, dimensions in a cube.

snowflake schema A single fact table which joins to many dimension tables, with each dimension normalized as two or more tables.

source attribute An attribute for which aggregated values are computed from its target attribute because the fact table does not contain a foreign key value for the source attribute.

star schema A single fact table which joins to many dimension tables, each of which is a single denormalized dimension table.

subcube A specific collection of cube cells.

surrogate key A redundant, unique key generated for a record in a data warehouse table to allow integration of data from multiple source systems and to support changing data over time.

target attribute An attribute, for which a foreign key value is contained in a fact table, and which is used to compute aggregated values for other attributes in a dimension.

tuple A multidimensional coordinate that refers to a specific value in a cube.

unary operator A custom aggregation based on an operator (+, -, *, /, and ~) that is stored in a column in a parent-child dimension table.

Unified Dimensional Model (UDM) The measure groups and dimensions that define your organization's business intelligence data. Essentially synonymous with a cube.

user hierarchy A collection of attributes placed into a hierarchy structure to help users drill up or down from one attribute to another.

visual totals The totals for the values displayed in a browser which might override actual values from a cube if security limits the visibility of values for specific dimension members.

workflow A connection between two tasks in a Microsoft SQL Server 2005 Integration Services (SSIS) package that determines under what conditions, or whether, the second task executes after the first task.

write-enable To permit a user to make dynamic modifications to a dimension or a measure group's partition.

Index

Symbols

* (asterisk)
  comments in MDX queries, 193
  multiplication operator, 135
  { } (braces), MDX queries, 191, 195
+ (plus) operator, 135
/ (slash) division operator, 135
/ (slash) character, 193
// (double slash) character, 189, 193
~ (tilde) 135

A

Absolute references, MDX expressions, 185
Account dimension
  Account Intelligence, 130
  adding Operating Profit Per Employee, 146, 149
  aggregating by account, 140–141
  browsing default aggregations of, 135–137
  creating, 130–135
  creating nonadditive measures, 145–149
  overview of, 129–130
  setting *UnaryOperatorColumn* property, 138–139
  using ByAccount aggregate function, 144
  using LastNonEmpty function with, 141–144
  using *Type* property, 135
  using unary operators, 135
Account Hierarchy option, 231
Account Intelligence, 130
Account Manager dimension, 223, 226, 228
Account Type attribute, 132
action expression, 246
Action tab, Cube Designer, 246, 249
action targets, 246
actions
  defined, 245
  drillthrough, 251–253
  overview of, 245
  reporting, 249–251
  standard, 246–249
  types of, 245
  URL, 246–249
Add/Remove Tables, 100
Addition, derived vs. calculated measures, 120
administration security
  creating roles, 291–293
  overview of, 291
  using local Administrators group, 271
aggregate functions
  DistinctCount, 117–119
  LastNonEmpty, 116–117
  Min or Max, 121
  overview of, 115–116
  semiadditive measures, 117
  Sum as default, 120
aggregate tables, 19
aggregated value vs. aggregation, 151
AggregateFunction property, 115, 141–144
aggregation
  Account dimension rules, 135
  aggregated value vs., 151
  browsing Account dimension, 135–137
  By Account, 27, 140–141
  defining, 28
  defining and using, 150
  overview of, 24
  processing cubes, 57
  relational, 305
  unchanging values of, 261
aggregation design
  adding attributes to, 160–161
  changing partition counts, 158–160
  inspecting aggregations, 155–157
  of user hierarchies, 165–167
  understanding, 149–151
  with Aggregation Design Wizard, 151–155
Aggregation Design Wizard, 151–155
  AggregationUsage property, 160
  caching options, 153
  changing partition counts, 158
  Count function, 153
  launching, 153
  opening SSAS Step by Step, 152
  overview of, 151
  partitions, 152
  performance gain setting, 153
  storage options, 153, 306
  viewing graph, 154
  viewing processing status, 155
aggregation optimization
  maintaining query log, 172–173
  overview of, 167
  using query log, 168–170
  viewing usage data, 170
  with Usage Based Optimization Wizard, 171–172
Aggregations tag, 157
AggregationUsage property, 160–161
All level
  removing in Parent Child dimension, 94–95
  summarizing dimensions at, 157
All member, 187
All Users role, restricting, 282–283

AMO (Analysis Management Objects)
 automating development tasks with, 28
 deploying multiple databases with, 336
 working with, 356
Analysis Services
 business intelligence and, 3
 speed and, 24
 understanding, 23–24
Analysis Services Deployment Wizard, 341–348
 Confirm Deployment page, 344
 Credentials, 343
 defined, 335
 Deploying Database page, 345
 final database files, 336
 Installation Target page, 341
 naming system, 345–346
 Select Processing Options page, 343
 Specify Configuration Properties page, 342
 Specify Options for Partitions and Roles page, 342
 Welcome page, 341
Analysis Services Processing Task, 358–359
Analysis Services Scripting Language (ASSL), 336
Analysis Services server role, 291
analytical reports, 4
application keys, 13
arithmetic operators, 135
asdatabase files, 336–340
Assemblies folder, 35
ASSL (Analysis Services Scripting Language), 336
asterisk (*)
 comments in MDX queries, 193
 multiplication operator, 135
attribute hierarchies
 modifying attribute properties, 76–77
 overview of, 25, 75–76
 restricting access to dimensions, 278–281
AttributeHierarchyEnabled property, disabling, 76–77
attributes
 Code Wizard, 41
 Cube Wizard, 45
 dimension. *See* dimension attributes
 granularity, 106
 hierarchy of, 116
 in aggregation design, 160–161
 indirect relationships, 110
 modifying properties, 76–77
 overview of, 25
 relationships, 110–112
Auto Build, 100, 165, 69–70
Automatic MOLAP, 323
AverageOfChildren, 116
Avg function, MDX, 198–200
axes
 executing MDX queries, 192
 report, 188

B

back ups
 as deployment method, 335
 creating, 365–366
Balance Sheet accounts
 LastNonEmpty working with, 144
 semiadditive aggregations for, 140
base dimensions, 105
Batch command, 354
BI (business intelligence), 3–4
BIDS (Business Intelligence Development Studio). *See* Business Intelligence Development Studio (BIDS)
bin folder, Build process, 338
bloomberg.com, 4
braces ({ }), MDX queries, 191, 195
Browser
 Cube, 57–59, 107, 109
 Dimension Designer, 74–76
Browser toolbar, Clear Results button, 114
bubble up formulas, 23
Build command, 336–340
business intelligence (BI), 3–4
Business Intelligence Development Studio (BIDS)
 opening SSAS Step by Step, 33–35
 overview of, 28, 31–32
Business Intelligence Wizard, 231
By Account aggregation, 27, 141, 144

C

Cable Lock, 248
caching
 defined, 28
 storage, 26
 proactive, 320–325
Calculate statement, 208
calculated measures
 creating, 120
 defined, 197
 derived measures vs., 120
calculated members
 defining, 28
 overview of, 27
 tuple-based, 177–182
calculations
 adding to cubes, 120–121
 conditional formatting, 126–127
 cumulative, 200–202
 display folders for, 236–238
 MDX for, 119
 naming conventions, 122, 183
 Percent of Parent, 186–188
 Percent of Total, 182–186
 Ratio, 123
 sequence of, 202–205

weighted average, 121–126
Category target attribute, 111
Category attribute hierarchy, 193
cell-level security
overview of, 287
read permissions for specific cells, 288–290
user writeback, 290–291
Child members, attributes, 116
Clauses, MDX query, 189
Clear Results button, Browser toolbar, 114
Client Initiated option, 325
Columns, fact tables, 10
COLUMNS, MDX query, 192
commands, menu, 35–36
comments, adding to MDX queries, 189, 193
commit transaction, 348
composite key, 224
conditional formatting, 126–127
connections, adding data source, 65
consistently fast response, OLAP, 18
context-sensitive, 35
ConvertToUnknown property, 77
coordinates, 181
Copy roles, 278
Count function, Aggregation Design Wizard, 153
count measures
added to cubes automatically, 114
building cubes and, 102
Create Deployment Script option, 344
Credentials, database, 343
CrossJoin function, MDX queries, 196
Cube Browser, 57–59
Cube Designer
Action tab, 246, 249
adding role-playing dimensions, 85
Browser tab, 107
creating KPI, 209
Cube Structure tab, 46–48
dimension usage and, 104
generating MDX queries, 188
opening, 36
Partitions tab, 297
renaming measure groups, 102
reviewing cube structure, 46–48
semiadditive measures, 113
testing translations, 235
Cube menu, 35
Cube Wizard, 39–46, 100–103
adding dimension tables, 101
adding dimensions, 41–42
adding fact tables to data sources, 100
adding measures, 40–41
adding special calendar, 43
defining time periods, 42–43
fact table selection, 101
finishing, 44–46
measure groups, 102–103
measure selection, 102
relating dimensions to measures, 43–44
relationship between dimensions and fact tables, 104
semiadditive measures, 113
specifying data source, 39–40
using Auto Build with, 165
Welcome page, 39
cubes
analyzing requirements, 37
browsing, 57–59
building, 100
Business Environment Development Studio, 32
Business Intelligence Development Studio (BIDS), 31–35
calculations added to, 120–121
creating new project with, 37–38
defining, 18, 28
dimension tables added to, 100
DistinctCount measures, 118
examining contents of project, 32–33
fact table selection for, 101
loading data into relational schema, 53–56
measure groups in, 102, 107–112
measure groups added to, 97, 113–115
measure selection for, 102
menu commands, 35–36
metadata, 25–26, 28
multiple measure groups in, 107–112
naming conventions, 102
opening SSAS Step by Step, 33–35
overview of, 31
processing, 56–57, 318–320
role access granted to, 276
write-enabling, 262
using Schema Generation Wizard, 50–54
cubes, localizing
adding translated captions and attribute values, 231–235
browsing translations, 235–236
currency conversions, 230
overview of, 231
cumulative calculations, 200–202
currency conversions, 230
currency measures, 230

D

dashboard reports, 4
data explosion
avoiding in database model OLAP, 19
controlling, 150
spreadsheet model OLAP and, 18–19
Data Source Designer, 34
Data Source View Designer, 100

Data Source View Wizard, 68–69
data source views (DSVs)
 overview of, 34
 selecting in Dimension Wizard, 70
 Time dimensions, 78–79
 Unified Dimensional Model, 67–68
 updating for many-to-many relationships, 225
 user hierarchies in, 162
Data Source Wizard, 49, 66
data sources
 adding fact tables to, 100
 adding to dimensions, 65–67
 building cubes without. *See* Cube Wizard
 defined, 65
data warehouse structure, 63–64
data warehouses, 5–16
 application keys, 13
 measures, 6
 multidimensional databases. *See* multidimensional databases
 overview of, 5
 primary key column, 11
 purposes of, 5–6
 star and snowflake schemas in, 14–15
 structure of, 6
 surrogate keys, 13–14
database model OLAP, 19
databases
 configuring proactive caching, 320–325
 monitoring, 326
 processing, 312
 processing cubes, 318–320
 processing dimensions, 313–318
Date attribute, Time dimension, 43
Date/Time column, 78
Debugging MDX scripts, 205–209
Decision Support System (DSS), 4
DefaultMeasures property, 46
default member, for dimensions, 284–287
DefaultMember property, 190
degenerate dimensions, 222, 226
DELETE query, 173
denormalizing data, 15
Deploy command, 335
deployment
 automating database processing, 356–364
 building database, 336–340
 creating SSIS package, 357–358
 handling task failures, 359–361
 managing, 335
 managing database objects programmatically, 351–356
 options, 335–336
 processing database, 348–351
 using Analysis Services Processing Task, 358–359
 working with AMO, 356
derived measures, 120
design
 aggregation. *See* aggregation design
 dimensions. *See* dimensions, designing
Design Aggregations link, 153
DimEmployee table, 64
dimension. *See* dimension relationships
dimension attributes
 Account dimension, 130, 132
 changing over time, 13–14
 dimension tables, 11
 groupable and nongroupable, 12
 hierarchies and, 12
 member properties, 12
 primary and foreign key, 11
 renaming, 73
 selecting, 72
 snowflake schema for storing, 15
 star schema, 15
 Time dimension, 43, 81–82
Dimension Data tab, 279
Dimension Designer
 testing translations in, 235
 using Browser to review members, 74
dimension metadata, 24–25
dimension relationships
 many-to-many, 222–229
 referenced dimensions, 217–220
 overview of, 217
Dimension Structure, 47
dimension tables, 11–13, 101
dimension usage
 correcting between dimensions, 125
 creating referenced dimension, 219
 defined, 104
Dimension Wizard
 Auto Build option, 69–70, 165
 creating currency dimensions, 230
 creating many-to-many relationship, 223
 defining parent-child relationship, 73
 finishing, 73
 overview of, 69
 renaming attributes, 73
 selecting attributes, 72
 selecting data source view, 70
 selecting dimension types, 70, 72
 selecting key columns, 71
 selecting Main Table, 70
 selecting related tables, 71–72
Dimension.Hierarchy.CurrentMember, 248
dimensional data warehousing, 17. *See also* multidimensional databases
dimensions
 attribute relationships in, 111

Build process creating files for, 337
cubes created with, 38, 41–46
currency, 230
data warehouse structure for, 63–64
default member for, 284–287
designing, 61–63
dynamically adding members to, 255–257
fully restricting access to, 278–281
granting access to roles, 277
in every project, 35
in multidimensional databases, 8–10
incremental updates on, 320
linked, 97
key attributes, 107
many-to-many relationships and, 221, 226
MDX vs. spreadsheet formulas, 23
members of, 9
one-to-many relationships and, 221
Parent-Child. *See* Parent-Child dimensions
processing, 313–318
processing cube with, 56–57
relationships between fact tables and, 104
relationships to measure groups, 104–107, 259
removing from browser grid, 114
restricting members of, 281–283
role-playing, 84–86, 105
Server Time dimension, 84
Standard dimension. *See* Standard dimension
user hierarchies added to, 162–165
visual totals for, 283–284
write-enabled, 254–255, 266
Time dimensions. *See* Time dimensions
UnknownMember property, 77
DimProduct table, 64
DimProductCategory table, 64
DimProductSubcategory table, 64
DimTime table, 64
direct attribute relationships, 110
Direct Hit Ratio performance counter, 330–333
disaster planning
creating backups, 365–366
overview of, 364
restoring database, 366–367
display folders, 236–238
DistinctCount, 117–119
drillthrough action
creating, 251–253, 266
defined, 245
DSS (Decision Support System), 4
DSV (Data Source View). *See* data source views

E

e-mail, 359–361
EIS (Executive Information Systems), 3
embedded scripts, 352
Employee dimension, 87–89
End Scope statement, 206
ErrorConfiguration property, 260
Estimated Count, 153
exception formulas, MDX, 23
Execute button, MDX, 190–191
Executive Information Systems (EIS), 3
expressions
creating key performance indicators with, 209
queries vs., 188

F

fact tables
adding to existing data source, 100
building many-to-many relationship, 226
changing estimated count of, 158–60
creating partitions based on, 296–301
creating unit forecast measure group from empty, 257–261
defining relationship with dimensions, 104
integer keys for reducing size of, 13
joining to dimension tables, 11
many-to-many relationships and, 221
one-to-many relationships and, 221
selecting for building cubes, 101
storing values for measures in, 10–11
using local currency, 230
FactAccountManager, 223, 226
FactInternetSales table, 64
FactResellerSales table, 64
Filters, 297–301
financial analysis tools, 129. *See also* Account dimension
financial applications
finance formulas, 27
spreadsheet-based OLAP tools for, 19
FirstNonEmpty, 116
fiscal years, 78
folders, 236–238
forecasts
creating unit measure group for, 257–261
interactive, 253
foreign keys
building many-to-many relationship, 225
column, 11
creating indexes on, 51
Schema Generation Wizard naming conventions, 52
Form View, 121
formats
calculation expressions, 123
measures, 104, 109
multidimensional database reports, 8
FormatString property, 104, 114

formulas
  Analysis Services, 26–27
  finance, 27
  MDX vs. spreadsheet, 22–23
Freeze statement, 208
FROM clause, MDX queries, 189
Functions, accessing external, 27

G

geometric progression, in OLAP, 19
GIS (Graphical Information Systems), 135
Goal expression, KPI, 209–210, 214
Grain, in cube metadata, 25
Grand Total, 283–284
granularity attributes, 106
graph, Aggregation Design Wizard, 154
Graphical Information Systems (GIS), 135
Grid View, 46
Group accounts
  adding to server role, 291
  creating, 272–273
  overview of, 272
groups, attribute, 12

H

Hierarchies
  attribute, 25
  defined, 29
  dimension attributes and, 12
Hierarchy drop-down list, 75, 89
HOLAP (hybrid OLAP)
  defined, 305
  storage option, 306
  vulnerability to changes in cell values, 312
hybrid OLAP (HOLAP). *See* HOLAP
hyphen characters (–), MDX queries, 193

I

icon, referenced relationship, 221
Impersonation Information page, Data Source Wizard, 66
implicit reference, 185
incremental updates, 296, 313–318
indexes, on foreign keys, 51
indirect attribute relationships, 110
Installation Target page, Analysis Services Deployment Wizard, 341
integer keys, 13
Integration Services. *See* SSIS (SQL Server Integration Services)
inventory control, 11
ISO (International Standards Organization) Codes
  8601 calendar, 43
  defined, 229
  storing for currency, 230
Item function, 286

J

joins
  dimension tables to fact tables, 11
  self-referential, 16
  slowing down queries, 15
joint checking accounts, 222

K

key attributes, 11, 107
key performance indicators (KPIs). *See* KPIs (key performance indicators)
KeyColumns property, 82
KeyErrorAction property, 77
KeyNotFound property, 260
KPIs (key performance indicators)
  business intelligence reports and, 4
  defined, 27
  developing, 209–213
  naming conventions, 210
  overview of, 209
  using MDX expressions with, 212–216

L

Languages, translations, 232
LastNonEmpty
  aggregation, 116–117
  overview of, 140
  with Account dimension, 141, 144
latency
  low-latency MOLAP, 324
  low-latency vs. medium-latency MOLAP, 325
  medium-latency MOLAP, 324
levels, 93–97
linked dimensions, 97
local Administrators group, 271–272
local currency, 230
low-latency MOLAP, 324

M

macros, values for cubes, 265
Main Table, Dimension Wizard, 70
manufacturing calendar, 43
many-to-many relationship, 222–229, 242
maps, 313
Materialize check box, 220
Max function, 121
MDX (multidimensional expressions)
  calculating for Percent of Total, 182–186
  calculating Percent of Parent, 186, 188

conditional formatting, 126–127
creating calculated members using set-based functions, 197–200
creating cumulative calculations, 200–202
creating default dimension member for role, 285
creating URL action, 247
enabling read permissions for specific cells, 288–290
executing queries, 188
executing queries with SQL Server Management Studio, 189, 193
for dynamic URLs, 248
formulas, 22–23, 27
functions of, 122
in Time dimensions, 78
overview of, 21, 119
queries, 193–197
terminology, 193
tuple-based calculated members, 177–182
using, 175

MDX scripts
adding script assignment, 205–209
developing KPIs, 209–213
managing sequence of calculations, 202–205
overview of, 202
using with KPIs, 213–216

measure groups
adding to a cube, 97
adding to existing cubes, 113–115
building cubes with, 102
creating from empty fact table, 257–261, 266
creating partitions, 297
defined, 29
granularity of, 106
multiple, 107–112
organizing measures into, 103
overview of, 25
properties, 103
relationship dimensions, 104–107, 259
renaming, 103

measures
adding DistinctCount measures, 118
aggregating semiadditive measures, 115–117
attribute relationships affecting aggregated values of, 112
calculated measures, 120
creating cube with, 40–41
currency, 230
DefaultMeasures property, 46
derived measures, 120
dimensions as way to subdivide, 9
display folders for, 236–238
dragging from metadata pane, 108
formats, 104, 109
in data warehousing, 6
in Grid View, 46
organizing into measure groups, 103
properties, 103
red lines in Measures pane, 45
removing from browser grid, 109, 114
selecting for cubes, 102
semiadditive, 113
storing detailed values in fact table, 10
subcategories of, 109
using Cube Wizard, 43–44
Tree View for, 46
viewing in Browser, 109
viewing in Grid View, 46

medium-latency MOLAP, 324
member key values, 147
member properties, 12

members
defining default, 285–287
designing custom, 197
dynamically adding to dimensions, 255–257
MDX query terminology, 193
of dimensions, 9
tuple-based calculated, 177–182

Members function, 286
menu commands, 35–36
merged partitions, 301–304

metadata
cube, 25–26, 28
defined, 20
dimension, 24–25
MDX vs. spreadsheet formulas, 23
MDX query window, Metadata pane queries based on, 20–21

Microsoft SQL Server 2005 Analysis Services. *See* Analysis Services
Microsoft Visual Source Safe (VSS), 28
Min function, 121
Mining Structures folder, 35
minus (-) operator, 135
Miscellaneous folder, 35

MOLAP (multidimensional OLAP)
creating aggregations in, 26
data warehouses not affected by, 310
defined, 305
HOLAP storage vs., 305
low-latency, 324
medium latency, 324
overview of, 228
Scheduled vs. Automatic, 323
storage options, 306–308

MSSQL.n naming convention, 345

multidimensional databases, 6–16
dimension tables, 11–13, 15
dimensions, 8
fact tables, 10–11
overview of, 6
report format options, 8
report values (dimensions), 7–10

star and snowflake schemas, 14
multidimensional expressions. *See* MDX (multidimensional expressions)
multidimensional OLAP. *See* MOLAP (multidimensional OLAP)
multiplication, 121

N

NameColumn property, 81
Name property, 104
Named Calculation
  adding, 120
  modifying data source view, 78
Named Query
  adding empty fact table to data source view with, 257
  creating data source view, 69
  creating unit forecast measure group, 257–261
  modifying data source view, 78
naming conventions
  calculations, 122, 183
  cubes, 102
  data sources, 67
  dimension attributes, 72
  key performance indicators (KPIs), 210
  measure groups, 103
  member names, 71
  MSSQL.n, 345
  renaming user hierarchies, 81
  Schema Generation Wizard, 52
  Time dimension attributes, 81
  User accounts, 273
NamingTemplate property, 95–97
natural hierarchy, 12
Net Income accounts, 144
New Measure wizard, 119
nonadditive measures, 145–149
Non-Empty Behavior, 123
normalization, 14
notification
  caching changes, 325
  SQL Server, 307
NT AUTHORITY\SYSTEM account, 307

O

octuple coordinates, 181
ODBC (Open Database Connectivity), 65
OLAP (online analytical processing)
  Analysis Services formulas, 26–27
  Analysis Services tools, 28
  business intelligence and, 3
  consistently fast response of, 18–20
  cube metadata, 25–26
  database model, 19
  defined, 29
  dimension metadata, 24–25
  history of term, 17–18
  MDX and, 119
  metadata-based queries, 20–21
  processing, 312
  speed, 24
  spreadsheet-based, 18–19, 22–23
OLE DB for OLAP, 120
OLE DB standard, 65
OLTP (online transaction processing), 17, 29
one-to-many relationship, 11, 221
online analytical processing. *See* (OLAP) online analytical processing
online resources, XMLA, 21
online transaction processing (OLTP), 17, 29
Open Database Connectivity (ODBC), 65
Operating Profit Per Employee, 146–149
OrderBy property, 82

P

Parent Account Key attribute, 132
Parent-Child dimensions
  Add/Remove Tables, 87
  adding Employee dimension, 87–89
  creating Account dimension, 131–132, 134
  creating level naming template, 95–97
  defined, 15
  defining relationship, 88
  managing levels within, 93–95
  non–leaf-level data members, 89–93
  opening SSAS Step by Step, 87
  overview of, 86–87
  renaming attributes, 88
  selecting attributes, 87
  Usage property, 88
parentheses
  executing MDX queries, 192
  using in tuples, 182
Partition Count, 153
Partition Wizard, 297
partitions
  Aggregation Design Wizard and, 152
  benefits of multiple, 296
  changing counts, 158–160
  creating, 296–301
  database deployment options, 342
  examining aggregations for dimensions in, 155–157
  executing XMLA scripts, 353
  in Analysis Services, 151
  merging, 301–304
  overview of, 295
  processing, 351
  write-enabling, 262–266
Partitions Storage Settings dialog box, 306

passwords
- creating database backup, 366
- restoring database, 367

Percent of Parent, 186–188
Percent of Total, 182–186
performance
- enhancements for Schema Generation Wizard, 51
- overview of, 326
- profiling queries, 326–330
- referenced dimension, 220
- setting in Aggregation Design Wizard, 154
- speed and disk space vs., 161
- storage options affecting, 305
- using Performance Monitor, 330–333

performance gain setting
- changing count for fact tables, 158
- setting in Aggregation Design Wizard, 153

Performance Monitor, 330–333
PeriodsToDate function, 200–202
permissions
- administrative, 291
- inheritance of cube, 279
- read, for specific cells, 288–290
- role, 276

perspectives
- creating and browsing, 238–242
- creating within cube, 26

pivot currency, 230
planning
- adding Scenario dimensions to forecasts, 254
- interactive forecasts, 253
- new scenarios, 255

plus (+) operator, 135
primary keys
- in data warehouses, 11
- Schema Generation Wizard and, 51–52

proactive caching, 320–325
Process command, 318
Process Data, 318
Process Full, 314, 318
Process Incremental, 318–320
Process Update, 314, 316
processing
- automating database, 356–364
- cubes, 56–57, 318–320
- databases, 343, 348–351
- dimensions, 313–318
- OLAP, 312
- using partitions for, 296
- viewing status in Aggregation Design Wizard, 155

Product Category attribute hierarchy, 187
Product Detail, 250
Product dimension, 37
product report by month, 7
production management. *See* security
production reports, 4
profit and loss accounts, 141
Project menu, 35
properties
- database deployment options, 342
- measures and measure groups, 103
- modifying attribute, 76–77

Q

quadruple coordinates, 181
queries
- joins slowing down, 15
- profiling, 326–330

queries, MDX
- basic, 193
- executing, 188
- executing with SQL Server Management Studio, 189–193
- overview of, 188
- use-sets and set-functions, 193–197

query log
- deleting records from, 173
- maintaining, 172–173
- populating, 168–170
- reviewing data in, 170
- using, 168–170

QueryLogConnectionString property, 168
QueryLogSampling property, 168
QueryLogTable property, 168
quintuple coordinates, 181

R

ratio calculations, 123
read permission
- granting to roles, 277
- MDX expressions enabling, 288–290

Read/Write permission
- enabling user writeback, 290
- granting to role, 277

Rebuild Interval, 323
recovery planning
- creating backups, 365–366
- overview of, 364
- restoring database, 366–367

red symbol, 122
referenced dimension, 218–221, 242
references, MDX vs. spreadsheet formulas, 22
referential integrity, 51
regular relationships, 106–107, 217
relational database, storage modes, 305
relational OLAP. *See* ROLAP (relational OLAP)
relationships
- attribute, 111–112

between dimensions and measure groups, 104–107, 259
defining, 107
regular, 106–107, 217
relative reference formula, 178
Report Path, 251
Reporting action
creating, 249–251, 266
defined, 245
Reporting calendar, 43
reporting currency, 230
reports
accessing through linking, 249
business intelligence, 4
requirements, project, 37
Reseller Sales Order Details dimension, 224, 226
Reseller Sales Order dimension, 224, 226
Restore command, 366–367
Retained Earnings Since Inception, 20
ROLAP (relational OLAP)
aggregations, 305
changes in cell values in, 312
creating writeback values with, 263
defined, 304
overview of, 26
storage options, 306–308
terminology, 306
Role Designer, 278, 290
role-based security
creating database roles, 291–293
creating default dimension member, 284–287
creating role for all users, 274–277
creating users and groups, 272–273
fully restricting dimensions, 278–281
managing roles, 277
overview of, 272
restricting members of dimension, 281–283
role-playing dimensions, 84–86, 105
roles, database deployment options, 342
Roles folder, 35
rolled back transactions, 348
rows, fact tables, 10
ROWS, MDX query, 192

S

sales cubes, 20
Sales Order Details dimension, 228
SalesOrderLineNumber, 223
SalesOrderNumber, 222–229
sampling frequency, 168
Scenario dimension
adding new scenario, 255–257
creating write-enabled, 254
Scheduled MOLAP, 323
schema
defined, 45
loading with data, 53–56
multidimensional databases, 14–15
Schema Generation Wizard
building cube with, 48–52
Connection Manager, 49
creating relational schema, 49
Data Source Wizard, 49
loading Time dimension with data, 51
naming conventions, 52
performance enhancements, 51
preserving data, 51
Progress window, 52
referential integrity, 51
Specify Target page, 49
starting, 45
Subject Area Database Schema options, 50–51
Scope statement, 206
Script command, 352
Script Organizer, 36, 122
scripts
assignment, 27, 202
deployment, 344
MDX. *See* MDX scripts
XMLA, 352–356
security
cell level. *See* cell level security
creating administrative roles, 291–293
creating default dimension members for roles, 284–287
enabling visual totals, 283–284
fully restricting access to dimensions, 278–281
overview of, 269
restricting members of dimensions, 281–283
role-based. *See* role-based security
writeback value permissions, 265
SELECT clause, MDX queries, 189
SELECT statement, 297–298
self-referential joins, 16
semiadditive aggregations, 140
semiadditive calculations, 27
semiadditive measures
functions, 115
LastNonEmpty function, 116–117
overview of, 113
Send Mail Task icon, 359
septuple coordinates, 181
Server Time dimension
Date/Time column, 78
designing, 84
Sessa, 18–19
sets, MDX queries, 193–197
sextuple coordinates, 181
Silence Interval setting, 323
Silence Override Interval, 323

single coordinates, 181
slash (/) division operator, 135
slash (//) character, 189, 193
slash (/) character, 193
snap shots, 113
snowflake schema
  creating referenced dimension, 217
  for storing dimension attributes, 15
Solution Explorer window, 32, 38
sources attributes, 110
special calendars, 43
speed, 24
spreadsheet model OLAP, 18–19
spreadsheet style formulas, 22–23
SQL (Structured Query Language)
  creating partitions, 296
  MDX queries vs., 21
  metadata problem with, 20
  Native Client, 65
Server Agent, 352
Server Import and Export Wizard, 53
Server Integration Services. *See* SSIS (SQL Server Integration Services)
Server notification method, 307
Server Profiler, 326–330
SSAS Cube Dimensions, 278–281
  WHERE clause, 297
SQL Server Management Studio
  executing MDX queries with, 189–193
  processing databases with, 348–351
  writeback values, 265
SSAS Step by Step
  adding data source to project, 65–67
  adding data source view, 68–69
  building many-to-many relationship, 222–229
  creating Account dimension, 131–135
  creating parent-child dimension, 87–89
  creating partitions based on fact tables, 297–301
  creating role for all users, 274–277
  creating URL action, 246–249
  creating write-enabled dimension, 254–255
  deploying dimensions, 74–76
  Dimension Wizard, 70
  executing MDX queries, 189
  loading schema with data, 53–56
  merging partitions, 303
  opening, 33–35
  overview of, 63
  possible combinations, 149
  referenced dimensions, 218–221
SSIS (SQL Server Integration Services)
  creating package, 357–358
  creating package schedule, 361
  handling task failures, 359–361
standard actions
  creating URL action, 246–249
  drillthrough action vs., 252
  using, 246
standard dimensions
  adding data source, 65–67
  adding data source view, 67–69
  building, 64
  deploying, 74–76
  modifying attribute properties, 76–77
  using Dimension Wizard. *See* Dimension Wizard
star schema, 15
Status expression, KPI, 209–210, 212, 214
storage
  choosing mode, 305
  creating partitions, 300
  options, 304
  Process Incremental vs. Process Full options, 318
  processing entire databases, 312
  setting options, 306–308
  Storage Options dialog box, 322
  warehouse data, 308–312
Structured Query Language. *See* SQL (Structured Query Language)
Subcategory, 109
subcubes, 206
Subject Area Database Schema Options, 50
Subtraction, 120
Sum function
  as default aggregation function, 120
  MDX, 197
  PeriodstoDate function vs., 200–202
  semiadditive measures and, 115
surrogate keys, 13–14
Synchronize Database Wizard, 335
Syntax button, Calculation toolbar, 124
System Administrator privileges, SQL Server, 307

T

tables
  adding to data source view, 79
  dimension, 11–13, 101
Tail function, 285
target attributes, 110–111
task failures, 359–361
tilde (~), 135
Time calendar, 43
Time dimensions
  as role-playing dimension, 105
  assigning table columns to specific properties, 80
  Auto Build option, 79
  creating, 37
  defining time periods, 42–43
  loading with data, 51
  modifying data source view, 78–79
  NameColumn property, 81

overview of, 77–78
renaming attributes, 81
renaming user hierarchies, 81
selecting as type, 79
sort order of attributes, 82, 84
SSAS Step by Step, 79
user hierarchies, 80
time periods, 42–43
time-dependency, in data warehouses, 309
transaction databases, 5–6
transactions, 230, 348
translations, 231–236
Tree View, 46
Trend expression, KPI, 209–210, 213
triple coordinates, 181
tuples
calculated members based on, 177–182
defined, 147, 181
MDX query terminology, 193
Type property
ByAccount aggregate function, 141
creating Account dimension, 134

U

UDM (Unified Dimensional Model)
advantages of, 67–68
cube as, 26
defined, 29
unary
defined, 135
code, 138–139
operators, 27, 135
UnaryOperatorColumn property, 135, 138–139
unit forecast measure group, 257–261
UnknownMember property, 77
Update Cube MDX statement, 261
Update Warehouse.sql file, 309
updates
dimension, 313–318
incremental, 318–320
URL action, 245–249, 266
Usage Based Optimization Wizard
Aggregation Design Wizard vs., 167
designing usage-based aggregations, 171–172
retaining old query logs, 173
usage data
browsing query log, 170
viewing, 170
Usage property, 88
Usage-Based Optimization Wizard, 160
User accounts
adding to server role, 291
creating, 272–273
creating multiple roles for, 277
creating role for all, 274–277
overview of, 272
user hierarchies
adding to dimensions, 162–165
aggregation, 165–167
creating, 162–165
designing, 161
in Time dimensions, 80
renaming, 81
use-sets, in MDX queries, 193–197

V

Value expression, KPI, 209–210, 214
Values, writing back cube, 261–266
Visible property, 123
visual totals, 283–284
VSS (Microsoft Visual Source Safe), 28

W

Wall Street Journal, 4
Warehouses, changing data in, 308–312
weighted average calculation, 121–126
Welcome page, Cube Wizard, 39
WHERE clause, 189, 297, 300
Windows Performance tool, 330
Workflow, controlling, 359–361
Working with Storage solution, 306
write-enabled dimension, 254–255
writeback
creating write-enabled dimension, 254–255
database deployment options, 344
database processing options, 349
defined, 245
dynamically adding members to dimension, 255–257
enabling user, 290–301
modifying cube structure for, 257–261
overview of, 253
values, 261–266
WriteEnabled property, 254

X

XMLA (XML for Analysis)
automating development tasks with, 28
inspecting aggregations with, 155
MDX query language for, 21
scripts, 336, 352–356

About the Authors

Reed Jacobson is a senior architect in Hitachi Consulting's business intelligence (BI) practice. He has more than 20 years' experience in providing software applications solutions to customers. Prior to working for Hitachi Consulting, Reed ran his own consulting firm for eight years, and worked as a Software Applications Specialist for Hewlett Packard for 10 years. Reed developed and delivered a world-wide prerelease course on Microsoft SQL Server 2005 Business Intelligence. He also developed the Microsoft Official Curricula (MOC) three-day Multidimensional Expressions (MDX) course for SQL Server 2000, and has authored several books including *Microsoft SQL Server 2000 Analysis Services Step by Step*, *Microsoft Excel Visual Basic for Applications Step by Step*, and *Excel Trade Secrets for Windows*. Reed lives a secluded life in Seattle with his piano, trumpet, drums, guitars, and home theater, but with no dogs, cats, or kids.

Stacia Misner manages Hitachi Consulting's education services practice, specializes in developing training and solutions for BI and enterprise reporting, and delivers BI training worldwide. She has more than 20 years' experience as an IT consultant and educator, with experience in project management, life-cycle data warehouse design and development, and software development life-cycle management. Stacia is the author of both *Microsoft SQL Server 2000 Reporting Services Step by Step*, and *Microsoft SQL Server 2005 Reporting Services Step by Step*, and coauthor of *Business Intelligence: Making Better Decisions Faster*. She lives in Las Vegas, NV, with her husband, Gerry, and their seven parrots.

As Hitachi, Ltd.'s (NYSE: HIT) global consulting company, Hitachi Consulting is a recognized leader in delivering proven business and IT solutions to Global 2000 companies across many industries. We leverage decades of business process, vertical industry, and leading-edge technology experience to understand each company's unique business needs. From business strategy development through application deployment, our consultants are committed to helping clients quickly realize measurable business value and achieve sustainable return on investment. Hitachi Consulting is also a Microsoft Certified Gold Partner for Business Intelligence, an exclusive provider of curriculum and instructors for Microsoft's SQL Server 2005 Business Intelligence Ascend training program, and an experienced systems integrator with successful SQL Server 2005 BI implementations at companies participating in Microsoft's Technology Adoption Program (TAP). We offer a client-focused, collaborative approach and transfer knowledge throughout each engagement. For more information, visit *www.hitachiconsulting.com*. Hitachi Consulting – Inspiring your next success®.

Contributing Authors

Mary Gianopoulos, a Senior Consultant at Hitachi Consulting, has over 20 years of comprehensive business and technical experience, including software engineering, financial analysis, project management, and sales management in the financial services and educational software industries. She started using Microsoft SQL Server with the 7.0 release and is delighted with the 2005 improvements and integration with Microsoft Visual Studio. She is an instructor of Hitachi Consulting's BI courses. Mary has a B.B.A. in Accounting from the University of Notre

Dame, and an A.A. in Information Technology from Bellevue Community College. She lives on the east side of Seattle with her husband, Tony, and daughters, Katie, Dee Dee, and Christy.

Aaron Solomon, a Business Intelligence Architect at Hitachi Consulting, has been developing BI solutions for over six years. He has taught SQL Server 2000 and 2005 BI courses throughout the United States, and teaches courses for the University of Washington's Certificate Program in Database Management. He has engaged with a wide range of client business groups including accounting, mergers and acquisitions, data warehousing, IT, tax, and legal, and has worked on numerous projects that involved performing complex analysis on large data sets. He has a B.A. in Economics from the University of Washington. Aaron lives in the Seattle, WA, metro area with his wife, Darla, and their cats, Omar and Henry.

Scott Cameron, a Business Intelligence Architect at Hitachi Consulting, has been developing BI solutions for nine years and has over 20 years' data analysis experience. He has over three years' experience working with SQL Server 2005 Business Intelligence components and has taught SQL Server BI courses in the United States and Europe. He has experience in the healthcare, software, retail, insurance, legal, vocational rehabilitation, travel, and mining industries. He has helped several large companies perform their initial implementation of Microsoft Analysis Services 2005 and helped several independent software vendors integrate Analysis Services into their products. He has a B.A. in Economics and Asian Studies from Brigham Young University; his M.A. in Economics is from the University of Washington. Scott lives in the Seattle, WA, metro area with his wife, Tarya, and beagles, Hunter and Si.

Joe Kasprzak, a manager for Hitachi Consulting's Business Intelligence practice, has over 14 years of comprehensive business, technical, and managerial experience providing consulting services for clients in the financial services, retail, telecommunications, healthcare, hospitality, manufacturing and government industries. He has helped architect, integrate, develop, and manage full life-cycle implementations of strategic BI analytical systems. Joe holds a B.S. in Mathematics and Chemistry from Assumption College in Worcester, MA, and has done post-graduate studies in Computer Science at M.I.T. in Cambridge, MA. He lives in Newburybort, MA, with his wife, Liz.

More Great Resources for IT Professionals

Published and Forthcoming Titles from Microsoft Press

Administrator's Pocket Consultant

- Practical, portable guide for fast answers when you need them
- Focus on core operations and support tasks
- Organized for quick, precise reference—to get the job done

Microsoft® SQL Server™ 2005 *Administrator's Pocket Consultant*
William R. Stanek
0-7356-2107-1

Microsoft Windows Server™ 2003 *Administrator's Pocket Consultant* Second Edition
William R. Stanek
0-7356-2245-0

Microsoft Windows® XP Professional *Administrator's Pocket Consultant* Second Edition
William R. Stanek
0-7356-2140-3

Microsoft Windows Command-Line *Administrator's Pocket Consultant*
William R. Stanek
0-7356-2038-5

Administrator's Companion

- Comprehensive, one-volume guide to system administration
- Real-world insights, procedures, trouble-shooting tactics, and workarounds
- Fully searchable eBook on CD

Microsoft Windows Server 2003 *Administrator's Companion* Second Edition
Charles Russel, Sharon Crawford, and Jason Gerend
0-7356-2047-4

Microsoft Windows Small Business Server 2003 *Administrator's Companion*
Charles Russel, Sharon Crawford, and Jason Gerend
0-7356-2020-2

Microsoft Exchange Server 2003 *Administrator's Companion*
Walter J. Glenn and Bill English
0-7356-1979-4

Microsoft Systems Management Server 2003 *Administrator's Companion*
Steven D. Kaczmarek
0-7356-1888-7

Resource Kits

- In-depth technical information and tools from those who know the technology best
- Definitive reference and best practices for deployment and operations
- Essential toolkit of resources, including eBook, on CD

Microsoft Windows Vista™ *Resource Kit*
Tulloch, Honeycutt, Northrup, and Russel with the Microsoft Windows Vista Team
0-7356-2283-3

Microsoft Exchange Server 2003 *Resource Kit*
Unkroth, Molony, Cherny, Reid, Strachan, English, and the Microsoft Exchange Server Team
0-7356-2072-5

Microsoft Windows Server 2003 *Resource Kit*
Microsoft MVPs and Partners with Microsoft Windows Server Team
0-7356-2232-9

Microsoft Windows Security *Resource Kit* Second Edition
Ben Smith and Brian Komar with the Microsoft Security Team
0-7356-2174-8

Self-Paced Training Kits

- Two products in one: official exam prep plus practice tests
- Features lessons, exercises, and case scenarios
- Comprehensive self-tests; trial software; eReference Library on CD

Implementing and Maintaining Microsoft SQL Server 2005 *MCTS Self-Paced Training Kit*
0-7356-2271-X

Designing a Microsoft SQL Server 2005 Database Server Infrastructure *MCITP Self-Paced Training Kit*
0-7356-2173-X

Microsoft Windows Server 2003 Core Requirements Second Edition *MCSE Self-Paced Training Kit*
0-7356-2290-6

Installing, Configuring, and Administering Microsoft XP Professional Second Edition *MCSA/MCSE Self-Paced Training Kit*
0-7356-2152-7

What do you think of this book? We want to hear from you!

Do you have a few minutes to participate in a brief online survey? Microsoft is interested in hearing your feedback about this publication so that we can continually improve our books and learning resources for you.

To participate in our survey, please visit:
www.microsoft.com/learning/booksurvey

And enter this book's ISBN, 0-7356-2199-3. As a thank-you to survey participants in the United States and Canada, each month we'll randomly select five respondents to win one of five $100 gift certificates from a leading online merchant.* At the conclusion of the survey, you can enter the drawing by providing your e-mail address, which will be used for prize notification *only*.

Thanks in advance for your input. Your opinion counts!

Sincerely,

Microsoft Learning

Learn More. Go Further.

To see special offers on Microsoft Learning products for developers, IT professionals, and home and office users, visit: *www.microsoft.com/learning/booksurvey*

* No purchase necessary. Void where prohibited. Open only to residents of the 50 United States (includes District of Columbia) and Canada (void in Quebec). Sweepstakes ends 6/30/2007. For official rules, see: *www.microsoft.com/learning/booksurvey*